SOCIALISM AND SUPERIOR BRAINS

This book provides a comprehensive critical account of the political ideas of Bernard Shaw, the master intellectual of British socialism and one of the most influential political commentators of the twentieth century.

Shaw assumed many roles as a thinker, among them those of artist-philosopher, clowning prophet and pamphleteer. This book explains the methods he employed, the levels of abstraction at which his thought operated, and the intentions which informed his epic engagement with ideas. Part I provides an intellectual biography, while at the same time analysing Shaw's key concerns in relation to his Fabianism, arguments for equality of income and ideas on democracy and education. Part II looks at those areas which Shaw approached as long-standing historical problems or as dramas requiring immediate thought or action: sexual equality, the Irish question, war, fascism and Sovietism.

Socialism and Superior Brains is directed at the general reader as well as at specialists. It will be central reading for anyone seeking to understand Shaw's life and literary and political writings, the development of political thinking in this century and the problems and potential inherent in socialism.

Gareth Griffith is Senior Research Officer at the New South Wales State Parliament Library.

SOCIALISM AND SUPERIOR BRAINS

The political thought of Bernard Shaw

Routledge

London and New York

First published 1993
by Routledge
11 New Fetter Lane, London EC4P 4EE

New in paperback 1995

Simultaneously published in the USA and Canada
by Routledge
29 West 35th Street, New York, NY 10001

Typeset in Garamond by
NWL Editorial Services, Langport, Somerset

Printed and bound in Great Britain by
Mackays of Chatham PLC, Chatham, Kent

British Library Cataloguing in Publication Data
A catalogue reference for this book is available from the British Library

Library of Congress Cataloguing in Publication Data
A catalogue reference for this book has been requested

ISBN 0–415–08281–1 (hbk)
ISBN 0–415–12473–5 (pbk)

For Sue and Sam
and in memory of the Great John I

CONTENTS

Preface   ix
Introduction   1

Part I

1 SHAW'S FABIANISM   23
2 SHAVIAN SOCIALISM   101

Part II

3 SEXUAL EQUALITY   157
4 THE IRISH QUESTION   191
5 WAR AND PEACE   216
6 FASCISM AND SOVIETISM   241

Part III

7 CONCLUSION   277

Notes   286
Bibliography   291
Index   300

PREFACE

I have four aims in writing this book. First, I wish to offer a comprehensive and critical account of Shaw's political thought which is of value both to specialists in the field as well as to students and general readers perhaps coming to these ideas for the first time. Central to the work is the understanding that, while Shaw is not a major figure in the history of social and political thought, he was extremely influential in the development and dissemination of socialist and progressive ideas in Britain and beyond for over half a century. He made a difference, albeit of a kind that cannot be expressed in quantitative terms. A critical assessment of his political thought is essential to a complete picture of social and political argument in the modern age. The lack of a comprehensive study of this kind prompted this work and guided its purpose.

Second, my aim is to characterize Shaw's thought, or, more precisely, to explain the methods he employed, the levels of abstraction at which his thought operated, and the intentions which inspired his work. He assumed many roles as a thinker, *inter alia* that of artist, pamphleteer, philosopher and clowning prophet. Was he a serious thinker, or a devil's advocate? Were his ideas intended to transcend the context in which they were formulated? These are among the perennial questions which are asked of Shaw. This study characterizes his thought not in terms of political theory but as a form of political argument, inherently controversial, having regard to context and audience, but not necessarily intended to function purely within the framework of controversy.

My third aim is to present a picture of the development of Shaw's thought without seeking to offer a standard intellectual biography. I should explain myself. In order to show the interrelations, the continuities and discontinuities in Shaw's work, and in part to suggest why he is a serious if not wholly successful thinker, I have chosen to organize this study along thematic lines. In the light of the sheer variety of Shaw's interests, interspersing discussion of his views on such issues as the state and sexual equality with consideration of the totality of his concerns in any period of his life would have led, I believe, to a disjointed and unsatisfactory critical account. My aim, therefore, has been to integrate the contextual and biographical elements into a form of presentation which transcends their limitations from the standpoint of critical analysis.

My fourth aim is to show the extent to which Shaw's work is a matrix of creative contradictions and, further, to indicate the representative quality of these for socialism and, more tentatively, for modern culture generally. In developing this representative theme, I acknowledge that I have not always explored the connections between Shaw's utterances and their wider linguistic context to an extent that would satisfy some exponents of the history of ideas. Part of the difficulty here is that a comprehensive study of that sort would require detailed analysis of almost every facet of modern history and culture from around 1870 to 1950; perhaps, too, its emphasis would be different, having as its aim a portrayal of the intellectual and political movements of the period, and using Shaw's intellectual odyssey primarily as the frame for that portrait. In this study, on the other hand, Shaw dominates the canvas.

I am indebted to the Society of Authors, acting on behalf of the Bernard Shaw estate, for granting permission to quote from copyright material. Parts of Chapters 2 and 5 first appeared in *History of Political Thought* and *Review of International Studies* respectively, and I am grateful to the publishers for permission to use them here.

An earlier version of this work was submitted as a doctoral dissertation, and my first acknowledgement is to my supervisor, Professor Paul Wilkinson, for his encouragement and advice. I should also like to thank Bob Osgerby, with whom I taught an MA course on Politics and Literature at the City of London Polytechnic, for his valuable insights into Shaw's plays; Dan H. Laurence for his help in tracking down sources relating to Shaw's ideas on the coupled vote; Belinda Yuen for typing the final draft of the manuscript; and my wife Sue who helped prepare the manuscript and provided such affectionate support during the years of its making.

Gareth Griffith
Sydney, Australia Day, 1992

INTRODUCTION

'Life levels all men: death reveals the eminent.'

(Shaw 1931f: 222)

Usually George Bernard Shaw is thought of as a playwright: author of such works as *Saint Joan* and *Major Barbara*; winner of the Nobel Prize for Literature in 1925. Failing that, his reputation rests on his scintillating work in music and drama criticism. What is sometimes overlooked, in the popular perception of him at least, is that he first achieved prominence in public life as a leading member of the Fabian Society, serving on its executive committee for over twenty years, acting as resident propagandist and original thinker, often tackling neglected themes. Even after he resigned from the executive in 1911 his interest in politics and political ideas never flagged. Only now it was developed more in his capacity as an independent thinker or world statesman. His achievement was considerable.

In his day he commanded both a large audience and a massive reputation in the socialist movement. His name appears at a critical stage in countless biographies and reminiscences of Labour politicians and socialist intellectuals. 'Shaw gallops away at the head of the author's field' was the conclusion Alexander and Hobbs reached from their research in 1962 into 'what influences Labour M.P.'s?'. He was the author cited most by those of all shades of political opinion in the Party, among left and non-left groups; nor did his popularity vary according to educational background, among those who had or had not attended university: 'Shaw, Wells, Cole and Marx emerged high in all lists, Shaw always first' (Alexander and Hobbs 1962: 11). He was, to use Kingsley Martin's phrase, the favourite intellectual father figure of an entire generation; 'Shaw, like Wells, dominated the world in which I grew up', wrote J.B. Priestley (Winsten 1946: 50).

Where the British labour movement was concerned, therefore, he was perhaps the most influential of all socialist propagandists. Together with his fellow polymath, H.G. Wells, he mapped out the contours of the progressive cause in Britain and beyond. Shaw was like a machine, producing ideas and opinions at a constant rate over seventy years, stretching and pulling the mind

1

of his audience, tugging at its conscience, trying its nerve and tweaking its prejudices. He was one of the master intellectuals of his age, a prince in the universe of progressive thought.

That intellectual mastery was short-lived. In a few decades his standing as a thinker has plummeted dramatically. How are we to account for this? E.J. Hobsbawm has written that the first post-Chartist generation of British socialists produced three thinkers of international stature, namely William Morris, Shaw, and the Webb partnership. He adds that Shaw's work, despite his superior intellect, seems in retrospect the least substantial of the three. Shaw's socialism is too hard to define or categorize and consequently the interpretations of his political ideas are so varied that he does not occupy a clear position in the history of socialist thought. His doctrinal legacy is so curiously scattered that he rarely makes a positive appearance in the contemporary debate on socialism, unless one of his illuminating or amusing aphorisms is used to couple one train of high-minded thought to another (Hobsbawm 1947: 324).

Is it then a case of unfulfilled potential? Or rather, is the ability to gain a significant degree of mastery over the mind of a generation to be distinguished from a talent for the complex task of doctrinal formulation? One species of conventional wisdom, associated with such writers as V.S. Pritchett and Edmund Wilson, holds that Shaw was more of a social critic or literary pundit than a purposeful thinker: he is too irresponsible, too erratic and inconsistent to be considered in any other context (Wilson 1962: 193). A variation on this theme, presented by Eric Bentley, argues that Shaw is basically an artist in politics – more of a devil's advocate, or a propagandist of unconventional or unpopular ideas than a serious thinker. Bentley's point is that the customary criteria of theoretical analysis cannot be applied to Shaw's politics because he deliberately overstated his case in order to make an impact on his audience. This line of reasoning is used by Bentley as a means of saving Shaw from direct responsibility for his own excesses (Bentley 1967: 16). Other writers are less apologetic: they simply stress that he was always the entertainer, the sprite, the raconteur who, in Leonard Woolf's opinion, failed to understand that: 'It is only by talking bleak, bare sense and converting the world to it that you can make the world sensible' (Woolf 1944: 188). It is not surprising therefore to find both Woolf and G.D.H. Cole discussing Shaw's sober Fabian output in terms of his post as amanuensis and mouthpiece to the Fabian 'Thinking Cabinet'. More particularly, they imply that his contribution must ultimately be considered in relation to his graphic presentation of Sidney Webb's facts and figures. The argument states that when Shaw's syllogistic mind was allowed to roam at will it immediately declined into eccentricity (Cole 1956, Woolf 1944). In a similar vein, Victor Kiernen writes of Shaw's political thought as an 'extraordinary medley of sense and nonsense' (Martin and Rubernstein 1979: 54). Shaw's waspish friend, H.G. Wells, reported, 'his is a fine intelligence which is always going off on the spree' (Wells 1932: 484).

2

There is some truth in all these arguments. Shaw's artistic temperament certainly encroached on his political thinking: one suspects, for instance, that despite his Fabian background he merely toyed with facts, relying instead on the power of intuition – 'I am not a complete apriorist', he was to admit, 'I always start from a single fact or incident. But one is enough'. He also relied on Webb and his fellow Fabians and he never tired of acknowledging the debt he owed to them. Through his commitment to Fabianism he was to become active in politics, speaking regularly and without payment at all kinds of public meetings, as well as serving as a councillor in St Pancras for many years. He was proud of this. In contrast to Wells, Chesterton and Orwell, those names most often associated with Shaw's in discussions of culture and society, he was no mere literary pundit, producing ideas in isolation without reference to the movement at large. For as long as he remained intimate in Fabian affairs he retained a foothold in the world of practical politics. Again, Shaw acknowledged Webb as the key influence here: 'without him I might have been a mere literary wisecracker, like Carlyle and Ruskin' (Shaw 1949b: 82).

There is some truth, too, in the contention that Shaw's argument was an exercise in self-dramatization: the making and mass distribution of a special universe of discourse, having at its centre the superior brain of GBS – unofficial Bishop of Everywhere. To write of Shaw's career is to trace the intellectual adventure of that superior brain, striving to understand, to explain, to delight and outrage, to extend the intellectual consciousness of the race. And to do all that he took the liberty of recreating life in his own image. Hence one figure dominates the plays and prefaces: the free-thinking progressive, the realist who can see life for what it is and so lives more abundantly than others. In Shaw's scheme of things, such unaverage individuals were the Word made Flesh, or the true instruments of the inner will of the world. Creation was but an extension of his own personality. In this way he associated the metaphysical truths of the Life Force philosophy with his own identity, so creating for himself a privileged role as interpreter of the purpose of the universe. True, statements to this effect were accompanied by the usual irony and extravagance associated with GBS. However, irony and extravagance can also mask a deeper commitment. 'Look at me!', he said in *Back to Methuselah*, 'I seem a man like other men because nine-tenths of me is common humanity. But the other tenth is a faculty for seeing things as they really are'. The superior brain represented life at its highest actual human evolution; as the propagandist of enlightenment Shaw conveniently believed that his own purposes had an important relation to the purposes of the universe.

This desire to participate in universal progress reveals a source of many complexities in his work, underlining as it does the importance of personality in politics in this instance. Shaw's personality is a curious alliance of idealism and realism and this basic diversity produced what Eduard Bernstein described as the seemingly paradoxical character of the critical ideologist, combining a rare degree of scepticism and devotion (Bernstein 1921). It is important to remember that Shaw's comprehensive iconoclasm was founded on a deep vein of utopianism. In fact, many of the idiosyncratic features of his politics (the connection with the religion of creative evolution, for example) are associated with this fundamental idealism which tended to divorce his work from the norms and values of the indigenous labour movement, thus complicating the nature of the influence he exercised over its members.

Fundamental to this book is the argument that, however eccentric or egocentric his ideas, whatever his methods and however great his debts, Shaw's estimation of his own powers as a thinker and of the seriousness of his intentions is not to be underestimated. It endeavours to look at Shaw on his own terms, recognizing the complications and pitfalls of his mixed style of argument, admitting that his motives were not always pure nor his methods always appropriate to the task at hand, yet still accepting that he sought ultimately to transform human consciousness and radically alter social institutions, rules and practices.

The creator of the ebullient, sparkling fiction of GBS was a man possessed by an awesome conviction of moral duty, compelled by intellectual earnestness to the pursuit of ideas. The amusing paradoxer of popular opinion, the owner of the absurdly pretentious title of World Betterer was, in fact, a man of substance, working primarily for radical change. 'My conscience is the genuine pulpit article: it annoys me to see people comfortable when they ought to be uncomfortable; and I insist on making them think in order to bring them to conviction of sin', he told Arthur Bingham Walkley (Shaw 1931f: viii). John Tanner of *Man and Superman* spoke for his creator when he declared, 'moral passion is the only real passion'. Shaw was a moralist. Not in the tradition of the dull, forbidding sort, but one filled with vitality and fun. Where there was Shaw there was sure to be ambiguity, a whiff of trickery, the showman's sign, a multiplicity of roles and perspectives. Yet fundamental to his many roles was that of moral revolutionary. Of the many perspectives on Shaw's work, the most striking is that which sees it as an argument for moral transformation.

This may seem a curious thesis. Shaw's reputation seems to contradict the very notion of him as a moralist. Instead, the popular perception of his work, certainly before the Great War, was that of an immoralist, seeking not to present a constructive alternative of his own, merely to undermine the moral order of Victorianism, leaving nothing in its place but a sort of Nietzschean state of anarchy. He was an archetypal 'missionary of discord'. As Louis Dubedat says in *The Doctor's Dilemma*: 'I dont believe in morality. Im a disciple of Bernard Shaw' (Shaw 1932d: 141). Shaw certainly enjoyed toying with this view of himself in his many public controversies, complicating any interpretation of his ideas by his deliberately provocative language. Writing to Robert Blatchford, the editor of *The Clarion*, for example, he declared that the case for socialism was as 'immoral as Ibsen's plays', whereas the case for unsocialism and inhumanity was perfectly moral, conforming to the impossible ideals of goodness, purity, honesty and sincerity (Shaw 1965a: 726).

Alternatively, a question mark must hang over the description of a Fabian as a moral revolutionary. Thus, in contrast to his reputation as a wild heretic, Shaw was also the sober Fabian socialist who argued only for piecemeal institutional reform, denying all claims that socialism entailed a change in consciousness, or even a compromise in middle-class respectability. So much for Shaw's picture of himself as a 'revolutionary in grain'. On this basis, he occupied an uncertain middle ground between revolution and reform, operating partly inside and partly outside the civil life of the British polity, as something of an outsider with inside information: 'if you rebel against high-heeled shoes, take care to do it in a very smart hat' (Shaw 1949a: 406).

This dualism in Shaw has been formulated in many ways. For example, Hobsbawm, Hulse and the MacKenzies all describe him initially as a rebel before qualifying this picture in some way. Hobsbawm distinguishes between the reformist and revolutionary elements in Shaw's work (Hobsbawm 1947: 314), while Hulse chooses instead the terms 'revisionist' and 'anarchist' to indicate the different strategies Shaw employed in his rebellion against the established order (Hulse 1970: 224). The MacKenzies prefer to tell of how the rebel was transformed into a prophet of his age. That transformation was facilitated, they say, by Shaw's 'intellectual arrogance' which was 'funda-mental to his character: the unconscious assertion of virtue by the man who knows the way to salvation' (MacKenzie and MacKenzie 1977: 295). Clearly, many strategies were adopted in that quest for salvation, some of a destructive and others of a constructive kind. Shaw was, to use the terminology of this present study, both a rebel and a lawmaker, the first determined to undermine conventional morality, the latter to create a new table of values. Ultimately, it is argued here, his political thought drifted toward the lawmaker's dream of a collectivist morality of service to the community as well as to life itself. That is not to suggest, however, that his rebellious individualism was ever overwhelmed completely, for the uneasy tensions between the polarities in his thought operated throughout.

Indeed, what emerges in this study is a picture of Shaw's thought as a matrix of creative contradictions. The ethical foundations of his political ideas were in fact scarred by so many conflicts: the utilitarian politics of welfare set against the republican politics of virtue; contrasting views of human nature; differing conceptions of goodness (as happiness or perfection); and the competing demands of individualism and collectivism. Discussion of these polarities offers an insight into the prevailing concerns of Shaw's thought, political and philosophical, revealing the links between his different activities over many decades, while still acknowledging the violent changes in direction and the ambiguities and contradictions which characterize his argument.

The perennial tensions in Shaw's political thought extended to his conception of the politcal itself, a point which can be illustrated by reference to the central metaphor of this book, namely, the notion of socialism and superior brains. As Shaw said in his usual ironic way, this was the title of a Fabian booklet he had written 'from personal experience'. The metaphor expresses the maverick style and ebullience he brought to serious matters. It also points to an attempt by men of his kind, the righteous intellectuals in politics, to impose the order of reason on an uncertain world. Through this metaphor we meet Shaw at his most playful and at his most pretentious. The cult of superior brains lies behind his reputation as an élitist who, in the words of G.D.H. Cole, 'did not care a button about democracy: he wanted things to be run by experts, not merely administrators but also as makers of policy, and he was apt to admire dictators, if only they would give the experts a free hand' (Cole 1956: 211).

This interpretation, which is in some ways consistent with many views of mainstream Fabianism, points to an outlook on the public realm which can be characterized as a form of technical élitism; where politics is dominated by the technicians of social reform, experts, bureaucrats, social engineers; where the chief demand is for 'brains and political science', as Shaw announced in *Fabianism and the Empire* (1900); where socialism is more a matter of legal rules than virtues.

Against this, there was an aspect to Shaw's thought which viewed the public realm as a place of discourse not science, presenting opportunities for self-discovery and collective agency, a forum for the search for rational consensus through argument and debate. In this context Shaw can be seen driving towards a more robust conception of citizenship based upon the republican virtues of civic pride and public honour. He described his plays as Shavio–Socratic dialogues to be seen as models of a dialectical mode of rational deliberation where common and uncommon understandings meet and fuse promoting new awareness, new visions and new questions, thus acting as agents of moral self-discovery and collective agency. The theatre was for Shaw the equivalent of the ancient forum, a place 'where two or three are gathered together', he called it 'a factory of thought, a promoter of conscience, an elucidator of social conduct, an armour against despair and dullness, and temple of the Ascent of Man' (Shaw 1932m: vi). And further, his mastery of language allowed him to transform the most technical issues into accessible subjects for a general audience. This was fundamental to what Maurice Dobb called 'the impelling quality' in Shaw's work 'that has fascinated the minds of three generations of readers' (Winsten 1946: 138). Holbrook Jackson, writing in 1909, said Shaw had 'become a modern Socrates – doing for England by means of stage-play and essay, lecture and epistle, what Socrates did for ancient Athens by conversation and example' (Jackson 1909: 92).

One danger to avoid is that in seeking out the serious side to Shaw encapsulated in the man of doctrine, we shall somehow drain the life, the joy, the sheer exuberance and variety from his work, so revealing only a famine where abundance lies. There is nothing to be gained by extracting a dry, formal set of theorems from this rich store of intellectual novelties. There is still less to be gained by creating a false unity or tidiness in his outlook. Just as his seriousness is to be accepted on its own terms, so must his waywardness. There is a kind of balancing act to be mastered wherein earnestness does not kill off playfulness, where the pursuit of doctrinal truth does not overwhelm the sense of experiment and development so crucial to Shaw's epic engagement with ideas. He simply did not care to fit his socialism (or any other facet of his argument) into an academically respectable system. He purposefully attempted to establish a flexible relationship between thinking and experience, believing that a useful idea or policy was to be retained even at the expense of consistency. His overriding concern for the immediate relevance of his ideas affected the tone and substance of his political argument, preventing him, as A.M. McBriar said, from scaling 'the higher ranges of theoretical speculation' (McBriar 1962: 347).

The term argument has been used in the general characterization of Shavianism. For that was precisely what it was – an argument for moral transformation, not a piece of analytical reasoning. Shaw did not deal in the necessary truths of logic, but in the likely, the plausible and the probable which belong to the domain of deliberation and argument. His concern was with persuasion, not proof. Whereas formal theory deals in logically inter-connected sets of propositions from which empirical uniformities or normative theorems can be derived, Shaw's work had to do with the making and unmaking of conviction, the moulding and breaking of opinion in specific contexts.

Richard Ohmann has offered a detailed analysis of Shaw's style of argument, which he describes as that of an unphilosophical philosopher whose ambience was one of 'disputatious voices, conflicting ideas, acceptable and unacceptable notions, trustworthy and untrustworthy advocates'. Ohmann's thesis is (i) that Shaw's plays-of-ideas were a natural extension to the rhetoric of opposition forged in the political arena in the 1880s, and (ii) that Shaw's habit of assigning each point of view to an imaginary speaker or to a disembodied voice was a sign of his humanitarian sense of the relevance of ideas to conduct and experience. In the latter, the picture is one of a practical moralist testing ideas in relation to character and circumstance; in the former, it is that of the 'cart and trumpet' philosopher engaging in conflict of ideas in his most energetically egoistic fighting style. There is nothing of the scholar's call in Shaw's prose style, concludes Ohmann, 'he wrote for the forum just as he debated in the forum' (Ohmann 1962: 115).

Commendable as Ohmann's work is, there are some areas of ambiguity. For example the notion of unphilosophical philosophy is unclear, inviting comment on the relationship between rhetoric or argument, on one side, and philosophy (however unphilosophical), on the other. In classical times, from Plato to Hobbes, these two modes of discourse were in direct opposition: argument being concerned with the immediate, the mutable; philosophy with truth. Hobbes called them contrary faculties, distinguishing between the 'powerful eloquence' of argument and the 'solid reasoning' of philosophy. Stated simply, the question is whether Shaw's argument raises the issue of truth and falsity, or is it somehow reducible to the context in which it was formulated? Can one ask whether equality of income, for instance, is a true or false statement of socialist doctrine, or only whether it was an effective or ineffective argument in the circumstances? Alternatively, can both questions be asked? The point is crucial. Was Shaw a serious thinker, a serious controversialist, or both?

Here the final option is pursued. Context is important in argument, but not to the exclusion of all other considerations. The conception of argument employed here has much in common with Ronald Beiner's recent characterization of political judgment as a 'living synthesis of detachment and involvement, of passionate commitment and critical distance'. Beiner's political judgment, like Shaw's moral argument, confronts 'an established structure of actualities and possibilities', yet it also brings to bear 'a concept of right that critically judges, and therefore distances itself from, the established reality' (Beiner 1983: 150). Such a synthesis of detachment and involvement was central to every aspect of Shaw's work. Though it operated in specific contexts, in relation to varying audiences, his argument still retained an external standard of critical judgment in terms of which Shaw sought to establish the truth of his views on subjects as diverse as evolutionary theory and economic morality. It was this doctrinal quality which lay at the heart of his genius for journalism, allowing for a critical distance to be established between the political commentator and the events under consideration. In this way, his critical journalism was not caught in the web of conventionality; otherwise suppressed interconnections between social factors were exposed in his work; prevailing practices and understandings were undermined. On this basis, Shavian discourse was a compound of persuasion and explanation, manipulation and enlightenment by the spoken and written word, a mixed mode of reasoning about facts and values which connected thought and action, philosophy and rhetoric, the realm of theory with that of chance and contingency.

This sounds grand, even masterful, nothing less than an invitation to enthusiasm. But care is needed here. Philosophy and rhetoric make poor bed fellows. A man might be a serious thinker without being a good one; he might even gain a great reputation without achieving his true aims. It has been suggested already that the nature and purpose of Shaw's argument were not constant. On occasions it was deliberately provocative and wayward, as in his journalistic statements on fascism, while elsewhere it was more sober, intended seemingly as an authoritative expression of his views: 'The golden rule is that there are no golden rules'.

The presentation of neat formulas and divisions in relation to Shaw's work represents another victory for temerity over prudence. However, they are unavoidable if some order is to be brought to bear on this vast universe of discourse.

Shaw's argument can be considered, if only schematically, at three distinct though related levels. First, it can be seen as a kind of guerilla war against established values and practices, using every device from his vast armoury of mockery and outrage to uncover and undermine the spiritual and material poverty suffered under capitalism. Shavianism was, in this respect, an essentially critical exercise, a daily commentary on the evils and follies of contemporary life: the work of a social critic operating in a variety of modes, including drama, journalism, political tracts and speeches. On these many platforms Shaw displayed his much publicized capacity for facing unpleasant realities, together with his gift for presenting those realities in an arresting, even dramatic light. Here he was at his most destructive, a pioneer in the spirit of Shelley and Ibsen, a critical realist intent on revealing the hypocrisy of conventional ideals. He could never be satisfied, he said in 1898,

> with fictitious morals and fictitious good conduct, shedding fictitious glory on robbery, starvation, disease, crime, drink, war, cruelty, cupidity, and all the other commonplaces of civilization which drive men to the theatre to make foolish pretences that such things are progress, science, morals, religion, patriotism, imperial supremacy, national greatness and all the other names the newspapers call them.
> (Shaw 1931g: xvi)

On the other hand, he did not 'see moral chaos and anarchy as the alternative to romantic convention' (ibid.). At a second level, he tried to formulate a constructive alternative to the sham ideals of the Victorian age. He too was an idealist in his way. Only his idealism was based on a vision of social justice conceived in terms of a classless and rationally-ordered society founded ultimately on the socialist doctrine of equality of income. He claimed that his idealism was of a superior kind, for it accorded with his own realistic assessment of the facts of social and political life. His political outlook was very complicated: part Fabian welfarism, part Shavian egalitarianism. At its heart, however, was a concern to connect the truths of doctrine to the 'realities' of political life, in particular to the tactical compromises and contradictions which belong to the political realm. His political thought was in this sense an exercise in socialist realism.

Finally, Shaw as artist-philosopher explored the preconditions and possibilities for generating a qualitative change in man. At his most visionary, he envisaged the evolution of humanity beyond man to the superman (the apotheosis of superior brains). He called himself a vitalist, or creative evolutionist, aligning his philosophy with the celebration of spontaneity over reason, will over intellect, as associated with the work of Schopenhauer and Nietzsche in Germany and Bergson and Sorel in France. Perhaps this sounds strange – something is out of place, a discrepancy has arisen between history and reputation. This is not to claim that Shaw's association with these writers has not been recognized for a long time. Shaw himself cited Schopenhauer and Nietzsche in 1903 as 'among the writers whose peculiar sense of the world I recognize as more or less akin to my own' (Shaw 1931f: xxviii). 'Coat, Mr Schopenhauer's; waistcoat, Mr Ibsen's; Mr Nietzsche's trousers' was Max Beerbohm's barbed comment from 1914 on Shaw's philosophical pretentions (Riewald 1977: 80). So there is no mystery surrounding the vitalist connection. Nevertheless, Shaw's precise intellectual affinities with these writers remains somehow tenuous. He is still often placed in the tradition of Diderot and Voltaire, those champion rationalists of the Enlightenment, not among those who seek to demonstrate the primacy of will over reason. Julia Briggs has argued that Shaw 'preferred to contemplate man within the clear and ordered perspective of the Enlightenment, to which, intellectually, or spiritually speaking, he might easily have belonged' (Briggs 1986: 15). For the moment, the easiest way out of this conundrum is to assert that Shaw's vitalism was of a peculiar sort, taking many unlikely intellectual turns, being expressed in a variety of forms. His stated aim throughout was to 'get at' the spiritual realities behind material facts. As he informed the Marxist H.M. Hyndman in 1900 'I am a moral revolutionary interested, not in the class war, but in the struggle between human vitality and the artificial system of morality, and distinguishing, not between capitalist and proletarian, but between moralist and natural historian' (Shaw 1972: 160). In this respect, his artist-philosophy was an exercise in vitalist realism.

The word 'realism' is fraught with confusion and controversy. So high a status does it confer on its owner, that schools of philosophy have fought for many centuries over its possession and meaning, like dogs over a bone. It is used here mainly because it is fundamental to Shaw's vocabulary, especially as a term of self-description. In this sense, realism relates as much to the intention or conceit behind Shaw's work as to its actual content, which can only be described as a curious mixture of critical and utopian elements. In speaking of realism, then, this book critically employs Shaw's own vocabulary of self-description and self-aggrandizement as a means of ordering his universe of discourse. In speaking of his moralism, it refers to that element which ultimately powered every facet of his argument, transcending the whims and vanities of personality. Be it as music or drama critic, playwright or pamphleteer, his role was that of a specialist in a heretical argument, working 'with the deliberate object of converting the nation' to his opinions.

Another constant feature of Shaw's argument at every level, and of argument generally perhaps, was its abiding interest in audience. According to Chaime Perelman, it is that concern with audience which connects argument to the classical notion of rhetoric: 'it is in relation to an audience that all argumentation is developed', the difference between modern argument and ancient rhetoric being that the former carries the art of persuasion and adherence far beyond the scope of oratory (Perelman 1977: 138).

Shaw certainly needed an audience. He once said he was 'like a child in that respect': a born actor, a compulsive performer playing to the audience he had longed for as a boy. Moreover, a sense of audience – of a specific address to a specific group of people – was essential to the conduct of his argument. Time and again he paused at the start of a book or lecture, or somewhere in a preface, to fix his audience, to establish what Richard Ohmann calls 'a minimum shared ground of assumptions upon which to build' (Ohmann 1962: 112). Shaw always spoke directly to his audience, though from many standpoints and in many guises, sometimes assuming the part of the scandalized moralist, at other times preferring instead to appear as the scandalous heretic. He could be harsh and indignant, playful and understanding. Often he was all these things, approaching his audience with a mixture of concern and criticism, highlighting its faults and limitations while yet attending to its needs and foibles, forever working his way into its confidence.

It is one thing to assert this concern with audience, it is of course quite another to try and identify Shaw's audience with some precision. This is partly because its scope and nature changed over time and according to circumstance: the audience he attracted as a young socialist agitator was different to that which later attended the lectures of the great man of English letters. And on a contemporary note, his audience changes still as succeeding generations encounter the work, finding in it new worth, new relevance and old frustrations. Attempts have been made to identify Shaw's audience with a particular group or class. Eric Bentley says that Shaw's political discussions were always directed toward 'the English people'; 'one can scarcely exaggerate his preoccupation with them' (Bentley 1946: 361). This is an important line of interpretation, casting a spotlight on Shaw's professed goal of converting 'the nation to his opinions'; he was, after all, to claim that he was a national socialist long before Hitler was born. The communist R. Palme Dutt, in a review of *The Intelligent Woman's Guide to Socialism, Capitalism, Sovietism and Fascism (The Guide)*, wrote that while the book is nominally addressed to the 'intelligent woman' without distinction of class, 'in fact, with rare exceptions, it ignores 90 per cent of the women of the country, and is addressed almost exclusively to the upper- and middle-class 10 per cent, with investments and servants, ladies of high social standing and gentle breeding whose fate "you" (who?) may share' (Dutt 1928: 392). These views are echoed in Margaret Walters's recent introduction to *The Guide*. Again, it is an important line of interpretation. Certainly it shows how the details of a writer's argument – its form and style – can complicate his address to what Richard Hoggart calls 'the intelligent layman' (Ingle 1979: 185). All the same, Shaw's audience was not confined to any one social class. In all probability the majority of those who read his books and attended performances of his plays had neither 'high social standing' nor much 'good breeding' to boast of. Despite the complications, intelligence was indeed the key to Shaw's perception of his audience. At its broadest, it was universal in scope, comprising all those with sufficient intelligence to engage in the pursuit of ideas. Shaw was back among the Encyclopaedists. His identification of that audience in *Everybody's Political What's What? (Everybody's)* shows a nice line in flattery and self-display: 'Behind Wells and Shaw', he declared, 'is a considerable class of persons intelligent enough to buy their books and enjoy reading them, or at least criticizing them. They are at present only an intelligentsia; but they contain material for a genuine aristocracy ready to our hand' (Shaw 1944: 44). Shaw's gospel was not only of, but also for, superior brains.

Cockiness and optimism were part and parcel of the Shavian canon. They were, however, sometimes a mask concealing a sense of deep frustration. It must be recorded that, despite his massive audience and reputation, a sense of failure and exasperation pervaded the moralist's later work, so much so that in 1932 he was to say 'For forty-eight years I have been addressing speeches to the Fabian Society and to other assemblies in this country. So far as I can make out, those speeches have not produced any effect whatsoever' (Shaw 1962b: 235). It was an outrageous exaggeration. The picture of the most celebrated living dramatist in the English speaking world as an abject failure was scarcely credible. Besides, by the 1930s the part he had played in undermining Victorian consciousness was readily acknowledged, as was his contribution to the raising and broadening of public interest and debate in matters too often dominated by experts and professionals in the field. Yet he remained frustrated as a moralist on a grand scale: there were few converts to the religion of creative evolution; prospects for the egalitarian order were dim. Perhaps in Shaw we see the revenge of classical austerity over modern licence. Brilliance in controversy may prove a corrupting accomplishment after all. Some of the many accounts of his limitations as a thinker have been discussed. Central to most is the claim that he was too engrossed in the exaggerated art of argument to succeed as a constructive thinker: he could destroy, but he could not build. Some of these accounts were written by active combatants, fresh from an engagement in Shavian controversy. He was to have many distinguished sparring partners, among them Wells, Chesterton, Belloc and Hyndman. The case for this much-provoked cohort was made by L.T. Hobhouse, who wrote of Shaw: 'Confident of his gallery, he takes his own whimsical arguments, his fanciful analogies, his strained generalisations, his distortions of his opponent's words, for serious reasoning. He most pitiably deceives himself, and the truth is not in him' (Hobhouse 1913: 384). In the same vein, Dan H. Laurence does well to remind us that Shaw's classicist friend, Gilbert Murray, charged him with 'the damnable vice of preferring rhetoric to truth' (Shaw 1962b: xiv).

This is not to deny that Shaw sought to establish a middle-ground between philosophy and rhetoric, combining the search for truth with the necessity of persuasion. It is only to hint at the difficulties and frustrations he encountered in practice. Aspiring to reconcile passionate commitment with critical distance is one thing; achieving the goal a very different matter. The sweet sound, the elegance and speed of Shaw's argument for moral transformation were no guarantees of ultimate success.

Arguably, it was as dramatist that Shaw made his greatest impact. Here his ebullient personality, his eclecticism, his wit and his disregard for system were at their strongest. Ideas were his stock-in-trade. He toyed with them and taunted them remorselessly, hoping always to make an impression on his audience. He played the part of intellectual circus master, displaying his fantastic menagerie with impeccable style. There seemed to be a novelty for every occasion. There were supermen, pioneers, gentlemen, world-betterers, splendid heroines and fallible anti-heroes. The animals squabbled and laughed, united in a moment and then were torn apart by a command from the prompter's box. There was no formal system. Yet Shaw manipulated the chaos of clear ideas with masterful precision. It is true, there were times when players and painted stage took all his love, but there was nothing haphazard about his performance. It was all Shaw, and there was always a purpose and a reason behind his antics, his loyalties and inconsistencies.

Shaw was adamant that his drama was only an extension of his more overtly political work. In the preface to *Man and Superman* and elsewhere, he portrayed himself as a didactic artist, concerned, like Bunyan, with the unities of the world, not its diversities. In contrast to Shakespeare and Dickens he claimed, his was the literature of constructive ideas: 'Effectiveness of assertion is the Alpha and Omega of style'; an original morality is 'the true diagnostic of the first order in literature', he declared (Shaw 1931f: xxxiv).

Surely commentators such as Robert Brustein are right not to take such declarations too literally, distinguishing between Shaw's utilitarian aesthetic theory and his artistic practice, 'separating his negative artistic rebellion from his affirmative philosophical doctrine' (Brustein 1964: 191). This is not to deny the relevance of one to the other – but the relationship is complex. Evidently, art and politics (or indeed any form of programmatic or philosophical discourse) invoke different criteria of success in argument. Whereas a literary text, in published form or in performance, thrives on ambiguity and openness which allows for competing interpretations, a programmatic work, on the other hand, must necessarily seek clarity and consistency. Despite Shaw's claims to the contrary, as an artist he sought to present a dialogue on the diversities of the world, whereas as an ideologist he sought instead to offer a discourse on its unities. Hence the uniqueness of art must be acknowledged when Shaw's political argument is under discussion, particularly in relation to any comparison between the content of a preface and a play. Different kinds of text and rhetorical strategy are under consideration here.

Indeed the locating of an authentic Shavian text in terms of his drama is itself problematical. Performances differ as do productions. It must also be recognized that a large part of his audience, especially in the early years, encountered the plays only in published form, with Shaw seeking to guide the destiny of his argument in the copious stage directions. Originally the decision to publish the plays with extended prefaces in the 1890s was partly an insurance against prolonged theatrical neglect, though at the same time it ensured that his audience was not somehow reducible to Shaftesbury Avenue, or to any combination of its equivalent throughout the world. Through publication and with the help of the public library service, Shaw too 'went native' in industrial England and beyond, reaching an audience that possibly had not heard of the brilliant music critic, Corno di Bassetto, only of a troublesome Fabian who had attended the inaugural conference of the Independent Labour Party in 1893. By the turn of the century many more had probably read the plays and their scintillating prefaces than had ever attended the scattered performances of his works.

Returning briefly to the theme of Shaw's audience, clearly in this respect there was no settled Shavian audience, nor even a settled Shavian literary text. His forays into the theatre, the *Plays Unpleasant* of the early 1890s, were all directed towards a minority audience of committed socialists. Indeed, far from appealing to the mass of theatre-goers, he took the opportunity in his early prefaces to undermine their pretensions and limitations: the shop assistants, typists and clerks who filled the English theatres were 'at home in the fool's paradise of popular romance' (Shaw 1931k: viii). Nor were his later experiments in artist-philosophy, the full texts of *Man and Superman* and *Back to Methuselah*, in particular, written for the ordinary theatre-goer. His ambition, he said, was to turn the theatre from 'the drama of romance and sensuality to the drama of edification'. He had always wanted to write for a 'pit of philosophers', a comment which fits neatly into Brustein's contention that 'the theatre of revolt is not a popular theatre, nor are its dramatists much concerned with instructing the middle classes' (Brustein 1964: 9). The same cannot be said of *Arms and the Man* or *Pygmalion* or *Androcles and the Lion* in which we encounter the populist side to Shaw.

Nor is the situation any more straightforward for any one play. Consider, for example, such issues as meaning and impact in relation to the minor play, *The Man of Destiny*, as performed in Croydon in 1897, New York in 1899 and in Berlin five years later; or, alternatively, as read by an English audience, provincial or otherwise, as against its Irish counterpart. Consider the variety of reactions to the play's statements on war, great men, republicanism, or to Napoleon's waspish speech on the English race and its colonial exploits. Surely its reception varied considerably between Croydon, Berlin and Dublin.

All of which is not to support outright relativism or complete openness in the interpretation of the politics of the drama. It is only to hint at the complications involved in any such analysis.

To pursue the matter a little further, what is often said of Shaw's drama is that it is characterized by a conflict between form and content. While the dialogue of the plays may have been radical in content, the form was decidedly conservative in nature; what he offered typically was a play of ideas presented in the form of a static comedy of manners. His radicalism, it has been said, was channelled into the eloquence of his characters who would expound their contrasting ideologies of life, sometimes at inordinate length, to an audience which barely had time to recover from one wave of words before it had to brace itself for the next. These articulate assaults on contemporary values were challenging enough in their time. But it is claimed that the context in which they operated – the customary drawing-room scenes replete with the solid artefacts of modern bourgeois life – created an aura of stability, even permanence, which effectively undermined the presumed radicalism of the dialogue. Shaw's drama, then, in its form and perhaps in the action it portrayed, was locked into the system it sought to destroy. Though it chipped away at the edifice of bourgeois values in its treatment of the family, romantic love and the military, it relied for all its devices of comic invention on the conventions of the established system. Edmund Wilson said that Shaw's comedy 'for all its greater freedom in dealing with social conditions, is almost as much dependant on a cultivated and stable society as the comedy of Molière'. And Wilson went on to argue 'Shaw, as much as Molière, must speak the same language as his audience; he must observe the same conventions of manners' (Wilson 1962: 219). Even Shaw's language was but a parody of conventional rhetoric, returning, as Andrew Kennedy has said, to the naturalism of the nineteenth century, instead of journeying towards an expressionistic theatre of word-music (Kennedy 1975: 47–84).

Now the relationship between form and content and its relevance to the kind of impact the drama made (and makes) on its audience is open to conflicting interpretations. Shaw's conservatism as a dramatist can be linked to the conservatism inherent in his Fabian gradualism and there are those on the Left who would see the two as equally futile undertakings, incapable of delivering, or even contributing to, fundamental change in man or society. If Wilson is right, if Shaw really does speak the same language as his audience (whatever that means exactly), then is it not likely that, despite the radical intent, his work reproduced or reflected conventional relationships of power? It is a tempting conclusion, especially for the academic world which has come rather to despise Shaw's elegantly orchestrated conflict of voices, seeing it as somehow inadequate and superficial, unable to break through to the psychological depths of human motivation, or to break out of the conventional parameters of moral discourse. 'As a wit and pamphleteer he was impressive: as a creative artist only a minor figure', writes T.R. Barnes in the influential *The New Pelican Guide to English Literature* (Barnes 1983: 279).

Again the matter is complex. Certainly the plays are flawed as vehicles of revolutionary change, though in fairness they are hardly alone in that respect. And in response to Wilson, it is hard to conceive how a moralist could make any kind of impact on his audience unless, in some minimal sense, he spoke the same language as it did. This is especially true of the dramatic moralist. Turning to T.R. Barnes again, 'The novelist or poet, who addresses the individual, can forge his own language, and hope that his readers will learn it. The dramatist must speak in terms they already understand; he has to use the language of his age, and this language reflects the condition of the society that speaks it' (Barnes 1983: 277). At least Shaw's voice was and is heard for the simple reason that his plays are popular among a wide public, where other, more innovative writers, must often rest content with a coterie of admirers capable of appreciating their experiments in form. None of which is to underestimate the problems involved in the presentation of radical ideas.

Interestingly, the relationship between thought and practice was a major theme of the plays. The difficulties encountered by moral and intellectual enlightenment in a world plagued by the illusions of tradition and governed by the forces of ignorance and interest were central to the plays of his middle period, *Man and Superman*, *Major Barbara* and *John Bull's Other Island*. It was also the major theme of the socialist realism of his political propaganda. In the plays there was no requirement to arrive at a distinctly socialist resolution to the problem, whereas in his programmatic work he had at least to offer a viable guide to action. The distinction is a simple one, serving only to emphasize that in literature and politics we are dealing with different kinds of rhetorical strategies.

The differences between literature and politics can be noted in the context of Shaw's outlook on human nature. This is of course fundamental to his argument for moral transformation, for human nature is the foundation on which the moral philosopher constructs his scheme of things. As Isiah Berlin explains, 'The ideas of every philosopher concerned with human affairs in the end rest on his conception of what man is and can be' (Berlin 1981: 298).

In the plays Shaw was able to present contrasting views on human nature for the sake of dramatic effect, without having to make a clear choice between the alternatives. The best example of this is found in the exchange between the Devil and Don Juan from Act III of *Man and Superman*. The Devil argued the case for the primacy of the egoistic, hedonistic and destructive qualities in man. Don Juan presented the opposing view, centred on man's instinct for creativity and his sense of service to the life force. No firm conclusion was required. None was forthcoming. All that was aimed at in the drama was to encourage thought by reproducing the main points of controversy in as entertaining a format as possible. The rhetorical strategy employed in the drama therefore was that of a relativist encounter, carefully orchestrated, between conflicting moral passions. Or, to put it another way, Shaw sought to emulate the 'unscrupulous moral versatility of a born dramatist' which Mozart had displayed in his Don Giovanni (Shaw 1932p: 32).

What was disturbing about Shaw as a thinker was that the same uncertain view of human nature was found in his political work. Part of the problem was bound up with the nature of argument itself; he tended to vary the emphasis of his thinking depending on audience and circumstance. When refuting Kropotkin's anarchism in 1888, for example, he was eager to show man as an 'obstinate and selfish devil' so underlining the sheer impracticality of any 'doctrine refusing to countenance social coercion' (Shaw 1888a: 379).

On the other hand, when addressing the more hard-headed Fabian audience two years later, Shaw allowed himself the luxury of presenting a more optimistic picture, announcing that 'the present system is not good enough for human nature' (Shaw 1971: 92).

But it was not just a question of convenient shifts in emphasis to suit the moment. Rather, important changes in the substance and temper of Shaw's argument occurred over the years. In 1894 in a modest article on 'How to become a man of genius', he divorced himself from idealism and cynicism alike, on the grounds that they both 'have as a common basis of belief the conviction that mankind as it really is is hateful' (Shaw 1965b: 345). Shaw did not agree. As a realist, he believed human nature was complex, a mixed bag of potential for good and harm, something which had to be understood on its own terms instead of those imposed on it by dogmatic moralists. Socialism was to be constructed in terms of human nature as it exists and not as it might exist in some utopian dream. In 1928, however, he was to fall into the very trap set for the idealists over thirty years before, arguing now that 'Capitalist mankind in the lump is detestable', so implying a need for radical change in human nature (Shaw 1949a: 489). Sixteen years on, in his desperate pursuit of a doctrine of hope, he was defending human nature against its critics, arguing now that with such material there were no limits to the possibilities of utopian change (Shaw 1944: 2).

To complicate matters still further, the complexities within Shaw's outlook on human nature were not only the products of changing times and audiences. They also derived from deep, ineradicable tensions in his spiritual and intellectual make-up. Fundamental to his vitalism was a conception of individual moral responsibility, founded on a belief in the free development of the autonomous self. Fundamental to his socialism was a contrasting emphasis on the social and environmental determinants of human character. In both instances he was convinced of the essential changeability of human nature, only in one change was due mainly to the operations of individual will, while in the other it was more a case of the malleability of man in relation to the processes of social engineering. As he announced in 1890 'Human nature is only the raw material which society manufactures into the finished rascal or the finished fellowman, as the case may be, according to the direction in which it applies the pressure of self interest' (Shaw 1971: 96). An extreme version of the socialist argument was made in the 1933 preface to *On the Rocks* where Shaw claimed 'There is nothing that can be changed more completely than human nature when the job is taken in hand early enough' (Shaw 1934d: 166). The contrary, vitalist argument was presented in a lecture in 1918 where evolution was described as a 'creative impulse, a living force seeking more life'. The following statement of faith was made: 'Men can change themselves into socialists by willing to be socialists; and, if the change requires eyes in the back of their heads and as many extra pairs of arms as an Indian god has, they could evolve them' (Shaw 1971: 325).

The many-sided and multi-layered reflections on human nature indicate still more problems involved in discussing Shaw's argument. His outlook was certainly flexible. At its best it operated as a critique of the fallacies of absolute morality – of man as essentially good or bad – allowing Shaw as a critical and socialist realist to offer sophisticated analyses of practical political dilemmas as diverse as war between the sexes, classes and nations. But he seemed to carry flexibility too far, touching on almost every possible viewpoint, from wild optimism to deep despair, switching from what Martin Hollis calls an 'autonomous' to a 'plastic' model of man with remarkable ease and rapidity (Hollis 1980). Perhaps in the light of this mercurial performance it would be more appropriate to deal in pluralities, speaking not of Shaw's argument but of his arguments for moral transformation.

Then again, perhaps it would be best to avoid such diversions altogether, keeping to the straighter roads of drama and criticism. But to do so would be to mistake the nature of Shaw's argument and its underlying mechanism. For every play he wrote, he made hundreds of speeches, wrote as many articles and essays, and edited an enormous quantity of Fabian literature. The nights of triumph in the theatre were more than matched by evenings spent in committee meetings in the St Pancras vestry. How many political false starts nourished the sudden glory of his drama? For all he said against dogma and system, the moral revolutionary still searched after faith and order. His drama criticism contained a body of doctrine. His plays were the dialectical expression of his compulsive intellectualism. However great the differences between literature and politics, Shaw's claim that his conversion to socialism in 1882 was the true basis of his success as an artist still has some validity. There can be no profit in the conscience of the pulpit unless one owns a gospel, even one as gloriously eclectic as Shaw's Fabian communism and creative evolutionism. Without that gospel his art lacked power and direction. Before his conversion to socialism he was but a contradictory youth with a critical mind and a certain literary knack. In the absence of the religion of creative evolution he was but a vain man with a talent to amuse. In his own words, he needed a clear comprehension of life in the light of an intelligible theory to set those qualities in triumphant operation. Shaw's argument was powered by his politics.

This study of Shaw's political thought is in two parts. Part I deals primarily with his broad doctrinal concerns and offers the outline of an intellectual biography designed to assist in the complex task of unravelling the overall development of his political thought. Chapter 1 discusses Shaw's Fabian socialism. In Chapter 2 his political ideas are pursued beyond the confines of his Fabianism, looking in detail at the key components of his two major independent statements on politics, namely, *The Guide* and *Everybody's*, published in 1928 and 1944 respectively. Discussion of the first is organized mainly around the doctrine of equality of income, while consideration of the latter concentrates on the issues of democracy and education. With regard to presenting an outline of an intellectual biography, Chapter 1 deals with the period from Shaw's conversion to socialism in 1882 to around the outbreak of the Great War, while Chapter 2 takes up the story from there to 1950.

Part II takes up those subjects which, though fundamental to Shaw's interests, were approached by him not so much as the core matters of socialist doctrine, but as developing historical problems or dramas requiring an immediate and intelligent response from the doyen of socialist realism. The subject of sexual equality was to become such an issue with the advent of the suffragette movement. The Irish question was quintessentially of this kind, although it also raised the broader doctrinal problems of nationalism and imperialism in an acute form. Analysis of foreign policy, the causes of war and the conditions of international order were not exactly forced on Shaw by circumstances, but only took firm root in his work as a consequence of his response to the Great War. Fascism and Sovietism were perhaps the most spectacular unforeseen products of that war and his reflections on both were very much in the nature of unscripted commentaries on exotic new growths in the political hothouse. Each of these chapters might, conceivably, be read as independent essays on distinct subjects. In fact the successive instalments of Part II present the breakdown of the stable Victorian order grounded on the commitment to reason and to progress through technical advancement in the natural and social spheres. The violent tactics of the suffragettes and subsequent government repression, the even fiercer violence and repression in Ireland, coupled to the waste and cruel passions of war – all these worked to undermine Shaw's relatively secure universe powered as it was by the force of rational persuasion, compelling him to reconsider the basic tenets of his thought. His success (or otherwise) in coming to terms with the brave new world of extremism is presented with cruel clarity in his attempts to understand and critically assess the meaning and importance of Mussolini, Hitler and Stalin for the realization of the Shavian vision of a new moral order. The picture to emerge is that of a long struggle on the part of the superior brain to engage the exigencies of power politics in meaningful discourse. Unhappily, the glaring demands of those exigencies were to cast a lengthening shadow across his work, leaving the balance he sought to attain between realism, on one side, and his rational and ethical socialism, on the other, in disarray. The adventures of the superior brain terminated in confusion – moral and intellectual.

A further point to note is that Part II relies more heavily on the drama as evidence of Shaw's views than does Part I. This is because his prose work – the Fabian tracts and essays, his speeches and newspaper articles, plus his book-length studies of politics – offer a more reliable (or at least less problematic) guide to his outlook on the core doctrines of socialism, whereas his views on those matters raised in Part II were in a sense inherently unstable and shot through with ambiguity and uncertainty, so making them good candidates for dramatic as well as prosaic formulation.

The chief aim of this study is to explain and critically assess the central components of Shaw's political thought. In doing so it is informed at many points by the views of other contributors to the field. Though his politics is overshadowed by his drama and consequently sometimes overlooked, especially in studies of a literary kind, it has not been neglected entirely. There exists now a substantial body of literature dealing, in particular, with the Fabian part of his career, though often extending beyond there to his output as a more independent thinker. A.M. McBriar and, more recently, N. and J. MacKenzie are perhaps the best examples here. In a more limited vein, J.W. Hulse and W. Wolfe have offered interesting accounts of Shaw's intellectual links with anarchism, while M.M. Morgan, following the example of E. Strauss and Alick West, has written perceptively on the relationship between his politics and literature. Also, Richard Ohmann's pioneering book on Shaw's style is a model of its kind, while A.J. Turco has brought new depth and cogency to the analysis of his moral vision. Building on these foundations, as well as on the biographical endeavours of Michael Holroyd and the invaluable editorial and bibliographic work of Dan H. Laurence, this study seeks to offer a comprehensive account of Shaw's reflections on politics.

Although this book sees Shaw as an important historical figure in the development of socialist thought and practice, it does not represent a concerted attempt at an intellectual rehabilitation; his theoretical failings are too obvious and too well documented for one to pretend that the innumerable copies of *Everybody's* can be snatched from their dusty graves. But, if his failings as a formal theorist are clear, so too are the strengths of his long discourse on the shifting realities of political life. In effect, Shaw's innate eclecticism (so often a source of ridicule) has a representative quality. His compound personality and the fiercely independent character of his thinking transformed him into something of a receptacle for the doubts and hopes expressed in the Second International and beyond. The unsystematic nature of his work makes him a good illustration in a historical picture of the period. Moreover, his contrasting experience as a critic and defender of Marxism and as the Fabian propagandist is especially pertinent if one accepts that most concrete and reasonably durable forms of socialism fit roughly into the Marxist-Leninist or Fabian models. The point is that different parts of his thought mirror the practices of both the social democrats and the communists. His personal dilemmas are reflected in their attempts to grapple with the perplexing realities of the modern world. Though socialism has governed a considerable part of the globe over the past seventy years or so, its achievements, when considered in relation to its aspirations, are also curiously scattered.

The tensions and creative contradictions which characterize Shaw's political thought bear upon the dilemmas at the heart of socialism and modern culture generally.

Part I

1

SHAW'S FABIANISM

THE COMPLETE OUTSIDER

Shaw was born in Dublin in 1856 into a Protestant family in financial decline: he was 'a downstart and the son of a downstart'; his class was that ephemeral social entity known as 'the Shabby Genteel, the Poor Relations, the Gentlemen who are no Gentlemen' (Shaw 1930: viii). It was a seemingly hopeless start to life with the Shaws possessing a good deal of snobbery and little else. The father drank and the mother appeared fonder of an orchestral conductor called George John Vandaleu Lee than of either George Carr or George Bernard Shaw. 'Sonny', as his family called him, and his sisters, Agnes and Lucy, inhabited an indifferent world, free of emotional, moral or intellectual substance. Shaw was to say years later that this lack of any strong sentiments or faith left a 'clear space for positive beliefs' to invade at some future date. That was the long-term case in its favour. Meanwhile the forgotten boy feasted on dreams. He wandered the art galleries alone. He read his favourite authors, Bunyan, Dickens, Shakespeare and Shelley, exploring the world of the imagination mostly in solitude, or perhaps in the company of his one close friend, Edward McNulty. There was always music, Lee made sure of that; it was Sonny's first love. Yet, even here there lurked a cruel irony, for it seemed the child, starved of affection, preferred this harmonious universe of abstractions to the bitter complexities of human relationships. It was not that he was dominated by his family, but that he was too free. It was not that he was abused, but that he was ignored. And so he dreamed his dreams imagining that his precocious intellect might somehow set him on the throne of English culture.

The reality was very different. At the age of fifteen he began his working life in an estate agent's office in an alien world of stifling routine. There he was a success of sorts. At a deeper level, however, the work was killing the soul of the irreverent and rebellious youth. To compound his misery, two years later, in June 1873, his mother and sister Agnes (Lucy was to follow shortly after) left for London in pursuit of the elusive Mr Lee. Their departure left Sonny in the company of an alcoholic father whose only gift to his son seems to have been an 'extraordinary sense of the ludicrous' (Shaw 1965a: 3).

Sonny was not to remain in Dublin. Early in 1876 he set sail for England in search of fame, fortune and identity. Up to that date the only public manifestation of his genius was an obscure letter attacking the travelling evangelists, Moody and Sankey, published in 1875 in the London weekly, *Public Opinion*. Undaunted he set out on his quest with nothing to declare but his ambition and his brains.

Shaw was to make London his own. For nearly seven decades he was to drive the Rolls-Royce of Shavian argument through its intellectual world at top speed, thus confirming the reality and power of the downstart's dream. At first, however, the road to success was slow and uneven. Shaw spent six years in London writing without success, experimenting with outlandish notions while living at the expense of his mother's better nature. These were the testing years for the shy and nervous young Irishman with an erratic beard and an even more erratic education, the impoverished rebel constantly excited by revolutionary ideas, the nuisance always at odds with the conventions and institutions of society. What was to be done with this quarrelsome youth? He would not work in the normal way. He spent long hours at public meetings or walking the streets at night constructing visionary plans of social reform. It was not that he lacked enthusiasm; he followed Shelley into vegetarianism, joined such radical debating clubs as the Dialectical and Zetetical Societies, studied the art of public speaking and dabbled in pugilism. But to what end? He had written four novels, all of which had been rejected. Far from being the original intellectual phenomenon of his heart's desire, he was, unhappily, but a typical member of the nineteenth century fraternity of shabby genteel radicalism: rootless and aimless, a repository for half-baked doctrines and ill-conceived projects. Shaw was to describe that young man as the complete outsider in search of a gospel of life that might liberate his genius for argument. Possession of a gospel of some kind was essential if the outsider was to play his unique part in the drama of human emancipation, allowing him to traffic in mockery with the earnestness of a prophet.

By 1880 Shaw had attained the status of an able-bodied pauper in a city teeming with ideas, causes and movements. It was a fortuitous coincidence which landed the argumentative Irish alien at the centre of a maelstrom of argument at a time of acute intellectual upheaval. The 1880s was a period of 'ideological cluster', not unlike the 1960s, when the young rebelled against the orthodoxies of their elders by experimenting in a host of alternative doctrines, from socialism to theosophy. Darwinism had caused a generational rift in consciousness and in its wake there followed a wave of radicalism which 'marked the coming of a great reaction from the smug commercialism and materialism of the mid-Victorian epoch, and a preparation for the new universe of the twentieth century' (Feuer 1975: 87). In addition, the economic depression of 1879 and the mounting evidence of urban and rural poverty aroused the guilty conscience of the middle class, sending the intellectual discontent in the direction of economic and social reform.

Upon this stage there arrived in 1882 the radical American agitator, Henry

24

George, armed with his timely doctrine of land nationalization. What George offerred in *Progress and Poverty* was a simple solution to the problem of social justice, encapsulated in the argument for the abolition of private property in land, an argument which he expounded with religious zeal. Instead of being the common property of all, the land was owned by a wealthy oligarchy and therein lay the source of injustice, argued George. Working with a theory of rent derived from Ricardo, he denounced landlords as idle sinners living off the unearned increment of the land they owned. He advocated imposing a single tax on the value of the land and using the revenue thus raised to establish a prototype of the welfare state.

George's only London lecture was delivered on 5 September 1882 in the Memorial Hall at a meeting sponsored by the Land Nationalization Society. Shaw was at that meeting and the address he heard fired his imagination. Henry George transformed his intellectual world by opening his eyes to 'the importance of economics' (Shaw 1949b: 49). Shaw arrived at the Memorial Hall with a batch of discordant radical sentiments, decidedly secularist in content and individualistic in tenor; an enthusiast for Shelley with a reasonable grounding in the fashionable thinkers of the period, Darwin, Herbert Spencer, George Eliot, Tyndall and Huxley. Shaw had read John Stuart Mill, in particular his reflections on the Irish Land question. As the MacKenzies suggest, Shaw's Irish background, the years he spent working in the office of a land agent, made him ripe for Henry George's message that the greed of landlords was the cause of poverty (MacKenzie 1977: 37). Shaw left the Memorial Hall convinced of its truth, on the threshold now of possessing a unifying social gospel. In the Autumn of 1882 his world was transformed. Of George, Shaw wrote 'He struck me dumb and shunted me from barren agnostic controversy to economics' (Shaw 1949b: 58).

His interest in the economic side of the revolutionary argument now awakened, Shaw decided to inquire into the newly-emerging socialist movement as represented by the Social Democratic Federation (SDF), formed in 1881 under the flamboyant leadership of the aristocratic H.M. Hyndman. It was there he learnt of Marx. Conscientious as ever, the rebel read volume one of *Capital* in the French translation and there found the powerful demonstration of the moral rottenness and practical inadequacy of commercial civilization he had been searching for. Conversion was immediate. *Capital*, he said, 'knocked the moral stuffing out of the bourgeoisie' (Shaw 1972: 558). Whereas other political economists treated the wicked nineteenth century as the culmination of human progress, Marx reduced it to but a transitory phase, a mere 'cloud passing down the wind, changing its shape and fading as it goes' (Ellis 1930: 109). Whatever criticisms Shaw levelled against Marx in later years, he always insisted that it was Marx that made him a socialist: 'From that hour I was a speaker with a gospel, no longer an apprentice trying to master the art of public speaking' (Shaw 1949b: 58). From that hour he was tireless in preaching: 'Economics are fundamental in politics: you must begin with the feeding of the individual. Unless you build on that, all your superstructure will be rotten' (Shaw 1962b: 138).

Shaw was a willing convert. Poverty and lack of social standing, his radical temper and compulsive intellectualism, all conspired to impress on him the truth of this most fundamental critique of established values, structures and practices. At a personal level, it showed that the outsider was not to be despised after all. Quite the reverse. Shaw and his kind were the real guardians of public morality, the bearers of the true vision of progress and justice. If they had been rejected by capitalism, it was because of its failing, not theirs (MacKenzie and MacKenzie 1977: 40). At last he had found his rightful place among moral and intellectual pioneers, a group of men 'burning with indignation at very real and very fundamental evils that affected all the world'. Socialism acted on the visionary and moralist elements in Shaw's character, producing a sense of personal salvation through service to a righteous cause. It was the key to the realization of genius and identity. Through socialism, a fusion of public morality and personal identity was achieved, transforming the outsider into an instrument of the *Zeitgeist*.

SOCIALIST FUNDAMENTALISM

An insight into the nature of Shaw's original socialism is gained through the last of the novels of his nonage, *An Unsocial Socialist*, written in 1883. As he explained later, it was intended to be 'only the first chapter of a vast work depicting capitalist society in dissolution, with its downfall as the final grand catastrophe' (Shaw 1932a: v). Whatever its faults from a literary point of view, the novel retains some interest as a political document, both in terms of Shaw's ideas and because of its reflections on the condition of society and the socialist movement at large. On the latter issue, it showed there was no socialist movement in any serious sense, only what Shaw was later to describe as a few 'pushing middle-class men and autocratic swells' (Shaw 1934b: 268). As the novel shows, the hardships encountered by the working class in the economic depression of the 1880s had not been translated practically into mass proletarian activism. The socialism of the period was essentially an intellectual affair, a collection of 'individual minds' as Engels said, 'with a hotch-potch of confused sects, remnants of the great movement of the forties, standing behind them and nothing more' (West 1974: 26). Shaw's hero, Sidney Trefusis, was an isolated intellectual of this kind. In many ways he was something of a prototype for Jack Tanner of *Man and Superman*, a revolutionary member of the idle rich, firm in his hatred of modern English public society which Trefusis described as 'A canting, lie-loving, fact-hating, scribbling, chattering, wealth-hunting, pleasure-hunting, celebrity-hunting mob, that, having lost the fear of hell and not replaced it by the love of justice, cares for nothing but the lion's share of the wealth wrung by threat of starvation from the hands of the classes that create it' (Shaw 1932a: 67).

Devastating though his critique may be, Trefusis is uncertain as to how that society is to be replaced. His strategy in the first part of the novel is to turn his back on his marriage and position in the world, changing his name to Smilash and his accent and clothes to those of a workman. In pursuit of a more authentic mode of life, he rents a 'hermit's cave' deep in the country and takes on odd jobs as a gardener and the like. That Shaw has his hero disappear into rural England and not the industrial North hints at the author's own lack of knowledge of England's industrial heartland and its people. That Trefusis is an isolated figure is only to be expected in the circumstances. The International Association of Labourers, Trefusis mentions, is a distant and unreal organization whose only function in the novel is to reveal the lack of working-class participation in revolutionary politics: 'Expenditure, four thousand five hundred pounds. Subscriptions received from working men, twenty-two pounds seven and tenpence half-penny', the Association's balance sheet reads. As Alick West, writing from a Marxist standpoint, comments, 'From the millionaire's son comes the respectable round sum; from the workers, the comic half-penny' (West 1974: 27). The hero's mission is clear: to liberate the Manchester labourers who were his father's slaves by persuading them to unite 'in a vast international association of men pledged to share the world's work justly'. He acknowledges that the mission will not be easy to fulfil, 'because working-men, like the people called their betters, do not always understand their own interests'. All this Trefusis tells his estranged wife, Henrietta, in an interlude during a prolonged wrangle over their broken marriage. 'We', by which he meant the minority of enlightened socialists, 'must educate the workers out of their folly', he says, though he admits he is far from confident that his own efforts are 'really advancing the cause'. Trefusis only knows he has no choice but to tread the path of righteousness.

For Alick West, Shaw's portrayal of the revolutionary suggests the 'negative individualism' at the core of his socialism: mankind is to be saved by the individual who sets himself apart from others and not by individuals acting in concert, still less by the operations of larger social and economic forces. Similarly, the MacKenzies argue that the portrait confirms Shaw's opinion of the proletariat as 'a useless tool for the would-be revolutionary: the world would be changed only by those who had superior brains and organizing skills' (MacKenzie and MacKenzie 1977: 43). Indeed, toward the end of the novel Trefusis says he now only helps those workmen who show some 'disposition to help themselves'. He also asserts that in creating men of his own kind, rich intellectuals discontented with the prevailing order, capitalism has produced its own gravedigger: 'our system of organizing industry sometimes hatches the eggs from which its destroyers break'. The destiny of man rests not with the masses, nor with hidden historical forces, but with the rebellious intellectuals.

Pertinent as these comments are, it must be acknowledged that here, as in

Man and Superman, the portrait of the would-be revolutionary is underscored by heavy irony. Shaw shares in the dilemmas of his hero and faces the same intellectual tensions. But while he may not have seen a way round them in 1883, he did see through their limitations as strategies of enlightenment. The novel's ultimate strength is that it sets out the contradictions between individualism and collectivism, populism and élitism in such a stark manner. It is not the downfall of capitalism that is depicted so much as the difficulties facing the socialist movement (such as it was) in seeking to translate thought into practice. In that sense, too, the novel is a prototype for Shaw's mature work.

To make too literal a connection between the impoverished Shaw and his wealthy hero is unwise. Nevertheless, Trefusis does seem to express the essence of the young Irishman's socialist faith when he denounces the idleness of the rich and the poverty of the masses in words fired by the power of deep conviction. The contrast between Trefusis's own circumstances and those of the poor aptly demonstrates the hypocrisy of the Victorian ideal of 'the rewards of abstinence': the cotton manufacturer's son who had not done a stroke of work in his life was overburdened with wealth, 'whilst the children of the men who made that wealth are slaving as their fathers slaved, or starving, or in the workhouse, or on the streets, or the devil knows where'. Trefusis had abstained from nothing, while

> the workers abstained from meat, drink, fresh air, good clothes, decent lodgings, holidays, money, the society of their families and pretty nearly everything that makes life worth living, which was perhaps the reason why they usually died twenty years or so sooner than people in our circumstances.

> (Shaw 1932a: 71)

If Shaw was sceptical of the revolutionary potential of the proletariat, he was on this evidence absolute in his condemnation of the condition of their life and the lives of their exploiters: 'under existing circumstances wealth cannot be enjoyed without dishonour, or foregone without misery,' he declared in 1884 in his first Fabian publication (Joad 1953: 72).

Shaw's approach to socialism was fundamentally ethical in nature. At its root was a critique of the evils of capitalism, in particular of the idleness and poverty endemic in commercial civilization. Hatred of idleness and of poverty was the central motif of his socialism; their eradication, its denouement. Idleness was a sin against society, a denial of duty and of man's creative power. Poverty, according to the famous dictum from *Major Barbara*, was the greatest of evils and the worst of crimes. In the socialist order there would be no poverty, none of the artificial barriers raised by class society against either material welfare or the development of the human spirit. There could be no argument: socialism's first duty was to secure sufficiency of means for the masses. Financial security would be assured in the new economic order, an

28

order where men would 'fight for ideas, not for bread and butter at one end and for corrupt domination and stolen luxury at the other' (Shaw 1971: 185).

The critique of poverty was really the common theme uniting the whole of British socialism from Robert Owen to the Fabians, with the entire movement being motivated by a simple and direct abhorrence of want and destitution. The first ever Fabian tract asked, *Why Are the Many Poor?*. Subsequently the Fabian response was in terms of such policies as the minimum wage and old-age pensions, all dedicated to the politics of welfare which had as its *raison d'être* the elimination of poverty.

In his hatred of poverty, Shaw uncovered the roots of an individualist morality of welfare based chiefly on a conception of goodness as happiness. In his hatred of idleness, he unearthed the seeds of the collectivist morality of service. The ideal of the 'gentleman', the essence of Shaw's mature political collectivism, was a direct reversal of customary usage of the word: 'instead of being the detestable parasitic pretention it is at present', he wrote in 1928, in a socialist society it will 'at last take on a simple and novel meaning and be brought within the reach of every able-bodied person'. Idleness was without virtue; the idler a symbol of the corruption that must end with the passing of capitalism. Service to community would be the hallmark of the new moral order, an ideal of citizenship founded on a higher conception of life.

Perhaps the exact terminology changed slightly over the years. All the same, the critique of idleness was a constant concern. His first socialist lecture delivered in a workman's club at Woolwich in 1883 was on the subject of 'Thieves' and in it Shaw tried to demonstrate 'that the proprietor of an unearned income inflicted on the community exactly the same injury as a burglar does' (Shaw 1949b: 59). A year later he was arguing 'that the socialist movement is only the assertion of our lost honesty', that it is 'the duty of each member of the State to provide for his or her wants by his or her own labor'. Again, idle shareholders and absentee landlords were castigated as thieves, highwaymen and public nuisances; private property was said to be the root of evil, leading inevitably to corruption and dishonesty. Neither 'the organization of labor by the State, nor the abolition of competition, nor an equal division of all existing wealth' were socialism's true goal, its essence being 'the essential principle of socialism is that men shall honestly labor for those who labor for them, each man replacing what he consumes, none profiting at his fellows' expense, and all profiting alike by the most economical division of labor. . . .' (Shaw 1971: 2). Behind this statement lay the assumption that socialism's political economy rests on ethical foundations. Shaw explained the connection in an address to the Students' Union at the London School of Economics in 1906, stating that 'Every economic problem will be found to rest on a moral problem: you can not get away from it' (Shaw 1976: 6).

In this critique of idleness Shaw drew not so much on Marx as on the indigenous radicalism of Ruskin and Carlyle, with their fundamentalist emphasis on the morality of labour. Ruskin was especially important in that he underlined the moral foundations of political economy. Like Shaw, he believed that too many workers were engaged in superfluous production instead of in meeting the vital needs of the community. Ruskin wrote that 'as long as there are cold and nakedness in the land around you, so long there can be no question at all but that splendour of dress is a crime' (Ruskin 1906: 60); and in the 1889 *Fabian Essays* (Shaw (ed.) 1948) Shaw supplied the instance of 'a New York lady ... having a nature of exquisite sensibility, orders an elegant rosewood and silver coffin, upholstered in pink satin, for her dead dog. It is made; and meanwhile a live child is prowling barefooted and hunger-stunted in the frozen gutter outside'. Such socially useless production Ruskin called *illth*. It is the negation of true wealth, for exchange value no longer represents utility but what Shaw described as 'the cravings of lust, folly, vanity, gluttony, and madness, technically described by genteel economists as "effective demand" ' (Shaw 1932e: 22). In this way Shaw joined Ruskin in setting a moral standard on industrial production.[1]

Thus Shaw convicted the capitalist system as both unjust and inefficient, producing in the modern era an obscene contrast of riches and misery, the piling up of luxuries for the idle rich while wealth and welfare decrease. What had capitalism produced? 'Only a monstrous pile of frippery, some tainted class literature and class art, and not a little poison and mischief' (Shaw 1932e: 23). Little wonder, then, that his first play dealt with slum landlordism. In Shaw's own words, 'In Widower's Houses I have shewn middle-class respectability and younger son gentility fattening on the poverty of the slum as flies fatten on filth' (Shaw 1931h: xxii). Such was the literature of transition; 'the poetry of despair will not outlive despair itself', predicted Sidney Trefusis (Shaw 1932a: 259).

In spite of all Shaw said about realism and relativism, the core concerns of his socialism seemed to embrace the substance and temper of Victorian fundamentalism. His rhetoric certainly excelled in its violent opposition to the existing scheme of things. As William Morris acknowledged, Shaw was the most damning critic of the false society of his day (Thompson 1955: 636). In the prophet's eyes, the idler was the common enemy of mankind. In 1912 he spoke of 'our ridiculous hesitation over the simple duty of killing these parasites', adding that under capitalism the real tragedy is that we are all possessed by the dream of joining the robber class, even though the odds against it happening are a million to one (Shaw 1976: 112). What was required was the 'inculcation of social responsibility to make every citizen conscious that if his life costs more than it is worth to the community the community may painlessly extinguish it' (Shaw 1936b: 16). Idleness was not to be tolerated. Behind the sardonic humour of the court jester, or the opportunism of the Fabian pamphleteer, there lay a deep-rooted and unyielding moralism.

FROM MARX TO WEBB

Marx converted Shaw to socialism. Shaw, however, was no typical convert who was trusting, uncritical, secure in his fundamentalism. He had too critical and eclectic a mind for that. From the outset he was questioning his new faith, pulling it into different shapes, testing its theoretical power against his sharp, quizzical intellect. As early as March 1884 he mocked Marx's theory of surplus value in an article in the SDF's *Justice*, which he signed G.B.S. Larking. It was a typical Shavian performance, the sort which prompted William Morris, as editor of *Commonweal*, to comment regarding a piece Shaw had submitted to him for publication, 'I think it is better, except as a joke, not to have articles which go dead against our received policy' (Shaw Papers: BM 50541). As Eduard Bernstein remarked of Shaw, 'he is conscious that he himself is a socialist ideologist, but his is too critical a mind to swear fealty to abstract ideas'. G.B.S. Larking, speaking in the name of common humanity, spoke against Marx's abstract notion of bourgeois civilization, pronouncing 'civilization is not the engine, the loom, or the pyramid; it is Man, the master of these things'. Bernstein commented 'In his ideology he is a realist; one might say, paradoxical though it may sound, a critical ideologist, and perhaps this paradox may serve as a key to many apparent contradictions in his behaviour' (Bernstein 1921: 228).

Shaw was always something of a trial to his comrades. H.M. Hyndman found him particularly hard to endure at times. The feeling was mutual. Hyndman's SDF was not exactly to Shaw's liking either. It was too sombre in tone, too authoritarian in its intellectual style, trapped somehow in a straight-jacket of Marxist dialectics. Shaw was not impressed, his comment being that Marx 'deserved something worthier from his pupils than idolatry' (Shaw 1889a: 135). Another major stumbling block from Shaw's standpoint was the SDF's membership, drawn as it was from every class in British society, with its middle-class leadership and proletarian rank and file. Whether it was snobbery or common sense that made him uneasy is open to debate. Either way, he was convinced that such a diffuse and emotionally charged gathering would not suit his own peculiar qualities of cool irony, civility and self-possession 'in the presence of the sufferings upon which socialists make war' (Shaw 1932e: 127). He knew he was capable of doing practical work for socialism, but not here, not in this mixed bag of zealots, idolaters and warm-hearted working men. Having found a gospel, what he now needed was a place of worship which could somehow accommodate the tensions within his personality, torn as it was between faith and doubt, fundamentalism and apostasy.

In September 1884 Shaw was pleased to join the newly formed Fabian Society which he described in a letter written a few weeks later to the Austrian émigré Andreas Scheu as 'a body of middle-class philanthropists who believe themselves to be Socialists' (Thompson 1955: 385). There was no Fabian doctrine as such. What appealed to Shaw about the Society was its ethos of tolerance, its critical intellectualism and its exclusiveness. Later he was to say that he was guided 'solely by an instinctive feeling that the Fabian and not the Federation would attract the men of my own bias and intellectual habits who were then ripening for the work that lay before us' (Shaw 1932e: 127). It was an intensely personal decision. The early Fabians were mostly men of Shaw's kind, unattached intellectuals searching for a spiritual home – teachers, journalists, low-grade civil servants – many of them drawn from the provinces and cast adrift in London, all of them misfits and outsiders in their way. These were men of the same class and age, tolerant of eccentricity and heresy, glad to have their meetings enlivened by Shaw's wit, consoled by his tact and stimulated by his intellect. This surely was the perfect theatre for a maverick socialist (to use J.W. Hulse's term) to stage his personal drama of redemption. What if the Fabians lacked a doctrinal understanding of socialism? That surely could be remedied by a little thought and manipulation. As luck would have it, Shaw had a manifesto he had written tucked away in his pocket, just waiting to be snapped up by a discerning socialist organization. He was especially pleased when the Fabians decided to adopt and print it, taking the decision to be a sure sign of superior brains at work.

Significantly, in a letter to Scheu he indicated that the *Manifesto* was for 'distribution among the middle class', which suggests that even here he was feeling his way towards an appropriate audience for his uniquely eloquent and sardonic brand of socialist argument. In a sense the Fabians themselves were a microcosm of what is often perceived to be the true Shavian audience: cultured, caring, concerned to bring the values of civic humanism to bear on socialist practice, yet still sufficiently at ease to enjoy the luxuries of style and humour. Where else would the smart criticisms he aimed against dogma, or his ironic understanding of the absurdities of political enthusiasm have found favour? His *Manifesto* ended with a clever, waspish declaration on British democracy which could only have appeared under Fabian auspices 'That the established Government has no more right to call itself the State than the smoke of London has to call itself the weather'.

And yet, in spite of his apparent sense of direction, the overall picture of Shaw we have from the early 1880s is that of a rebel with a cause, but still unclear as to how to translate that commitment into a practical strategy of social transformation. At one level these years were the golden age of GBS, the intellectual rebel personified. He threw himself into London's radical world with tremendous energy, so much so that his name was synonymous with the progressive cause. Within months of his conversion to socialism, the poor, self-educated outsider found himself at the centre of the small stage which sufficed for the socialist movement. It was his university. His intellectual curiosity knew no bounds.

Shaw came into contact with so much and so many in this period. He knew all the leading members of the SDF, among them Karl Marx's youngest daughter, Eleanor Marx Aveling and her common-law husband, the unsavoury Edward Aveling. From Shaw's diaries there emerged a picture of frequent social intercourse with the Avelings in the mid-1880s, which turned upon mutual intellectual interests in Ibsen and a concern for the relationship between socialism and sexual equality.

Another SDF recruit was Belfort Bax, a freelance journalist from a wealthy non-conformist background who had come to Marxism via a study of Hegelian philosophy. Bax's Marxism was unusual in so far as he tended to differentiate historical periods in terms of their metaphysical and ethical outlooks (Pierson 1973: 92), a tendency which Shaw replicated when he came to formulate his vitalist philosophy in *The Quintessence of Ibsenism* (1891) (*Quintessence*). Bax was in fact an important influence on Shaw's philosophical education (Whitman 1977; Griffith 1979).

William Morris, the Pre-Raphaelite poet, painter and publisher who held the extraordinary opinion that *An Unsocial Socialist* was a good novel, was another member of Hyndman's SDF, before quarrels over strategies and personalities in 1884 persuaded Morris to form his own anarchistic organization, the Socialist League. Shaw was to become close to Morris, as well as to his beautiful daughter, May, with whom Shaw shared an unfulfilled love affair.

Beside the SDF, there were several other venues for the ubiquitous Irish rebel to meet the luminaries of radical thought in this period, including the Wheatsheaf Restaurant, where vegetarians satisfied their intellectual hunger, and the Land Reform Union, a body founded on the ideas of Henry George. In the latter Shaw met the Christian Socialist, Stewart Headlam, and James Leigh Joynes, the former Eton master who had accompanied George on his controversial visit to Ireland in 1882. Joynes was a fellow vegetarian, a humanitarian and Shelleyan; he was, besides, the brother-in-law of Henry Salt, another former Eton master of similar political persuasion who, with his wife Kate, had opted for the simple life in a Surrey cottage. Shaw and the Salts became close friends and through them he forged a link with the humanitarian side of the progressive movement. Intimate in the Salt household was the like-minded simple lifer and sexual radical Edward Carpenter, a co-member of the Humanitarian League founded by Henry Salt and fellow Fabian until 1900 when Carpenter parted company with the Society due to its stance on the Boer War. As Shaw commented, in the Salt circle 'there was no question of Henry George or Karl Marx, but a good deal of Walt Whitman and Thoreau' (Shaw 1949b: 67). At the other extreme, Shaw rubbed shoulders with Marx's collaborator, Frederick Engels, a fact which astounded his Russian hosts in the 1930s.

According to J.W. Hulse, Shaw was the 'most eclectic member of the London socialist community in the last fifteen years of the nineteenth century', sampling 'the several varieties of socialism then available' (Hulse 1970: 111–37). Hulse's main interest is in Shaw's leaning towards anarchism.

This can be traced to many sources, including his friendship with Morris and the radical individualism he inherited from his youthful regard for Shelley. Connections can also be made with Shaw's critique of duty in his early novels and with his later advocacy of individual wilfulness in *Quintessence*. This anarchistic element in his intellectual make-up was to play a constant part in his work, especially in the plays which, according to Hulse, were essentially vehicles for the expression of his heretical individualism. This interpretation of Shaw deserves consideration, especially as it offers a way of accounting for the contrast between the apparent individualism of the plays and the collectivism of his politics. Hulse, however, is careful to avoid the claim that Shaw's radical individualism entailed a more formal commitment to anarchist theory as such.

Shaw certainly flirted briefly with anarchism in the mid-1880s, submitting an article to *The Anarchist* in 1885 entitled, 'What's in a name?'. There he criticized state socialism, warning that 'Slavery is the complement of authority and will disappear with it'. But this flirtation with individualist anarchism was of an equivocal kind. The article, for example, was subtitled 'How an Anarchist might put it', and, as Shaw informed the paper's editor, Henry Seymour, prior to publication, it was 'written more to shew Mrs [Charlotte] Wilson my idea of the line an anarchist paper should take in England than as an expression of my own convictions'. Nevertheless, he added 'there is nothing in [the article] that I object to commit myself publicly to' (Shaw 1965a: 109). In the article Shaw asserted:

> the Collectivists would drive the money-changers from Westminster only to replace them with a central administration, committee of public safety, or what not. Instead of 'Victoria by the Grace of God', they would give us 'the Superintendent of such and such an Industry, by the authority of the Democratic Federation', or whatever body we are to make our master under the new dispensation.
>
> (Shaw 1885: 2)

After its publication, Shaw sought to defend himself against too literal an interpretation of the statement, stating in 1887 that he only employed anarchist arguments as a counterweight to Hyndman's authoritarian form of collectivism (Shaw 1887a: 8). The record is confusing, Shaw's performance certainly made a curious impact at the time. Perplexed, the American anarchist, Benjamin K. Tucker, told him in 1885 'Sometimes I wish you would be either a State Socialist or an Anarchist a little more steadfastly and consistently, but generally forget this in admiring the vigor of your assault on existing evils' (Shaw Papers: BM 50511).

Shaw's relationship with individualist anarchism has been discussed more stridently by Willard Wolfe. He, in fact, claims that Shaw embraced the anarchist standpoint more or less wholeheartedly in the mid-1880s. Wolfe argues that the basis of all Shaw's early socialist thought 'was his vision of a free trade Utopia in which every man would be his own master and all goods and services would exchange "honestly – at cost price" ' (Wolfe 1975: 128). In defence of the claim, Wolfe marshalls an apparently impressive array of sources, purporting to show how these views developed not only from Shaw's reading of Ruskin and the English radicals, but also from an early acquaintance with Proudhon's work. Wolfe explains how Shaw was introduced to Proudhon by an ex-Communard named Richard Deck, an acquaintance Shaw had made at the Zetetical Society. From Proudhon, Wolfe claims, Shaw acquired a 'Radical-individualist Utopianism' founded on the notion of 'giving all workers free "access" to the means of production and thus the opportunity to "produce for themselves" whatever they needed'. This was the libertarian side to Shaw, wary of the new masters that would arise under collectivism, eager to secure free competition among free men. His friendship with Morris strengthened this vision. Morris was 'Shaw's socialist mentor' in 1884, Wolfe asserts. Wolfe's argument is supported by Morris's contention that Shaw's 'real tendencies are towards individualist anarchism', which itself echoed Shaw's own admission to Andreas Scheu that he was at 'heart an Anarchist' (Wolfe 1975: 133, 138).

Much of what Wolfe says in this respect is stimulating and original. The problem is that he overstates the case. It is not that he denies the ambiguity in Shaw's outlook entirely, only that he insists it can be explained away in terms of a distinction between Shaw's economic and political doctrines (Wolfe 1975: 140). In economics Shaw favoured a form of competitive individualism operating on anarchic lines. Wolfe quotes the Fabian *Manifesto* of 1884 to this effect 'That since Competition among producers admittedly secures to the public the most satisfactory products, the State should compete with all its might in every department of production'. As this does not seem terribly anarchic, Wolfe explains that the state's only role was to 'stimulate *real* competition among producers'. But Shaw did not say that in the *Manifesto*, nor in the lecture, 'The New Radicalism', Wolfe's alternative source for his interpretation. In the former, the state was to compete with parents 'in providing happy homes for children'. More directly, it was to 'secure a liberal education and equal share in the National Industry to each of its units'. This was a long way from economic individualism, owing more perhaps to the later works of J.S. Mill than to either Proudhon or Morris. Further, in the lecture the state had a duty 'to compete with all its might in every department of production until the maxima of industrial efficiency and national welfare are attained' (Shaw 1971: 33). Shaw might well have been an anarchist at heart, but in his statements of socialist doctrine – economic as well as political – his tendencies were less clear-cut. His Fabian *Manifesto* was really a monument to his eclecticism.

If Wolfe's case is overstated, it does point us toward an important theme of Shaw's early socialism, namely, the paradoxical decline of competition in modern capitalism which was the result of the growth of monopolies in almost every industry. The argument was stated in detail in a letter he wrote to his friend Edward McNulty in 1884 'Everywhere the large capitalists are swallowing up the small ones', he declared, rounding off the paragraph nicely with the Marxian (and anti-Trefusis) prediction 'It is in this way that the capitalist system has evolved from its own essential principles of competition the instrument of its own destruction'. Clearly, the private monopolists who 'exercise all the powers of a government without its responsibilities' had to be dismantled (Shaw 1965a: 86). But how exactly, and what would replace them, was another matter.

If Shaw is to be believed, it was 1886 before he realized that none of the pioneers 'knew what Socialism was', that they were all but 'violent reactionaries against the existing system'. The issue at stake was the relationship between thought and practice, aims and means. Within a year or so that issue had been more or less resolved. By the end of 1887 he had abandoned, albeit reluctantly, Marx's theory of surplus value for the more respectable marginal utility theory of Stanley Jevons. Also, under the influence of Ferdinand Lassalle, the founder of the General Association of German Workers who had died in a duel in 1864, Shaw was to embrace political collectivism in a decisive way. There were to be no more flirtations with any form of anti-statist socialisms. Lassalle, not Marx, was to show the way toward social democracy. The Fabians were to add 'only pure detail' to his politics, Shaw admitted in 1889 (Shaw 1971: 45).

There was also a decisive rejection of insurrectionary tactics in 1887. At least that was how Shaw explained it. The events of Bloody Sunday in May of that year, when a rally of the unemployed was easily routed by a small group of disciplined policemen, revealed to him the impossibility of mass revolutionary politics. We are prompted to believe that before then Shaw was inclined to look upon 'the evolution of socialism as a miraculous catastrophe, with alarms, excursions and red fire' (Shaw 1888b: 39). 'The young socialist is apt to be catastrophic in his views – to plan the revolutionary programme as an affair of twenty-four lively hours, with Individualism in full swing on Monday morning, a tidal wave of the insurgent proletariat on Monday afternoon and Socialism in complete working order on Tuesday afternoon', he noted in an apparently autobiographical aside from *Fabian Essays*. Many commentators (especially those who emphasize his connections with Morris) tend to accept this line of argument more or less uncritically. Hulse, for example, says Shaw was impatient and uncertain about the gradualist method 'that might eventually be used', emotional in his commitment to the cause of justice; it was thus Shaw appended a 'half-warning, half-threat on to the end' of his 'Transition' contribution to *Fabian Essays* (Hulse 1970: 118):

> Let me, in conclusion, disavow all admiration for this inevitable, but sordid, slow, reluctant, cowardly path to justice. I venture to claim your respect for those enthusiasts who still refuse to believe that millions of

their fellow creatures must be left to sweat and suffer in hopeless toil and degradation, whilst parliaments and vestries grudgingly muddle and grope towards paltry instalments of betterment. The right is so clear, the wrong so intolerable, the gospel so convincing, that it seems to them that it *must* be possible to enlist the whole body of workers – soldiers, policemen and all – under the banner of brotherhood and equality; and at one great stroke to set Justice on her rightful throne.

(Shaw 1932e: 60)

Powerful as the statement is, it is worth noting that the evidence regarding Shaw's youthful commitment to an insurrectionary strategy is not entirely convincing. It is true that Morris in his review of *Fabian Essays* saw Shaw's conversion to gradualism as something of an aberration. Writing in *The Commonweal* in 1890, Morris said 'Mr Shaw does not love opportunism for its own sweet self; for in his second lecture he definitely proclaims his shame of the course to which, as he thinks, circumstances have driven him'. However this interpretation may have owed more to their friendship than to a deep insight into Shaw's politics. The Fabian *Manifesto* does close with the assertion 'That we would rather see a civil war than such another century of suffering as this has been'. But it was hardly a serious proposition. Long before the events of Bloody Sunday, Shaw had said the unemployed did not want a revolution, they wanted a job; they were 'as great a nuisance to socialists as to themselves' (Shaw 1886: 4). Writing in the journal *Our Corner* he had caricatured revolution as 'Misery having a holiday with civilization to play with', which would seem to point towards the gradual parliamentary road to socialism (Shaw 1887b: 164). This is not to deny the militant fundamentalism at the heart of Shaw's socialism. It is only to suggest that it was tempered by the spirit of the critical ideologist. The story of the insurrectionary youth of the early 1880s was to some degree a myth created by the master of self-dramatization.

Doctrinally, Shaw's performance before 1887 was a perplexing show that travelled between radical individualism and collectivism, militancy and reformism, fundamentalism and scepticism. He was never really an advocate of revolutionary catastrophism, but among the leading Fabians he was unique in his personal links with the Marxian tradition. His ideas were somehow representative of all the forms of socialism on offer, from the collectivist SDF to the libertarian Socialist League. Often the tone and substance of those ideas changed to suit context and audience, his latest enthusiasm or the threat of riot by the unemployed could tilt the balance of his rhetoric, just as his argument could change when speaking in the drizzle at the dock gates, as against lecturing in the relative comfort of the Liberal and Social Union. 'I cannot for the life of me escape from the influence of my audience', he confessed in 1891 in a fascinating account of how the style and substance of his argument depended on the nature of his audience (Shaw 1891: 9). For many commentators, Wolfe and the MacKenzies among them, the assumptions underlying his socialism were broadly the same as those of Morris. So they might have been when lecturing to the militants who gathered at Kelmscott House in Hammersmith. Even then the doctrinal connection between Shaw and Morris can be overplayed. More persuasive is Ingle's account of the divergences between the two, in particular regarding their respective visions of what man is and what socialist man can be: Morris's socialist man finds fulfillment through his creativity, Ingle argues, whereas Shaw's highly differentiated creature achieves fulfillment by acting out a specific social function (Ingle 1975: 92). It is true that Shaw later elevated Morris to the status of a saint of socialist fundamentalism, but this kind of eulogizing should not dominate the interpretation of their intellectual relationship which was complex and subject in many ways to the ruses and foibles of Shavian political argument. Certainly, the differences between the two became apparent when Shaw gained a platform among more traditional liberals and radicals: then he cut his rhetorical cloth accordingly, arguing that socialism should be made respectable and formidable by 'the support of our class', that it should be organized in 'a party informed at all points by men of gentle habits and trained reasoning powers', so avoiding the unpleasantness that would accompany revolution by the ignorant and uncivil poor (Shaw 1962b: 11).

This was the path the polemicist of gradualism was to take. It has long been acknowledged that his full acceptance of the parliamentary road to socialism was facilitated by his propaganda work in the circuit of London's radical clubs and societies in this period. This activity was largely the result of still another association, this time with the radical orator and fellow Fabian, Annie Besant. In the 1870s she had achieved notoriety on a national scale through her work with the militant atheist, Charles Bradlaugh, both for their agitation for secularism and for their defence of birth control. Their republication in 1877 of Charles Knowlton's banned book on birth control, *The Fruits of Philosophy, or The Private Companion of Young Married People*, resulted in prosecution, which in turn incited the young Shaw to offer to campaign on their behalf by distributing the book. In 1884 their roles were very different, for then Shaw was instrumental in converting Besant to socialism; in April 1885 he shepherded her questing soul into the Fabian fold (MacKenzie and MacKenzie 1977: 45). Intense in her commitment to the cause, she was a great asset to the fledgling Fabian Society. She alone among its early members had both a ready-made reputation as a radical agitator and close links with the network of London's radical groups. Whilst her contribution to *Fabian Essays* was the least impressive theoretically, her very participation in the project broadened its appeal, lending it an immediate legitimacy in progressive circles. Annie Besant was irresistible – she even published her own monthly journal, *Our Corner*.

One way or another, Shaw could not resist her. Soon after she joined the

Fabian Society tongues started wagging on the subject of their personal and political relationship. The incorruptible Morris considered Besant to be a bad influence on Shaw when, during the controversy in 1886 surrounding the formation of the Fabian Parliamentary League, he found the incorrigible Irishman defending parliamentarianism – 'as if he were ashamed of himself' (Arnot 1964: 35). What is clear is that through his association with Besant, Shaw gained access to more moderate middle-class audiences than those he encountered at the Dock Gates, which in turn hastened his drift toward gradualism and permeation.

The upshot was that he was never tempted to join Morris's Socialist League. His rightful place was with the tolerant Fabians who welcomed such an atypical member as Shaw in the manner of a wayward son of a respectable family, stimulating if unpredictable, surprisingly useful, even loyal and sensible in his own fashion. By 1888 the Fabians had come a long way doctrinally from the group of well-intentioned, if muddled enthusiasts of 1884. They were now firmly committed to economic and political collectivism, and armed with their own non-Marxian theory of economic exploitation. The theory was hammered out over many years at the Hampstead Historic Club among a coterie of friends, notably Shaw, Graham Wallas, Sydney Olivier and of course 'the ablest man in England', Sidney Webb. This, to use Shaw's phrase, was the Fabian Thinking Cabinet where he played D'Artagnan to the Three Musketeers of Fabianism. He said it served as an 'incomparable critical threshing machine for his ideas', knocking much of the provincialism out of him, smoothing out the rough edges in his education.

Shaw first met Webb in 1880 at the Zetetical Society when Webb was still a government clerk. He was shy, stocky and prosaic, with a socially-inhibiting Cockney accent which suggested his relatively humble middle class origins. But if Webb's origins were modest, his talents were prodigious and his meteoric ascent was in keeping with these. Within a few years this unlikely star had entered the upper division of the Colonial Office and established the effective beginning of Fabianism with his tract *Facts for Socialists* (1887); more remarkable, he was to form a unique partnership with the imperious social researcher, Beatrice Potter, with whom he now shares a reputation as one of the chief architects of the welfare state. Shaw knew at once that Webb was a phenomenon and nurtured his friendship accordingly, persuading him to join the Fabian Society in 1884.

Sydney Olivier, too, was a civil servant at the Colonial Office when Shaw first came across him at the Land Reform Union in 1883. There was nothing modest in his background. Olivier's father, a wealthy Anglican Minister, sent his son through the best public schools and on to Oxford, expecting him to make his mark on the world of the English Establishment. His son, as unconventional a civil servant as one could hope to find, went far indeed, but in his own way and in his own time. Like Webb, he died a peer of the realm, having achieved political eminence, first as Governor of Jamaica, and in the

1920s as a member of the first Labour Government, in which Olivier served as Secretary of State for India and his friend Webb as President of the Board of Trade.

Olivier had known the third Fabian Musketeer, Graham Wallas, since his days at Oxford. Their family backgrounds were similar, as were their intellectual and religious dilemmas and they became good friends. Both came to socialism with a guilty conscience, heavy with the presumed sins of wealth. As with Shaw, their socialism was driven by their moralism, with Wallas especially representing the connections between Fabianism and the Christian humanitarianism which underpinned so much of the socialistic faith of the British labour movement.

In Webb, Olivier and Wallas we find, both in terms of personalities and ideas, the subtle convergences and divergences within Fabian socialism. All three owed a strong intellectual debt to the later works of John Stuart Mill in which a commitment to individualist radicalism seemed to find expression in a nascent form of socialistic collectivism. Webb and Olivier nurtured their collectivist sentiments on the positivism of the French philosopher August Comte, who argued the case for the moralization of capitalism. The influence of Comte's historicism and social organicism was deepened by the vogue of evolutionary theorizing in England, so that in Webb's contribution to *Fabian Essays* we find him urging the individual to look upon his self-development in terms of the filling 'of his humble function in the great social machine' (Shaw 1948: 54).

All three Musketeers were regular attenders at the Hampstead Historic Club in 1885. Meetings were held fortnightly at the home of the anarchist sympathizer, Mrs Charlotte Wilson, with the purpose of discussing Marxian economic theory. Shaw was encouraged to join the circle by Webb who told him that without an 'unscrupulous socialist dialectician' like himself they would have discarded *Capital* within a month' (MacKenzie and MacKenzie 1977: 63). Something of the tone and substance of the club's proceedings is gained from Shaw's account of them written in the May 1889 issue of the socialist journal, *To Day*:

> A young Russian lady used to read out *Capital* in French to us until we began to quarrel, which usually occurred before she had gone on long enough to feel seriously fatigued. The first chapters in particular were of extraordinary efficacy in setting us by the ears. F.Y. Edgeworth as a Jevonian, and Sidney Webb as a Stuart Millite, fought the Marxian value theory tooth and nail; whilst Belfort Bax and I, in a spirit of transcendent Marxism, held the fort recklessly, and laughed at Mill and Jevons. The rest kept an open mind and skirmished on either side as they felt moved.
> (Shaw 1889a: 129)

Central to their discussions were the respective merits and de-merits of the Marxian and Jevonian theories of value. The case for Stanley Jevons and against Marx had first been made in the October 1884 issue of *To Day* by the Revd Philip H. Wicksteed, a unitarian minister with an interest in abstract economics. Shaw gamely offered a rejoinder in January 1885, but soon found himself under Wicksteed's tutelage at yet another economic discussion group, which was later to become the British Economic Association. He was joined there by Wallas. The tone here was abstract and academic, unlike at the Hampstead circle where the task at hand was to formulate a distinctly Fabian theory of surplus value. The upshot was that by 1887 Shaw had accepted the superiority of the Jevonian theory of value and the Fabian Musketeers had worked out their own theory of rent; Shaw achieved the amalgamation of the two in his 'Economic' contribution to *Fabian Essays* in 1889.

Shaw had foreshadowed his dissatisfaction with Marx's theory in the G.B.S. Larking article of March 1884 in which mock outrage was expressed at Marx's supposed reduction of the entire middle class to a class of thieves. The critical ideologist did not go on to question whether labour power was indeed the source of value. That was Wicksteed's contribution, who demonstrated, on Jevonian grounds, that the 'value of a commodity is a function of the quantity available, and may fall to zero when the supply outruns the demand so far as to make the final increment of the supply useless' (Shaw 1948: 116). Armed with the calculus of marginal utility, Wicksteed concluded that the Marxian determination of value by working time is false, as is the labour theory of surplus value and with it the whole edifice of Marx's prognostications regarding the inherent contradictions of capitalism. Commenting years later, Shaw said that he became:

> a convinced Jevonian fascinated by the subtlety of Jevons' theory and the exquisiteness with which it adapted itself to all cases which had driven previous economists, including Marx, to take refuge in clumsy distinctions between use value, exchange value, labour value, supply and demand value, and the rest of the muddlements of the time.
>
> (Pease 1963: 276)

Picking up on such statements as this, commentators have spoken of Shaw's conversion to Jevons's theory in the Spring of 1887. In fact the tenor of Shaw's public position on the issue was relatively circumspect. Developing mostly in the context of Shaw's debunking of Hyndman in the columns of the *Pall Mall Gazette* in May of that year, and later in a review of *Capital* for the *National Reformer* of 7, 14 and 21 August, the thrust of his position was (i) that socialism does not stand or fall with either the Marxian or Jevonian theories of value (Shaw 1887f: 11); (ii) that the ultimate verdict on Marx's political economy must await the publication of the third volume of *Capital* (Shaw 1887e: 85); but that (iii) certainly in the first volume of *Capital* Marx treated 'raw material without reference to variations of fertility' and the difference between 'the product of labor and the price (wage) of labor power as "surplus value" without reference to its subdivision into rent, interest, and profits' (Shaw 1887e: 85). Provisionally, then, Jevons had the edge on Marx in abstract economics, though Shaw was quick to remind his audience that the 'extraordinary impression' Marx makes 'does not depend on the soundness of his views, but on their magnificent scope and on his own imperturbable conviction of their validity'.

Privately, Shaw was more forthcoming. In a letter drafted to Edward Aveling on 17 May 1887 he conceded that Marx's theory of value was wrong, and admitted that he had tried to throw it overboard as gently as possible, claiming only that socialism was not based on it and, in a veiled reference to his own G.B.S. Larking article, that its rejection had been anticipated by the socialists themselves (Shaw 1965a: 168).

The episode was an interesting one, suggesting as it does Shaw's reluctance to break with his Marxist intellectual heritage, thus confirming Olivier's picture of him as a desperate representative of the Marxist viewpoint in the early Fabian economic debates (Henderson 1956: 212). The difficulty for Shaw was that his understanding of economic exploitation, and with it the moral and scientific case for socialism, was grounded on Marx's theory of surplus value. An alternative theory was needed if Marx was to be set aside; the Fabian rent theory was that alternative as formulated by Webb and Olivier in the latter part of 1886 or the early part of 1887 (McBriar 1962: 36). Original to it was its extension of the radical theory of rent, as expounded by Ricardo and J.S. Mill and vulgarized by George, to embrace a critique of capitalists as well as landlords.

In Fabian circles Shaw played George to Webb's Mill, with Webb presenting rent theory in a technical form in the *Quarterly Journal of Economics* in January 1888 and Shaw putting forward a more accessible version a year later in *Fabian Essays*, a version described by George Lichtheim as 'lively, albeit somewhat slap-dash' (Lichtheim 1975: 210). Shaw's essay opens with the assertion that 'All economic analyses begin with the cultivation of the earth', and proceeds to offer several definitions of the rent of land from J.S. Mill, Marshall and Sidgwick, all of which were said to be elaborations of Ricardo's conception of rent as 'that portion of the produce of the earth which is paid to the landlord for the use of the original and indestructible powers of the soil'. Reaching back to the Bible for its rhetorical power, Shaw developed his analysis of the origins and development of private property based on the story of Adam and his descendants, with each generation of men slipping more and more into the grasp of the landlords as the land available for cultivation diminished in size and quality. Eventually, Shaw explained, there emerged the landless worker whose only option was to sell his labour to the highest bidder, while the landlord, richer than ever, lived on the fruits of that labour. In this way 'the proletarian renounces not only the fruits of his labor, but also his right to think for himself and to direct his industry as he pleases. The economic change is merely formal: the moral change is enormous'. The resulting association of prosperity with idleness was noted and followed by an exposition of exchange value based on the marginal utility theory of Jevons. From there the argument moved to the subject of wages in industry, with Shaw concluding in a Marxian vein that the 'shareholder and landlord live alike on the produce extracted from their property by the labor of the proletariat'. A rapid endorsement of Ruskin's critique of conspicuous consumption in the form of *illth* concluded with the assertion:

> This, then, is the economic analysis which convicts Private Property of being unjust even from the beginning, and utterly impossible as a final solution of even the individualist aspect of the problem of adjusting the share of the worker in the distribution of wealth to the labor incurred by him in its production.
>
> (Shaw 1948: 22)

Ricardo identified the three factors of production to be land, labour and capital. The Fabian theory of surplus value, as explained by Webb, held that higher productivity resulting from superior soil or the application of capital and skilled labour is divided up between different types of rent, with the landlord and capitalist receiving a disproportionate return in the form of an unearned increment whilst the measure of the wages paid to unskilled workers is established by the wages paid to workers employed on the worst soil or with the minimum of capital (McBriar 1962: 31; Lichtheim 1975: 211). Eclectic to the last, Shaw cited Marx when formulating the theory of surplus value, stating that the types of economic rent are 'paid out of the difference between the produce of the worker's labor and the price of that labor sold in the open market for wages, salary, fees, or profits' (Shaw 1948: 25).

In the second 'Transition' essay Shaw explained that the achievement of socialism economically involves the transfer of rent from the class which now appropriates it to the whole people; envisaged was the taxation of unearned income and the gradual socialization of the sources of production 'by the expropriation of the present private proprietors', with the state acting as the trustee of the people in this process. Through rent theory the Fabians forged a theoretical justification for their commitment to economic and political collectivism. Thus, when introducing the essayists in 1889 as communicative learners not authoritative teachers of socialism, Shaw was able to assert as an article of faith that 'The writers are all Social-Democrats, with a common conviction of the necessity of vesting the organization of industry and the material of production in a State identified with the whole people by complete Democracy'.

More important in hindsight was the strategic value of rent theory to the Fabians, for it tapped into the established language and concerns of British radicalism, as against the off-putting foreign innovations of Marx. Rent theory fostered the cause of the Fabian permeation of radical liberalism; so, too, did the political economy of Jevons, again due largely to the familiarity of its concepts and concerns. Thus, Shaw wrote of the 'tremendous effectiveness' of Jevonian theory 'as a weapon in the hands of Social Democracy' in the July 1889 issue of *Justice*.

Probably as a result of his protracted conversion to it, Shaw was inclined at times to overstate the theoretical importance of Jevonian theory, in particular his suggestion in *Fabian Essays* that it was a necessary component of rent theory rather than being merely compatible with it. But even there the treatment was ambiguous, with the influence of Jevons forming one part of the eclectic puzzle. Indeed, in Shaw's work the overwhelming tendency was to use Jevons as a weapon of political controversy against Hyndman not as a genuine contribution to the cause of scientific socialism, still less as a weapon against the enemies of socialism generally. None the less, Jevons does seem to have confirmed Shaw's drift away from Marx's fundamentalist critique of the middle classes, with its class war implications, towards a more gradualist and marginalist approach to socialism, a socialism of 'more or less', based upon an incrementalist view of distributive justice, to be achieved by means of a policy of progressive taxation, and where the expropriation of private property was to be sweetened by the pill of compensation. The influence of Jevons was another nail in the coffin of the vision of socialism as a grand theatre of noble rebellion.

Through such influences and the workings of his Fabian associations Shaw found an empirical key to English politics. He said that Webb in particular saved him from becoming a mere literary social critic, making him a practical political proposition, a working socialist with a wealth of data at his disposal to support his ethical critique of the contemporary order. Webb was a bureaucrat in a bureaucratic age, one of the few socialists with real knowledge of local and central government. He was, in short, Shaw's passport into the hard-nosed world of English power politics: 'The difference between Shaw with Webb's brains, knowledge, and official experience and Shaw by himself was enormous' (Shaw 1949b: 66). Now Shaw was the outsider with inside information, fully equipped to agitate and permeate with a vengeance.

By the end of 1888 Shaw was editing *Fabian Essays*, the success of which made him a national celebrity in socialist circles. From that moment he was at liberty to describe himself as 'thinker and tactician' to the British labour movement (Shaw 1965a: 389).

FABIAN REALISM

Socialism is not an elaborate game with prizes for theoretical sophistication, but a practical philosophy offering a definite programme for changing the economic and political structures of society. What matters for the active socialist is the way ideas perform in practice, the part theory plays in forging an effective transition to socialist power and its role in practically transforming society in socialism's own image. Good intentions are of no value unless they can be expressed in the context of a viable policy of transition.

This, in essence, is the Fabian approach to politics. The early Fabians were certainly not renowned for theoretical sophistication. As Shaw explained, their chief interest was in locating the next practical step to collectivism, not in cultivating exotic or subtle visions of emancipation. Their reputation, such as it is, rests chiefly on the practicality of the social reforms they designed to secure the welfare of the masses. If Fabianism evokes any lasting impression among socialists, it is that of the perversion of an emancipatory doctrine into a dull bureaucratic creed. Often Fabian policy is identified with Webb; earnest but unimaginative, a study in caution and respectability, in an unwillingness to venture too far into theoretical territory. Initially at least, Fabian social democracy was projected as a form of socialism uniquely suited to British conditions; in the absence of a revolutionary tradition the best that could be achieved was a pragmatic approach emphasizing the institutional and essentially unphilosophical view of socialism as a set of economic measures to be enacted by local and central government. Their socialism was all 'gas and water', the small change of political reformism – municipal industry, progressive taxation, the eight-hour day. 'This, then, is the humdrum program of the practical Social Democrat today. There is not one new item in it. All are applications of principles already admitted, and extensions of practices already in full activity. All have on them that stamp of the vestry which is so congenial to the British mind,' Shaw concluded in 1889 (Shaw 1932e: 60).

The distinctive insight of the Fabians into the process of transition was quite straightforward. Transition to socialism, they believed, would not follow a clear programmatic course because it would be subject to all the false starts, missed opportunities and compromises which belong to the untidy world of practice. Transition would be slow and meandering, keeping pace with changes in popular opinion, with socialism solving its problems by the method of trial and error. 'No individual or society can possibly be absolutely and completely right', Shaw said, 'nor can any view or theory be so stated as to comprise the whole truth and nothing but the truth'. Others had said as much, but the early Fabians built their whole outlook around the prospect of implementing an imperfect programme of reform in an imperfect world. Modesty did not prevent Shaw from expounding the virtues of their realism: 'The Fabian wisdom, such as it is, has grown out of the Fabian experience; and our distinction, if we may claim any, lies more in our capacity for profiting by experience (a rarer faculty in politics that you might suppose) than in any natural superiority on our part to the follies of incipient Socialism' (Shaw 1932e: 125).

There is an important point here. Influential as Webb undoubtedly was in taking Fabianism towards a careful empiricism, it was Shaw who was responsible for explaining and expounding Fabian policy to the movement and to the public at large. He was at the forefront of the debate with Hyndman, Aveling and others over the theory of value in the late 1880s. It was Shaw who wrote the *Fabian Election Manifesto* in 1892 and in the same year lectured on the Society's history to the new recruits from the provinces. The dubious honour of explaining *The Impossibilities of Anarchism* (Shaw 1932e) fell into his lap in 1893, as did the task of formulating a *Report on Fabian Policy* (Shaw 1932e) for the Second International three years later. He was, in effect, the chief polemicist, star speaker, literary editor, mediator between competing factions, troubleshooter and heart-throb: the virtuoso of every public Fabian performance. He was the brash showman who brought a zest and eloquence to bear on the most mundane subjects.

It was not a question of exposition alone. On the contrary, as chief polemicist Shaw was required to consider the philosophical implications of Fabianism's pragmatic approach to politics. This was evident in the kind of public image he created for Fabianism, very much in keeping with his own public persona of the realist with the capacity to adapt the aims of doctrine to the possibilities of circumstance. What was apparent to the Fabians, he said, was that social democracy could not progress in conformity with abstract principles (Shaw 1932e: 65). It was thus that these righteous moralists gained reputations as trimmers and opportunists, their characters 'mildewed by expediency', to which Shaw replied, revelling in his bad eminence, that they at least were prepared to risk their souls for the millions of poor devils too poor to afford any character at all (Joad 1953: 184). Surely this was the authentic voice of pragmatic welfare socialism, aggressively defending its corner against the reproaches of the spiritual toffs and moral dandies. As Shaw explained in *Death of an Old Revolutionary Hero* (1905), the 'all or nothing' principles of absolute morality were the chains used by the governing classes to tie up the men of radical intent 'tighter than they could tie a hooligan with a set of handcuffs'.

Many of the qualities of Shaw's Fabian realism were to be found in three very different works from this period, namely the 1891 *The Quintessence of Ibsenism*, the 1893 *The Impossibilities of Anarchism* and an essay from 1896 entitled *The Illusions of Socialism*. Of these *Quintessence* is the most complex and the most atypical from a Fabian standpoint, presenting as it does the original version of Shaw's vitalist philosophy, with its nascent transcendentalism and advocacy of ethical individualism fitting very oddly with Sidney Webb's scheme of things. Central to the essay was the argument for a new Protestantism against the Victorian cult of duty, the assertion of the need for individual responsibility in every sphere of life.

Echoes of this line of argument were to be heard in Shaw's earliest work. Rebellion against the Victorian cult of duty was, after all, the quintessence of Shavianism. Hence the four novels he wrote before 1882 were fully armed to fight in the guerrilla war against conventional morality (if only they could find a publisher). Owen Jack, the musician hero of the third novel, *Love Among the Artists*, never complied with 'the laws of society' which in his opinion were 'designed to make the world easy for cowards and liars'. And he did more than rant. Defying her father's wishes, the young Madge

Brailsford received instructions in elocution from Jack, and this was to be the basis of her career as an actress, of her transformation from the 'pretty domestic toy' of her father's dreams into 'an independent woman and an accomplished artist' (Shaw 1932g: 191). Even clearer echoes were to be heard in the second novel, *The Irrational Knot*, so much so that Shaw was to claim in 1905 'I seriously suggest that *The Irrational Knot* may be regarded as an early attempt on the part of the Life Force to write *A Doll's House* in English by the instrumentality of a very immature writer aged 24' (Shaw 1931d: xix).

Still earlier, in the short essay written in 1878 *My Dear Dorothea* (Shaw 1956), Shaw warned an imaginary five-year-old girl of the cruelty, intolerance and stupidity of the adult world and sought to instruct her in the many virtues of selfishness: she was to preserve her identity and autonomy at all costs, he argued. In this context, Shaw was drawing on the indigenous tradition of radical individualism; he was Shelley's disciple. What happened between then and 1891 was that his individualism acquired a philosophical framework; and here, probably through the influence of Bax, he was Schopenhauer's disciple. Essentially the difference between Shaw's early radical individualism and the vitalist variety was that the latter redefined the role of the will as the key determinant of historical change. Social evolution was not, therefore, to be explained by impersonal factors of an economic or structural kind. Human vitality, the willpower of such maverick individuals as Shaw himself, that was the fundamental postulate of progress. In 1891 Ibsen was said to be among the first to assert 'afresh the old Protestant right to private judgement in questions of conduct as against all institutions' (Shaw 1932h: 129). Pronouncing the rebel's code, Shaw informed his Fabian audience in 1890 that 'The message of Socialism at present is one of rebellion, of implacable self-assertion, of resolute refusal to be unhappy in any avoidable fashion on any terms' (Shaw 1971: 101).

From this basis Shaw launched into a critique of materialism and rationalism in *Quintessence*, claiming that neither could offer a satisfactory explanation of 'the crablike progress of social evolution, in which the individual advances by seeming to go backward' (Shaw 192h: 18). Instead of looking to either historical causation or to reason, emphasis should be placed rather on the power of the individual will as the prime motor of historical change. While historical causation was an 'indispensable tool of socialist analysis', it was hardly satisfactory so long as the will was not explained. What positive science lacked, Shaw argued, was a 'phraseology of the spirit of the will', without which science could not begin to understand discovery and creation. In isolating the mystery of consciousness and the will to live, materialism and rationalism had only made these more conspicuous than before: 'We thought we had escaped forever from the cloudy regions of metaphysics; and we were only carried further into the heart of them' (Shaw 1932h: 21). It is not because of reason that we live, Shaw said, for, rationally considered, 'life is only worth living when its pleasures are greater than its pains'; no, we live instead in fulfilment of that mysterious will to live. Citing Schopenhauer, Shaw wrote that the will is the universal postulate.

These were not obvious views for a socialist to hold. By way of contrast, when writing in *Fabian Essays* of 'our irresistible glide into collectivist Socialism', Sidney Webb implied that Fabianism's evolutionary socialism was founded on alternative philosophical assumptions, neither voluntarist nor individualist in nature but based rather on a positivistic conception of the *Zeitgeist*.

For the moment the emphasis is on the connections between *Quintessence* and Shaw's Fabian realism, however. Originally the essay was one in a set of Fabian lectures on 'Socialism in Contemporary Literature' delivered in the summer of 1890. Shaw said he saw it merely as a *pièce d'occasion* at first, little more than a footnote to his career as a political controversialist, couched in the 'most provocative terms' (Shaw 1932h: 11). The main thrust of the lecture was a defence of political realism or opportunism, packaged in the form of a consequentialist argument to the effect that the social reformer should judge actions according to their practical outcomes and not in relation to the ideals of dogma. In essence it was yet another Shavian tirade against Hyndman's SDF. Ibsen was a convenient instrument for that tirade. As a realist, Shaw said the political activist must divorce himself from moral absolutes or principles and organize his work instead around the pursuit of welfare. This, according to Shaw the Fabian propagandist, was precisely what the Marxist faction did not understand. Ibsen understood. He knew that individual happiness counted for more than dogmatic loyalty to such principles as duty or self-sacrifice. Nora's closing of the door on her family was the perfect expression of that understanding. He claimed that Fabianism operated along similar lines, taking individual welfare or happiness, not doctrinal purity, as its goal. The portrait of Fabianism presented by Shaw was of a consequen-tialist doctrine of socialism, compatible with narrow utilitarian assumptions based on a conception of goodness as happiness and committed in its social policy to individual welfare and self-development.

When the essay appeared in its published form in 1891 the more overtly political references had all been stripped away. In its place was an abstract style of argument which was itself underpinned by the new vitalist philosophical outlook. The essay was in two parts, the first dealing with broad philosophical issues, the second concerned with a detailed critique of Ibsen's plays. These two were not entirely compatible. Underpinning the philosophical section was the suggestion of a transcendental conception of goodness as perfection, a conception which was linked to Shaw's perennial concern for collective progress. It was introduced by reference to 'the two pioneers – pioneers of the march to the plains of heaven (so to speak)'. These were the archetypal Shavian realists or rebels, one declaring that 'it is right to do something hitherto regarded as infamous', the other that 'it is wrong to do something that no one has hitherto seen any harm in'. Shelley, who was a

48

'pioneer and nothing else', belonged to both categories. Ibsen was primarily a pioneer of the first kind, a liberator from the constraints of conventional morality, the one man in a thousand who dares to face facts and tell himself the truth. Initially the point was that pioneers of this kind were the agents of social progress which, in Shaw's words, take 'effect through the replacement of old institutions by new ones; and since every institution involves the recognition of the duty of conforming to it, progress must involve the repudiation of an established duty at every step' (Shaw 1932h: 13–24). In presenting his model pioneer as a destroyer of idols who judges every custom or practice by its effect on his own self, Shaw was operating with an essentially emotivist conception of the self as sovereign in its own realm and free of all traditional boundaries. The pioneer's self-interestedness was not anarchical in nature, however. On the contrary, in seeking out the new truths and destroying old illusions the pioneer was prosecuting the righteous cause of spiritual progress; 'Shelley, the realist, was an idealist too' (Shaw 1932h: 29).

In the second section of *Quintessence* the approach to the perfectionist strivings of the heroic rebels was essentially critical in nature. Here all notions of that kind were branded as forms of dangerous idealism likely to undermine individual happiness. 'What Ibsen insists on is that there is no golden rule – that conduct must justify itself by its effect upon happiness and not by its conformity to any rule or ideal', Shaw wrote, outlining the consequentialist doctrine behind his discussion of the plays (Shaw 1932h: 125). There was not a good word for the likes of Ibsen's Brand, whose passionate commitment to an alternative ideal encapsulates all the pitfalls involved in the extremism of the man of principle. Evidently Shaw was continuing his Fabian polemic against political idealism by other means. Moderation was the order of the day, in wilfulness as in all else. Of Brand's attempt to persuade his congregation to worship God in the mountains Shaw notes unsympathetically, 'After a brief practical experience of this arrangement, they change their minds, and stone him'. Shaw's concern was now with the majority who must suffer the consequences of the pioneer's heroic striving. According to Turco, it was these pioneers, or heroic idealists as Turco calls them – 'Brand, Solness, Mrs. Alving, Robeck – persons who in terms of his own prior definition have as much claim to be considered realists' – who were the real targets of the essay's critical section (Turco 1976: 49). Shaw's treatment of the conventional idealists in Ibsen's plays was comparatively tolerant, again suggesting a link with his Fabian claim that socialism was perfectly consistent with middle-class respectability. Turco's argument is that Shaw arrived ultimately at a pragmatic conclusion in 1891, a conclusion which was in line with the individualist morality of happiness and one that, true to the essay's origins, had strong connections with his political outlook: 'Shaw insists that the prospect of implementing his own reformist goals will depend upon an ability to resist grand designs foredoomed to failure by the nature of the world' (Turco 1976: 53).

The argument was developed in Fabian Tract No. 45, *The Impossibilities of Anarchism*, a work based on a series of articles published in the September and October 1888 issues of the journal *Our Corner*, then re-written to be presented as a paper to the Fabians in October 1891 before being published by the Society in 1893. The tract opens with the claim that once the practical policy of socialism began to shape itself into the 'program of Social Democracy, it became apparent that we could not progress without the greatest violations of principles of all sorts' (Shaw 1932e: 65). There followed an account of the debate between the Impossibilists and the Trimmers among the British socialists of the 1880s, with Shaw asserting in his most aggressively realist manner that

> My own side in the controversy was the unprincipled one, as Socialism to me had always meant, not a principle, but certain definite economic measures which I wish to see taken. Indeed, I have often been reproached for limiting the term Socialism too much to the economic side of the great movement towards equality.
>
> (Shaw 1932e: 65)

The first target of Shaw's critique was the individualist anarchism associated with Benjamin Tucker, an American follower of Proudhon and editor of the anarchist journal, *Liberty*. Shaw's controversialist tactic was to highlight the affinities between individualist anarchism and the liberalism advocated by Herbert Spencer, and then to use rent theory in order to explain how a society organized on Tucker's principles would only reproduce the evils of capitalism on a still grander scale. As McBriar has commented, this was to be one of the rare occassions when rent theory had some practical significance, albeit of a limited kind. Tucker's contention was that *laissez-faire* would work justly once equality was established; against this, Shaw contended that, even though society began in a state of equality, differential returns would automatically arise and lead to inequality once more (McBriar 1962: 44). Having rejected the state, individualist anarchism had no effective theory of distributive justice, Shaw concluded: 'The economic problem of Socialism is the just distribution of the premium given to certain portions of the general product by the action of demand' (Shaw 1932e: 76). As individualist anarchism not only fails to distribute these, but deliberately permits their private appropriation, individualist anarchism is the negation of socialism and is, in fact, unsocialism carried as near to its logical conclusion as any sane man dare carry it. Shaw was adamant that in utopia alone 'would occupying ownership be just'. Clearly his flirtations with Proudhon's individualist anarchism were at an end.

The next target was the communist anarchism advocated by Kropotkin and Morris. Here the task of demolition was undertaken with regret, for their vision of a moral polity had much to commend it. Indeed, from the standpoint of the moralist, that vision represented a truer statement of the socialist ideal than did social democracy itself. In the 1888 version of the paper, Shaw said

'The main difficulty in refuting Kropotkin lies in the fact that his Communism is finally right and inevitable' (Shaw 1888a: 374); by 1893 it was said to be 'cheap and expedient', a phrase more in keeping with the tone of contemporary Fabian propaganda (Shaw 1932e: 76). Shaw offered this statement of his socialist faith 'For my own part, I seek the establishment of a state of society in which I shall not be bothered with a ridiculous pocketful of coppers, nor have to waste my time in perplexing arithmetical exchanges of them with booking clerks, bus conductors, shopmen and other superfluous persons before I can get what I need' (Shaw 1932e: 78). He said he was looking forward to a time when our 'superior humanity' would allow for a new system of exchange, when 'a just distribution of the loaves and fishes becomes perfectly spontaneous' (Shaw 1932e: 78). Here Shaw was looking towards the politics of virtue in a moral polity based on the ideal of service to the collectivity.

The problem was human nature. As Hulse remarks, Shaw was sympathetic towards Kropotkin, but he was 'too Hobbesian in his view of man' to embrace communist anarchism as a realistic strategy (Hulse 1970: 118). Socialism had to contend with human nature in its current selfish and degenerate state. The limited doctrine of social democracy, concerned not with grand notions of superior humanity but with mundane schemes for the municipalization of industry, aiming not toward some perfectionist ideal of a moral community but only toward the elimination of poverty and the goal of individual happiness, was the only feasible option in the circumstances, the realist concluded. To underline social democracy's limitations, Shaw stressed:

> Even under the most perfect Social Democracy we should, without Communism, still be living like hogs, except that each hog would get his fair share of grub. High as that ideal must seem to anyone who complacently accepts the present social order, it is hardly high enough to satisfy a man in whom the social instinct is well developed.
>
> (Shaw 1932e: 78)

Strictly speaking, then, the social democratic state was only a second-best state, where the rational perception of individual self-interest, not the selflessness preached by the socialists, was the key to human motivation. That was to be changed through a transition system founded on compulsory labour, the key to the collectivist morality of service. The critical ideologist thus arrived at a compromise between the conflicting forces of his moralism and his realism, his absolutism and his desire to get things done. That compromise was Fabianism.

Through work of this kind, inherently controversial in nature, Shaw was to gain an expertise in the dynamics of socialist thought and action, culminating in the essay *The Illusions of Socialism* from 1896. Here he was to offer a new and in some respects alternative dimension to his Fabian realism. The essay can in fact be read as a companion piece to *The Quintessence of Ibsenism*. In both, he confronted the relationship between ideals and reality, principles and practice. The central theme was the dilemma found in his critique of Ibsen's *Brand*, namely that men would not, on the one hand, be persuaded to join together for the sake of a progressive cause unless they were inspired by illusions or ideals, by a melodramatic conception of social life, but, on the other hand, ideals, if carried to their logical conclusion, were capable of great injury against human welfare. It was a question of creating an argument at once scientifically sound yet still capable of inspiring the kind of sociological rage he had felt on reading Marx. The imaginative qualities of argument and illusion were essential to the socialist cause (Shaw was to identify these qualities with the god, Loki, in 1898 in *The Perfect Wagnerite*) (Shaw 1932h). Yet these qualities were to be handled with the utmost care lest they distort the whole project of enlightenment. This, in Shaw's mind, was the ideological dilemma which faced every active socialist as a potential instigator of a mass political movement.

His strategy in 1896 was to begin by discussing those 'necessary illusions' behind the socialist cause, in particular the class-war illusion which 'presents the working class as a virtuous hero and heroine in the toils of a villain called "the capitalist", suffering terribly and struggling nobly, but with a happy ending for them, and a fearful retribution for the villain, in full view before the fall of the curtain on a future of undisturbed bliss'. Shaw, like Sorel later, saw the greatness of Marxism in terms of the social poetry embedded in its central myths, though unlike Sorel he did not advocate unqualified support for such dramatic myths. Though socialism 'is founded on sentimental dogma, and is quite unmeaning and purposeless apart from it', he wrote, nevertheless from a programmatic standpoint socialism must yet 'come into the field as political science' (Shaw 1965b: 412). Though fundamental to socialist doctrine, such metaphysical illusions as man's natural rights cannot supply the basis for a political programme. Shaw therefore proceeded to argue the political case for the Fabian approach which considered the whole question to be one of 'political science and practice, and of them alone' (Shaw 1965b: 414). Dramatic illusions may be necessary at the crude, initial stage of propaganda, but, then, neither the propagandist nor his audience could begin to transform society on a heady mixture of melodrama and first principles. A similar case was made by Lavinia on behalf of Christianity in *Androcles and the Lion*. The Roman Captain tells her, 'one of your fellows [Spintho] bolted and ran right into the jaws of the lion. I laughed. I still laugh'. To which Lavinia responds that the Captain had failed to understand what it meant: 'It meant that a man cannot die for a story and a dream. None of us believed the stories more devoutly than poor Spintho; but he could not face the great reality. What he would have called my faith had been oozing away minute by minute whilst Ive been sitting here, with death coming nearer and nearer, with reality becoming realler and realler, with stories and dreams fading away into nothing' (Shaw 1931a: 136). This was the lesson to be learnt by all converts to all faiths.

Back in 1896 the realist's message was that socialism, if it was to have any hope of success, must eventually be appreciated in its most prosaic form, in terms of the complexities involved in creating a collectivist order in an industrial age. Socialism would, in all probability, be statist and bureaucratic in nature, organized in terms of a mixed economy and involving considerable inequality of condition. Shaw ridiculed the 'consistent levellers'. He was even prepared to treat 'the question of private property as one of pure convenience'. The details of the matter were not to be settled in principle, but in practice, 'as long as the livelihood of the people is made independent of private capital and enterprise the more private property and individual activity we have the better'. At the close of the *The Illusions of Socialism*, the contrast was drawn between 'the fanatics who are prepared to sacrifice all consideration of human welfare and convenience sooner than flinch from the rigorous application of their principles', and 'the more or less practical men' who accept diversity of opinion on points of detail. The argument was for tolerance and welfare against dogma and any form of cathartic moralism.

The essay was not only an original account of the dynamics of socialist thought and action, of the problems and limitations encountered in any project of rational enlightenment. It was also a powerful exposition of the positive, humanitarian qualities of pragmatic welfarism. Shaw's classic formulation is found in a letter to Benjamin Tucker from 1894:

> I am not a man with a theory, binding myself to all the logical conclusions of that theory; and you will find, if you study my polemics against anarchism, that I deal, not with the theories of the anarchists or the logical conclusions of those theories, but solely with the actual measures they advocate and the concrete results of those measures. The world was not made to fit anybody's theory, nor can our misfits be remedied by any mortal power.
>
> (Shaw 1894: 5)

DEVELOPMENTS AND COMPLEXITIES

The essay on *The Illusions of Socialism* was written at the very point when Shaw's social democracy was showing signs of strain and wear. In particular, fractures appeared in the foundation work as the belief in the inevitability of progress, which had underpinned his acceptance of Fabianism's sordid and slow path to justice, started to crumble. In the general election of 1895 the progressive cause, as represented by the Independent Labour Party (ILP) and the Liberal Party, fared badly, sending a wave of disappointment and frustration through the ranks of the socialist pioneers. Apparently the transition to socialism was going to be more sordid and far slower than even the Fabians had imagined; the working class was, it seemed, not only anti-revolutionary but also anti-socialist in outlook, wedded to the illusions of empire. Weariness and pessimism hung over the movement. They even clouded corners of Shaw's essay, casting a shadow over the gaiety of its verbal brilliance and its tough veneer of realism. There was poignancy in the portrayal of the socialist orator, mentally exhausted by long campaigns for justice, reduced to a hopeless windbag, 'opinionated without opinions, and conceited without qualities' (Shaw 1965b: 416). The point was pursued further in his portrayal of the Revd James Morell in the play, *Candida*, a man whose sermons were mere phrases that he cheated himself and others with every day. Shaw had to admit that propaganda has 'an unfortunate effect on the character of the propagandist'. And to what end? In the essay, he hinted at his growing disillusion with democracy, stating 'By the illusion of Democracy, or government by everybody, we shall establish the most powerful bureaucracy ever known on the face of the earth, and finally get rid of popular elections, trial by jury, and all the other makeshifts of a system in which no man can be trusted with power' (Shaw 1965b: 429).

Of course it could be argued that, as Shaw had never placed much faith in the working classes as the prime movers of socialism, preferring instead the stage army of Fabian social engineers, then the failure of the masses to rush into the arms of the ILP should not have dismayed him in the least. Far from constituting a betrayal of his ideals, the election result was confirmation of the view he expressed in *Fabian Essays* that 'an army of light is no more to be gathered from the human product of nineteenth-century civilization than grapes are to be gathered from thistles'.

Convenient as this is, the truth of the matter is more complex. Between 1888 and 1895 a debate raged in Fabian circles as to the relative merit of the policy of permeating the Liberal Party, on one side, as against that of founding an independent Socialist Party on the other. Shaw, in his capacity as chief polemicist, was effectively caught between the two factions, led by Webb and the eccentric Tory socialist, Hubert Bland, respectively, having in some way to satisfy both sides in his public pronouncements if the Society was not to be split on the issue. As A.M. McBriar said, such documents as Shaw's *Fabian Election Manifesto* (1892) were masterpieces of compromise and conciliation, being sufficiently flexible to accommodate the internal divisions while still presenting an appearance of clarity and unanimity to the world (McBriar 1962: 247).

On a more personal note, many of the tensions within Fabianism which lay behind this debate were encapsulated in Shaw himself. Permeation, with its aura of exclusiveness, its secretive wire-pulling and manipulation, certainly appealed to him, for it pandered to all that was superior and Machiavellian in his character. Besides, he had no wish to lead a mass movement. He was not politically ambitious in that sense. In 1891, for example, he turned down the invitation of the Bradford and District Labour Union to stand as its parliamentary candidate, disqualifying himself on the grounds that working men should learn to trust their own kind: 'seats in Parliament ought not to be made the prizes of fluent speakers and smart writers' (Pugh 1984: 42). The beauty of permeation was that it allowed him to work for socialism while still permitting other interests and ambitions to impinge on his life.[2]

Occasionally, the more populist and expansive strategy found its way into Shaw's propaganda, most notably in his address to the Fabian conference convened in 1892 to welcome into the fold new provincial members who had joined the Society as a result of the success of *Fabian Essays*. When explaining Fabian tactics he emphasized that the London Society had never aimed to establish an army 'any bigger than a stage army', drawn mainly from the middle classes. Eager not to alienate his provincial audience, however, Shaw closed on a different note, one designed to warm the long winter's journey back to the North of England: 'You know, too', he said, 'that none of you can more ardently desire the formation of a genuine Collectivist political party, distinct from Conservative and Liberal alike, than we do'; he then added the rhetorical flourish:

> Whilst our backers at the polls are counted by tens, we must continue to crawl and drudge and lecture as best we can. When they are counted by hundreds we can permeate and trim and compromise. When they rise to tens of thousands we shall take the field as an independent party. Give us hundreds of thousands, as you can if you try hard enough, and we will ride the whirlwind and direct the storm.
>
> (Shaw 1932e: 160)

That unlikely vision, formulated for a special occasion, was not repeated. More typically, in his correspondence he wrote of repudiating Gladstone in 'express terms'; or, as he told Sydney Olivier in 1890, wary now of being outflanked by the SDF:

> We must fall back on the Worker's Political Program to show that we also said so all along; and it is a definite Social Democratic Party, prepared to act with the Radical Party as far as that party pursues its historic mission of overthrowing Capitalist Liberalism in the interests of the working classes.
>
> (Shaw 1965a: 276)

The combination of tactical and doctrinal concerns embedded in this statement underline the fluidity in Shaw's outlook. Some have seen it as a sign of confusion; others of the opportunist abrogation of ultimate ends (Shaw 1965a: 275). Publicly he tried to accommodate both permeation and independence in his polemics, carrying this uncertain attitude even to the inaugural conference of the ILP in 1893, where his contribution was so equivocal that he won for the Society a reputation as an 'isolated knot of London perverts' (Field 1893: 2). Not that Shaw's contribution to the Bradford Conference was just that of a Fabian trouble-maker. That view has been dispelled by David Howell's explanation of the important role Shaw played in the making of the ILP's policy on social and fiscal reform. This was the constructive side to Shaw, a side so often obscured by the antics of the flamboyant controversialist. As Howell says, the irony was that the two principal figures in developing the ILP policy, Shaw and Aveling, had few subsequent dealings with the Party (Howell 1983: 296–8).

The Fabian outlook on the ILP generally was anything but stable and clear-cut. Almost immediately the conference ended Shaw was instructed by Webb to switch direction by declaring the failure of permeation in the rousing article, *To Your Tents, Oh Israel!* published in the *Fortnightly Review*, November 1893. By the Autumn of 1893, therefore, they were sounding the call for a mass movement, having severed their ties with the Liberal Party. There was only one problem. The masses were in no mood to heed the call, thus leaving the Fabians in a tactical cul-de-sac of their own making. As Beatrice Webb concluded, 'We have to some extent raised our natural enemies without having secured our natural allies' (Webb 1975: 117). Little wonder, then, that frustration and disappointment lurked beneath the glossy surface of *The Illusions of Socialism*.

Central to Shaw's social democracy was the appeal to the rational self-interest of the ordinary man which meant that, under capitalism at least, political affiliations were 'based on the pocket' (Shaw 1891: 11). If socialism was to have any chance of success then it must first explain to the masses how it will secure their material well-being. What was needed, he said, was propaganda urging the working class to be resolutely selfish in its politics, to assert its will in the interest of its own happiness. Rational education was the key to progressive politics. Fabianism's task, at its broadest and most ambitious, was to enlighten the masses as to their self-interest and, ultimately, to show how this was related to the collective interest of society as a whole. That at least was how Shaw framed the matter in 1891, the year he published *Quintessence*. Five years on, however, he was not so convinced. Now politics could not be conceived as the simple pursuit of instrumental rationality. Behind the veil of Fabian realism he glimpsed a deeper reality where the political arena was a place of conflicting illusions, or a madhouse of ignorant enthusiasm. Before he had thought the working class apathetic (in his Fabian propaganda at least); now he knew better. The prospects for the politics of welfare were not altogether encouraging, even in such capable hands as those of the Fabians. What price enlightenment now?

THE PERFECT WAGNERITE AND BEYOND

Strategically, a number of options lay before the Fabians in 1896. One was to depart from the pragmatic style of politics by formulating a uniquely Fabian illusion capable of inspiring faith and action. Shaw's transcendental myth of the superman could be seen as one response in this vein. He certainly used the myth in this way when introducing his doctrine of equality of income to the Society in 1910. Of course that is not the whole story. Embedded in the superman ideal was a deeper critique of socialism itself and its vision of progress. Shaw's intellectual world had always been a complex place. The vitalist doctrine he formulated in *Quintessence* cut across the grain of his Fabian evolutionism. Its emphasis on individual selfishness contradicted the altruistic faith of the Webbs and their kind: *Major Barbara*, the play which deals most directly with this theme was 'amazingly clever' in Beatrice Webb's view, but it was also a 'dance of devils' ending 'in an intellectual and moral morass' (Webb 1975: 313–15). Shaw's tendency to equate social democracy with the politics of private desires was a minority position in Fabian circles. His outlook was never orthodox or straightforward.

Now it was more complex still. By *Man and Superman* in 1903 he had apparently rejected the substance and ethos of his Fabianism, writing off the whole of capitalist humanity as unfit for socialism and incapable of progress (the illusion of illusions, he called it). Socialism was subsumed under a eugenic scheme; 'The only fundamental and possible Socialism is the socialization of the selective breeding of Man'. So, too, was democracy; 'King Demos must be bred like all other kings'. Fabianism itself, with its administrative approach to socialism, was singled out as 'fundamentally futile', having drawn the teeth of insurgent poverty it had 'saved the existing order from the only method of attack it really fears' (Shaw 1931f: 190).

The shifts in Shaw's outlook in this period were formulated in the 1898 *The Perfect Wagnerite* (Shaw 1932h), a critical work on Wagner's *Ring Cycle* which, in the event, was to reveal as much if not more about Shaw's own moral and philosophical outlook than about its purported subject. In this sense, as in others, the *Wagnerite* was a natural successor to *Quintessence*. Both were forerunners of the Life Force philosophy Shaw presented first in *Man and Superman* (1903) and then in more detail in *Back to Methuselah* (1921). Fundamental to the *Wagnerite* was Shaw's sudden loss of faith in progress which generated a harsher and sterner tone in his thought, a Nietzschean element which gave rise to what can be identified as a doctrine of evolutionary righteousness. Shaw's view was that the majority of men resist progress and that as a result, 'we must, like Prometheus, set to work to make new men instead of torturing old ones' (Shaw 1932h: 222). At his most strident, Shaw announced:

> The majority of men at present in Europe have no business to be alive; and no serious progress will be made until we address ourselves earnestly and scientifically to the task of producing trustworthy human material for society. In short, it is necessary to breed a race of men in whom the life giving impulses predominate, before the New Protestantism becomes politically practicable.
>
> (Shaw 1932h: 215)

The key words here were 'no business to be alive'. Apparently the rebel had now set himself up as the prophet of evolutionary righteousness with himself as the arbiter of the right to life. It is certainly true that, while Shaw's interest in eugenicism varied over time, signs of his moralistic concern with the justification of individual conduct in terms of his or her contribution to life's purpose were to remain in his work, surfacing in many places, indicating the ruthlessness of the pure heart fed by the commitment to perfectionism. In *The Guide* he was to say 'The working classes, the business classes, the professional classes, the propertied classes, the ruling classes, are each more odious than the other: they have no right to live' (Shaw 1949a: 490). Thus spoke the new voice of Shavian consequentialism.

In statements such as these we find the quality of hard, even brutal moralism of Shaw's evolutionary righteousness. This quality certainly affected many areas of his political thought, fuelling his interest in eugenicism, adding credence to his argument for the death penalty for all incurable criminals (a policy which he defended in terms of 'the ruthlessness of the pure heart') (Shaw 1932c: 199). Moreover, its brutal optimism allowed him in the 1930s to write euphemistic reports on the short-term casualties among the Kulak class in Stalinist Russia. The mind of the socialist was not to be 'disabled by excessive sympathy' (Shaw 1949a: 489). Shaw may have been a vegetarian and active in the campaign against vivisection, yet he was no ordinary humanitarian. In the preface to a book on *Killing for Sport* (1915), he embarrassed its editor, the gentle Henry Salt, when he wrote that he could see no 'logical nor spiritual escape from the theory that evolution (not, please observe, Natural Selection) involves a deliberate intentional destruction by the higher forms of life of the lower' (Salt 1915: xvii).

Not surprisingly, bearing in mind Shaw's consequentialist approach to ethics, individual rights did not hold a secure place in his scheme. In the *Wagnerite* the case for individual liberty of opinion was offered within a broadly evolutionary framework, specifically in terms of the contribution of immoral and heretical doctrines to a nation's progress. 'History', he said, 'as far as we are capable of history (which is not saying much as yet) shews that all changes from crudity of social organization to complexity, and from mechanical agencies in government to living ones, seem anarchic at first sight' (Shaw 1932h: 222). It was the case for the rebels and pioneers, presented, however, as a functional requirement for the evolution of the social organism, not in terms of an inviolable individual right. In other words, the principles of civil liberty held an uncertain place in his thought, especially as he assumed that the masses were either indifferent or even hostile to the toleration of unconventional views.

There was an element of deliberate exaggeration in much of this, employed as always to incite comment or provoke thought among his audience. Statements on the destruction of the lower forms of life and the extermination of the working classes were evidently the work of a controversialist. What is more, like Nietzsche, Shaw took a certain delight in deconstructing his own arguments, especially in the plays where the problems and contradictions of doctrine were explored. This was apparent in his treatment of the ethics of eugenic experimentation. In the preface to *Man and Superman*, for example, he offered a glib formula which held, 'Being cowards, we defeat natural selection under cover of philanthropy: being sluggards, we neglect artificial selection under cover of delicacy and morality' (Shaw 1931f: xxv). The debate in Act III, however, concludes on a different note, with the Devil positing this warning in opposition to the righteous advocates of selective breeding:

> Beware of the pursuit of the Superhuman: it leads to an indiscriminate contempt for the Human. To a man, horses and dogs and cats are mere species, outside the moral world. Well, to the Superman, men and women are a mere species too, also outside the moral world.
>
> (Shaw 1931f: 129)

None the less, it would be wrong to discount Shaw's evolutionary righteousness simply as the disturbing hyperbole employed by a controversialist. Shaw was far more than that and far more complex. Concealed within the excessive rhetoric was an influential element of his argument, designed to reconcile or combine individual responsibility with a sense of collective duty, the requirements of order with those of enlightenment and virtue. The controversialist was also a moralist and self-appointed arbiter of the right to life with a commitment to social and spiritual progress.

In the light of his doubts about progress and the politics of reform, the tangled relationship between theory and practice, always a central feature of Shaw's thought, was raised in an especially intense and poignant form in the *Wagnerite*. In particular, in his interpretation of Wagner's allegory of the dwarfs, giants and gods, Shaw revealed new insights into his own vision of a new kind of social order, as well as into his thoughts on the problems involved in its realization.

Without delving too deeply into the details of Wagner's plot, the main point to emerge from Shaw's initial analysis is that the allegory is a dramatization of 'the three main orders of men: to wit, the instinctive, predatory, lustful, greedy people; the patient, toiling, stupid, respectful, money-worshipping people; and the intellectual, moral, talented people who devise and administer states and churches' (Shaw 1932h: 189). Alberic, the dwarf, who steals the Rhinegold, is the representative plutocrat in Shaw's estimation; Fafnir, the giant, who hoards the gold, having neither the ambition nor the wit to use it constructively, stands broadly for the masses, the working and lower middle classes enslaved by their own stupidity; Wotan, Loki and Fricka, on the other hand, are the gods, the lawmakers, the superior brains striving to create order out of chaos.

Shaw believed that the real drama of the opera arose from the limitations and problems faced by each of these orders of man as each strove to fulfil its destiny. The gods, Wotan (the god of gods) especially, were the focus of Shaw's attention. This was because Wotan cared not for his own interests, but for the interests of life itself, even if that entailed his own destruction, 'Life itself, with its accomplished marvels and infinite possibilities, is the only force that Godhead can worship', Shaw tells us (Shaw 1932h: 182). There are hints here of his own Life Force philosophy and, as the argument develops, we are offered something like the original of the Shavian superman. Wotan, we are told, seeks to realize his vision of an intensely and joyously vital man, and of a new kind of order, featuring neither law nor coercion. Wotan was, therefore, seeking to make himself redundant, and, in Shaw's view, it is this quest which is the central impetus behind the dramatic action. Wotan's vision can be encapsulated in the phrase, 'a true republic of free thought', described by Shaw as a commonwealth of 'men whose wills and intelligences may be depended on to produce spontaneously the social wellbeing our clumsy laws now aim at and miss' (Shaw 1932h: 125, 175). The vision reminds us too that in Wagner's scheme the gods were not the highest possible order of men. On the contrary, as Shaw explains, on his own as well as on Wagner's behalf, 'history' points us towards the still higher possible order of heroes. The heroes will be capable of transcending the realm of the gods precisely because they have no need of the laws, conventions, commandments and punishments which is the destiny of the gods to impose on the world (Shaw 1932h: 189). Shaw was only too pleased to develop the argument on behalf of the Wagnerian hero, Siegfried, noting how he makes 'straight for truth and reality', so redeeming man from 'the lame and cramped government of the gods'; in the heroic age, social life will be the expression of 'the pure law of thought', not the reflection of a mechanical law of commandments as at present. Whereas the gods, as lawmakers, must engage the contingent and sordid realm of politics on its own terms, compromising, manipulating, destroying the disobedient, the heroes, as the guardians of pure will and true principle, will fashion their actions in accordance with their ideals, so transforming the political realm itself. The dilemma Wotan faced in having to choose between evils, the pact he was forced to make with Loki, the god of lies and illusions, in order to secure his aims – these disgraceful bargains will be of no relevance in that future day when, to use Shaw's analogy, the average man will be as superior to Julius Caesar as 'most of our English professional men are to Australian bushmen' (Shaw 1932h: 189).

The notion of a community of heroes, introduced in this very Shavian commentary on Wagner, was the prototype of that republic of free, thoughtful and superior brains which in 1903 Shaw was to call the democracy of supermen. There order and welfare would be created spontaneously in the natural fusion of theory and practice, of individual aims and collective needs. Politics, understood in terms of rules, conflicts and compromises, would be eradicated. Though Shaw argued that his superman was not the just man made perfect, on this basis he certainly had sufficient will, intelligence and virtue to render the coercive paraphernalia of politics irrelevant. The superman and the attendant vision of a democracy of supermen were, in that respect, the ultimate formulations of his transcendental theoretical optimism.

The relevance of the superman or heroic ideal for Shaw's political thought is far from straightforward. At worst, perhaps, it points to his occasional enthusiasm for the intervention of the great man in political affairs. Writing in 1896 in his most provocative manner, Shaw said he found it 'impossible to live in England without sometimes feeling how much that country lost in not being conquered' by Napoleon as well as by Caesar (Shaw 1931g: 146). Four years on he was to back this up with the prophecy that soon, 'the country will become unbearable for all realists, Philistine and Platonic', adding 'When it comes to that, the brute force of the strongminded Bismarckian man of action, impatient of humbug, will combine with the subtlety and spiritual energy of the man of thought whom shams cannot illude or interest' (Shaw 1931k: xx). This was Shaw at his most frustrated and frustrating, apparently seeking a man of destiny who might effect some dramatic change in events, similar in kind to the sort of impact such characters as Saint Joan make in the plays.

Alternatively, the ideal of a democracy of supermen represents Shaw's true republic or commonwealth of morally responsible individuals dedicated to the cause of collective progress, a utopian notion, perhaps, lying outside the mainstream of his concerns, yet still fundamental to the ultimate values of his socialism, finding expression in his discussions on communist anarchism and elsewhere. It cannot be ignored because Shaw's political thought, like Plato's, was haunted by his idealism, by his perfectionist desire to transcend the sordid realm of conflict. In this respect, the material well-being to be gained under socialism was only the basis for a broader programme of spiritual and moral reform.

Of course, the superman ideal can be seen as marginal to his politics. As a socialist realist he sought to address the public realm on its own terms, knowing that order would depend on the hard-pressed lawmakers and not on the romantic rebels. Interestingly, in his eagerness to present a political interpretation of Wagner, Shaw contrived to switch the focus of the opera away from Siegfried, the rebel hero, and on to Wotan, the lawmaker; Wotan is the opera's real hero, he says. It is the dilemma the god faces, the compromises and pacts which he must make, his violence and his manoeuvrings which provide the dramatic tension. It is his suffering which lends to the work its emotional power (Shaw 1931h: 217). Fundamentally, Shaw made the problems involved in translating theory into practice, in relating the ideals of doctrine to the complex realities of power politics, the central theme of the drama. In doing so, he was using the commentary on Wagner as a commentary on his own dilemmas as a socialist. Like Wagner, he was an idealist with a dream of a just and progressive order. It was a question of how to transform the vision into reality, giving full consideration to the expediences of political action, taking account of the moral and intellectual state of the human raw material with which he had to work. Again, like Wagner, he could escape into utopian speculations on heroes and supermen. But that was hardly satisfactory. As a socialist realist Shaw had to accept the challenge of bringing the power of thought to bear on the world of power in a forthright way: 'it is one thing to understand the aim of socialism', he wrote in 1928, 'and quite another to carry it into practice, or even to see how it can or ever could be carried into practice' (Shaw 1949a: 98).

Back in 1898 that seemed especially difficult. If on one side the superman ideal was the ultimate formulation of his theoretical optimism, on the other it was the ultimate statement of his strategic pessimism. In the closing comments from the *Wagnerite* Shaw implied that Alberic, the plutocrat, was the master of events in real life, controlling the masses with the help of Loki, the chief illusionist, who spins out the myth of capitalist legitimacy endlessly in the press. Strategically, then, the prospects for socialism and the politics of virtue generally were poor in 1898.

As if to underline the despair, the themes of doubt and the want of power were central to the plays of the period. The portrait of the wrangling social democrats from Act III of *Man and Superman* was hardly calculated to inspire confidence. Socialism itself was in retreat, apparently. Also, it could be argued that in *Major Barbara* the forces of radicalism were overwhelmed by the powers of capital and convention – are we really to believe that Cusins and Barbara will withstand the pressure put on them by the subtle Andrew Undershaft and the domineering Lady Britomart? In the *Wagnerite* Shaw suggested that if the rule of virtue was to be realized then Siegfried 'must learn Alberic's trade and shoulder Alberic's burden'. That too was his concern in *Major Barbara*. His view in 1898 was that the rebellious Siegfrieds of this world were too romantically impracticable to see that 'Alberic can never be superseded by a warrior, but only by a capable man of business who is prepared to continue his work without a day's intermission'. The closing scene of *Major Barbara*, where the unconventional scholar, Cusins, and his gospelling wife-to-be are all set to take over the reins of industry, was, by way of contrast, something of a step in the right direction; but for all that it remained an ambiguous response to the tensions between thought and action. This uncertainty was even more explicit in *John Bull's Other Island* where Father Keegan's vision of a new commonwealth was but an impossible dream. The predicament of John Tanner, the would-be revolutionist of *Man and Superman*, was every bit as hopeless as that of Sidney Trefusis twenty years earlier, only now the hero's 'negative individualism' was overpowered by the wiles of the mother-woman. In all three plays Shaw enquired into the relationship between thought and action, aims and means, arriving, seemingly, at the negative conclusion that capitalism is too powerful, culturally and politically, to be undermined by the radical; arguably, all three were Shavian tracts on the impossibilities of gradualism. Alberic's rule was to be long and cruel.

The temptation is to impose a more or less rigid dualism on Shaw's work from the late 1890s onwards, with the critical pessimism of the drama contradicting the shallow optimism of his Fabian politics. Hulse does something of the sort. So too does Martin Meisel who charts Shaw's growing awareness of the failure of Fabian gradualism, noting the drift towards 'apocalyptic catastrophism' in the plays, starting with the apparent advocacy of violence in *Major Barbara* and culminating in *Heartbreak House* where Shaw paints his vision of the decline and fall of European civilization (Meisel 1971: 226). It was the politics of desperation. Sometimes it struck a personal note. In the preface to *Major Barbara* he said his preaching and pamphleteering were of no use, 'we paper apostles and artist-magicians have succeeded only in giving cowards all the sensations of heroes whilst they tolerate every abomination, accept every plunder and submit to every oppression'.

This strand of desperate pessimism certainly existed in Shaw, growing out of his fundamentalism and, so it is argued here, operating as something of a sub-text behind his commitment to rational, gradual change, gathering force in his propaganda, until, by the 1920s, it threatened to engulf his political outlook. The distinction between his Fabian politics and his drama is too neat, however. The relationship was rather a complex network of form and content, agreement and tension, open to conflicting interpretations and varying from one play to another. That relationship was at its most complex in *Man and Superman* where a conventional comedy of manners accompanied the exposition of the transcendental myth in Act III. Further, its eugenic theme was very much in keeping with the thinking of other leading Fabians at this time; the Webbs, especially Beatrice were for once unstinting in their praise, 'genuinely delighted at his choice of subject' (Webb 1975: 256). As a good Fabian, the solution he sought to the eugenic problem was essentially administrative in nature, taking the form of 'a State Department of Evolution with a seat in the Cabinet for its chief'.

This is not to suggest that the tensions between Shaw's transcendentalism and Fabianism can be reconciled entirely. The former was in many ways a genuine alternative to the latter, calling the very foundation of his socialist faith into question. The superman was concerned with the search for more abundant life, while Shaw's social democracy was essentially about the search for money and more individual happiness. Implicit in the superman ideal was a rejection of politics, while in his social democracy Shaw still pursued his political goals with almost religious fervour. The gulf between the many aspects of Shaw's character and outlook were at their most obvious here. But so too were the connecting links. What is clear is that the creative contradictions and dilemmas at the heart of his work reached a new pitch of intensity in this period, leading toward a lively if unpredictable debate on strategy conducted by the rebel turned lawmaker and prophet.

NATIONAL AND INTERNATIONAL SOCIALISM

Grand designs of transcendental politics were to enter noisily upon the Fabian stage a few years later with the arrival of H.G. Wells. In the mid-1890s, with the Old Gang still in charge, the more viable strategic option for the Society

63

was to revert to permeation, with its paternalistic overtones and its mechanical commitment to social engineering. Only now of course the policy would be underpinned by a suspicion of democracy, based on the view that ordinary people – Mrs Webb's 'average sensual man' – were not merely ill-informed, they were also fundamentally irrational and incapable of enlightenment. These were not merely Shavian concerns. Graham Wallas was then starting work on *Human Nature in Politics* which seemingly confirmed Shaw's speculations on the irrationality of mass man, so undermining the whole project of liberal enlightenment. Similarly, the research of the Webbs into the trade unions and professional associations pointed toward the inevitability of oligarchy in any large complex organization. Such evidence seemed to confirm Shaw's predicition from 1894 that social democracy would have 'its helpless dependence on a minority of able men, and its mass of people, capable of nothing beyond their own immediate concerns, taking advantage of the higher wages, shorter hours and better education obtainable under Social Democracy without in the least understanding it' (Shaw 1894: 5). Apparently, his republicanism was being crushed by the forces of ignorance and unreason.

While there is again a danger of overstatement here, it is the case that the Fabians adopted this second option, eschewing any faint ambitions of acting as either generals or advisers to a mass movement. It was assumed that reform would come from above, perhaps even against the express wishes of the people. To add a further twist to the tale, what was of paramount importance now was not individual happiness, or even that of the working class, but instead the efficiency of the nation. The politics of social democracy was gliding towards the politics of national efficiency. Traces of this collectivist morality of efficiency had been evident for many years in Fabian literature, for example, in Sidney Webb's 'Historic' contribution to *Fabian Essays*. After 1896, however, it gained new impetus from the fresh injection of social Darwinist notions into the main arteries of Fabian thought. By the turn of the century national efficiency was all the rage and the Fabians were eager to reconsider the key concepts of their moral socialism in the light of the major shift in political argument. Writing in 1898, in the preface to *Plays Unpleasant*, Shaw picked out the concepts of 'discipline, subordination, good manners, and selection of fit persons for high functions' when describing the essentials of his socialist faith. In *Caesar and Cleopatra* (Shaw 1931k) the tensions in his outlook were worked out in relation to the topical question of empire. 'Rome is a madman's dream', Caesar tells the Sphinx, the Romans 'cannot even govern themselves'. And in the prologue added in 1912, the god Ra laughs at Rome, 'for the minds of the Romans remained the same size whilst their dominion spread over the earth'. Progress is nonsense, power an illusion. Yet, there is a subordinate theme in the play, a hidden agenda perhaps, which points to an affirmation of Roman power, through its prosaic superiority in organization and discipline over the Egyptians, qualities encapsulated in the soldier, Rufio, who Caesar appoints governor of Egypt on his departure. That affirmation was evident in Caesar's response to the claim that Rome will produce no art of its own: 'What! Rome produce no art! Is peace not an art? Is war not an art? Is government not an art? Is civilization not an art? All these we give you in exchange for a few ornaments'. The conquered peoples were to have the best of the bargain.

The parallels with contemporary England on the eve of the Boer War were clear. The story of the Fabian Society's reaction to that war and of the role Shaw played in the unusually torrid proceedings has been told many times. Commentators mostly agree that he was instrumental on this occasion in leading the Society towards a distinctive position, very different from the traditional radicalism which informed much of the doctrinal spirit of British labourism. Culminating in *Fabianism and the Empire*, a manifesto written for the Khaki election of 1900, Shaw forged an original socialist view of empire as the foundation of a 'commonwealth of nations' (a term he may have coined) (Porter 1984: 65). Typically, he was prompted by both doctrinal and tactical considerations. On the doctrinal front, he was perhaps of all the leading Fabians the most determined to carry British socialism beyond its reliance on liberal principles, especially those relating to the cause of national self-determination. His impatience with that cause was evident in several contexts. For example in the ridicule he heaped on the cultural pretensions of the backward Bulgarians in *Arms and the Man* (Shaw 1931g). More explicitly in a speech delivered to the Fabians in February 1900 he declared, 'the most governed state over the largest area is preferable to a number of warring units with undisciplined ideas'. To which he added the note of grim realism, 'The world is to the big and powerful states by necessity; and the little ones must come within their borders or be crushed out of existence' (Halévy 1961: 105).

On the tactical side, Shaw saw the manifesto, and more directly still Sidney Webb's 1901 tract, *Twentieth Century Politics: A Policy of National Efficiency*, as foundations for a new initiative in Fabian permeation, aimed at the new faction in British politics, the Liberal Imperialists, under the leadership of Lord Rosebery. Shaw's correspondence with the Webbs from this period suggests that it was he who pushed the reluctant partnership in this direction. Rosebery was Shaw's man of destiny. In Shaw's estimation he was an able politician who had captured the public mood in his speeches on national efficiency, with its concern for racial fitness and scientific progress. What Rosebery lacked was a definite programme, and in this respect he presented a golden opportunity for the Webbs. 'If Lord Rosebery wishes to become a political entity he must become a personified programme', Shaw told them (Shaw 1972: 234). That programme should be Fabian in nature, using an enlightened commitment to empire as the foundation for a policy of social reform. Having popularized the term 'national efficiency', Lord Rosebery was about to learn its exact collectivist implications.

The policy Shaw presented in *Fabianism and the Empire* was designed to rescue Britain and her colonies from the power of plutocracy. It was concerned 'not specifically for the wage earning class', but for 'the effective social organization of the whole Empire, and its rescue from the strife of classes and private interests'. The introduction was laced with social-Darwinist assertions on the inevitability of Great Power domination over the globe, as well as waspish remarks on the masses, who were, the manifesto remarked, 'in so deplorable a condition that democracy in the popular sense of government by the masses, is clearly contrary to common sense'. Evidently it was not a populist document. In keeping with the mood of Fabian permeation, its prospective audience was of a limited and peculiarly enlightened kind.

The manifesto was in two parts, Part I dealing with foreign affairs and concentrating on Britain's imperial policy towards India, South Africa and China and Part II concerned with home affairs and dealing with the standard Fabian obsessions – the housing question, municipal trading, the drink question and education. Its final conclusion ran along meritocratic lines. What the British Empire wanted was 'not Conservatism, not Liberalism, not Imperialism, but brains and political science' (Fabian Society 1900: 93).

In Part I, the manifesto offered a set of practical suggestions construed so as to 'make inclusion in the British Empire a privilege to be earned instead of a yoke to be enforced'. The British had to learn that a 'Great Power, consciously or unconsciously, must govern in the interest of civilization as a whole'. No general solution was forthcoming. Practically, the issues were different in each case, with neither democracy nor bureaucracy offering a clear-cut answer to the problems of colonial government. The racial issue, for example, made South Africa more complicated than India. In the latter, such suggestions as 'the further Indianization of the higher grades of the Civil Service' would suffice. In South Africa, on the other hand, 'we are confronted there with colonies demanding democratic institutions in the midst of native races who must be protected despotically by the Empire or abandoned to slavery and extermination'. The answer here was to offer constitutional reform to the white settlers – including an imperial council representing the entire empire – with safeguards for the black population, some political, others industrial, and bound up with the policy of bringing the mines under public ownership. The case of China was different again. There the central issue was the restriction on trade and travel caused by its anachronistic civilization. The manifesto concluded that the Powers had a duty to ensure that such minimum international rights were established and maintained by an active interventionist policy. It was to be a socialist policy – 'We must lay the foundations of International Socialism, as we are laying the foundation of National Socialism, by making the British flag carry with it wherever it flies a factory code and a standard of life secured by a legal minimum wage' (Fabian Society 1900: 54).

This odd statement suggests the broader context of Shaw's view on empire. 'Theoretically', he said, the world's resources 'should be internationalized, not British imperialized; but until the Federation of the World becomes an accomplished fact, we must accept the most responsible Imperial federations available as a substitute for it' (Fabian Society 1900: 24). Again, it was a second-best policy that Shaw presented – only the best outcome possible in the circumstances. He was all too aware that the working class was not internationalist in outlook, that the world state was merely a theoretical construct. The empire existed and socialism required a constructive policy to deal with the many practical dilemmas facing the statesmen of the future. At any rate, the negative radicalism of the ILP would not suffice. British industry was in decline, its education system outdated, its values antiquated, its empire in disarray. Bold initiatives were needed if the tide of national and imperial degeneration was to be turned.

Considerations of this kind informed Shaw's next major Fabian publication, *Fabianism and the Fiscal Question* (Fabian Society 1904). This dealt with the newly aroused controversy over free trade and protectionism, instigated by Joseph Chamberlain. In *Fabianism and the Empire* Shaw had viewed free trade almost as an economic law of nature. By 1904 his stance was far less settled. Socialism was in many respects 'Ultra-Protectionist', he said, advocating 'the deliberate interference of the State' with trade as well as the general 'subordination of commercial enterprise to national ends'. The emphasis on 'national ends' suggests the tensions inherent in his outlook. For example, the tract acknowledged that 'Socialism is internationalist in tradition and sentiment' and that its 'pre-possessions are not on the side of aggressive nationalism'. Yet, it also pointed towards a policy of socialism in one country. 'The Fabian Society knows very well that British Socialism must develop nationally as a British product on British initiative', it declared (Fabian Society 1904: 4). Exactly how this was to be reconciled with the imperialization policy was not explained. Indeed the 1904 tract was equivocal in the extreme, designed not to present an authentic Shavian statement of doctrine, but to defuse the cross current of opinion within Fabian ranks. It was, in short, another masterpiece of compromise.

The temper of Shaw's own response is better gauged from his correspondence from the period, as well as from a series of articles he published in *The New Age* (Shaw 1976) between October 1907 and January 1908, collectively entitled 'On Driving Capital out of the Country'. There the bias was towards national socialism (the focus was on England in particular), with the empire either being ignored or treated in a critical and negative way. Shaw warned of the 'unpatriotic internationalism of Capital' which sent money abroad to modernize the industries of England's competitors, leaving her under-invested, under-nourished and under-worked. 'The weakest point in our Capital system is its failure to secure the application of our national capital, as fast as it is accumulated, to the provision of our national needs in the order of their urgency,' he said. It was a new twist to J.A. Hobson's tale. Shaw challenged his opponents 'to name a single proposal made by English

Socialists that would not have the effect of investing English capital in England' (Shaw 1976: 81). The empire had returned to the shadows; it was again (as it had been before the Boer War), a 'non-socialist point of policy'. Internationalism was in retreat. This emphasis on 'national ends' was to become a perennial theme of Shaw's socialism, leading him ultimately to the assertion 'I was a National Socialist before Hitler was born' (Kaye 1958: 193).

COMMENTS AND EVALUATIONS

These texts, *Fabianism and the Empire* in particular, have excited more comment than any other of Shaw's avowedly political works. Comment has varied from the derision of Lenin who saw the manifesto as indicative of Fabianism's 'social chauvinism', to the view of A.M. McBriar, for whom it was something of an uncomfortable aberration in the Society's affairs, a *pièce de circonstance* interrupting their 'proper business' of domestic reform (McBriar 1962: 130).

Of course the work was not Shaw's alone. The contributions of S.G. Hobson, F. Whelen and Hubert Bland to the manifesto have long been established. More recently, Patricia Pugh has shown that without Graham Wallas's intervention 'there would have been no reference to the non-white races in the analysis of the South African situation, nor the defence of Britain's bureaucratic rule in Africa as preferable to government by white traders' (Pugh 1984: 80). All the same, commentators generally identify both the manifesto and the tract with Shaw, and rightly so. He was ultimately the prime-mover in the formulation of Fabian policy on these neglected themes. What is more, their core tenets stuck fast in his work. Of all the early Fabians, it was Shaw who pursued their implications for socialist doctrine far beyond the temporary craze over national efficiency.

What do these texts tell us of Shaw's tactical acumen? The initiative was a failure. Lord Rosebery was not so powerful a political tool as Shaw had thought. There was to be no man of destiny, only the usual round of humdrum permeation. Rosebery was too weak to be relied on, the Webbs decided. The idea of forming a centre party around the cause of national efficiency simply petered out. According to Lisane Radice, the Fabian involvement with Rosebery and their 'neglect of the infant LRC [Labour Representation Committee], was a serious miscalculation' (Radice 1984: 144). An un-sympathetic reading of events might well conclude that this miscalculation was the product of Shaw's flawed grasp of current politics, deriving ultimately from the arrogance embedded in his self-styled political realism. How like him to prefer the dramatic prospects offered by Rosebery to the steady progress of the working-class movement, it might be said. Was his erratic socialism not the result of his lack of faith in that movement? This reading of events has much to commend it. Shaw was not the grand tactician of his dreams, the new Machiavelli. He was too busy with other projects and too impatient for that. All the same, the interpretation can be tempered by the thought that the Fabians really lost very little ground through this adventure. History surely shows us that when the Labour Party was poised to gain power, then the Fabians permeated it with a vengeance.

They lost nothing but their reputation, it could be argued. Shaw certainly received and still receives a torrent of abuse from fellow socialists as well as such radicals as J.A. Hobson over *Fabianism and the Empire* (Griffith 1979: 573–80). The case for the prosecution was encapsulated in a letter from an old associate, Walter Crane, who said Shaw's application of revolutionary ethics to practical politics 'works out uncommonly like what is termed as "hunting with the hare and running with the hounds" ' (Shaw Papers: BM 50531). Only Robert Blatchford's eccentric voice in *The Clarion* and that of the conservative press were heard for the defence. It is in this context that many commentators first speak of Shaw's socialist realism degenerating into *realpolitik*. That was G.D.H. Cole's interpretation of his stance on empire, a stance which Cole found deeply shocking (Cole 1956: 191).

More recently, however, *Fabianism and the Empire* has been championed (albeit from within the Fabian fold) as the work of a prescient realist prepared to deal with issues other socialists preferred to ignore; as tactically unsound perhaps, yet still doctrinally significant. Both Pugh and Bernard Porter pursue this line of argument. Hindsight has been cruel to the 'imperio-internationalist dream', Porter states, yet the 'diagnosis that lay behind it' was sound (Pimlott 1984: 54–64); and Pugh reminds us that 'an evil is not undone simply by withdrawing from the scene of the crime' (Pugh 1984: 241). Bernard Semmel, writing from outside the Fabian fold, has also championed Shaw's stance: 'the social imperialists saw the needs of the time more clearly than their opponents', he says, adding that the Labour Party was to revert to the Shavian model of the national interest in the 1950s (Semmel 1960: 592).

Perhaps the appropriate response lies somewhere between these ultracritical and overly sympathetic approaches. Shaw certainly raised many important and neglected issues. However, the tensions in his work are not to be ignored, especially those between the nationalist and internationalist perspectives in his outlook. These were considerable and of considerable importance, too, in relation to the dilemmas facing the Second International. And further, beneath the humanitarian argument for a Commonwealth of Nations there ran darker undercurrents of thought, deriving from the shift towards a harsher realism in his work at this time. As the rebel turned lawmaker so he became more concerned to see the world from the viewpoint of the holders and not the victims of power. The shift in perspective was far from absolute, but it was real and it was to have serious repercussions in later years.

One footnote can be added to the debate. For some the whole episode confirmed Shaw's commitment to the British cause, summed up in the assertion from *Fabianism and the Empire* that 'the British Empire, wisely governed is invincible'. Complex as it was, his relationship with England was perhaps the most vital feature of his creative life. England, with all its failings and all its power, was the context in which his creative work was produced. Though England and the English were the favourite stalking-horses of his wit, they were yet indispensable to Shaw. Through the manifesto on empire and the tract on the fiscal question we are led to a view of Shaw, later encapsulated by St John Ervine, as 'the most jingoistic West Briton that ever came out of Ireland' (Shaw Papers: BM 50533).

HAPPINESS AND WELFARE

Fabianism has been aligned so far more or less consistently with the individualist morality of happiness or welfare on the understanding that 'Its ethic was the outgrowth of the rationalist liberal ethic of enlightened self-interest' (Berki 1975: 229). Now it appears this is too simplistic an approach. From the manifesto of 1900 Fabianism emerges as a paternalistic doctrine of an élite armed with its own collectivist morality of service, offering salvation to the poor. 'Missionaries among savages' was how Shaw described the Fabians in his retrospective account, 'a minority of cultural snobs' working apart from the proletarian movement, having 'learnt that cultural segregation is essential to research' (Shaw 1948: 229). Fabianism also had its anti-liberal tendencies. In their colonial policy they assumed not only that reform would come from above, but perhaps against the express wishes of the colonial people. It was a question of good government and not of the satisfaction of popular aspirations.

It seems a distinction must be drawn between the conception of goodness as happiness, on one side, and as welfare, on the other – the former belonging to the tradition of *laissez-faire* utilitarianism, the latter having more paternalistic overtones, representing the demanding side of the utilitarian outlook. Shaw at least was clear on this. In 1928 he explained that the principle of happiness was not sufficient as a guide to public policy. The poor, he said, may be perfectly happy in their poverty – 'the objection to it is not that it makes people unhappy, but that it degrades them; and the fact that they can be quite as happy in their degradation as their betters are in their exaltation makes it worse' (Shaw 1949a: 42). As Alfred Doolittle announces jauntily in *Pygmalion*, 'I aint pretending to be deserving. I am undeserving; and I mean to go on being undeserving. I like it; and thats the truth'. Human welfare, therefore, is not synonymous with happiness, because welfare must be concerned with the quality of life and so requires criteria of judgment distinct from mere personal satisfaction. 'Never give the people anything they want; give them something they ought to want and don't' was how Shaw formulated the welfare principle in his *Socialism for Millionaires* (Shaw 1932e), so setting the scene for the interpretation of Fabianism as an authoritarian doctrine of collectivist socialism. As for the happiness principle, that was expressed in the maxim 'Do not do unto others as you would that they should do unto you. Their tastes may not be the same'.

Fabianism, like Shavianism, has really a complex character, being something of a halfway house between liberal and socialist, individualist and collectivist morality, changing its complexion in response to shifts in the terms of political argument and the exigencies of power. Around this time, some Fabians (Shaw included) discussed seriously the perfectionist notion of an openly discriminatory eugenic policy, restricting procreation among the poor and unfit. On this basis, rational selection to secure maximum efficiency was the key to Fabian policies; the application of disinterested brains and political science to social problems was the myth underlying the Fabian mentality. It is thus that a link can be made between Shaw's rationalist élitism and his Fabian socialism.

Recently, commentators have tended to emphasize this controversial side to Fabian affairs.[3] Yet the bulk of their activities was still directed towards the pursuit of humdrum reforms. Webb was at work in the London County Council. There were tracts on municipal bakeries, hospitals and steamboats; *Life in the Laundary* was one title and *Small Holdings, Allotments and Common Pastures* another. Shaw in this period produced two Fabian publications, *Women as Councillors* in 1900 and *The Common Sense of Municipal Trading* in 1904, neither of which owed much to the prophet of the Life Force, deriving instead from his work as a vestryman of St Pancras. It was the practical means of gaining a fair and efficient system of sanitary accommodation for the women of London that was at issue in *Women as Councillors*, not some grand notion of welfare or perfection. As he told Lady Mary Murray in 1898, as a Fabian he cared only to ensure that 'the wants of the community are supplied in the best possible way'. Personally he considered many of these wants pernicious and ridiculous: 'horse traction, tall hats, furs and feathers, starched cotton shirts and 99/100ths of what people call art, I regard as more or less damnable', he said (Shaw 1972: 61). That was of no immediate account. His concern as a Fabian vestryman was to ensure that the trades servicing these wants operated along humane lines. On this more democratic basis, Fabianism was about securing happiness not presenting impossible schemes of improvement.

The nature of Shaw's commitment to efficiency as the goal of Fabian policy also needs to be qualified for (in contrast to the Webbs and H.G. Wells) he never considered efficiency to be an end in itself. Thus, in 1901, around the time Sidney Webb was preparing his tract on *Twentieth Century Politics*, Shaw counselled Beatrice:

> The Maximum Efficiency of the Nation is a good phrase for a treatise, but for a political article it is hardly succulent enough. And it is tremendously open to the sort of criticism that Bentham's formulae encountered. It may be that the Maximum Efficiency is only to be attained as the bees attain it; and unfortunately Maeterlinck has just described that method with a fullness that is hardly calculated to

71

popularize it. The truth is that efficiency is obviously not a final term
& cannot be held up as an end. So dont commit yourself.

(Shaw 1972: 235)

Such a statement suggests that Fabian political argument was in a state of flux
at this time, with different members of the old gang incorporating the new
vocabulary of national efficiency into their socialistic creeds in different ways.
In case anyone doubted what he understood to be the true end or goal of
progressive thought, in 1903 Shaw organized the reprinting of William
Morris's egalitarian lecture on *Communism* as a Fabian tract.

There are perhaps as many potential interpretations of Fabianism as there
are individual Fabians – is it a form of radical liberalism or labourism; a form
of national collectivism or a kind of incipient authoritarian socialism? By way
of a response to this debate, it can be said that it would be wrong, given the
evidence of the Fabian tracts and essays, to overstate the distinction between
happiness and welfare in Fabian socialism, or to overplay the Society's
departure from a piecemeal welfarism in the name of a doctrinaire science of
society.

The peculiarly Shavian contribution to the Fabian outlook on the central
issues of transition can be considered under four headings; (i) the state, (ii)
social conflict, (iii) labourism, socialism and the working class, and (iv)
socialism and the middle class.

The State

'The socialism advocated by the Fabian Society is State Socialism exclusively',
Shaw wrote in 1896 (Fabian Society 1896). There was no room for doubt. The
state was the key to socialist transition; it was the hub of power, the focus of
organization. Whereas their opponents on the left, the Marxist SDF and the
anarchist Socialist League, were either equivocal or downright hostile in their
outlooks on the state, the Fabians on the other hand built their conception of
socialist transition around the prospect of harnessing the authority of the state
to the socialist yoke. State socialism was not a matter of convenience for them,
but one of necessity. Indeed the maxim of Fabian strategy could well have
read 'If the state did not exist it would be necessary for socialism to invent it'.
As Rodney Barker says, 'the State, with a capital "S", strides through' *Fabian
Essays* 'like a romantic hero, regulating and controlling, and replacing the
anarchy of individualism with the good sense of collective social
responsibility' (Barker 1984: 28).

In fact the Fabian legacy in this instance is a frustrating one. They were
unusual in looking at the state when other socialists preferred mostly to ignore
it. But their sight was impaired. They are seen as collectivists who failed to
enquire deeply enough into the roots of their faith and so did not appreciate
its implications fully. The Webbs in particular are said to have presented an

administrative form of socialism which did not confront the problem of power on its own terms; their infatuation with the Soviet Union in the 1930s was the product of their naïve collectivism, it is claimed. Barker appends this warning to his discussion of the Fabian state: 'although the progress of the state is equated with that of socialism, early Fabian writing contains scant examination or description of what that state might actually be'.

The point is well made. It was Shaw who presented the official Fabian view of the state, originally in his 'Transition' essay, then adding to it in such tracts as *The Impossibilities of Anarchism* (Shaw 1932e) and *Report on Fabian Policy* (Fabian Society 1896). After his journeyings among Marxists and anarchists, he was, of all the early Fabians, the best placed to formulate the Society's position on the state. He at least had partially digested the arguments of their opponents and knew how best to refute them. From a theoretical standpoint, however, his work was a limited success only. Perhaps this was because his discussion always bore the hallmark of polemical debate, substituting the tricks of the controversialist for hard analysis. As he warned in the preface to *Fabian Essays*, the case for the social democratic state was put 'not as an author would put it to a student, but as a speaker with only one hour at his disposal has to put it to an audience'.

Whatever the reason, at the most abstract level Shaw's analysis of the state was sparse and unsatisfactory. Fabianism was a doctrine of political collectivism. But of precisely what kind? The classic formulation was presented in the 'Transition' essay, the theme of which was the gradual development of socialism in Britain over the preceding forty-five years. Central to the argument was the assertion 'What the achievement of Socialism involves economically, is the transfer of rent from the class which now appropriates it to the whole people'. 'How is it to be done?', Shaw asked rhetorically, 'Who is their trustee, their guardian, their man of business, their manager, their secretary, even their stakeholder?' (Shaw 1932e: 40). The answer was close at hand, for the practical socialist must learn to view 'the State as the representative and trustee of the people'.

At this point Shaw's argument took a curious turn. In his search for theoretical justification he invoked Hegel's name, stating that 'outside economics' the socialists were 'pupils of Hegel' who 'expressly taught the conception of the perfect State; and his pupils saw that nothing in the nature of things made it impossible, or even specially difficult, to make the existing State, if not absolutely perfect, at least practically trustworthy'. Practical trustworthiness was to be ensured through representative democracy. Gathering the strands of the argument together, Shaw concluded with this full-blown statement of Fabian collectivism:

> Consequently, we have the distinctive term Social Democrat, indicating the man or woman who desires through democracy to gather the whole people into the State, so that the State may be trusted with the rent of the

country, and finally with the land, the capital, and the organization of the national industry – with all the sources of production, in short, which are now abandoned to the cupidity of irresponsible private individuals.
(Shaw 1932e: 42)

Some of the questions and loose ends arising from this can be considered in relation to Shaw's lectures and unpublished essays from the late 1880s; for in these more speculative discussions he did go some way towards describing the social democratic state of the future. For example, its ultimate goal was seen in egalitarian terms and not just as a matter of just distribution; its object was to secure an 'individual's welfare coordinately with that of every other member' of society – 'perfect equality is the consummation of Social Democracy' (Shaw 1971: 100).

Again, the path towards this idealized version of the democratic state ran in a Hegelian direction. Shaw's mentor here was Lassalle who had, in Shaw's estimate, successfully related Hegel's abstract account of the state to the actual processes of history. Shaw explained the relationship in a Fabian lecture in 1889, starting with Hegel's abstract conception of the perfect state:

the conception in which all discordant categories negate themselves by their own immanent contradictions until a final category is reached which reconciles all contradictions. Thus, if the State is a structure of hostile classes, then at any moment the uppermost class is the common oppressor of all the rest. Then the uppermost-but-one, high enough to be powerful in itself, and able to count on the assistance of all the classes beneath it in opposing the uppermost, turns on its oppressor, overthrows it and absorbs its units, thus becoming itself the uppermost and the common enemy. In its turn it is overthrown and absorbed by the class beneath it; and the process continues until the turn of the lowest class comes. When *its* revolt is accomplished, there is only one class, and so you get the perfect State, the criterion of perfection being equality.
(Shaw 1971: 43)

Lassalle's achievement, according to Shaw, was to show how that final step entailed the overthrow of the middle class by the working class, not by bloody revolution, but through the ordinary processes of representative democracy. The account was rather different to the one offered in *Fabian Essays*, revealing the tensions inherent in Shaw's socialism. Whereas in the latter the process of social evolution was seen in terms of organization and efficiency with the state acting as the rational arbiter between conflicting interests, in the lecture the analysis revealed a residual militancy, where the state was a mirror of the conflicts in a divided society, with resolution only being attained in a classless order. Also, by way of a footnote to the debate, there is an indication here of the differences between his own and the Webbs's conception of administrative socialism. All three viewed a large and efficient bureaucracy as indispensable to socialism. Shaw, unlike the Webbs, was less inclined to place his faith in the civil service as an agent of transition. The road to socialism required the right sort of political leadership for him as well as the right economic base to favour the growth of a civil service dedicated to the common good. Administration was vital, but ultimately secondary to other factors such as economics, ideology and, increasingly, the superior brains and dynamism of the political élite.

A still more pressing issue, certainly in the context of the political argument of the day, was the relationship between the individual and the social democratic state: would such a state transgress the boundaries of individual liberty in its pursuit of equality? Shaw considered the matter in an unpublished essay written in July 1888. His opening proposition was that the notion of a 'self-regarding action', as conceived by J.S. Mill and Spencer, should be swept away into the 'limbo of decaying superstitions'. Actions of this kind were not possible in any form of state, democratic or otherwise. That having been established, he then presented this formula on the citizen and the state: 'Theoretically, the right of the community, organized as a democratic state, to interfere with the individual is boundless. Practically, the state has neither time, capacity, nor inclination to relieve the individual of more than a small share of the responsibility of guiding his own conduct'. Shaw's argument was that while there can be 'no theoretic limit to [the state's] right of interference', so long as the individual does not infringe the principle of equal welfare then his liberty is secure. He also assumed that no opposition of interests would arise between the individual and the state, for they both seek the same goal of welfare. In this way, Shaw arrived at the happy conclusion that

> The abstract proposition that the property of the individual is the property of the State; that the liberty of the individual is at the disposal of the State: that individual liberty and private property should be totally abolished; and that the right of the State to interfere with the individual is unlimited, are found, when reduced to practice, to be perfectly consistent with all the freedom of action, possession and enjoyment which so extreme an individualist as Mr Herbert Spencer claims for the individual.
>
> (Shaw 1971: 53)

The argument was extreme and paradoxical. It was also flawed as a defence of collectivism, based as it was on the naïve assumption (perhaps deriving from the British experience of government) that there is something like a natural limit to the state's desire to interfere in the lives of its citizens. Such apparent naïvety was to serve Shaw very badly indeed in the 1930s, when he was to accept the totalitarian theory of the state as a mere tautology (Shaw 1949a: 488). In this temper he represented the most extreme kind of collectivism in Fabian circles, eventually winning for himself the reputation of a state-worshipper, careless of individual rights, an advocate of all the terrors associated with revolutionary republicanism.

75

As always with Shaw, there was another side to the tale. In *Quintessence*, for example, the rebel declared 'All abstractions invested with collective consciousness or collective authority, set above the individual, and exacting duty from him on pretence of acting or thinking with greater validity than he, are man-eating idols red with human sacrifices'. Of course this can be seen as an untypical work, dedicated to the vitalist philosophy of individual wilfulness. To have imposed a collectivist conclusion on the argument here would have been to invite the charge of intellectual chaos. The alternative vision cannot be dismissed on those grounds, however. It represented a real and lasting element in Shaw's political outlook, informing many by-ways of his thinking. Thus, his discussion of education in the preface to *Misalliance* (Shaw 1932i) had strong libertarian overtones. So too did his defence of tolerance for heretical opinions (at least when he was not seeking to force that defence into a social Darwinist mould).

Yet, this libertarianism tended to be swamped in his programmatic work by the collectivist argument, with all its pitfalls and ambiguities. In time that argument also overwhelmed the case for the devolution of power to local or municipal government common in Fabian literature. 'A democratic State cannot become a Social-Democratic State unless it has in every centre of population a local governing body as thoroughly democratic in its constitution as the central Parliament', he said in the 'Transition' essay in *Fabian Essays*. Such arguments serve as mitigating factors where the case of Fabian collectivism generally is under consideration. However, despite his lengthy tract on municipal trading and his experiences as a vestryman, in contrast to the Webbs, the cause of local government does not seem to have struck deep roots in Shaw's thought (neither *The Guide* or *Everybody's* have chapters on local democracy).

Democracy itself had an uncertain status in Shaw's work. At best, his argument for 'complete democracy' referred to the limited, representative kind. His socialism was in that sense alien to the participatory tradition associated with Morris and G.D.H. Cole. When the controversies with the syndicalists and, more particularly, the Guild Socialists broke out in Fabian circles between 1910 and 1920, Shaw was among the first to recognize their importance for the socialist conception of 'practical democracy' (Fabian Papers: A1/2). Yet, he was unable to revise his own conception of democracy sufficiently to allow for fundamental change. In his appendix to Edward Pease's official history of the Fabian Society he sought to side-step the problem of democracy and participation raised by the Guild Socialists, arguing that their critique of Fabian collectivism 'was an imaginary one'. He said the requirements of distribution would inevitably reintroduce 'the whole machinery of collectivism' into the socialist state (Pease 1963: 281). Though valid in its way, it was hardly an adequate response to the issue, leaving Shaw open to the charge that in his state the worker 'would be a passive recipient rather than an active participant. It would be the Servile State predicted by Belloc, or the Selfridge State anticipated by Cole' (Wright 1979: 50–71).

76

The nature of the problem was outlined in *The Impossibilities of Anarchism*. The tract included a formal commitment to democracy together with dire warnings against authoritarian forms of socialism. 'Establish a form of socialism which shall deprive the people of their sense of personal liberty, and, though it double their rations and halve their working hours, they will begin to conspire against it before it is a year old', he declared. It was a fair warning. Still the project of enlightenment was as complex as ever. In particular, there remained his low estimate of current public opinion, 'educated to regard the performance of daily manual labour as the lot of the despised classes'. A new, more altruistic social morality had to be produced as a basis for the democratic state of the future, and its production involved, *inter alia*, a system of compulsory labour. According to the MacKenzies, the new order was to be achieved by 'something very like a Positivist State inspired by a Religion of Humanity and governed by a disinterested elite' (MacKenzie and MacKenzie 1977: 112). This was only implicit in 1893. By the 1930s the crucial part played by an energetic minority of political leaders in Shaw's scheme of things was all too obvious, prompting Rodney Barker to suggest a 'real difference' between Shaw's responses to the Soviet Union and those of the Webbs: 'The Webbs saw a seamless tapestry of consultation, advice and discussion. Shaw saw Bolshevik tories getting things done' (Barker 1984: 34).

Back in July 1888 Shaw indicated that his approach to the theoretical debate on freedom and the state was less than entirely serious. All 'abstract propositions' on issues of this kind, though valid in principle, were 'by themselves perfectly barren', he said. His real interest was not in such abstractions as the perfect democratic state, but in the problems encountered in practice. The state's practical trustworthiness was all that mattered. Again, his approach was flawed. What was lacking here, as elsewhere, was a clear account of the scope and nature of the moral authority of the practically trustworthy state, or indeed of any state operating under less than ideal circumstances. In 1914, for example, in a Fabian lecture on 'Redistribution of Income', his attempt to explain the state's right 'to do that which is wrong for private individuals and corporations to do' was ludicrously inadequate. He simply asserted that 'Governments may do what individuals may not because they can do things that individuals cannot. They enjoy a unique power in virtue of which they are allowed a unique license' (Shaw 1971: 276). All that this achieved was to make the degree of moral authority dependent on the extent of the power enjoyed by the state. This was socialist realism at its worst, simply reasserting the dilemma at the heart of the subject. Within this confusion, moral and theoretical, there lay the seeds of the facile statism which characterized his sympathy with the totalitarian governments of the 1930s. Such were the pitfalls of the Fabian neglect of theory.

By declaring the barrenness of abstract propositions, Shaw was effectively revealing his eagerness to proceed to practical discussion on strategy.

Excursions into Hegelianism, one suspects, were no more than embellishments, bits and pieces of theoretical finery, worn at a time when Shaw was casting-off the coils of Marxism and anarchism. The realm of strategy was his chosen domain and here, though we may not expect consistency, we might hope to find the substance which was lacking in his theoretical analysis.

In fact two alternative strategies (each connected to the tensions inherent in his theoretical discussion) emerged from Shaw's work: one relatively moderate both in aims and means, concentrating on the politics of welfare; the other more militant, more inclined towards the politics of conflict. Both strategies agreed as to the indispensability of some organization capable of administering the process of transition and of performing the functions of management identified with the modern state. The difference related to the details of transition.

The moderate strategy was the standard Fabian approach identified with the rationalist socialism of the Webbs. As formulated in the 1896 *Report on Fabian Policy*, it stressed the suitability of existing state machinery in England for the socialist cause; 'The difficulty in England is not to secure more political power for the people but to persuade them to make sensible use of the power they already have'. Marx had said as much in The Hague in 1871, but it was the Fabians who formulated a reformist doctrine of socialism founded on the British parliamentary system, described in the *Report* as a 'first rate practical instrument of democratic government'. Behind Fabian gradualism was an underlying commitment to the utilitarian conception of representative democracy as the only viable form of government in modern society, and behind that commitment was the assumed identification of the state with rational society. All that was required, it seemed, was for the majority to elect a parliament representative of the general interest.

In its own provocatively moderate way the *Report* was quite a faithful picture of Fabian politics: limited in scope, anti-theoretical in outlook, concerned solely with 'practical Democracy and Socialism'. Of course its very moderateness was tailored to suit a particular context. The work must be read, in the first instance, as an official statement presented to a suspicious and mostly hostile audience. Large sections of the Second International to which the work was addressed were contemptuous of Fabian social democracy and Shaw, in stating the Society's case in the most respectable terms, was striking an aggressively independent note in the movement. And further, the Report's defiant tone cannot be divorced from the Society's ignominious return to the paths of permeation after 1896. In this respect, the work was part of an attempt to rehabilitate Fabian fortunes among the established parties in British politics. To this end the story of transition was told in terms of rational enlightenment with the capitalist state playing a supportive and creative role in the educative process.

A version of the moderate strategy was also used in *Fabianism and the*

Empire. There Shaw asserted the autonomy of the state from the prevailing economic interests, or from class bias of any kind, writing of Britain's 'public-spirited imperialism'. Again, the work had to be understood in relation to the policy of permeation. Yet it also has considerable doctrinal and historical significance, because it highlights the problematical relationship between socialism and the nation state, especially at a time of war. Concealed within its national socialism are the warning signs of the chaos and defeat of the Second International in 1914 when national unity and loyalty to the state outranked the policy of class confrontation. This at least is one perspective on the moderate strategy of rational socialism (see also Chapter 5).

Elsewhere, a different story was told. In *The Impossibilities of Anarchism*, Shaw stated 'The state at present is simply a huge machine for robbing and slave-driving the poor by brute force' (Shaw 1932e: 96). In this context, where the premium was on combining practicality with militancy, the state was an organ of coercion, the strategic implication being that socialism must recognize the necessity of controlling the state in order that it might use its coercive power on behalf of the people against the classes. Transition, therefore, was not just a question of education, but of coercive force carried out by the 'impartial' police and armed forces against the former ruling class. This was the sting in the tail of parliamentary socialism. Though evident in his earlier work, it was the turn of the century before Shaw started to give full publicity to this aspect of his argument on strategy. Doubts about progress and the possibility of piecemeal reform, coupled to a growing awareness of the ideological strength of capitalism operating through the press and every facet of public life, fuelled new interest in the more militant approach. In 1904 Shaw warned against the identification of revolutionary socialism with Marxism: 'It implies that there are two courses open to us: Parliamentary action and physical force, each of which excludes the other. That is not so: Parliamentary action is usually the first stage of civil war' (Shaw 1904c: 1). And two years later, in the preface to *Major Barbara*, he seemingly condoned the terrorist, with his 'appalling courage and resolution' in his war against the state which 'is constantly forcing the consciences of men by violence and cruelty' (Shaw 1931e: 232–5). It was not the Fabian way, but revolutionary terror was a legitimate response to state terror. In the 1908 preface to *Fabian Essays* Shaw wrote: 'The Fabian knows that property does not hesitate to shoot, and that now, as always, the unsuccessful revolutionist may expect calumny, perjury, cruelty, judicial and military massacre without mercy'. The message was that when the shooting starts the Fabians intended to be at the state end of the gun.

It was an outlook on strategy which represented the extreme left-wing of Fabian socialism, a version of the politics of conflict which is too often associated exclusively with the more orthodox and less adventurous reformism of Karl Kautsky.

Social conflict

The details of the militant strategy were formulated in *The Clarion* of 30 September, 21 October and 4 November 1904 (Shaw 1904b, 1904c, 1904d). It was here Shaw first presented his unique analysis of social conflict in response to the Adler-Vandervelde resolution on class war which proclaimed 'the simple stratification of society into two classes with diametrically opposed interests'. The three-cornered debate that ensued between Shaw, Hyndman and Keir Hardie was really a first-class example of the style and temper of Shavian argument: fiercely independent, castigating both the Marxist orthodoxy of Hyndman and Hardie's pacifism. The argument was not founded on principle but on the realistic appraisal of 'actual social facts', Shaw claimed. His purpose was to explain the true economic and subjective grounds affecting the structuring of interests and patterns of conflict, thereby correcting the oversimplified class-war thesis which prevailed in the Second International.

The question in Shaw's mind was not 'whether there are social antagonisms or not, but who are the parties to it'. If Marx was wrong, if class was not the basis of such antagonism, then how were the patterns of conflict to be defined? Shaw's alternative was founded on a form of modified materialism. The difference between himself and Marx was that for Shaw the economic criteria determining conflict were conceived not in terms of property ownership, but according to types of services rendered. Shaw's prediction was that the following groups would engage in the socialist struggle: the productive proletariat and their socialist sympathizers on one side, the plutocrats and the parasitic proletariat on the other. Or stated in allegorical terms, 'we have three main social divisions, comparable to the fish, the seagull who swallows the fish, and the skua who makes the seagull vomit the fish again and hand it over to him. Now clearly both the fish and the skua are enemies to the gull, but they are not therefore friendly to one another: on the contrary, the fish is sacrificed to two appetites instead of one'. The fish was the productive proletariat, the producer of 'food, clothing and everything else that is needed by the workers of the world'. The seagull was the plutocrat. The skua, meanwhile, represented that 'corrupt class of workers' – tradesmen, hotel-keepers, gamekeepers, domestic servants, the makers of fashion and the products of luxury – created by the vast surplus profits of capitalism to pander to the whims of idleness. These were the parasitic proletarians of whom Shaw declared:

> Capitalism has created, as it formally did in Rome, an irresistible proletarian bodyguard of labourers, whose immediate interests are bound up with those of the capitalists, and who are, like their Roman prototypes, more rapacious, more rancorous in their Primrose partisanship, and more hardened against all the larger social considerations, than their masters, simply because they are more needy, ignorant and irresponsible.
>
> (Shaw 1904b: 5)

There was no question of false consciousness. In the plays, characters of this class were invariably presented as the most skilful role-players, operating perfectly within the limits of their station in life. The would-be shopkeeper, Nicola, from *Arms and the Man* knows exactly how to manipulate his servant's soul to his best advantage; so skilful is he that Bluntschli declares him to be the ablest man in Bulgaria. William Collins, the greengrocer from *Getting Married*, makes a similar impression; not that he is servile in manner, only that he contrives by this tone to imply that all he says and does is 'with your kind permission'. The relationship between this parasitic class and those it serves was expressed perfectly in Mrs Bridgenorth's comment 'What a bond between us, Collins'. On a more prosaic note, Shaw was to explain that the parasitic proletariat 'understand that their incomes, while the present system lasts, are bound up with those of the proprietors whom socialism would expropriate'. This kind of statement shows the grip that 'rational man' assumptions still held over Shaw's socialist politics. Despite the incursions of vitalism, his political outlook still centred around the politics of the pocket. But not entirely so. The author of *Pygmalion* was too perceptive an observer of social mores to imagine that the relationship could be explained solely in economic terms. Other, more subjective, more illusory qualities of snobbery and status were also involved; the rich 'do something more than employ the poor', they also 'reflect their glory on them'. Socialism, therefore, must recognize 'the enormous force of snobbery that fortifies property and privilege'. It must also understand that the economic and cultural parasites represent the real conservative opposition against its own onward march. The capitalists, Shaw wrote in 1907, are 'so few and negligible that there are already avowed socialists enough in the country to guillotine them in a week, if that summary method were still in fashion' (Shaw 1976: 70).

Such exuberance was natural to Shaw. It was indeed part of the whole style of his propaganda. But what of the value of his ideas both in terms of practical strategy and as an explanation of the 'actual social facts' of modern capitalism? Do his ideas constitute a realistic updating of Marx, as he suggested, or do they belong among the vain boasts of argument?

The record is uneven. From the strategic standpoint, his militancy was neither entirely plausible nor unequivocal as a guide to action. In particular, to assume the impartiality of the armed forces seems naïve in retrospect. More generally, the notion of a middle way between the parliamentary and insurrectionary roads to socialism has little credibility, especially on Shaw's terms which seem decidedly hazy as to detail. The prospect of Brighton tradesmen and their clients manning the barricades in the fight against socialism was not the most convincing of his prognostications. The forecast of the gamekeeper combining with the fashion designer against the common enemy bordered on the absurd – the mad climax to an Ealing comedy. Hence, though the militant strategy was central to the uniquely Shavian brand of socialism, playing a vital part in the argument of *The Guide*, it was never accepted as official Fabian doctrine, nor is there any evidence of it making an appreciable impact on any other part of the socialist movement. On balance, the more militant groups – the Guild Socialists and Syndicalists – were openly hostile to Shaw: critics in *The New Age* described his plays as inoffensive, as evidence of Fabianism's capitulation to the reactionary classes. He was simply too inconsistent in his advocacy of the politics of conflict, liable always to betray the cause by hoisting the ensign of rational propaganda: 'Fortunately, when a habit of thought is silly it only needs steady treatment by ridicule from sensible and witty people to be put out of countenance and perish' (Shaw 1932d: 68). Strategically, then, Shaw's work was too equivocal, the doctrine of conflict but a small and seemingly elusive component of his total argument.

However, his ideas had more to offer when viewed as a source of insight into the problems facing socialism, particularly in terms of an explanation of the relationship between economic and cultural factors affecting class consciousness. Shaw's thoughts on the confusing, reactionary role of the parasitic proletariat, especially the vast army of domestic servants in the Edwardian years, were surely a timely reminder to all socialists of the hurdles to be surmounted in the race for power and emancipation. And if the hurdles have changed since 1904, the significance of economic parasitism for socialism remains. Indeed, if the 'embourgeoisement of the working class' thesis is to be believed, then the entire work-force of the western world is now a parasite on capitalist luxury. The argument was not Shaw's (at least not until 1929 in *The Apple Cart*), yet it does give some indication of the value of his unorthodox attempt at updating the socialist theory of class formation.

Perhaps his error was not that he lacked faith in the working class but rather that he was enticed by his residual economism to place too great a faith in the socialist potential of the productive proletariat. He was really too eager to limit the 'angels in marble' to that corrupt class of workers in the service industries. Elsewhere, of course, he took a very different view. In *The Illusions of Socialism*, for example, he wrote that the greatest stumbling block to socialism was the stupidity, narrowness and idiocy of 'the class which suffers most by the existing system'. There is no neat conclusion to the issue. If Shaw was not altogether consistent, neither was he complacent. If his reflections were not always plausible, he at least showed an independence of mind which allowed him to explore the complexities of class consciousness. Despite their limitations, his reflections were an all too rare attempt to analyse the relationship between class categorization and class formation, between objectively determined and subjectively perceived interests from the standpoint of creative socialist realism. His unorthodox reflections are as pertinent and powerful today as when he wrote in *Our Corner* in September 1887 that:

The division into classes with various standards of comfort which always occurs among slaves, and which is due to the necessity of educating and maintaining the slave who is a doctor or barrister very much better than the slave who is a mere hewer of wood and drawer of water, makes the highly skilled slave despise the unskilled, the unskilled hate and envy the skilled: makes the upper regard classification with the lower an intolerable degradation, and the lower spurn classification with the higher as a hypocritical effort to reconcile him to his inferiority.

(Shaw 1887b: 175)

Labourism, socialism and the working class

Shaw's socialism was a meeting place for so many tensions and dilemmas: the pragmatic regard for welfare set against the concern for the principles of equality and justice; the attempt to reconcile the exigencies of power politics with the moral idealism whose goal was a rationally ordered, classless society founded on the morality of service. To use Peter Clarke's terminology, his socialism was a curious mixture of mechanical and moral reformism (Clarke 1978: 5), at times emphasizing the institutional path to change so dear to the Fabian social engineers, at others seeking to turn the hearts and minds of men and women away from the squalid narrowness of capitalism towards the light of socialism: the politics of welfare set against the politics of virtue.

These competing perspectives on socialist politics were to produce in his Fabian propaganda an extraordinary variety of thoughts on the spectrum of issues relating to the working class and the process of transition to socialism. How can one reconcile the views expressed in *The Illusions of Socialism* with those of *Quintessence* where Shaw insisted that the working class, 'by its freedom from the characteristic bias of the middle classes, has escaped their characteristic illusions, and solved many of the enigmas which they found insoluble because they wished to find them so'. At one moment the working class was the villain, at another the hero of the Shavian tale of enlightenment.

And how can one reconcile the contradictory perspectives on the role of conscious understanding in the transition process? The same Shaw who championed the unconscious gradualism associated with Sidney Webb's formulation of Fabianism could also stress the importance of developing a theoretical understanding of social reality. In his provocative epistle to the Second International in 1896, for example, he ridiculed the Marxian conception of a 'class conscious movement', arguing that its practical achievements were minimal when compared to the advances made by the atheoretical and pragmatic trade unions in England (Shaw 1896: 664). Within a decade, however, he was to change his tune, asserting now that trade unionism was potentially anti-socialist in nature, representing 'not socialism, but the interest of the seller of labour as against the buyer' (Shaw 1904b: 5). On this basis, consciousness of class interest was not to be equated with

83

socialist consciousness. The former led only to the policy of labourism, which was simply an attempt on the part of the exploited to maximize their welfare within the existing scheme of things, without regard for the interests of the community at large, without any thought for the morality of service. Now the call was for a doctrinally-inspired movement, free of trade union domination.

Shaw's thoughts on the trade unions act as a barometer of his shifting views on socialism and the working class. Before 1896 he was more or less content in his Fabian propaganda to restrict his argument to the trade unionist or labourist level, accepting the basic regard for wage differentials and working-class allegiance to the moral and cultural apparatus of the bourgeois state. *To Your Tents, Oh Israel!* was the classic example. Despite the radical reputation it gained for its fierce attack on the Liberal Party, it was in fact an essentially labourist text. Its imagery was traditional (Biblical and Dickensian). Its appeal was to the older, more conservative unions representing the aristocracy of British labour. The article ignored the 'new unionism' of the period, spoke of progressivism not socialism, and invoked none of the grand terminology nor the fierce rhetoric of moral and spiritual transformation. Shaw put it most succinctly in a lecture on 'The Political Situation' from 1895, asserting that the article 'asked nothing that the most conservative of the older Trade Unionists would not have asked, and nothing that was not immediately and easily practicable' (Shaw 1895: 7). Such was the realism appropriate to the moderate strategy in which the progressive cause was viewed in terms of our 'irresistible glide' into economic collectivism, in which it was assumed that the interest of the proletariat and those of the community at large were driving in the same direction. In this light it is not surprising to find that in Bradford in 1893 Shaw was among the fiercest critics of the proposed Fourth Clause advocating a more exclusive and ideologically-inspired constitution for the ILP (Howell 1983: 296–8).

As always the full story was complex, with a discrepancy arising between his public pronouncements on labourism and his private appeals for a full programme of social democracy. Before 1896 his political faith had a buoyancy which kept the many-headed craft afloat in the troubled waters of party politics. After 1896, however, when his socialism grew more ambitious and expansive as he sought to express his contempt for the status quo in a 'mind-changing manner', the tensions within his work increased until the craft itself seemed in danger of breaking up on the rocks of moral idealism and pragmatic instrumentalism.

Traces of a more critical outlook on the working class and its socialistic potential always existed in Shaw's work. He shared with H.G. Wells a shabby-genteel loathing for the poor and their poverty, a loathing arising perhaps out of fear over their own uncertain prospects. Only between 1887 and 1895 or so, when he placed his hope in social democracy, did Shaw offer a suitably tempered version of his views. This was especially true of his Fabian publications of the period in which he tended to omit his more colourful and fundamentalist criticisms of the working class. Contrast, for example, the original article on anarchism from 1888 with his subsequent Fabian tract of 1893. In the first, he asserted that

> all the detestable fruits of inequality of condition flourish most rankly among those who suffer most by it. The notion that poverty favours virtue was invented to prove that the poor gain in the next world what they lose here. *Material degradation inevitably brings moral degradation; and this is the real grievance of the proletariat* [emphasis added].
>
> (Shaw 1888a: 337)

In the Fabian tract the assertion was so watered down as to disguise the inevitable moral degradation of the proletariat. It read,

> all the detestable fruits of inequality of condition, flourish as rankly among those who lose as among those who gain by it. In fact the notion that poverty favours virtue was clearly invented to persuade the poor that what they lose in this world they would gain in the next.
>
> (Shaw 1932e: 81)

After 1896 Shaw was less circumspect, more eager to beat the hard drum of his evolutionary righteousness. His nurse had taken him as a child to visit her poor friends in the Dublin slums, and he had thought them horrible people. To be poor was to be weak, ignorant, a nucleus of disease, a standing exhibition and example of ugliness and dirt, he said in the preface to *Major Barbara*. Mustering his resources of provocative rhetoric, he declared in *Death of an old Revolutionary Hero* that he 'had no other feeling for the working class than an intense desire to abolish them and replace them by sensible people'. Or again 'The attitude of Socialism towards the poor man is always that the poor man is necessarily a bad and dangerous man' (Shaw 1962b: 55). Ironically, he claimed that the only people to really appreciate the argument were the poor themselves (Shaw 1976: 14). Fellow socialists were too often cocooned in middle-class delusions, born of pity and guilt. Neither the romantic, naïve faith in the poor as the liberators of mankind so common among Marxists, nor the sentimental philanthropy common among social democrats were appropriate responses in Shaw's mind. Such notions were dangerous and misleading. The ignorance and corruption of the poor were entailed in the logic of capitalism.

In this uncompromising mood he refused (or so he said) to toy with labourism. His relations with the newly formed Labour Party were those of hostility and mutual distrust. When the Party first scored some electoral success in 1906, Shaw was among the first to disparage the achievement: 'a nominally Trade Unionist and Radical Group' was how he described the Party, lacking doctrinal vision and leadership (Shaw 1906: 5). Whereas in 1893 the unions were the great hope of progressive politics, now they were cast in the villain's role as corruptors of the authentic aims of socialism. 'Trade Unionism is not Socialism', he declared in *The Guide*, 'it is the capitalism of the Proletariat'. He believed that a party dominated by the unions would operate only within the doctrinal confines of radical liberalism at best. Writing in *The Clarion* in 1907 Shaw said, 'Socialism must achieve its independence of the Labour Party as the Labour Party has at last achieved its independence of the Liberal Party' (Shaw 1907a: 1). Only the Fabian Society, he announced in all seriousness, headed straight for socialism, and he cited successive policies on protectionism, education and imperialism as evidence of the Society's determination to formulate a doctrine of national socialism free of liberal prejudice.

There was almost certainly some sour grapes in all this. For Shaw, having set himself up as thinker and tactician to the labour movement, had now to accept that he had not only failed to divine the changing mood of the electorate, but also that the Labour Party had prospered without his assistance and in spite of total neglect by the Fabian Society. On this basis his complaints were those of an upstaged tactician. In 1906 he warned of the Labour Party's neglect of socialism; but had he not himself said two years before that socialism could be ignored as long as 'the class of the Parliamentary majority could be changed.'

From a different standpoint, the doctrinal gulf between himself and the political and industrial organs of the working class was real enough. It derived from deep dissatisfaction with the political capacity of the masses, as expressed in his ideas on eugenicism and in his critique of democracy. In the 1892 *Fabian Election Manifesto* (Fabian Society 1892) he refused to accept want of 'education and opportunity' as a valid excuse for 'not understanding party politics'; the same working man 'is at no loss when the subject is football or racing, or pigeon-flying, or any subject, however complicated, that he really wants to understand'. Shaw also argued that the working man should be represented in parliament by men of his own class. This relatively generous outlook was to prove short-lived, however. When in 1914 he explained why representatives of the working class were not suitable material for serious drama, his terms of reference were such as to cut this class adrift from the moral and spiritual foundations of his socialism; 'Everybody, including the workers themselves, know that they are dirty, drunken, foul-mouthed, ignorant, gluttonous, prejudiced: in short, heirs to the peculiar ills of poverty and slavery, as well as co-heirs with the plutocracy to all the failings of human nature' (Shaw 1932i: 225). Shaw's dramatic perception of the working man seemed to be locked into a Dickensian vision of London's undeserving poor. In Alfred Doolittle he produced one vigorous and likeable representative of this class at ease in the world, cut adrift from the strictures of middle-class respectability. But Doolittle was a special case, very different in character and outlook to the ordinary working man. All in all there did not seem to be much hope for the socialistic potential of the average quarryman or cotton spinner.

The tangle was complete. Strictly speaking the working classes were no longer a proper subject for Shaw's socialism. Being poor, they were not to be seen as agents of radical change, but as unfortunate creatures to be abolished by sensible reforms. Steven Ingle has responded to this aspect of Shaw's socialism, arguing that his 'hatred of poverty was simply part of a more general hatred of the poor and in this we find a complete break with the normal socialist tradition'. Ingle goes on to say:

> When we remember that Shaw also believed the workers to possess little potential for revolution or even sustained militancy, we begin to realize that when Shaw spoke of abolishing the working class he was not being profoundly humane and far-sighted; he was callously dismissing a range of problems with which he would prefer not to deal. One cannot escape the conclusion that at heart Shaw believed that nobody was poor who did not deserve to be.
>
> (Ingle 1975: 85)

Harsh as Ingle's judgement is, it is worth citing as an extreme version of a view of Shaw's socialism that is quite common, especially within the socialist movement itself, but is it correct? Only in the sense that it pushes one aspect of Shaw's argument to its logical conclusion. Contrary to Ingle, Shaw's critique of the poor and their poverty was neither simple nor dismissive. If the critique had its limitations, it also had its strengths. For example, his discussion of the relationship between dialect and class in *Pygmalion* raised important and neglected issues for socialism. In creating a new speech for Eliza, Higgins claimed he was 'filling up the deepest gulf that separates class from class and soul from soul' (Shaw 1931a: 248). Nor were Shaw's views on working-class culture entirely unsympathetic. As Ian Britain reminds us, Shaw's early reflections on the music halls were quite supportive; writing in 1883 he said they 'do more to educate the people artistically than all the nimminy-pimminy concerts in the world' (Britain 1982: 240). Traces of a less sympathetic attitude were also apparent in his early music criticism. On hearing a performance of Gounod's Redemption at the People's Palace in April 1889, Shaw was compelled to write 'I understand that various members of the industrial classes of Mile End pretended to enjoy it, which shews how the hypocrisy of culture, like other cast-off fashions, finds its last asylum among the poor' (Shaw 1937: 95). Views of this kind do not please every socialist. They cannot be easily rejected as 'callously dismissive' on that account alone. There is an important issue at stake here which Shaw does well to raise.

His critique of the poor after 1896 should be seen, too, in relation to his declining faith in progress. It was then his socialism felt the strong pull of perfectionism which accompanied his general despair of capitalist humanity, rich and poor alike. The poor had further to go than the rest, if only because they arrived at the starting point with so many handicaps. It was also then that his socialism acquired the hard edge of social Darwinism. From this perspective, extermination of the poor was Shaw's original and daring variation on the theme of national efficiency, guaranteed to raise eyebrows among both friends and foes in progressive circles.[4] The fundamentalist critique of the poor was therefore both part of the development of the distinctly Shavian doctrine of socialism and of his performance as an innovative controversialist, seeking to employ the language of political argument in a heightened way (especially at the time of the agitation for the reform of the Poor Law between 1909 and 1912). But, simple or not, this critique certainly meant that the working classes were not obvious candidates as agents of enlightenment. At best all they could muster was the trade union consciousness which Shaw now considered anti-socialist in nature, representing no more than a sectional interest within the capitalist scheme of things.

Another perspective on his views on the working class is gained from the dramatic text of *Major Barbara*, with its contrast between the scenes at the Salvation Army shelter and those at Undershaft's munitions factory in the final act. The former is filled with an air of pathetic charity, violence, squalor and dishonesty, seemingly representing the working man in his most anarchic and degraded state. In contrast, the latter points toward the brave new world of work – clean and dignified and secure, 'all horribly, frightfully, immorally, unanswerably perfect' in the opinion of the scholar, Adolphus Cusins. Undershaft's heavenly city had everything: libraries, schools, a nursing home. So different was it from the normal working environment that when the respectable Peter Shirley was brought there from the shelter he was too ashamed to use the facilities which seemed beyond his station in life. So much was provided that it prompted Undershaft's son, Stephen, to open the debate with the remark 'I cannot help thinking that all this provision for every want of your workmen may sap their independence and weaken their sense of responsibility.... Are you sure so much pampering is really good for the men's characters?' To which Undershaft replied that those who are organizing civilization do not believe that 'trouble and anxiety' are good things. Thus, order and enlightenment were not to be gained through struggle; they were to be delivered courtesy of the superior brains of Andrew Undershaft and his like.

In this brief exchange Shaw uncovered a major dilemma of his socialism. As a moralist, he sought to transform consciousness by developing a new and positive sense of responsibility. As a socialist, especially in his more élitist phase, he appeared interested only in efficient management by a hierarchy of experts, with responsibility being understood (for the masses anyway) in a negative sense. In this way, argued critics such as G.D.H. Cole, he undermined the means by which his republican vision of emancipation might be realized, because the experience of responsibility required for the development of character was divorced from the day-to-day lives of ordinary working people.

Shaw understood the relationship between character and responsibility. Writing in 1894 he offered the hypothetical example of two soldiers, both of equal ability, with one being made a commander-in-chief, the other left as a private: 'After a year the difference in ability between the man who had been doing nothing but sentry duty, under no strain of responsibility, and the man who had been commanding the army would have been enormous', he predicted (Shaw 1932e: 271). Clearly, responsibility begets ability and enhances character. Shaw argued that capitalism operates with an artificial system of responsibility, wherein the opportunity to exercise authority is limited by class. Conservatism's standard strategy, he said, is to conclude from observation of the character of the average agricultural or industrial labourer that people of this class are unsuited to the burdens of respectable life. Shaw, on the contrary, seemingly believed that a man's ability could not be properly judged apart from the exercise of responsibility.

From this one might have expected Shaw to support a form of participatory democracy in industry as well as in politics. As noted in the discussion on the state, he did not draw this conclusion. Certainly in *Major Barbara* the emphasis was on strict hierarchy in working relations. Striking a particularly cynical note, Undershaft says of his workmen 'Of course they all rebel against me, theoretically. Practically, every man of them keeps the man just below him in his place'. Even the more militant speeches of Cusins, now the heir apparent, have a curiously hierarchical twist to them: 'I want a power simple enough for common men to use, yet strong enough to force the intellectual oligarchy to use its genius for the general good'. Why not seek a power which might allow the common man to use his own genius for his own good? The play closed with Barbara tugging at her mother's skirts and imploring her to tell her which home to take in the model village. What conclusion are we to draw? Must the young and poor alike relinquish responsibility to those who know best? Not that *Major Barbara* can be taken as conclusive evidence of Shaw's views which, taken as a whole, offer conflicting possibilities for the young and poor. Around the same time as he was writing the play with its picture of a tame and contented work-force, he was also publishing 'The Class War' articles in *The Clarion*, where part of the proletariat, the productive proletariat, were supposed to form the backbone of the socialist movement in its militant phase. This last option suggested that he could not just abandon interest in proletarian consciousness in favour of reform from above. Perhaps the obvious way out of this tangle of strategies was to emphasize the importance of industrial conflict, using the unions or some variation on unionism to awaken the working class to the realities of its exploited position under capitalism. An obvious solution perhaps, but one which Shaw could not adopt. Every bone in his Fabian body warned him of the dangers of unregulated working-class activism; every imperative of his morality of service condemned strikes as a form of anti-social activity, with the right to strike being viewed as the worker's right to idleness. He had no difficulty in

89

endorsing the Fabian proposal to substitute compulsory arbitration for the turmoil of industrial conflict. So opposed was he to the strike weapon that his critique of syndicalism was every bit as intense as his critique of capitalism itself; compared to the anarchy of syndicalism, even Mussolini's regime was considered a healthy reaction towards 'devotion and discipline' (Henderson 1925: 31). Unlike the Webbs, Shaw never found a place for the right to strike in his socialism (Webb and Webb 1975: 297).

Despite their apparent waywardness, his ideas on working-class consciousness and the trade unions were essentially Fabian in nature. From the Webbs he learnt the value of the unions in the war against poverty. Though in time he was to challenge their hold on the labour movement, he never ceased to advocate their cause from the pragmatic standpoint of the politics of welfare (he was at the forefront of the agitation for white-collar unionism). Shaw's view was that the working class cared for money and not for those fastidious visions of the good life produced by the likes of William Morris (Shaw 1931e: 213). And rightly so. Yet, Shaw's advocacy was qualified by the proviso that the unions must play the 'welfare game' according to Fabian rules; in no way was the pursuit of self-interest to be allowed to contradict the common interest of society as a whole. Such were the restrictions he placed on the lower morality of self-interest, restrictions which derived from the subtle interaction of individualist and collectivist principles in his Fabian socialism.

And Shaw's militancy? – if he was a militant then he was strictly a corporate militant. Social antagonisms would not be expressed in the industrial sphere where the uneducated proletariat would operate without sufficient guidance; rather, they should be expressed in terms of the state militant. If there was really any fighting to be done, then it would be the police and the armed forces who would be involved, not the productive proletariat. But even that seemed far-fetched. *The Revolutionist's Handbook* (Shaw 1931f) was really anything but revolutionary in the accepted sense; 'The constitution of England is revolutionary', it claimed, 'Revolution is therefore a national institution in England'. Turning again to the evidence of the plays for a moment, the last act of *Major Barbara* rings with such militant assertions as 'the ballot paper that really governs is the paper that has a bullet wrapped up in it'. This appears consistent with the militant strategy, only it was said by Undershaft and, in the context of the play, there was no prospect of his own work-force doing anything but making and wrapping up bullets for other people to use. The only example of active proletarian militancy from the plays was in the political comedy, *On the Rocks* (1933), where an unemployed mob breaks into Downing Street singing 'England, arise' and smashing windows (the wrong ones). Nothing comes of it and nothing will come of it, because a leaderless and undisciplined mob can be no match for the coercive forces of the state. Again the emphasis was on order, hierarchy and discipline.

Socialism and the middle class

Writing in 1912, in the first issue of the *Daily Citizen*, Shaw noted 'a complete change in the class of [his] audience' as between the early pioneering days and the Edwardian years. By way of illustration he contrasted his first visit to Walsall in the 1880s when he spoke to rows of black-faced men, colliers and workers in grimy industries, with a second visit when he spoke to 'rows of ladies sitting in a flood of electric light in the smartest hats the wealth of Walsall could procure'. The shabby workmen had given way to 'a collection of young toffs and old geezers' (Shaw 1976: 110). Whether the change pleased Shaw, he did not venture to say. He offered instead an explanation which had to do with his growing popularity as a dramatist and critic, together with the rising cost of admission to any of his lectures which effectively barred the working man from attending them. Added to which, by the early 1900s his socialist message was itself addressed as much, if not more, to a middle-class audience as to the industrial worker. And as Shaw was quick to point out, the 'immediate interests' of the toffs and the working classes were too sharply opposed for there to be any question of a common political purpose: 'They hated one another like poison. They would not speak to one another; would not eat with one another; would not sit in the same part of a theatre; would not intermarry; and would not believe any good of one another, though, underneath their clothes, they are exactly the same animal' (Shaw 1976: 110).

That was the plain truth. The same could not be said of his claim that it was twelve years after his first appearance on a socialist platform before the 'plight' of the middle class engaged his interest as a propagandist, for occasional overtures to this class are found in his early work. It is fair to say, however, that his outlook in this period was overwhelmingly critical and fundamentalist in nature, as in this warning to the Fabians in 1890:

> I do not see how a man is to be a candid Social Democrat with the approbation of the middle class. He cannot stir up the people mightily against inequality and all its bitter fruits if he is also to win golden opinions for his moderation by finding polite excuses for the ignoble ruck of place hunters who have as much intention of abolishing inequality as a pirate has of scuttling his own ship.
>
> (Shaw 1971: 150)

All the same, middle-class respectability invariably played the whipping boy to Shaw's moral assaults. Even though he accepted that the revolt against capitalism starts with those in the middle station in life, his work still bristled with contempt for his own class which as a whole was locked into the ethical and economic structures of capitalism, unable and unwilling to break free.

It was only at the turn of the century, and after 1906 in particular, that Shaw explored the socialistic potential of the middle class in a concerted way, and then partly as a response to the gains made by the Labour Party at the general election. His purpose was to carve out a new and vigorous programme for the Fabian Society, a programme suited to its unique style, membership and pre-occupations: he informed Webb:

> before the Labour Party has been blazing away in Parliament for another year, there will be the beginning of a big middle-class demand for an educated middle-class handling of the new problems in Parliament. . . . We must spend the next five years in educating these chaps in committee work and public life; then throw the whole thing into their hands as a Federation of Fabian Socialist Associations; formally wind up the old Fabian and make our bow, as we shall both by that time be too wise, too various and too old to play with them any longer.
>
> (Shaw 1972: 661)

It was a revealing statement, personally and politically. There were hints here of a drift away from the grind of politics and the murky affairs of the Fabian Society towards the more splendid and carefree role of the man of letters at liberty to pronounce on any aspect of world affairs. Soon he would have outgrown the Fabian nursery, he suggested, and would not miss the constraints and demands that it placed on his energy and intellect.

Politically, the statement was an indication of the adjustment in Shaw's socialist propaganda towards the neglected middle class. Concealed in this change was the attempt to mark out a distinctive and independent place for the Fabian Society in British political life by forming a Fabian Parliamentary Party, or something of the kind – how else was the Society to avoid the fate of becoming a research department for the Labour Party and therefore yet another adjunct of the trade union movement, with all that entailed for Shaw?

Furthermore, Shaw's reflections on these matters must be seen in the light of the alternative proposals put forward by H.G. Wells for the reorganization of Fabian affairs. The story of this 'storm in a Fabian tea cup' has been told many times. In essence, Wells's scheme was to use the Society as a basis for a new order of the Samurai élite. The Society would receive a new title – the British Socialist Party – and its policy, now far more doctrinally-inspired than before, would be formulated by a triumvirate of its most influential members. In this way it would become the dynamic centre of progressive socialism in a technocratic age, with Wells at the helm setting the course indicated by his fantastic imagination (or something along those lines).

Given what has been said about Shaw's commitment to socialism and superior brains, one might have expected him to have welcomed the Samurai scheme with open arms. 'Why dont you see how entirely I am expressing you in all these things', Wells told him (Shaw 1972: 653), hoping to enlist the support of his fellow artist-philosopher in transforming socialism into a large, imaginative project made in 'transparent living matter' in place of the 'china or cast iron' favoured by the Webbs (Wells 1970: 164). Shaw could not accept the invitation. He too believed that Fabianism had to be made 'interesting again' and saw Wells as a useful recruit in that respect. But Wells's big schemes for the Society and, especially important, the manner in which he propounded them, did not win Shaw's approval. Too often Wells's political objectives were mixed with personal abuse and this was something Shaw could not accept, especially when that abuse was directed against Sidney Webb. There was also his own vanity to contend with. Though outwardly friendly and often encouraging in his correspondence with Wells, there was a sense of personal conflict behind the words of honey, a locking of horns between two literary stags, with Shaw determined to show who was the master technician where political in-fighting was concerned. He was more than a little piqued at the prospect of being ousted as chief strategist and polemicist by the upstart Wells.

Shaw was cast in an unfamiliar role in this affair, no longer was he the rebel leading the young into battle, but instead the aged defender of the established order, holding the fort against the youthful enthusiasts for change. He was getting old and steady, and Wells was not too much of a gentleman to prod at this vulnerable spot in the Shavian armour. He said Shaw was willing enough 'to play about with ideas like a daring garrulous maiden aunt', but when the test came in real life he showed 'the instincts of conscious gentility and the judgement of a hen' (MacKenzie and MacKenzie 1977: 362). Wells was not an orthodox pugilist, he did not care overmuch for the rules of the game but he knew how to hurt.

It was as much a problem of personality as of policy. The old gang calculated (rightly) that Wells had no stomach for the hard grind required to turn enthusiasm into practical action. They feared his revolution would destroy the Fabian Society and ruin the work of over twenty years. Wells did not understand the unique qualities of the frail Fabian craft, they reasoned. He would make a bad navigator and an even worse captain. If Fabianism was to be made interesting again without being undermined, then a less ambitious scheme was needed. In the event Shaw argued, albeit intermittently and with uncertain success, for using the Society as an instrument for raising the class consciousness of the middle classes. This too was a Wellsian theme, but more modest and so better suited in Shaw's mind to the Fabian Society created by the old gang. And Shaw prevailed. The conclusion reached by the Special Committee on Socialist Representation in Parliament had a well-worn and reassuring feel to it: 'We want to make those who have enjoyed the advantages of education and leisure desire Socialism for its own sake and their own' (Fabian Papers: A1/5).

The details of Shaw's middle-class propaganda were as complex as they were confusing. At times, between 1906 and 1908 especially, his call was for a 'Middle-Class Socialist Party'; at others it was for a socialist party to the left of Labour; and very often it was for something more modest, such as the 'Federation of Fabian Socialist Associations' mentioned in his letter to Webb. Shaw almost certainly saw his role not so much in organizational terms as in the dissemination of ideas, using his notoriety as a dramatist to stir things up a little in middle-class circles. As a propagandist, he directed his message to two distinct audiences within the middle class, namely, those he called the middle-class proletariat and those more favourably characterized as the intellectual proletariat. The middle-class proletariat was a broad grouping including small tradesmen and clerical assistants, the entire army of people who were being dragged down by advanced capitalism into the more mundane areas of non-manual labour. He called these 'skidders', the weaklings of the middle class, subjectively identifying themselves with the culture and wealth of the rich, while in reality standing on a par or even below the material level of the productive proletariat, performing 'slave labour of a very abject kind' (Shaw 1976: 60; Parkin 1975: 53). Blenkinsop, the impoverished GP from *The Doctor's Dilemma*, speaks on behalf of this class when he says that his 'patients are all clerks and shopmen. They darent be ill: they cant afford it'. The best example in the plays of this class of person was the prudish and socially gauche cashier, Gunner, from *Misalliance*. Gunner was perhaps the most pathetic character in all the plays: worn down by his tedious work, his poverty and ignorance, goaded by his inadequacy and embittered by his expectations. 'Of all the damnable waste of human life that was ever invented, clerking is the very worst', he says. His frustration finds expression in a moral fundamentalism which fires the most banal prophecy of socialist upheaval: 'The writing is on the wall. Rome fell. Babylon fell. Hindhead's turn will come'. There is a poignancy in the portrait deriving from the author's personal experience. Had Shaw not spent many years as a clerk in Ireland before coming to London to dream his wild shabby genteel dreams of social reform? Had he not longed for respect and status as Gunner longed for it? As Shaw was to confide to his old friend Edward McNulty, 'Gunner is immense. Gunner is Me . . . Gunner is the impecunious middle class' (Shaw 1985b: 233).

Shaw's strategy with regard to this class was to appeal directly to its self-interest. Despite Gunner's romantic outburst, little or no attempt was made in the articles and speeches to appeal directly to a truly socialist consciousness. All that could be hoped at this stage was to develop in the middle-class proletariat a consciousness of their exploited class position. It marked something of a return to the non-doctrinal, broad-based propaganda of his early labourism, with the call for the 'Middle-Class Socialist Party' being coupled with an appeal for the formation of a 'National Union of Clerks'. Unless they organized in defence of their interests, they would be 'fleeced' by the plutocrats to pay for a reform policy aimed at pacifying the working class, Shaw warned. He introduced socialism to his audience in an ultra-gradualist form: 'it is only a little question of taxation', he told the Liverpool Fabians; it is a 'very elastic thing: it is a thing which comes on gradually, and you can stop it whenever you like' (Shaw 1976: 100). As to the impact of his propaganda, Shaw informed Webb:

I find that my line of telling the middle class that they are getting badly left between Labor and Plutocracy in Parliament and that the cost of pensions and all other reforms extorted by Labor will be thrown on their rates and taxes if they dont organize, is effective; and it involves emphasising the limitations of Labor; but it seems to me that what we want is a couple of years of this sort of talk rather than any immediate attempt to organize anything or formulate anything.

(Shaw 1972: 717)

That was in 1907. Privately he was cautious about the prospects of his middle-class propaganda where the skidders were concerned. He realized that the forces of snobbery, status, differing habits, dialects and styles of life were too formidable to be routed by the verbal assaults he could muster. Clerks, like women, were almost 'impossible to organize', because neither expected to stay in their position for long: the clerk 'either hated business and meant to get out of it and become a great man . . . or else, if he was keen on business, he meant to set up for himself unless the boss took him into partnership' (Lloyd and Scouller 1919: 5). Shaw was certain that economic interest would eventually compel the new class of office workers to organize themselves, and he saw his own work and that of Wells, Masterman and others as the first step towards that goal. He pioneered socialist concern for the middle-class proletariat. When two Guild Socialists, J. Henry Lloyd and R.E. Scouller wrote a tract on *Trade Unionism for Clerks* in 1917, it was Shaw, as the major spokesman in the neglected field (along with J.R. Clynes), who supplied the Introduction.

The distinction between this grouping and the intellectual proletariat was never that clear or pronounced in the Edwardian years (for that we must wait until the 1930s). All the same there was no way that so shrewd an observer of social life as Shaw could have equated one group with the other. Nor was there much prospect of so able a propagandist approaching the two groups in quite the same way. The intellectual proletariat were professional men and women of all kinds, managers of industries, technicians and civil servants, all those representing the new class of administrators and researchers required by the changing nature and structure of capitalism. Unlike the skidders, the managerial stratum enjoyed a relatively prosperous and comfortable life-style, with considerable status. What is more, because of their technical skills they were potentially the most dynamic and powerful class in the modern world. Shaw never tired of expounding the virtues of the professionals, starting with *Socialism and Superior Brains* in 1894 and culminating in the statement from *The Guide* where they are said to act 'as a sort of Providence' to both rich and poor alike:

if the landlords and capitalists can neither make anything nor even tell others how to make it; and if the workers can do nothing until they are told what to do, how does the world get on? There must be some third class standing between the propertied class on the one hand and the propertyless class on the other, to lease the land and hire the capital and tell the workers what to do with them.

There is. You can see for yourself that there is a middle class which does all the managing and directing and deciding work of the nation, besides carrying on the learned and literary and artistic professions.

(Shaw 1949a: 168)

This, basically, was the intellectual proletariat, the brains of the outfit without whom all the paraphernalia of modern life would grind to a halt. Shaw's sympathy with this class was a distinguishing feature of his socialism. It made his outlook seem very modern while at the same time, because of its regard for superior brains, gaining for him a reputation as a technocrat. Together with the Webbs and Wells he forged the outline of a socialist response to the brain-workers, changing the contours of his socialism to suit its special gifts and qualities. He was the champion of bureaucracy, the prophet of a centrally-planned, rationally-conceived system in which sound administration was a necessity of life. It was in this context that he first wrote of socialism as a paradise of the able man. And further, he believed the intellectual proletariat to be uniquely adapted to the consciousness of service that was fundamental to his conception of socialism. Like the Webbs, he not only emphasized their importance to the modern economy, but also viewed the salaried professionals as expressing (potentially anyway) an ideal of public service. There were those Fabians, as Hobsbawm has claimed, who saw in the intellectual proletariat 'a sort of anticipation of the ethos of communism', the key being that their work was inspired, not so much by financial gain, as by the joy of discovery and elucidation or by the pursuit of order and efficiency (Hobsbawm 1964: 258). The propaganda directed towards them had to be adapted accordingly. Shaw at least argued that a myth of service and a conviction of sin against commercial morality were required if their full socialist potential was to be realized. He explained that in order to make a professional man class conscious

you have first to explain to him that as organizer of production to the community he is so vitally necessary and important that no revolution could possibly enable the state to do without him. This pleases and reassures him, though it would please him more if he understood his own business better. Second, that the commercial method of organizing production condemns him to be a cad who does everything for pay and nothing for honour, love or patriotism. And this he is apt to get huffy about; but he cannot rub it off; and it is the shame of it that will finally convert him to socialism if anything will.

(Shaw 1976: 111)

A consciousness of exploitation was not sufficient therefore. Instead, between

1908 and 1914, when his interest in this class was at its height, Shaw's work was littered with references to the stern republican virtues of citizenship. It was at this time that he formulated the ideal of the 'gentleman' 'who asks no more than a sufficient and dignified subsistence in return for the best service he is capable of giving to his country and to the world' as the cornerstone of the myth of service for this very Fabian class of persons (Shaw 1932e: 252).

Considerations of this kind also informed his analysis of what he called the 'rent of ability', that is, the advantage or profit that accrues to an individual from the possession of a natural skill or talent for invention, artistic creation, management, or whatever. Shaw's views on the subject were first expounded in *Fabian Essays*. But it was in *Socialism and Superior Brains* that he looked at the matter in detail. The pamphlet was in fact written as a response to the conservative critic of Fabianism, W.H. Mallock, who held that, as the advance of civilization was due to the inventiveness and sagacity of the intellectual proletariat, the causes of justice and efficiency alike insisted that they should be allowed to retain the profits arising from their abilities. Shaw could not agree. Turning Mallock's argument on its head, he said the analysis was flawed in two respects. First, though the intellectual proletariat was indeed essential to any economic system, no one could seriously argue that they actually received the full rewards of ability under capitalism. According to Shaw, Mr Mallock was confusing the productive classes with the proprietary classes, the holders of ability with the holders of land and capital. Second, the analysis offered a false picture of motivation. Far from stifling initiative, socialism would provide the framework for the true development of ability in line with the real needs of society instead of as a response to fickle and unenlightened market forces. Far from inhibiting responsibility, socialism would encourage it. Anticipating the doctrine of equality of income, he said 'If an ordinance were issued tomorrow that every man, from the highest to the lowest, should have exactly equal pay, then I could quite understand difficulties arising from every man insisting on being head of his department'. Under socialism, therefore, the abilities of the intellectual proletariat would be developed for their own sake, as well as for that of the community at large.

In time Shaw's sympathy for the intellectual proletariat hardened into a form of technical or vocational élitism. At the outset, however, it was a positive contribution because he was breaking new ground in a way which showed him to be among the most perceptive of socialist agitators. His work was not theoretically sophisticated, but it did help to establish an important trend in socialist thought, culminating in the 1950s in the revisionist belief in a neutral technocracy standing above the conflict of classes, motivated by a professional desire for efficiency and service to the nation. His record as a propagandist in this context is surely impressive. How many teachers, lawyers and professionals of all kinds, from bureaucrats to fellow writers did he convert to socialism? It is as hard to calculate as it is to overestimate his contribution to reconciling the romance and passion of socialism to the practical world of technology and administration, for with the help of his propaganda these essential skills gained legitimacy in an otherwise complacement movement.

Because it was part of his personal guerrilla war against commercial civilization – its ethics, structures and practices – his middle-class propaganda operated at many levels and across many dimensions, defying neat analysis. The moralist would never be reconciled to middle-class ideals. On the other hand, Shaw the Fabian was content to explore the socialist potential of his own class, which surely constituted the majority of his audience as playwright and pamphleteer. It was a strange marriage, charged with creative tension; something of a love–hate relationship, sealed with a kiss of convenience, sanctified by the cult of superior brains.

CONCLUSIONS

What conclusions can be offered on the Fabian section of Shaw's socialism? Setting aside the brilliance, the delightful mischief and power of his rhetoric, how is his contribution as a thinker to be assessed? Should it be that he was not altogether convincing or consistent? Certainly his reflections on the state were hardly satisfactory considering their importance to the whole scheme of his socialism. Should it be that his pursuit of realism led him along dangerous and unwholesome trains of thought? As a Fabian he supported British imperialism in South Africa and seemed almost to revel in his own disillusion with democratic processes. All this is true. Yet what is clear is that Shaw in his imperfectly flexible, tough-minded way, produced an arresting account of the great issues to be faced by socialism in the modern age. He offered no infallible guides to action, it is true, nor were his reflections very sophisticated pieces of doctrinal analysis. And he was inconsistent. But then he worked so near to the heartbeat of politics that his ideas were invariably coupled to tactical considerations. As a Fabian he believed practical relevance and the concern for the politics of welfare to be more important than the niceties of theory. If he could not supply all the answers, he at least hoped to pose the major questions, too often obscured, he believed, by crass moralism and dogma. The Fabianism he outlined was, despite its many faults, a rare form of socialism in so far as it was uniquely adapted to the modern world, dealing with the key problems of the state, bureaucracy, class-consciousness and welfare in a forthright way. Shaw and his Fabian colleagues were the chaperons who brought socialism into the Age of Bureaucracy – not properly dressed perhaps, missing the essential doctrinal undergarments – but a working proposition all the same, honestly and openly formulated in plain language. The prediction that socialism would, by the illusion of democracy, establish the largest bureaucracy ever known on the face of the earth, is hardly pretty, still less inspiring. Yet, it seems in its hard simplicity to carry more weight than all the delightful visions of Marx and Morris combined.

But Shaw was not an uncritical advocate of bureaucratic socialism. Far from it. He was too various and too erratic for that. The moods of militancy which fuelled his opposition to the Labour Party in this period were real enough, surfacing time and again in different aspects of his argument, even spilling over, in *Man and Superman*, into a critique of Fabianism itself: Fabianism was the respectable face of socialism and as such it had 'drawn the teeth of insurgent poverty'. And had not Shaw himself been sucked into the system he sought to undermine? The rebel and outsider was now the pampered and honoured guest of the Establishment, with ready access to the conservative section of the press. His plays from this period, *Getting Married*, *The Doctor's Dilemma* and *Misalliance*, were not so much the works of a moral revolutionist as those of a respectable gadfly operating within the confines of bourgeois society. All of which made Shaw feel uneasy. Having entered the new century determined to state his case in a mind-changing manner, he found himself struggling to regain the militancy which was essential to the persona of the radical outsider. This latent militancy and frustration found its way into his middle-class propaganda. In 1907 he wrote a series of provocative articles in *The Clarion* featuring a socialist party of 'professional men and gentlemen employees . . . openly bent on abolishing property, breaking up the family . . . and (incidentally) criticizing the Labour Party on all possible occasions with studied arrogance and without the slightest regard for its feelings' (Shaw 1976: 47). In *Man and Superman* he went much further, arguing that the whole of capitalist humanity was unfit for socialism and incapable of progress. Less spectacularly, he appeared to strike at the empiricism of the Webbs when, in *The Common Sense of Municipal Trading*, he said that counters of a spiritual kind must be added to the facts and figures when stating the balance sheet of a city's welfare (Shaw 1932e: 163). Socialism was about human welfare, but human welfare was now entangled in a transcendental web. In this way Shaw's politics grew more complex, trapped somehow between the rival claims of happiness and perfection.

Clearly Shaw needed to look again at the foundations of his socialist realism, hopefully to find a unifying doctrine that might dispel the mounting tensions in his argument. He needed also to look again at the institutional focus of his socialism, in particular to reconsider his position with regard to the Fabian Society. For a quarter of a century he had worked in harness with his colleagues as editor and chief polemicist, often tailoring his own ideas to suit their collective approach to practical socialism. But increasingly he found it hard to fit his idiosyncratic views into the Fabian mould. That was evident in the preface he wrote for the 1908 reprint of *Fabian Essays*, with its departures into violence and vitalism. And increasingly he felt he could not operate at full power so long as his argument had to wear the official Fabian stamp of approval. The Society needed new blood, he argued, to reinvigorate its policy and reputation. He wanted his freedom to develop into a world statesman. In March 1911 he wrote to the secretary, Edward Pease, resigning his post on the executive committee; 'I think the moment has arrived for the old gang to make room for younger men. I always intended to do it myself when I completed my quarter of a century service, but what with Wells and one thing and another, the moment was not propitious; and I had to wait for an opportunity at which I could resign without any fear of having a political significance attributed to the move' (Shaw 1985b: 12).

2

SHAVIAN SOCIALISM

SHAW'S MORAL VISION

A concept of right and faith in a true and progressive doctrine were essential to Shaw's socialist realism. In his Fabianism he had typically pursued a pragmatic, welfarist approach to politics, devaluing theory as a guide to action, viewing realism more in terms of an empirical account of the immediate consequences of policy for the happiness of the individual and the efficiency of the nation, than in relation to any grand scheme of social reconstruction. That approach to politics and the policy of compromise and permeation it entailed bore many fruits. Because of it, the Fabians were to gain a reputation as the ultimate technicians of reform. Of course like any other policy it had its faults and pitfalls; the most crucial for Shaw was that in practice it tended to blur the critical distance between himself and the established reality. Through Fabianism, the radical outsider came to participate in the civil life of British politics at many levels; he served as a vestryman in St Pancras for six years, in 1904 he stood (albeit unsuccessfully) as a Progressive candidate in the London County Council election; and, in harness with the Webbs, he sought to influence the doyens of high politics – including Earl Rosebery and Balfour. In this way, Shaw's vision of the realities of political reform was more and more construed in terms of the established parameters of power.

Eduard Bernstein described the Fabianism of the period as but a 'series of socio-political measures without any connecting element that could express the unity of their fundamental thought and actions' (Kilroy Silk 1972: 70). It was that connecting element, that concept of right formulated as a clear and forceful doctrine of socialism which Shaw now sought; a theoretical departure capable of injecting new direction into his radicalism, so rescuing him from the swings and roundabouts of militancy and reformism. In his metaphysical speculations he had already constructed that new departure in the Life Force philosophy, as expressed in *Man and Superman*. After 1910 or so, and throughout the war years, he was concerned to translate the tenets of his artist-philosophy into a religion dedicated to the vision of individual service

101

to the cause of progress, a process which culminated in the 1921 *Back to Methuselah* (Shaw 1945), Shaw's Bible of vitalism, complete with its own elaborate iconography.

An alternative vision was harder to construct in the realm of politics, primarily because proximity to the day-to-day contingencies of political life and the complexities and contradictions they generated always seemed to Shaw an essential feature of his socialist realism. And yet the balance shifted in his work (at least in relation to its central doctrine) away from the hard-nosed empiricism and opportunism of the Fabian years, towards a more expansive and doctrinal approach to politics. Hence in 1914 he described the realistic imagination not in terms of its relevance to what he had once called 'objective or real' life, but as 'a means of foreseeing and being prepared for realities as yet unexperienced, and of testing the feasibility and desirability of serious Utopias' (Shaw 1932i: 103). Further, all the explicit references in his work to the new vogue of pragmatism in the twentieth century were hostile in nature. In the 1915 preface to *Androcles and the Lion*, for example, he aligned it with the mindless drifting characteristic of the politics of a neo-Darwinist age (Shaw 1931a: 77). Even if the relativism or scepticism it entails is philosophically correct, he said four years later, it would serve no useful purpose for the statesman. By the 1920s Shaw was convinced that a healthy polity requires common adherence to a political and religious creed. In a lecture delivered at the Hampstead Ethical Institute, he advised the statesman:

> when you come to governing a country, there is no use in talking pragmatism. You have to come back to your old Platonic ideals. You will have to use your reason as best you can, to make up your mind there are certain things that are right and certain things that are true.
>
> (Shaw 1962b: 115)

A restatement of the development of Shaw's moral vision, as well of its central tenets, can be offered at this point by way of an introduction to the detailed discussion of his argument for equality of income. Regarding the development of his moral vision, it has been shown that happiness was the key term in Shaw's formulation of his consequentialist doctrine in the 1891 edition of *The Quintessence of Ibsenism*: the idea that 'conduct must justify itself by its effects upon happiness and not by its conformity to any rule or ideal'. In the 1913 edition, happiness had been replaced by the much more demanding notion that conduct should justify itself by its 'effect upon life'. This seemingly minor alteration indicates an important change in emphasis in Shaw's moral outlook, away from happiness towards perfection, from individualism to collectivism, from pragmatic welfarism to an ideal utilitarianism concerned with collective duty. From the standpoint of the doctrine of evolutionary righteousness, life's purpose and the individual's contribution to that purpose was the standard for judging the rightness or wrongness of human actions. The rebel had joined forces with the lawmaker.

Underlying this change was Shaw's loss of faith in progress in the mid-1890s, with a new pessimism replacing the sometimes ill-defined evolutionary optimism of his earlier work. In *Quintessence*, for example, he differentiated historical periods in moral and metaphysical terms. The age of duty in ethics, he said, is 'correlative to the rationalist stage in the evolution of philosophy and the capitalist phase in the evolution of industry'. Behind the statement lay an optimistic view of the processes of evolution, together with a desire to equate socialism with the liberation of the will from the shackles of Victorianism. Turco writes that 'Shaw's book operates within the conceptual framework of evolutionary assumptions' and adds '*Quintessence* was a work he could expect to ride the crest of the *Zeitgeist*' (Turco 1976: 38). In this context, worship of self was the 'last step in the evolution of the conception of duty' (Turco 1976: 23).

The pillars of this *weltanschauung* collapsed in 1896 or so. Progressivism was fundamental to the persona of GBS, modernity was his watchword. Now that cosy metaphysical world was torn apart, with the result that Shaw's consequentialist ethic had to be reformulated. As Turco puts it, 'Shaw's pragmatism could not outlive his optimism' (Turco 1976: 119).

The pragmatic welfarism of the early Fabian years had assumed, more or less, that a consensus of opinion existed concerning 'good effects'. This indicates the extent to which at one level Shaw's social democracy operated within the broad parameters of established values, accepting these values as positive expressions of the forward march of civilization. That at least is one perspective on his Fabian welfarism (it is based on the assumption that Fabian welfarism operated with a conception of goodness as happiness). Shaw's dilemma in this respect was that, in reducing the problem of moral action to a consequentialist measurement of facts relating to happiness or welfare, he was ignoring the hard question of how to judge good and bad consequences by standards other than those implicit in the established order. Also, as a socialist realist he recognized that an individual's perception of happiness would be conditioned by the totality of his existence in the capitalist order. In this way the critical distance between Fabianism and the existing society was undermined precisely because of the inadequacies of happiness as an alternative concept of right. As a full doctrine of moral transformation, welfarism was both flawed and limited. It had seemingly committed what Shaw now called the cardinal rationalist error of 'making happiness instead of completeness of activity the test of the value of life' (Shaw 1965b: 359). He was not to abandon welfarism, but he was to readjust its position within the total framework of his thought. In keeping with the new spirit of radicalism, Shaw was to inform his Fabian colleague Graham Wallas in 1898: 'My contempt for the status quo grows from year to year; and I do not despair of expressing it in a mind-changing manner' (Hobsbawm 1950: 215).

It was more a question of emphasis than of a change in outlook. All the same, real and lasting changes did occur in Shaw's thought after the mid-1890s, altering the basis of his consequentialism and forcing him to clarify the relationship between the individual and the community in his work. In 1891 he assumed that the seemingly warring causes of individual self-interest and that of the common good would be somehow magically reconciled; that they would work together to fulfil the common goal of social evolution. By 1913 this cosy line of argument had to be explained, not simply assumed, for now the relationship between his New Protestantism and his collectivism was not so obvious. In the event, he opted for the line of least resistance, arguing that 'the actual history of the nineteenth century' showed that 'the way to Communism lies through the most resolute and uncompromising Individualism'. In his search for evidence he hit upon the case of J.S. Mill who, Shaw tells us, was educated by his father to be 'the arch-Individualist of his time'; the result, however, was that he 'became a Socialist a quarter of a century before the rest of his set moved in that direction'. Happy with this dubious evidence, Shaw then offered this statement of faith:

> There is no hope in Individualism for egotism. When a man is at last brought face to face with himself by a brave Individualism, he finds himself face to face, not with an individual, but with a species, and knows that to save himself, he must save the race.
>
> (Shaw 1932h: 102)

In this way his New Protestantism glided effortlessly into his collectivism, selfishness thus served the cause of the morality of service. The essentials of that morality were to be found in the ideal of the gentleman, again formulated in 1913, which encapsulated Shaw's mature conception of citizenship. That ideal was organized around the notion of a 'handsome and dignified existence' free of the disabling threat of poverty and ennobled by the morality of service to the community. The gentleman, according to Shaw, is the man who declares 'I want to be a cultured human being; I want to live in the fullest sense; I require a generous subsistence for that; and I expect my country to organize itself in such a way as to secure me that'. The real gentleman, however, does not stop there, Shaw explains, he goes on to say:

> In return for that I am willing to give my country the best service of which I am capable, absolutely the best. My ideal shall be also that, no matter how much I have demanded from my country, or how much my country has given me I hope I shall strive to give my country in return more than it has given to me; so that when I die my country shall be richer for my life.
>
> (Shaw 1976:143)

The man who does not take this debt of honour seriously 'is not worth talking to', Shaw told his audience at the City Temple in 1909 (Shaw 1962b: 81). The good man was by definition the good citizen, citizenship was by implication the exclusive domain of the righteous, those 'possessed of a genuine conviction of sin and of salvation'. The task then that Shaw formulates for the pioneering realist in 1913 is that he must 'save the race' by raising 'the general level of life'; he must understand 'he can have no life except a share in the life of the community; and if that life is unhappy and squalid, nothing that he can do to paint and paper and upholster and shut off his little corner of it can really rescue him from it' (Shaw 1932h: 102). The pioneer must seek the welfare of his city, his state, his nation and, ultimately, his race. Such was the lawmaker's creed.

This was the republican side to Shaw, the side which disavowed the emotivism and relativism implicit both in *Quintessence* and in the individualism of the plays, arguing instead for the politics of virtue founded on a new conception of citizenship. For Chesterton it was the 'nobler side' of Shaw's complex character, revealing that part of him which 'cares more for politics than for anything else'. Chesterton says of Shaw that while he is not a democrat, 'he is a splendid republican'. It was intended as a compliment, for the democrat, in Chesterton's eyes, is an all-too-familiar and corrupted figure, trading on the debased coinage of modern political rhetoric,

> But a republican is a rare bird, and a noble one. Shaw is a republican in the literal Latin sense; he cares more for the Public Thing than for any private thing. The interest of the state is with him a sincere thirst of the soul, as it was in the little pagan cities.
>
> (Chesterton 1910: 86)

Shaw can be seen driving towards this vaguely republican conception of citizenship in the 1896 essay, *The Illusions of Socialism*. There he argued that socialism, of a humane and civilized kind, would require 'more and more of that quality which is the primal-republican material – that sense of the sacredness of life which makes a man respect his fellow without regard to his social rank or intellectual class, and recognize the fool of scripture only in those persons who refuse to be bound by any relation except the personally luxurious ones of love, admiration, and identity of political opinion and religious creed'. We all have some of this republican quality, Shaw suggested, even in the corrupted world of capitalism: it is a latent quality, a reserve of goodwill waiting to be tapped. Of the good republican, Shaw wrote: 'To such a man alone can Equality have any sense or validity in a society where men differ from one another through an enormous compass of personal ability, from the peasant to the poet and philosopher' (Shaw 1965b: 426).

This republican theme was to find its fullest expression in the ideal of the gentleman and in the argument for equality of income with which that ideal was associated: central to both were the republican virtues of civic pride and duty, with public honour and merit replacing financial incentive as the motivating force behind its vision of social justice. Of course the tensions in Shaw's thought continued to operate, and therefore the collectivist politics of virtue never supplanted the individualistic politics of welfare in any

105

categorical sense. None the less, Shaw drifted closer to the politics of virtue in the twentieth century, caring more for perfection, duty and life's purpose than before. At least he was more explicit and insistent in their advocacy, confirming the portrait we receive of him from the Christian Socialist, Stuart Headlam, who describes Shaw as 'an *idealist* with romantic notions of life and conduct, and evidently most sincerely impressed with an awful sense of *duty*' (Shaw 1962b: xv). It was these qualities which fuelled Shaw's advocacy of his own serious utopia.

SHAW'S POLITICAL UTOPIA

The first unequivocal statement of his serious political utopia and its attendant principle of right was presented in a lecture, delivered on 9 December 1910 to a Fabian audience, on the subject of 'equality' (Shaw 1971: 155–94). It was there he unveiled the argument for equality of income which was to become the hallmark of the distinctly Shavian doctrine of socialism (at least until the late 1930s). The major formulation of the argument was in *The Guide*, Shaw's political testament from 1928, where equality of income was introduced as the 'essential diagnostic of socialism'. But before then, both during and after the war years, he bombarded his audience with lectures and articles explaining his views on economic egalitarianism as the necessary postulate of permanent civilization. Equality of income was the way to a new moral order, to a just and progressive state which will attend to the individual's material well-being, as well as to the moral and spiritual excellence of the community as a whole. It was the central doctrine connecting aims and means, the guiding thread in his running commentary on the daily follies of capitalism. Shaw is not renowned for consistency, but in equality of income, it seemed, he had found a doctrine that pulled together all the threads of his politics, making one tightly woven cord. 'Socialism translated into the concrete terms', he wrote in 1913, 'means equal division of the national income among all the inhabitants of the country, and the maintenance of that equal division as the invariable social postulate, the very root of the Constitution' (Shaw 1976: 117).

That seems to be perfectly clear and straightforward. However, his advocacy of this form of literal economic egalitarianism was puzzling in its way. Partly because its seemingly primitive fundamentalism contradicted much of the spirit and substance of his early Fabianism, founded as it was on an incrementalist policy of compromise and permeation, in which actions were not governed strictly by a priori rules or principles, but rather by considerations of welfare and contingency. Having previously argued against a too theoretical approach to politics, he had now embraced (apparently) precisely such a strategy, rushing headlong from one extreme to the next. Was he really in earnest? Did he believe, for a time at least, that equality of income was the only plausible as well as moral socialist standpoint on distributive justice, or was it a piece of propaganda set in a typically exaggerated form to capture attention and stir things up a little in socialist circles, as conventional wisdom maintains? All the difficulties involved in taking Shaw seriously as a thinker are at their most intense and insistent where the egalitarian doctrine is concerned. Acting under the influence of Stalinism in the 1930s, he eventually abandoned the doctrine, returning to a pragmatic standpoint where the claims of any rules or principles were carefully weighted against the case for efficiency, an approach that was reminiscent of his Fabianism. As a Fabian, indeed, Shaw was unequivocal in his critique of equality of income; 'The Fabian Society', he declared in the 1896 *Report on Fabian Policy*, 'resolutely opposes all pretensions to hamper the socialization of industry with equal wages, equal hours of labour, equal official status, or equal authority for everyone. Such conditions are not only impracticable, but incompatible with the equality of subordination to the common interest which is fundamental in modern socialism'. Equality of income was neither feasible nor desirable.

Was the change of heart in 1910 to be taken seriously? Does the argument belong, to use Hobbes's distinction, to the mutable realm of rhetoric, dealing only in opinion, or does it strive to present a true philosophical principle of socialist justice? Was it another escapade in controversy, or a genuine attempt at doctrinal exposition? As explained in the Introduction, the view taken here is that the argument represented a middle-way between the two, being an attempt, however flawed, at combining the art of controversy with that of doctrinal exposition.

Such an approach is not without its difficulties. For one thing, Shaw himself seemed eager to spike the guns of those seeking to make grand claims on his behalf. *The Guide* opens with the statement that 'Socialism is nothing but an opinion held by some people' as to how wealth should be distributed in a respectable civilized country. The use of the word 'opinion' at this juncture would appear to place the work firmly within the mutable, uncertain realm of rhetorical persuasion, eschewing any mention of philosophical exposition. However, there is room for an alternative interpretation which states that, while we should be sensitive to his use of the word 'opinion' at this critical point, we should not conclude that he was necessarily reducing his argument for equality of income to a propagandist exercise. It arose rather from his views on the essentially controversial nature of political discourse itself, admitting no final or ultimate proof, subject to conflict and change, with knowledge deriving from assumptions of a metaphysical kind. Hence at the heart of his case for equality was the distinction, described by Shaw as the 'eternal conflict', between the socialist or human outlook on man as a being possessing a soul with potential for development and worthy of care and respect on one side, and the commercial outlook and which regards a 'human being as a mere instrument for producing commercial profit' on the other (Shaw 1971: 203). It was not that all opinions were of equal value. On the contrary, *The Guide*'s purpose was to persuade its audience of the moral and empirical superiority of the egalitarian principle of distributive justice over all its opponents in current discourse, with those claims made on its behalf then being submitted to the test of practice, always on the understanding 'that the Settled Questions are never really settled, because the answers to them are never complete and final truths'. On this interpretation, the opening pages of *The Guide* were not so much the confessions of a propagandist, as a plea for tolerance and a warning against dogma, to be read in relation to the pragmatic, provisional, trial-and-error conception of truth which prevailed in Shaw's work.

PROPAGANDA AND CONTROVERSY

On this basis, the argument for equality of income was necessarily the work of a propagandist and controversialist, though it was not on that account to be explained wholly in terms of persuasion or adherence, or with regard to its success in inciting thought and debate among a particular audience in a particular context. In the egalitarian doctrine, it can be said, rational argument was laced with irony, eloquence and propaganda, those ingredients necessary to fortify and sustain the truth of doctrine in a hostile and uncertain world.

The propagandist element in the argument was apparent in the Fabian lecture of 1910 in which Shaw again urged the Society to re-establish a strong and distinctive position with the socialist movement. They should avoid, he argued, too close an association with the welfarist policies of social security and the minimum wage, policies that were identified in the public mind with the new 'social liberalism' of Lloyd George. Nor should they rest content with an image of Fabian socialism as an 'idolized bureaucracy of experts', for this was out of step with the rising mood of militancy as expressed in the nascent movements of Syndicalism and Guild Socialism. In this context equality of income was a means of outflanking opponents on the right and left in politics, designed to maintain Fabian independence of labourism and liberalism alike. 'The task of the Fabian Society in the future', he declared, 'must be to work out the practical path towards equality', thereby regaining the initiative at the head of 'the general Progressive movement' (Shaw 1971: 190).

In a sense it was Shaw's parting gift to the Fabians; his last attempt, at least as a member of the executive committee, to offer a new and dynamic policy initiative, sufficiently radical and fundamentalist to dispel the Society's reputation as a centre for oligarchic socialism. With such a doctrine the old gang could yet strike back at their young critics on the left – G.D.H. Cole, Orage and their kind. In the event, the doctrine was not endorsed by the Fabians, nor did they jump at Shaw's proposal to produce 'a new volume of *Fabian Essays* working out the application in economics, in morals, in politics, in art and so forth, not this time merely of Collectivism, as we did before, but of Equality' (Shaw 1971: 193). Instead, they settled down to the more immediate task of campaigning on behalf of the National Committee for the

Break-Up of the Poor Law. Shaw, in all probability, must surely have known as much. He must have calculated that this was an opportune moment to launch a new argument for redistribution, coming as it did on the heels of Beatrice Webb's *Minority Report*, a work he described as 'big and revolutionary and sensible and practical at the same time' (Shaw 1909: 685). His egalitarian doctrine was in a way an extension of this, a drawing out of a scheme of redistribution, big and practical in his mind, to its ultimate conclusion. All his rhetorical skills were employed in the lecture, with equality of income being presented not only in terms of its morality, but also as a practical proposition. 'The line of practical progress, roughly speaking, is the advocacy of a minimum wage. On that path we are already afoot', he said. It was not a question therefore of a completely new departure in policy. Equality of income entailed only the full realization of the socialist potential inherent in current practice. And Shaw tugged at the middle-class conscience of his Fabian audience when he declared: 'Until we can see the expediency as well as the justice of this, we are not socialists: we are only pitiers of the poor and rebels against unpleasantness' (Shaw 1971: 191).

In 1910 Shaw might still have hoped to use the egalitarian argument as a means of securing Fabian independence from the Labour Party; he knew perfectly well a movement dominated by the trade unions would not entertain for a moment so fundamental an attack on traditional scales of differential payment. But of course the political landscape is subject to upheaval. By the 1920s Fabian fortunes were bound up with those of the first Labour administration, the Liberals were in decline, the Syndicalist threat had been averted. Now the argument's immediate role was to undermine complacency among Labour supporters by presenting them with an avowedly socialist programme, by way of a reminder of the gulf between themselves and those who sought only to exploit collectivitist and welfarist policies in order to prolong the lifespan of capitalism, and by way of an invitation to socialists to consider the fundamental tenets of their faith. According to Shaw, too many in the movement shared the 'craving for an easy-going system which, beginning with 'the socialization of the means of production, distribution and exchange', will then work out automatically without interference with the citizen's private affairs' (Pease 1963: 282). Shaw maintained that, through the egalitarian doctrine, the movement would learn that there could be nothing 'easy-going' about socialism.

This is not to imply that the argument of *The Guide* was directed solely toward a relatively exclusive audience of committed socialists. Rather, it was aimed at all those with sufficient tolerance and intelligence to engage in the pursuit of ideas, irrespective of party allegiance; at those among the educated classes eager to consider 'the condition of England' from a novel and challenging standpoint in the wake of the moral and intellectual upheavals of the Great War.

Shaw did not underestimate the problems involved in such a programme of re-education. The Great War had reinforced his view that socialism must engage in the ideological struggle against capitalism in the most vigorous way. The governing class manipulates information in the press and so organizes the messages propounded in the schools and churches so as to make its creed of idleness and exploitation seem somehow pre-ordained in the nature of things; capitalism is so sustained by a powerful and insidious ideology as to render the gradual transformation of consciousness a far more exacting task than the early Fabians had every imagined it would be, Shaw argued. Socialism 'must get at people's minds' (Shaw 1976: 160). It too must organize itself as an alternative creed or religion capable, on the one hand, of inspiring and guiding an energetic minority of socialist agitators, while on the other making a sufficient impact on the masses to dispel some of the 'bewildering and bedeviling' nonsense peddled by the agents of plutocracy.

At the core of this creed was the argument for equality of income. It was thus a flexible instrument of propaganda. In the most general terms, Shaw claimed it was the common man's view of socialism and so would serve as the kind of 'simple mental handle' required by any mass movement (a point he explained in the essay on *The Illusions of Socialism* (1965b)). It was, in short, an invaluable addition to his armoury of verbal extremism, to be fired against the faint-hearted, the beguiled, the curious, the adventurous, the corrupt and muddle-headed apologists of capitalism. Its simplicity and clarity made it a wonderfully provocative and stimulating tool of Shavian argument, inciting debate on the fundamentals of morality and justice at every level of sophistication. An article in *The Morning Post* and a lecture to the Political and Economic Circle of the National Liberal Club in 1913, for example, sparked off heated controversies with Harold Cox and L.T. Hobhouse, and eventually even inspired a competition organized by the *Metropolitan Magazine* in America for the best rejoinder to Shaw's case for equality. Armed with equality of income, the master controversialist could annoy and instruct, guide and stimulate his wide and varied audience, while always prompting speculation on the key concept of socialist doctrine.

THE CASE FOR EQUALITY

Though crucial to any interpretation, the contextual and propagandist elements need not provide the only nor the dominant perspective on Shaw's argument for equal incomes; the argument can also be seen as an attempt to articulate the essential character of Shaw's vision of socialism as a rational moral order without class, poverty, idleness or waste. Service to community would be the hallmark of the new moral order, founded on an ideal of citizenship based on 'the obligation of every man to leave the world in his debt, or at least to pay his way'. The vision of the gentlemen, the republican symbol of the morality of service, was at the heart of the argument for equality of income.

110

Shaw's underlying commitment to equality as the goal of socialism was evident even in the early Fabian years, especially in those lectures where he sought to remind colleagues that a man could not 'be a candid Social Democrat with the approbation of the middle class'. Hence, beside standard Fabian accounts of socialism as but a secular expedient for securing human welfare by means of a combination of a basic material minimum with rough equality of opportunity, there were statements of a very different kind which spoke of the need for a new religion of equality and embodying a view of social democracy as the consummation of 'perfect equality' (Shaw 1971: 100). The true goal of the social democratic state, he told the Fabians in 1890, was to secure the welfare of an individual 'co-ordinately with that of every other member' of society (Shaw 1971: 41). Socialism would throw on 'all an equal share in the inevitable labor imposed by the eternal tyranny of nature' in return for securing 'to every individual no less than his equal quota of the nation's product' (Shaw 1932e: 93).

It would be wrong to present too unified a picture of Shaw's socialism which was a curious and unstable mixture of pragmatism and idealism, militancy and reformism. However, it is right to note that the argument for equality surfaced many times in his work, especially after the turn of the century, as he edged his way towards a more radical fundamentalism. In Shaw's politics these fundamentalist moods often took the form of an appeal to the authority of William Morris. In a 1910 lecture he was to confess 'I always recognized that our goal was equality, and was forgiven for much Fabian opportunism by William Morris on that account'. Seven years earlier he had edited Morris's lecture on *Communism* as a 'warning to the Fabians that it is one thing to formulate on paper a constitutional policy and another thing to induce people to carry it out when the Equality and Communism to which it leads are abhorred instead of desired by them' (Shaw 1903: 4).

Further, in a series of newspaper articles from 1904 Shaw presented the case for equality explicitly in terms of equality of income, though not in any detail (Shaw 1904a: 8; Shaw 1904f: 12). And in the preface to *Major Barbara* two years later he was again in a fundamentalist mood, denouncing the evil of poverty, declaring money to be 'the most important thing in the world', celebrating the 'sacred mystery of equality'. Yet, equality of income itself was not on the agenda.

Socialism was basically about equality, the question was how to translate that general article of faith into an article of doctrine, so connecting means and aims in a fuller, more militant conception of socialist realism. Shaw considered the idea that individuals are in fact equal in powers and dispositions nonsensical. Also inappropriate for the good Fabian was the idea of political equality, variations in aptitude and skill combined with the requirements of political division of labour were such as to guarantee failure in practice. As for the prospect of combining equality of opportunity with inequality of condition, it was an absurdity. By 1910, in fact, he was clear in his own mind that the socialist commitment to equality could only take the form of equality of income. Perhaps, as Harold Laski noted, Shaw would in practice 'rest content with an approximation to his ideal', and Laski cited the exclusion of artists from the egalitarian rule in *The Guide* as evidence of this (Laski 1928: 68). But that does not of itself undermine the seriousness of Shaw's commitment to equality as the goal of socialism, nor does it destroy the value of exploring the implications of that commitment in terms of a clear and consistent principle of distributive justice. By 1914, in another Fabian lecture, Shaw was speaking of equality of income as a utopia for practical men, to be arrived at by gradual means – subject to delay and imperfection, but operating always as an ideal by which current practice might be gauged and criticized (Shaw 1971: 278). It can be argued that through equality of income Shaw reformulated the critical distance from established reality essential to his radical argument.

THE INTELLIGENT WOMAN'S GUIDE TO SOCIALISM AND CAPITALISM

There is evidence to suggest that during the Great War Shaw arrived at a working agreement of sorts with the Webbs, whereby he was to concentrate on matters relating to distributive justice, while they turned their attention more to constitutional and institutional issues (Winter 1974: 59).[1] In 1920 the Webbs duly produced *A Constitution for the Socialist Commonwealth of Great Britain* (Webb and Webb 1975). Eight years later Shaw published *The Guide*, a work too often read from either a feminist standpoint[2] or as an untimely restatement of Fabian socialism, instead of as the most elaborate and authoritative account of equality of income in socialist literature. *The Guide* may have started life as a response to his sister-in-law's request for some ideas on socialism for the benefit of a local women's group, but it turned quickly into a vast enterprise occupying at least three years of Shaw's time, with the tough reasoning of doctrine displacing the romance and invention of drama in his life (Shaw Papers: BM 50519). In 1925 he was to write 'This terrible book on Socialism, which is costing me more labor and thought than half a dozen plays, makes it impossible for me to attend to anything else until I have sent it to the printer' (Shaw 1985b: 921). A year later he was to add 'It is a tremendous job of real literary work: not like playwriting' (Shaw 1988: 11). *The Guide* was, in effect, Shaw's political *magnum opus*, which he completed, much to the relief of his entire household, on 16 March 1927.

This is not to deny the original request's influence on the work. Rather, it is a warning against any overstatement of that influence. As noted in the Introduction, R. Palme Dutt and Margaret Walters remind us that *The Guide* was addressed mainly to women of the middle and upper classes, noting that this affected the style and substance of its argument, with its gallant, drawing-room manner implying a 'well-bred and highly respectable' reader, with the book's structure giving 'more space to the managing of investments

112

and a household with servants than to the working woman' (Walters 1982: xxii). Relevant as these insights may be, they should not entice us into too literal or specific a view of the Shavian audience, nor into making too strong a connection between style and substance. The book may be distinctly genteel in tone, but its conclusions were not substantially different from those advocated elsewhere; Shaw had always maintained that socialism was a matter of law not of personal righteousness and that nationalization should be accompanied by adequate compensation; he had never advocated the egalitarian doctrine on the grounds of equality of misery – 'Only in a settled and highly civilized society with a strong Government and an elaborate code of laws can equality of income be attained or maintained'.[3]

The address to the intelligent woman was essentially a device of argument employed to lend a novel perspective on the dry, abstract subject of political economy, thereby gaining the reader's immediate attention, and retaining it by the lively eccentricity of examples used, ordinary yet extraordinary because of their concentration on the world of women as mothers and housewives. The form of address was a means by which the practical moralist was able to demonstrate the relevance of ideas to conduct and experience. Whatever else Shaw sought to achieve in *The Guide* the work remains, in Walters's own words, 'Shaw's attempt to give his ideas systematic and comprehensive expression' in the light of his 'recognition of an impending crisis in England and Europe'. And further, Walters accepted that equality of income was 'the central idea round which he organizes all his other insights and suggestions' (Walters 1982: vi, xxv).

A valuable and interesting perspective on the work is found in Beatrice Webb's diary where she declares waspishly that Shaw lacks 'the necessary equipment alike in the knowledge of facts and in the power of thought' for systematic political theorizing (Cole 1956: 170). The comment's value derives from the intimacy of their working relationship in political matters. Its interest lies in the implication that he was engaged on a large philosophical enterprise for which he was unsuited, quite different in scope and nature to the glittering plays and prefaces with their quick insights and lack of system, an enterprise more or less doomed to failure because it was too ambitious an undertaking. It was not Shaw's seriousness of purpose that was in doubt, so much as his aptitude for the task at hand.

This is a good sounding-board from which to launch a consideration of the details of his argument for equal incomes. The argument can be reconstructed around four salient issues: (i) the positive economic argument for equality of income and the critique of alternative economic arrangements, (ii) the critique of communism and the defence of compulsory labour, (iii) the political argument, and (iv) the biological argument for equality of income.

The economic argument

The economic argument was based on the notion of natural or vital needs. All human beings share the same vital needs, Shaw argued – of sustenance, shelter, medical care – and society has a duty to meet the requirements of the vital economy before turning to the production of luxuries. This was Shaw at his most fundamentalist and Victorian, railing against the evil of poverty. Like Ruskin before him, he looked forward to a time when 'There would be less ostentation, less idleness, less wastefulness, less uselessness; but there would be more food, more clothing, betting houses, more security, more health, more virtue: in a word, more real prosperity' (Shaw 1982: 85). This was a long-standing feature of Shavian socialism. He believed the feeding of the individual was fundamental to all things and that unless a society builds on that its moral, spiritual and cultural superstructure would be rotten. There can be no question of human excellence unless human welfare is first cared for in material terms: 'We must serve mammon diligently and intelligently before we can serve God, as anyone may prove by trying to substitute prayers for meals' (Shaw 1971: 169). Clearly, the capitalist system of distribution which has 'million-dollar babies side by side with paupers worn out by a lifetime of unremitted drudgery' could only be described as 'wildly and monstrously wrong' (Shaw 1982: 82–5).

However, Shaw's egalitarian argument was not just about the satisfaction of vital needs, for this would have been no more than a restatement of Fabian welfarism. Rather, he claimed that equality of income alone could satisfy the criterion of rationality which is at the root of justice. The only fair distribution, in his view, was that of equal access to an equal value of scarce goods (Barry 1965: 43). He sought to demonstrate its truth in *The Guide* by a critique of six alternative proposals: (i) to each what she produces, (ii) to each what she deserves, (iii) to each what she can grab, (iv) oligarchy, (v) distribution by class, and (vi) *laissez-faire*.

Proposals (iii), (iv) and (v) were simply the cannon fodder of Shavian propaganda. That current distribution is unfair and in need of reform was axiomatic for Shaw. Hence *laissez-faire* was not a principle of justice but an expression of the moral corruption of the 'men of business'. Similarly, to each what she can grab had nothing to do with justice, everything to do with the anarchy of the Hobbesian state of nature. Proposal (iv), meanwhile, for oligarchy, or to each according to her rights, was said to be a conservative doctrine founded on a view of the world as one of fixed stations and fixed entitlements. If it had once gained moral credence by serving practical ends in a static, rural order, that credence had now departed along with its practicality. The idea that an economic oligarchy – aristocratic or plutocratic – was essential to the nation's cultural and financial well-being was but a confidence trick. 'We must go on with our search for a righteous and practicable law' was Shaw's conclusion.

Such a law was not to be found in proposals (i), (ii) and (v), all of which represented variations on liberal principles of justice founded on merit or desert. His analysis of proposal (i), to each what she produces, was in fact a critique of the evaluation of merit by a system of piecework, a suggestion canvassed by L.T. Hobhouse in his controversy with Shaw in 1913. The response was straightforward. Even if piecework had some credence as an inducement to industry, it was quite inappropriate as a means of evaluating 'natural differences in human worth'. The variety of work performed – from the housewife to the fashion model – at varying rates of intensity and status was such as to undermine its feasibility. From this vantage point Shaw proceeded to discuss the principle of desert generally, first in terms of present arrangements and, second, as a goal to be attained. His argument was that the market system at present does not allow the free interplay of natural worth. Far from distributing goods according to desert it 'makes a few idle people very rich, and a great many hard-working people very poor'. And further, no amount of social reform could render the principle less arbitrary because desert could not be measured in money terms. By way of a practical exercise, the intelligent woman was asked to apply the principle to her local blacksmith and clergyman to determine 'how many verses of the Greek Testament are worth one horse-shoe' (Shaw 1949a: 28). A trite example perhaps, but one which underlined the problems of evaluating the merits and demerits of different beings and their different occupations (the work of the housewife was a particularly good instance). It was precisely the impossibility of calculating the varying social utilities of the professions which Shaw sought to demonstrate in relation to proposal (v). Differences in income, he told the intelligent woman, are not the product of rational evaluation, only of power and convention. Clearly, to include the principle of desert in the design of the new moral order (and this was exactly what was at issue in Fabianism's commitment to equality of opportunity) was to build the arbitrariness of capitalism into its foundations, thus undermining its character and purpose. Equality of income was the only form of equality nature would allow, the only pattern of distribution morality could endorse.

But what of efficiency? Does the egalitarian doctrine not treat the issues of motivation and incentive 'rather cavalierly' as C.A.R. Crosland suggested, so inviting inefficency and a decline in material well-being into the socialist order? (Crosland 1956: 210). Shaw's response was many-sided. Basically, however, his argument was that the acquisitive instinct is vastly overrated as the mainspring of human activity, being dominant only in a few individuals. What the vast majority of people desire is not unlimited opportunity for pecuniary gain, but job security and security of welfare. It is not that they lack enterprise, only that enterprise is normally (and rightly) channelled into those higher pursuits which belong to the leisure hours. Indeed the value Shaw placed on leisure was such that shorter working hours, early retirement and longer holidays would be used as inducements to engage in 'the less agreeable

115

employments'. Most modern occupations are in fact routine in nature, he wrote, and reasonably pleasant under the right conditions, hence requiring no special rewards for their efficient completion. This was not to say that the state would be the sole employer. On the contrary, he argued in the best Fabian tradition that all non-routine and experimental work should be left to private enterprise (presumably on the understanding that the entrepreneur's only reward would be in terms of public honour, not financial gain). Whatever work remained would be done by 'those who are never happy unless they are working', on the one hand, and, more importantly, by the natural increase in voluntary labour which would occur in a community versed in the morality of service, on the other. Many people, he wrote, after completing the standard four-hour working day, would engage 'for fun' in 'nationally beneficial work that we cannot get done at present for love or money' (Shaw 1982: 112). This, in essence, was the economic argument for equal incomes.

Communism and compulsory labour

In advocating equal incomes Shaw was also setting communism to one side and this, for a man converted to socialism by Marx and committed by sentiment and emotion to Morris, was no small matter. It is worth remembering that in his critique of anarchism in 1893 and elsewhere there are clear indications that Shaw viewed the communist-anarchist conception of equality of condition as an ultimate ideal to be attained by a purely moralized humanity (Shaw 1931a: 62). In *The Guide* he was more critical in his approach, noting that the communitarian vision ignores such problems as scarcity and pays insufficient attention to the liberty of the individual. Tastes differ so radically in relation to such non-essential goods as pet dogs, gramophones and bicycles, he argued, as to render equal distribution wasteful and planned production quite impossible to achieve in a large and complex society. Failing conditions of utopian abundance, the state (or some equivalent) would either have to engage in a huge research programme into individual wants, so detailed as to constitute a threat to liberty, or else personal choice would be severely restricted. Giving people money and letting them buy what they like, on the other hand, would not only solve the demand–supply problem for non-essential goods but also reduce collective interference in personal choice. The use of money, Shaw wrote, 'enables us to get what we want instead of what other people think we want' and is therefore a necessary part of our freedom (Shaw 1982: 63). Equality of income may not be a perfect solution to the problem of personal choice, but in Shaw's mind it had many practical and moral advantages over its communist rival when applied to any complex society.

Libertarians do well to treat such appeals to personal choice with caution, reminding us of the restrictions on liberty implied in any conception of justice which views human abilities as collective assets. Whatever their differences, communism and Shavianism share an organic conception of society in which the individual is obliged by the morality of service to contribute according to his or her abilities. Marx (it seems) assumed that all individuals would contribute without incentive or coercion. But then, as Michael Lessnoff has said, 'One need not take this utopia seriously. Anyone practically concerned with the real world must recognize that to propose the socialist principle of distributive justice is to propose that it be *enforced*, if necessary' (Arthur and Shaw 1978: 142). This leads into a debate on the relationship between the duty to labour – a standard feature of all practising socialist constitutions – and the positive right to work which is unique to socialism.

Shaw certainly did not offer a systematic account of the relationship between rights and duties. Nevertheless, he is of some interest because he was at least clear that equal incomes would have to be supported by a doctrine of compulsory labour. Again, this was a long-standing feature of Shavian (and Fabian) socialism, being a corollary of his hatred of idleness and his advocacy of the morality of service; 'I submit then, to our Communist Anarchist friends that Communism requires either external compulsion to labor, or else a social morality which the evils of existing society show that we have failed as yet to attain', wrote Shaw in *The Impossiblilities of Anarchism* (Shaw 1932e: 82). Ideally, of course, the Shavian alternative was to be realized in terms of the gentleman who makes certain claims on his country 'for a handsome and dignified existence and subsistence' (including the right to work), while in return giving his country the best service of which he is capable, striving to give more than he has received (Shaw 1976: 143). The extension of such right social conduct until it became 'habitual and conventional with all' was crucial to the moral vision behind the egalitarian doctrine. Yet, prudence demanded that socialist justice must contend in the forseeable future at least with man as a creature of limited sympathies, with refusal to work being treated as a social crime. Shaw understood that this would not be popular among a powerful section of the labour movement, in particular the trade unions, let alone among the class of wealthy parasites. But in this context he was more interested in presenting the authoritative case for Shavian socialism than in pleasing his immediate audience. His argument, contra Rousseau, was that 'man in society is not born free but is born in debt and must always seek to justify his existence: not until that debt is paid can any freedom begin for the individual' (Shaw 1932i: 35). Coercion was to be the last resort, the ultimate sanction of the economic argument which maintained that moral freedom exists only beyond the satisfaction of need-claims. In this way the egalitarian doctrine was supported by an unequivocal doctrine of social responsibility.

The political argument

Shaw's view was that only a socialist state could assume the moral authority over the lives of its citizens implied in the doctrine of compulsory labour, because only socialism could hope to formulate and implement policy on a rational or impartial basis, with regard to the common good. Without socialism there is no common good, only the rival goods of competing interests; bias and corruption replace the spirit of rationality crucial to social justice; the intellectual conscientiousness required for finding the 'right way' in politics through observation and analysis is distorted by 'pecuniary temptation' (Shaw 1982: 497). Shaw believed that the strains set up by the divisions of interests destroy 'peace, justice, religion, good breeding, honour, reasonable freedom, and everything that government exists to secure'. As he stated in 1910 'one of the most powerful arguments against our existing system is that it fails to produce as much political virtue as we need' (Shaw 1971: 117).

Equality of income was, in short, an argument against class government, with its false democracy and legality, its sham eminence and cruel inferiority. Shaw, never one to understate his case, even used distinctions in income as a means of categorizing distinctions in class. Of course, there was no guarantee that equal incomes would eliminate all distinctions in status. Similarly, it would not guarantee the resolution of political conflicts on a rational basis. But at least an egalitarian community would have some advantages in the elimination of sectional interests from the policy-making processes. At least a community characterized by moral consensus regarding the material facts of life might steal a march on those enemies of enlightenment eager to deny the masses any possibility of developed existence.

There was also the possibility that economic equality would allow for the recognition of real merit, that is, for the rise of a genuine meritocracy in social and political life, in place of the conventional oligarchy founded on inheritance and privilege: 'Between persons of equal income there is no social distinction except the distinction of merit. Money is nothing: character, conduct and capacity are everything', Shaw wrote. Instead of class distinctions based on money, there would be the natural distinction of merit between the great, the average and the small-minded (Shaw 1982: 102). In this way, Shaw presented an egalitarian doctrine dedicated to the pursuit of inequality, a doctrine founded on a conception of the natural order which owed more to the Callicles than to Rousseau. Whereas critics of egalitarianism often see it as leading to drabness and uniformity, in Shaw's case it was the problem of combining equality with excellence which was at issue.

The biological argument

Nowhere was the conflict between equality and excellence clearer than in the biological argument. When it was first formulated in 1910, Shaw claimed that it was the most urgent and compelling of all arguments for equal incomes. Equality of income, he told the Fabians, is the prerequisite for racial improvement, the precondition for the breeding of the superman – an argument with 'a hundred times the leverage of the surplus value demonstrations of Marx'. Speaking as a good moralist among the righteous protagonists of the morality of service, Shaw announced 'We are all ashamed of ourselves as we are: we all want to reach forward to something better; but we none of us care twopence whether we receive the whole value of our labor or not, provided that what we get is enough to keep us going' (Shaw 1971: 190). Whereas Marxism was founded on the economic model of man as motivated primarily by rational self-interest, Shavianism emphasized the vitalist motive of commitment to evolutionary progress as the true basis of socialist thought and practice.

It was a message for its time. It was precisely then, in those years before the Great War, that the debate on eugenics reached its dizzy heights. 'For social reformers to ignore eugenics and its claims about heredity in the early-twentieth century would have been to opt out completely from one of the major controversies about social welfare', wrote Greta Jones (Jones 1980: 98). In Shaw's case, the eugenic dimension to social reform survived into the 1920s and beyond. *The Guide* included a chapter on the subject which insisted on the need to consider 'what effects equality of income would have on the quality of our people as human beings'.

One interesting feature of the argument on the population question in *The Guide* was its reassertion of the idea, common among advocates of eugenics at the turn of the century, that the 'defectives,' the slum stocks degraded by their wretched circumstances, 'are appallingly prolific'. Like Sidney Webb in *The Decline in the Birth Rate* (1907) and the eugenicist, Karl Pearson, Shaw did not doubt that 'the inferior stocks are outbreeding the superior ones' (Shaw 1949a: 90). By getting rid of poverty, he said, 'we should get rid of these circumstances and of the inferior stocks they produce; and it is not at all unlikely that in doing so we should get rid of the exaggerated fertility by which nature tries to set off the terrible infant mortality among them' (Shaw 1949a: 90). Part of the interest derives from the fact that in Shaw's work, at least, such an explicit identification of inferior stocks with a particular class or group had not occurred before. It may have been implicit in the claim made in *Man and Superman* that 'we must either breed political capacity or be ruined by democracy'; but there the argument for the elimination of the 'Yahoo' was clothed in a wider critique of capitalist humanity.

The biological argument invites much speculation, especially in terms of Shaw's enthusiasm for state intervention into racial breeding, and also as symptomatic of his pessimistic outlook on humanity generally. The enthusiasm for state intervention was evident in *Man and Superman* where he called for the formation of a 'State Department of Evolution, with a seat in the Cabinet for its chief, and a revenue to defray the cost of direct State experiments, and provide inducements to private persons to achieve results'. It was to surface again in the 1930s, particularly in relation to his reflections on the Jewish question. Thus, writing to Beatrice Webb in 1938, Shaw offered a telling statement both of his continued commitment to a eugenic programme and of the legitimate scope of state power in this respect, he said:

> I think we ought to tackle the Jewish question by admitting the right of States to make eugenic experiments by weeding out any strains that they think undesirable, but insisting that they should do it as humanely as they can afford to, and not shock civilization by such misdemeanours as the expulsion and robbery of Einstein.
>
> (Shaw 1988: 493)

By way of contrast, in relation to the argument for equality of income Shaw's outlook on the feasibility and desirability of a eugenic programme, the selective breeding of man, was more modest and humane. In essence, it took the form of an argument for intermarriageability which, though it accepted the need for racial improvement, rejected state intervention as impractical. Writing in *The Guide*, Shaw stated:

> It takes all sorts to make a world; and the notion of a Government department trying to make out how many different types were necessary, and how many persons of each type, and proceeding to breed them by appropriate marriage, is amusing but not practicable. There is nothing for it but to let people choose their mates for themselves and to trust to nature to produce a good result.
>
> (Shaw 1949a: 54)

Equal incomes, Shaw maintained, would allow the most extensive choice in sexual partnership by breaking down all class barriers to free association between men and women. Natural evolutionary–sexual selection would replace class or money selection. Shaw's claim was that, if the race did not improve under such conditions, then it was simply unimprovable. To which he added, even if that proved to be the case the increase in happiness for the majority of people would in itself justify the equalization of incomes (Shaw 1949a: 56).

Intermarriageability played a vital role in Shaw's scheme of things, keeping alive the perfectionist concern for racial improvement without committing the legislator to any ideal-regarding discrimination between wants, or even to any distinctive views on excellence or fitness other than the moral excellence of service to community. Intermarriageability, by facilitating a form of *laissez-faire* perfectionism, allowed for the combination of the principles of individual happiness and collective progress within a socialist order founded on equality of income.

RECEPTION AND REPUTATION

In the event, *The Guide*'s fortunes and that of its central doctrine were mixed. Taken simply as the work of a controversialist intending to trigger-off debate on distributive justice among a broadly-based audience of the educated and self-educated, it had immense prestige and success, even inspiring a conservative rejoinder by a Mrs Le Mesurier, entitled *The Socialist Woman's Guide to Intelligence*. Within ten years *The Guide* was to run through five editions, including a Pelican edition with chapters on Fascism and Sovietism. Over 60,000 copies of the latter were printed at 6d each, in stark contrast to the 16,000 or so copies of the expensively bound first edition which sold at 15s (a popular edition was published in 1929). In the USA the first edition received enormous publicity, with 56,800 copies being distributed through the Book of the Month Club alone (Laurence 1983: 172).

But whether the work was 'learnt, marked and inwardly digested' was a very different matter. Though widely read and praised, it had little success as a programmatic text seeking to sway opinion, particularly in the labour movement, toward a more egalitarian conception of distributive justice. This was not entirely surprising. The critique of differentials was not calculated to gain support among trade unionists or among the new breed of meritocrats and careerists – teachers, professional people, former liberals – in Labour circles. Ramsay MacDonald sent a note of congratulation (Shaw Papers: BM 50519), but there was really never any prospect of the work having a great effect on the forthcoming general election as Shaw once hoped (MacKenzie 1978: 300).[4] Writing from Cliveden in December 1927 to his old Fabian colleague, Graham Wallas, he said he hoped the book would cure some of the 'wretched wobble' that afflicts the Labour Party: 'As none of them knows what Socialism is, it is necessary to plonk something definite down and say "let that be Socialism", very much as Queen Elizabeth plonked down the prayer book'. Stoically, he was to add, 'But I suppose they will go on wobbling' (Shaw 1988: 81). Shaw's sense of disappointment was genuine and severe. The author's note to the popular edition of the *The Guide* was an unusually rancorous document which stated: 'I have, at great cost of labor eliminated from this book all the common adulterations of doctrine by mush, gush, nonsense, hypocrisy and humbug, only, it seems, to make it unfit for human consumption'. In *The Guide*, he told H.G. Wells in 1932, he 'worked the thesis out carefully and exhaustively and, so far, unanswerably', only to see it rejected by arguments so crude they could belong to a retired colonel in Cheltenham (Shaw 1988: 280).

Shaw was especially scathing toward the reviewers, most of whom had been prepared to celebrate the work as that of a great humanist, as a powerful moral appeal for the egalitarian state (Anon 1928: 56), but not so ready to take it seriously as a work of doctrinal formulation. There were those who simply found Shaw's socialism uncongenial, stating that he 'wrote of government as though people had never cared for liberty' (De Wolfe Howe 1953: 1072) while others were concerned about his 'surprisingly feeble sense of institutions' (Laski 1928: 67). More generally, however, criticism centred on the nature of Shaw's argument, on its attempt to somehow combine rhetoric and philosophy, the populist art of controversy with that of doctrinal exposition.

Brilliance in controversy can of course prove a corrupting accomplishment. Rebecca West, for example, said he had little regard for facts, too much regard for exaggeration: 'he has a propagandist habit of allowing himself the extremist latitude of statement, provided he can hit off something telling and inspiring' (West 1928: 514). Similarly, Harold Laski noted:

> It would be in vain to look in him for a systematic philosophic exposition. He takes rather convincing aspects of his problem and presents them to his public as situations of inescapable interest. He is almost uninterested in the logic of his process; rather he is concerned with making the impress of that aspect, shown in its most dramatic significance, pierce the mind of the attentive reader.
>
> (Laski 1928: 68)

The same point was made on behalf of a different generation by A.M. McBriar, who writes 'the argument is highly entertaining, but not one that would be likely to convince an opponent. Its main merit, as is often the case with Shaw's writing, is that its challenging 'reasonableness' leads one to examine commonly accepted assumptions' (McBriar 1962: 58). Hugh Dalton, speaking on behalf of the politicians, said he found equality of income 'too absolute to be convincing'. Shaw's value, he said, was as an ally in destructive propaganda 'against stodgy, stupid, selfish opposition', rather than as a constructive thinker (Joad 1953: 257). Shaw could destroy, but he could not build. Though Shaw is said to be the single greatest influence on the post-1945 generation of Labour MPs, equal incomes was never a candidate for inclusion into the official party programme (Alexander and Hobbs 1962: 11–14).

It seems Beatrice Webb was right in her judgement. *The Guide* was simply a non-starter as a work of formal theory. While it was ambitious in scope and intent, it was also flawed in exposition, marred by internal ambivalences and limitations, contradicted by unexplored inconsistencies between its egalitarian doctrine and other aspects of Shaw's thought (the Fabian theory of rent, for instance) (McBriar 1962: 59).[5] It never faced the relationship between equality and liberty in a clear or plausible way but simply side-stepped the matter by equating liberty with leisure. At its worst, it indicated the extent to which Shaw's political thought was based on a facile romance of rationalism; the belief in the power of verbal extremism, the tendency to push an idea to its logical conclusion with no regard for practical feasibility. Surely the requirement of strict equality of income was too extreme as a condition of social mobility, certainly in those societies with a less rigidly-defined class system than the United Kingdom. Surely, even if we accept that a society which relies primarily on the profit motive as the incentive to effort will pay insufficient attention to human needs, it does not follow that it can be dispensed with entirely, especially in the kind of mixed economy envisaged in *The Guide*.

Yet the argument for equal incomes should not be dismissed altogether. It certainly served a useful purpose in lending a clear focus to Shaw's socialism during a period of growing disillusion with standard Fabian politics. Also, though it never scaled the heights of formal philosophic exposition, the argument goes a long way toward refuting the conventional picture of Shaw as no more than an amusing paradoxer or devil's advocate. It was not perfect or even terribly sophisticated, but it had a coherence and a clear structure and purpose which deserve to be recognized on their own terms. From a doctrinal standpoint (in terms of the relationship between thought and action) it can be seen as an instructive failure because it questioned the nature of socialism's commitment to equality in a forthright way, asking how this fundamental tenet of socialist faith was to be translated into concrete terms. By concentrating attention on distribution and offering so unequivocal a guide in the matter, Shaw succeeded in presenting a useful 'diagnostic of socialism' by which the claims of individuals, parties and societies could be gauged; his argument put equality on the offensive in doctrinal terms by requiring an explanation for every and any inequality of income. His views on compulsory labour would not meet with universal approval, yet they are relevant to socialist practice and constitute a clear response to the vital and thorny problem of social responsibility. Though of limited value as a sociological theory, Shaw's categorization of class by distinctions in income was a good rule-of-thumb measure of any supposedly egalitarian order.

R.H. Tawney is generally considered as a reliable guide to an outlook on equality that is both sensible and trenchant. Shaw, on the other hand, is seen more as representing the tendency in socialism, primitive or juvenile, to a wayward fundamentalism which broaches no (or very few) restrictions on its ideal conception of justice, to be realized in a society versed in the morality of service. But Shaw was neither primitive nor juvenile. He certainly did not welcome simplistic or one-dimensional accounts of the nature and purpose of his utopia for practical men and women, which stands at the very least as a courageous effort to keep the socialist movement alive and militant.

DISMANTLING THE EGALITARIAN DOCTRINE

It has been said of Shaw that he profited too much from experience, so much so that he was constantly revising his fundamental principles to fit the sensations of the hour (Irvine 1968: 368). He revised the egalitarian doctrine to fit the sensation of Stalinism. When Shaw himself posed the question as to whether equal incomes is a true statement of socialist doctrine, his final answer was 'no, it is not'.

The reasons behind the change of heart were many-sided. There existed in him a deep tension between an idealistic moralism which established a critical distance between his thought and contemporary practice, and a pragmatic realism that sought an accommodation between principle and power, seeking to move with the times in the manner of a good trimmer. For three decades equality of income guided his path between these extremities. Stalinism, however, acted on both these elements of his thought and character, producing a heightened regard for *realpolitik*, on the one side, and an upsurge of idealism, on the other, thus upsetting the delicate balance of Shaw's critical utopianism. In essence, Shaw's view was that Stalin was a model Fabian, being 'entirely opportunist as to *means*, discarding all doctrinaire limitations, and confident that Russia is big enough to achieve Socialism by itself independently of the capitalist world, which can follow his example or go its own way to perdition' (Shaw 1988: 269). Stalin was a national socialist and a realist to boot. Shaw's respect for him rested on the pragmatic grounds that he 'delivered the goods', or at least that he would do so in the immediate future. This necessitated a change in doctrine for Shaw, because these goods would evidently be delivered in a manner contrary to the egalitarian argument. Moreover, that argument actively prevented Shaw from proclaiming the virtues of the Soviet Union as an authentically socialist order in an unequivocal way. Paradoxically, equality of income stifled his idealistic fervour. There is a danger of over-statement here because Shaw was alive to the limitations of the Soviet regime. Even so, beside this critical vein there seemed to lie a faith in Stalin personally as a new standard of right conduct by which established reality was to be judged. In this sense, Stalin turned Shaw's critical world upside down and in doing so ousted the concept of equality from the centre of his scheme of things.

By the 1940s Shaw was highly critical of those equality merchants who 'sacrifice life to logic' by mistaking socialism for a 'mathematical abstraction like equality of income' when its real goal is a 'basic income sufficient to eliminate ignorance and poverty' (Shaw 1944: 57). In this seemingly innocuous way – was it no more than a return to Fabian welfarism? – Shaw reintroduced classes to the socialist order, and he did so along technocratically élitist lines. Now income stratification was to be determined by the state in terms (considered impossible in 1928) of the varying social utilities of the different occupations. Immediately, only the 10 per cent belonging to the intellectual proletariat, the bureaucrats and managers, would enjoy the basic income: 'Only what is left can be distributed among the ninety per cent who in the factories and mines, the ships and trains and city offices, have only to do what they are told and need not think about it' (Shaw 1976: 242). Such was Shaw's account, circa 1944, of the rent of ability as it related to the intellectual prole-tariat. It was in marked contrast to his original discussion of the subject in *Fabian Essays*. There he had predicted 'Social Democracy would not long be saddled with the rents of ability which have during the last century made our born captains of industry our masters and tyrants instead of our servants and leaders'. To which he added 'It is even conceivable that rent of managerial ability might in course of time become negative' (Shaw 1932e: 58). In 1889, therefore, it was thought that, given the right circumstances, the manager could actually receive 'less for his work than the artisan' without any adverse effects on economic efficiency. Fifty years on all that had changed. Socialism was to be organized by its superior brains who were to be rewarded accordingly. The statesman's first rule was that, having fixed the appropriate income for higher brain work, 'he must maintain the incomes of the bureaucracy and the professions at the fixed figures as a first charge on the national income'. In the meantime the artisans had suffered a demotion; they were now coupled with the unskilled labourers and told they must accept rough equality between the two groups.

The case should not be overstated. Intermarriageability remained on the agenda as did the general aim of producing a basic income of £5,000 a year for the entire population. Equality of income was still mentioned even in *Everybody's*, though its exact meaning and status were uncertain: at one moment it was asserted that it could yet be attained, 'virtually if not mathematically'; a page later it had been ousted altogether by the goals of sufficiency of means and equality of opportunity. Amidst the confusion the suspicion remained that Shaw's brave new world was neither classless or egalitarian, having as its *raison d'être* the planned elimination of waste.

The fate of the egalitarian doctrine highlights the difficulty involved in assessing the nature, purpose and significance of Shaw's political argument. Why should anyone take the doctrine seriously when Shaw himself treated it with so little respect? Would it not be best to keep discussion of it within the bounds of controversy and propaganda as history and reputation seem to dictate? For he not only excluded artists such as himself from the egalitarian rule, but also complained long and loud against paying supertax on the money he made as a dramatist.

Curiously, his dismantling of the egalitarian doctrine served only to prove its importance as the principle around which his socialist militancy was organized. Without it his politics seemed to degenerate into little more than a combination of a pragmatic welfarism with a coarsely grained managerial élitism. Equality of income was pivotal to the distinctly Shavian doctrine of socialism. It is true that his achievements as a constructive thinker were of a strictly limited kind, being compromised by the habit of controversy and generally overshadowed by his contribution as an intellectual raconteur and propagandist of heretical opinions. But, for all that, the scope and seriousness of his intentions when formulating the argument for equality of income should not be neglected entirely. Shaw was a complex man and his political ideas should be approached accordingly. As for the charge of special pleading, the most that can be said is that he carried such shortcomings on his sleeve, never seeking to conceal the gulf between doctrine and conduct.

THE RELIGION OF CREATIVE EVOLUTION

At the end of the Great War, addressing a Fabian audience ravaged by personal loss and eager for a message of hope and liberation, Shaw delivered a lecture on 'Socialism and Culture' in which his argument for political change was infused with a barrage of metaphysical speculation. Taking careful aim, and having the practical men of the trade union movement in his sights, Shaw argued that socialism requires statesmen, not mere opportunists; he added that 'Socialism will not be the work of so-called practical men, meaning mostly ignorant men: it will be the work of statesmen educated by those metaphysicians and those theorists in economics and sociology who are also Socialist and mean to establish Socialism' (Shaw 1971: 315). In this vein, the need for a religion, a creed, an alternative vision of things in the fullest and grandest sense became an important and insistent theme of Shaw's reflections in the post-war years. He declared:

> Socialism must have a positive religion, characteristic of and proper to the epoch which it is to inaugurate, with articles of faith and command-ments based on it and accepted as the foundations of the Socialist State.
>
> (Shaw 1971: 323)

What the lawmakers had to understand was that 'all communities must live finally by their ethical values', and that these must have a firm metaphysical foundation. But would the Labour Party understand? In March 1918, in a letter to the parliamentarian, Charles Trevelyan, we find Shaw once again toying with the idea of a new political party, stating that 'it must have a common religion, which nowadays means a philosophy and a science, and it must have an economic policy founded on that religion' (Shaw 1985b: 542). Always the intellectual *provocateur*, Shaw posed the question, 'Well, why not a creative-evolutionist party?'.

The religion of creative evolution was the central plank of Shaw's argument for a social creed; looking under the plank we find the Life Force philosophy of *Man and Superman* and *Back to Methuselah*. In the formulation of that philosophy Shaw was locking into the nineteenth-century obsession with evolutionism. At the same time he was also seeking to offer a radically different view of evolutionary theory, namely one that would rescue the claims of individual moral responsibility from the ethical chaos of Darwinian natural selection. Following Samuel Butler, his mentor in this field,[6] Shaw argued that natural selection was an amoral creed which not only obscured the part played by the individual in historical change, but actually banished mind and any element of design from the universe. Evolution for Darwinism was but an amoral, nihilistic chapter of accidents, a series of unthinking adaptations to circumstance. Shaw, on the other hand, wanted to return to the Lamarckian conception of evolution as an 'open-eyed intelligent wanting and trying', with progress resulting from the desire or will to live more abundantly. Shaw's doctrine was one of purpose against chance, choice against determinism, design against opportunism. Central to the doctrine was the metaphysical notion of the life force as a tireless power which is continually driving onward and upward, growing from within itself into ever higher forms of organization, a power which is driving at a larger, higher, more intelligent, more comprehensive consciousness.

126

Paradoxical though it may seem, the most powerful link between Shaw's socialism and his vitalist Life Force philosophy was to be found in his regard for reason and the intellect. Socialism is fundamentally a doctrine of rationalism, intending to create a just society through the planned elimination of waste. The vitalist philosophy, on the other hand, was supposedly a celebration of the primacy of will over intellect, spontaneity over reason, heralding the revolt against positivism and the recovery of the unconscious. Shaw, to put it simply, was a peculiar vitalist. All that was entailed in his critique of rationalism was the notion (reminiscent of Hume) that reason does not and cannot supply the motive for action (Shaw 1949b: 75). What lies at the root of existence is the desire or want for a more complete, more abundant life, and it is that desire or want which constitutes the spiritual reality behind all material facts. But if rationalism cannot supply a full explanation of human motivation, it does not follow therefore that we should devalue the importance of reason and intelligence in human affairs. On the contrary, Shaw confessed that for him intellectual passion was the noblest and most lasting and enjoyable of all the passions, which dovetailed neatly into his argument that life's ultimate purpose was to advance the intellectual power of comprehension. In Act III of *Man and Superman* he explained that the life force is 'evolving a mind's eye that shall see not the physical world, but the purpose of life and thereby enable the individual to work for that purpose instead of thwarting and baffling it by setting up short-sighted personal aims as at present'. Life is driving at brains, commented Don Juan, 'an organ by which it can attain not only self-consciousness but self-understanding!'

This striving for intellectual excellence was underscored in *Back to Methuselah* where Shaw pursued his vitalist romance of rationalism to its ultimate conclusion. Following the lead of the French philosopher Henri Bergson, Shaw established there an adversorial contest between 'Life and Matter', with life's conquest of matter being conceived in terms of the intellect's increasing capacity for understanding and organization. The origin of being was in thought itself, he claimed; 'In the beginning was the Thought and the Thought was with God: and the Thought was God' (Shaw 1945: 297). Further, he believed as an article of faith that life is pressing on 'to the goal of redemption from the flesh, to the vortex freed from matter, to the whirlpool in pure intelligence, that when the world began was a whirlpool in pure force'.

Shaw sought to avoid the pitfalls of historicism by claiming that, in contrast to the Fabian *Zeitgeist*, for example, his vision of evolutionary progress lacked any sense of certainty. 'The driving power behind Evolution is omnipotent only in the sense that there seems no limit to its final achievement', Shaw wrote in 1921 (Shaw 1931b: lix). There was no predestined path to progress because the life force had to rely on individual human agency with all its imperfections. The individual, therefore, had direct responsibility for advancing the purpose of the universe. Man was the righteous prophet of the life force. To accompany this revelation Shaw presented a metaphysical equivalent of the collectivist morality of service, stating in the preface to *Man and Superman*:

> This is the true joy in life, the being used for a purpose recognized by yourself as a mighty one; the being thoroughly worn out before you are thrown on the scrap heap; the being a force of nature instead of a feverish selfish little clod of ailments and grievances complaining that the world will not devote itself to making you happy.
>
> (Shaw 1931f: xxxi)

Through vitalism Shaw learnt to 'lay more stress on human volition and less on economic pressure and historic evolution as making for socialism' (Shaw 1948: xxxviii). Neither economism, nor fatalism, nor yet the mechanical utilitarian reformism often associated with Fabianism offered a sound philosophical basis for the socialist and vitalist realist. 'I, as a Socialist, have had to preach, as much as anyone, the enormous power of the environment', Shaw told the novelist, Henry James, in 1909, 'But I never idolized environment as a dead destiny', he explained. The doctrine 'that Man is the will-less slave and victim of his environment' was pernicious; 'What is the use of writing plays?', Shaw asked, 'what is the use of anything? – if there is not a will that finally moulds chaos itself into a race of gods with heaven for an environment, and if that will is not incarcerated in Man' (Shaw 1972: 827). Through arguments of this kind Shaw placed the individual at the centre of the political stage, whilst at the same time emphasizing the role of individual responsibility and personal righteousness in his progressive argument.

His message to the Fabians in 1918 was that if men are to become socialists it is not enough to change the social environment or to believe that this environment, once established, 'would force the human organism to adapt itself to it, and thus become Socialist whether it meant to or not' (Shaw 1971: 324). 'Men can change themselves into Socialists by willing to be Socialists', Shaw declared, and he added with a kind of desperate optimism 'and, if the change required eyes in the back of their heads and as many extra pairs of arms as an Indian god has, they could evolve them' (Shaw 1971: 325). He urged the Fabians to encourage the will to socialism.

There was an odd sting in the tail of Shaw's religion of hope for, as a moralist and a consequentialist to the last, he warned that if humanity proved incompetent as an instrument of evolutionary progress, then the life force might scrap the species altogether. 'Nature holds no brief for the human experiment: it must stand or fall by its results', Shaw warned in *Back to Methuselah*. In 1918 he commented, 'There is really a law of the survival of the fittest: not the survival of the fittest to slay and destroy, but the fittest to evolve and attain' (Shaw 1971: 324).

What emerges from the 1918 Fabian lecture is a profound belief that if socialism could be combined with a moral order founded on socialism and creative evolution, then man might yet survive the scrutiny of the life force.

The religion of creative evolution effectively sealed the bond of moral duty at the heart of Shaw's argument. Without it he was left to journey between the destructive relativism which informed his work as a critique of contemporary values on one side, and the appeal to enlightened self-interest which fuelled his welfarism on the other. Neither would suffice for the moralist, because neither infused a Calvinistic conception of duty into his politics. His argument for individual responsibility required ultimately a metaphysical foundation. The difference between his vision and (to offer a bold comparison) that of John Locke's, was that Shaw envisaged punishment for failure, not in individual terms, but in relation to a collectivist nightmare where the entire species would be destroyed for its common neglect of a duty to progress. Put in this grandiose way, his evolutionary righteousness was the focal point of his metaphysics, politics and ethics.

Shaw's obsession with the complimentary notions of metaphysical duty and metaphysical judgment indicate the fate that awaited his vitalist philosophy once it was transformed into an instrumental social creed operating under the title of the religion of creative evolution. Originally, both were introduced as doctrines of liberation for the individual from the ethical wilderness of natural selection. However, the transaction had its costs and these seemed to increase as Shaw's search for hope grew more desperate in the post-war years. Having set himself up as the iconographer of an emancipatory creed based on free agency, he was to find himself entangled ever more in Wotan's dilemma, cast as the oppressive lawmaker among a race of moral dwarfs, trading the liberating symbols of the vitalist philosophy for the necessary illusions of social order.

The political implications of Shaw's vitalist creed, infused with a commitment to superior brains, were hinted at in his account of the allegory of the dwarfs, giants and gods from *The Perfect Wagnerite*, in particular in Shaw's advocacy of Wotan's power of Godhead which represents the forces of intellect, creativity and progress in the world. Shaw explained:

> The mysterious thing we call life organizes itself into all living shapes, bird, beast, beetle and fish, rising to the human marvel in cunning dwarfs and in laborious muscular giants, capable, these last, of enduring toil, willing to buy love and life, not with suicidal curses and renunciations, but with patient manual drudgery in the service of higher powers. And these higher powers are called into existence by the same self-organization of life still more wonderfully into rare persons who may by comparison be called gods, creatures capable of thought, whose aims extend far beyond the satisfaction of their bodily appetites and personal affections, since they perceive that it is only by establishment of a social order founded on common bonds of moral faith that a world can rise from mere savagery.
>
> (Shaw 1932h: 174)

The passage is important because it unveils the essential features of Shaw's creative evolutionism. On one side, it is suggested that all creatures are equal in so far as they participate in the Godhead of life. On the other, there is an indication that a relatively exclusive class of creatures are more equal than others because of their superior reasoning powers and moral sense. In fact such a division of humanity into different types according to mental and moral powers was to become typical of Shaw in the 1920s and 1930s. He was especially fond of distinguishing between the 5 per cent or so capable of management and administration and those capable only of obeying rules and following instructions. His republic of free thought was to be the paradise of the able man. In 1932 he envisaged a scientific classification of humanity in terms of 'three quite distinct classes with distinct mentalities', with the classification forming the basis of a rationally-constructed social order geared towards a strict division of labour according to intellectual ability (Shaw 1964: 8). In *The Guide* the cult of superior brains was offered in an even more challenging form: 'The more power the people are given, the more urgent becomes the need for some rational and well-informed superpower to dominate them and disable their inveterate admiration of international murder and national suicide' (Shaw 1949a: 454). Shaw had nothing but praise for the Leninist conception of the dictatorship of the proletariat, commenting in 1919 that conferring the benefits of socialism on the working man 'will be very like forcibly feeding a ferocious dog with a bad sore throat' (Shaw 1919: 1).

There were two sides to Shaw's argument for a social creed. One was that it was required to guide and keep in check the intellectual élite of lawmakers. Another was that the creed was needed to inculcate into common humanity the values appropriate to a collectivist order. The latter was to take Shaw's vision down some strange paths, all of them bleak and inhospitable, leading to the conclusion that common man is lazy and incompetent, fearful of liberty and the responsibility it entails. Shaw had said in *Man and Superman* that 'the right to live is abused whenever it is not constantly challenged'. So concerned was he in the 1930s that he thought of introducing an inquisition (of all things) to judge whether an individual was more a social asset than a social nuisance. In his drama the same concern was expressed in the fable play *The Simpleton of the Unexpected Isles*, described by Shaw as an up-to-date vision of judgement based 'on the ancient fancy that the race will be brought to judgement by a supernatural being coming literally out of the blue' (Shaw 1936b: 15). The ultimate penalty at the disposal of both the temporal and metaphysical inquisitions was the threat of extermination. Evidently, the masses could not be trusted to enter the Shavian republic of free thought by the narrow gate.

The dire threats and warnings in Shaw's post-war work suggest the themes of the sub-text which lay behind his political rationalism. Yet it must be emphasized that his vitalism brought him few insights into the irrational recesses of the human psyche. It is true that his work contains the occasional philosophical statement on the unconscious self, along with appeals for political spontaneity, for action based on the promptings of instinct instead of deliberation, but to claim on the strength of this that his vitalism brought him close to something like Sorel's politics of cathartic violence and unreason would be altogether misleading. In his metaphysics Shaw argued that the problem of evil should be understood in the context of errors or unsuccessful experiments of a fallible life force which struggles with matter and circumstance by the method of trial and error (Shaw 1931b: lv). In his politics he built a wall of rational hope or theoretical optimism around himself in order to guard his faith against the forces of discouragement. As the years passed so the wall grew, until by the 1940s it had achieved its maximum height. Hence, when he opened *Everybody's* with the question 'is human nature incurably depraved?', he was able to give an immediate assurance to the contrary. The atrocities of capitalism, far from being expressions of human vice and evil will, were instead the product of an antiquated system of education as well as of a host of misdirected virtues and enthusiasms. The road to hell really was paved with good intentions. Demonstrating the depth of his commitment to a progressive doctrine founded on rationalist premises, Shaw offered this counsel of perfection:

> Capitalism is not an orgy of human villainy: it is a Utopia that has dazzled and misled very amiable and public spirited men, from Turgot and Adam Smith to Cobden and Bright. The upholders of Capitalism are dreamers and visionaries who, instead of doing good with evil intentions like Mephistopheles, do evil with the best intentions. With such human material we can produce a dozen new worlds when we learn both the facts and the lessons in political science the facts teach. For before a good man can carry out his good intentions he must not only ascertain the facts but reason on them.
>
> (Shaw 1944: 2)

With this faith, these doubts, in the company of an army of intellectual tensions, Shaw encountered the hostile political universe of post-1918 Europe, dominated by Mussolini, Hitler and Stalin.

THINGS FALL APART

Lord Halifax held the view that 'long life giveth more marks to shoot at, and therefore old men are less well thought of than those who have not been long upon the stage'. It was certainly true of Shaw. If he had died in 1930, in his early seventies, his stock as a humanitarian seeking to redraw the map of human consciousness and reform the structures of our social and political institutions would have been high indeed. His ship of death would have been lighted by the glory of *Saint Joan* and furnished with the triumph of the Nobel Prize for Literature. The egalitarian doctrine would still have been in one piece, enshrined in *The Guide*, which would be seen as the brave, if ultimately unsatisfactory, political last will and testament of a tireless fighter for welfare and justice. Of course not everyone would have admired his work, either as a political thinker or as a dramatist. But really, considering the sheer quantity of his output, there was very little in it of a downright objectionable nature. In his politics at least, there were relatively few marks to shoot at. His last major work would have been *The Apple Cart* where he could be seen, not at the peak of his powers admittedly, yet still vibrant and witty, as technically proficient as ever, still eager to relate his art to the issues of the day. The critique of democracy therein would have upset a part of his audience, but the damage to his reputation would not have been great; any doubts would have been set beside his dubious reflections on fascism from 1927 and explained away as the last desperate effort on the part of the independent troublemaker to shock his audience out of its complacency. Even at this stage, it could have been argued, the socialist realist did not flinch from tackling the major problems facing the world, even if his grasp of those problems was not all that it might have been. In short, he would have made a dignified exit to the sound of loud applause.

It was not to be. Shaw lingered on the stage, fretful and verbose, for another two decades, his long life giving as many marks to shoot at as would satisfy the most voracious of his critics. *The Apple Cart* was not the final fling of a mischievous devil's advocate. Instead it signified the approach of a more difficult era in his career: his political thinking grew more wayward, less civil and less sound in its judgement; a shrillness, the extremities of desperate hope, seeped into his thinning prose.

In the 1930 preface to *The Apple Cart* (Shaw 1932q), his critique of democracy in a capitalist system effectively manipulated by big business and the civil service 'without the slightest regard to the convenience or even the rights of the public', was trenchant enough. Yet, for all that, it remained essentially civil, sober and constructive in tone. That was to change within the space of a year. In 1931, in a symposium on the contemporary crisis in *The Political Quarterly* which included contributions from Harold Laski, J.A. Hobson and W.A. Robson, Shaw's voice was of them all the least restrained in its analysis of the failings of constitutionalism, arriving at the conclusion: 'There is no apparent way out except in Marxian Communism' (Shaw 1931i: 457). And in the same year, in yet another preface to the inexhaustible *Fabian Essays*, he turned again to the authority of William Morris, this time to question the feasibility of constitutional change, not, it must be said, in so manic a tone as that adopted in *The Political Quarterly*, but still vibrating with a sense of political failure and informed by the approach of crisis and imminent collapse. 'Morris was right after all', Shaw informed Emery Walker in January 1932, 'The Fabian parliamentary programme was a very plausible one; but, as MacDonald has found, parliament and the party system is no more capable of establishing Communism than two donkeys pulling different ways, one at each end, is capable of moving a modern goods train of 70 ten ton trucks' (Shaw 1988: 274). A few months later he was to say that the real 'danger is that Capitalism, instead of crashing, may peter out without ever producing a revolutionary situation. We may get no further than a succession of Kerenskys or MacDonalds trying to make omelettes without breaking eggs' (Shaw 1988: 295). Was there really no hope save in revolution?

Though rhetorical in kind, the question still signals the frustration Shaw felt at the state of things in the world and at his own impotence to change their course. Of course the feeling was not entirely new. It was the central theme of the 1919 *Heartbreak House* (1931c), where the old and irascible Captain Shotover tells of a ship of state that is drifting toward the rocks of disaster: of England, he says, 'The captain is in his bunk, drinking bottled ditch-water; and the crew is gambling in the forecastle. The ship will strike and sink and split'. The sense of powerlessness in the face of impending crisis, born in the Great War and nurtured through the troubles in Ireland, was contained in the 1920s to a degree – the hope Shaw derived from the egalitarian doctrine was in this respect a good companion in a vexatious age. But hope is generally a wrong guide. By 1931 Shaw had to admit that equality of income had not made the impact on the socialist leaders he once thought it would. Indeed, the experience of the two Labour Governments under MacDonald's leadership and packed full of Fabians, had served only to convince him of the futility of present constitutional arrangements. And further, the onset of economic depression coupled with the rise in unemployment and the mass idleness it entailed, served only to rouse Shaw's fundamentalist instincts. Writing at the end of the Great War, Beatrice Webb said of him that he had become 'more serious in his concern for the world', and that he was 'really frightened that civilization as we know it is going bankrupt and not so sure that he knows how to prevent it' (Cole 1952: 228). Some of his prescriptions were fanciful in nature. In *Back to Methuselah*, for example, longevity was peddled as a cure for our irresponsible attitude to life. Throughout his work there was a quest for a solution to man's spiritual and political plight, but it was more desperate after 1918, less inclined to dissolve into jollity and paradox. At every turn his political ideas were assailed by metaphysical claims. The urgent need was for a creed to rescue European civilization from the moral wilderness associated with the all-pervasive doctrine of natural selection. A decade later, Shaw's predicament was much worse again, his speculations much more capricious and extreme.

Opinion differs as to why Shaw appended a long speech by the preacher, Aubrey, to the closing scene of *Too True to Be Good*. What is not in dispute is that the speech itself exudes an air of melancholy unique in Shavian literature. There Aubrey speaks of the post-war generation as hopeless and faithless, reeling under the shock of mass destruction, incapable of believing in the old truths, devoid even of the illusion of hope; a generation made in the 'fiery forcing house of war' and growing 'with a rush like flowers in a late spring following a terrible winter', growing into the desolation of reality. He speaks of the human soul standing naked and vulnerable, with no creed to soothe the spirit or calm the nerves. And the preacher? Aubrey confesses that his gift for rhetoric has possession of him; 'I must preach and preach and preach no matter how late the hour and how short the day, no matter whether I have anything to say'. Not content to end on such a negative note, Shaw added the comment in the published version that while the author has allowed the professional talk-maker the last word, his own 'favourite is the woman of action'. This attempt to steer the fate of his argument, to conceal or retract what might be seen as weakness from a doctrinal standpoint, was typical of Shaw. What is more, the terms of the debate reveal the conflict between the realist and idealist elements in his nature, the destructive critic of illusion set against the man of faith seeking a life-enhancing creed as a mask for the naked soul. Aubrey has no such creed to offer. Shaw, it seemed, had only a belated and none too convincing appeal to the woman of action (the patient), a character already demolished by Aubrey as fantastic and unreal, perverse and profoundly unsatisfactory, falling endlessly and hopelessly through a void in which she can find no footing. Was this the nemesis of realism? Is Shaw's predicament to be constructed out of this matrix of talk and action, the reality of relativism and alienation, the illusion of hope and the quest for order?

At least it is one canvas against which to trace his visit to the Soviet Union in the summer of 1931 when he is said to have discovered 'the almost perfect state'. Shaw and his travelling companions, the Astors, arrived in Moscow on 20 July to a grand reception fit for a hero of the revolution, with a brass band and a military guard of honour in attendance. Once there his varied schedule included a speech at the Central Hall of Trade Unions, visits to the races (in honour of Shaw's seventy-fifth birthday), to a penal colony for young offenders (where Shaw was much impressed by the cabbage soup) and to the theatre, together with much hand-shaking and smiling. However the undoubted highlight of the visit was the four-hour interview with Stalin of which, unfortunately, no record exists. The impact the visit made on Shaw and its implications for his political argument are discussed in Chapter 6. For the moment it is enough to note the change in the temper of his work before and after that trip, as perceived through the play *Too True to Be Good* and its preface respectively. Whereas in the play his vivacious humour was under-scored by a sense of loss and foreboding, the preface fairly hummed with the working of his brash optimism. There Shaw proclaimed the need for a 'science of happiness' founded on the axiom that well-being is not to be found through the pursuit of wealth, but in service, duty and labour for the common good. The central proposition was that the road to happiness was by way of a strong collectivist government, organized around a vanguard of vocationally-qualified leaders dedicated to the inculcation of a common faith, encompassing metaphysics, politics, and economics. The creed's task was to resolve 'the paradox of government' which Shaw described in these terms: 'as the good of the community involves a maximum of individual liberty for all its members the rules have at the same time to enslave everyone ruthlessly and to secure for everyone the utmost possible freedom'. In the preface Shaw used the Soviet regime as his working model. His analysis was not restricted to a single system of government, however. The preface culminates with the claim: 'Stalin and Mussolini are the most responsible statesmen in Europe because they have no hold on their places except their efficiency; and their authority is consequently greater than that of any of the monarchs, presidents and prime ministers who have to deal with them'.

Interestingly, equality of income was not mentioned in the preface to *Too Good to be True* (in its place Shaw offered equality of leisure as the goal of socialism). Nor was the egalitarian doctrine mentioned in *The Rationalization of Russia*, a work written in 1932 on his return from the Soviet Union, but not published in his lifetime. There again the text was permeated by a kind of righteous optimism. It was here he first called for a new understanding of class, different to the economic approach of Marx, concerned instead with a psychological classification of mankind according to mental abilities and vocational capacities. Fundamental to this ultra-rationalist scheme of things was the intellectual proletariat: 'Communism does not alter the natural division of modern mankind into 95 per cent who have their work cut out for them and 5 per cent who can cut it out'. In the 1930 preface to *The Apple Cart* concern for the rights of the public had been high on the agenda. Now efficiency and order were paramount. The Enlightenment vision – dream or nightmare – was on full beam. Mankind was to be saved by a science of happiness operating in harness with a science of extermination. Suddenly, it seemed all that was worst in Shaw technocratic élitism, state-worship, the tendency to divide the species according to some form of differential rationality – came to dominate his outlook, just as arrogance and vanity took control of his public persona. The one-time iconoclast, the destroyer of cant and pretentiousness, was now the outraged moralist and disciplinarian, peddling his own kind of cant and pretentiousness in the vulgar language associated with his evolutionary righteousness. The rebel was now the republican lawmaker condoning the terror required by the politics of virtue in a degenerate age.

Of course Shaw is not so easily pinned down. Not all his work from this period should be viewed in so negative a light. In fact, the notoriety of one aspect of his performance has resulted in the neglect of other, more positive elements in his work. By Shaw's standards, the 1930s was a time of decline for him, artistically and intellectually. In comparison with almost anyone else it was still a time of high achievement. *On the Rocks* (Shaw 1934d) had a sharpness and relevance which belied the rumour of its author's failing powers. The 1938 political extravaganza, *Geneva* (Shaw 1946), was a huge, popular success. What is more, *The Simpleton of the Unexpected Isles* (Shaw 1936b) revealed an appetite for experimentation in new forms, with fable, myth and iconography replacing the usual diet of social and political satire. As Margery M. Morgan says, the sheer variety found in the plays confirms the fertility and adroitness of his mind in this period. The plays also highlight his predicament perfectly. *The Simpleton*, as Morgan argues, 'balances a steady philosophic optimism against the realistic awareness of how wrong things were in the actual world of politics, which was expressed in *On the Rocks*' (Morgan 1972: 286). And on a slightly different tack, the 1932 short story, *The Black Girl in Search of God* (Shaw 1934b), is certainly not a major work, yet it has a charm of its own, an innocence, a sense of tolerance and self-mocking humour which belies the picture of Shaw as an arrogant and dogmatic old man. Also, against the glare of the Enlightenment vision, the superiority of non-Western civilization was hinted at in both *The Simpleton* and *The Black Girl*. There is no easy access into Shaw's world.

Nevertheless, the decline (if not actual fall) into a harsher sensibility is not to be denied. The 1935 *The Millionairess* (Shaw 1936b) is a clever comedy in its way, full of pace and contrasts. Yet it remains particularly unsatisfactory at an emotional level. The central character, Epifania Ognisanti di Parerga, has all the vivacity and self-confidence associated with the Shavian woman of action, but the portrayal is somehow shallow and brutal. She is a Saint Joan without a religion, fighting for fighting's sake and not for any cause. There is violence in her soul. She married her husband because he was a boxer; she throws a man downstairs for daring to insult her father. Her character is sufficiently flawed to allow comedy to operate, but what follows is neither appealing nor satisfactory. As a personification of the life force, Epifania is a two-dimensional caricature, lacking the extra qualities of vision and comprehension which lend credence to action. Whereas in *The Black Girl* and *On the Rocks*, the way to progress, beyond ignorance and hypocrisy, is through an initial stage of contemplation and withdrawal into the private realm, here progress is identified almost entirely with the pragmatic vitalism of the born boss, determined to create a perfectly clean and orderly world. Of course Epifania's limitations as an agent of the life force are recognized in the play. The contrast between her and the Egyptian doctor dedicated only to service is based on that awareness. Epifania is only a capitalist manifestation of the life force, subject to waste and incoherence. It is even suggested at the close that she will only find true fulfilment in the Soviet Union. All the same, the focus remains on her. It is her aggression, her arrogance and brashness which must prevail. There is a sublimated ruthlessness in the play and a sardonic humour which finds expression in violence and cruelty. The old couple who managed the Pig and Whistle so inefficiently before Epifania bought them out do not survive the experience in tact; the old man suffers a stroke and is close to death and the woman goes 'a bit silly'. Not even their son, who relates the tale, shows any sorrow. He is instead content to be employed by Epifania as the new manager; 'it was best for them', he says, 'and they have all the comforts they care for'. He expresses a social Darwinist ethic encapsulated in the phrase, 'It was hard, but it was the truth', which suggests that mankind must and will welcome any intervention by the born bosses. Similarly, when the doctor suggests to Epifania that she should make the British Empire a Soviet republic, her response is: 'By all means; but we shall have to liquidate all the adult inhabitants and begin with the newly born. And the first step to that is to get married' (Shaw 1936b). The very last words of the play are spoken by Patricia, or Polly Seedystockings as she is called, who represents the safe, conventional woman who can only offer happiness to a man, not perfection or welfare on any grand scale. 'Congratulations, darling', she says, failing to understand Epifania's radical conception of marriage, so confirming the gulf that exists between the bosses and the common people. Even allowing for a degree or rhetorical excess, the play, in short, portrays all that is most facile and dangerous in Shaw's evolutionary righteousness.

Those facets of his argument were mirrored in the dimissive comments he made on the treatment of dissidents in the Soviet Union. These were especially evident in his attempts either to allay or undermine the concerns expressed by Nancy Astor on this matter. In September 1931, shortly after returning from Russia, he advised her:

> Dont worry about the sorrows and terrors of the poor things in Russia who are still foolishly trying to be ladies and gentlemen: it does not hurt them half as much to be governed by Communists as it hurts you to be governed by distillers and brewers and publicans and doctors and 'forty millions, mostly fools'.
>
> (Shaw 1988: 260)[7]

In particular, the decline in Shaw's socialist realism can be seen clearly in the contrast between his reflections on the First and Second World Wars. Comparison of 'Common Sense about the War' (1914) with 'Uncommon Sense about the War' (1939) shows that decline most markedly. The former was among his finest achievements as a pamphleteer, while the latter was little more than an apology for Stalin and a misguided plea for peace with Hitler: 'He actually owed his eminence to us', declared Shaw, still obsessed with the debacle at Versailles:

> so let us cease railing at our own creation and recognize the ability with which he has undone our wicked work, and the debt the German nation owes him for it. Our business now is to make peace with him and with all the world instead of making more mischief and ruining our people in the process.
>
> (Shaw 1939b)

To which he added, 'I write without responsibility, because I represent nobody but myself and a handful of despised and politically powerless intellectuals capable of taking a catholic view of the situation' (Shaw 1939b: 484). On one level, that could be read as an admission of his alienation from the core of any political movement. True, Shaw was still a Fabian, though not very active in the Society's affairs. As for his post as self-appointed tactician for the Labour Party, that had long since lost even the fictional credibility it once had. As early as 1930 Beatrice Webb was of the opinion that Sidney and herself were really his last resting place in the labour movement. Hence, whereas 'Common Sense about the War' set the seal on his career as an independent world statesman, in 'Uncommon Sense about the War' he was drifting out into political irrelevance with only his genius for company. At another level, however, the comment that he was writing 'without responsibility' could be taken as an indication of a lack of seriousness, even a lack of sincerity on Shaw's part. Was this a particularly elaborate and foolish move in the game Shaw played with his audience? Was it a coded message from a reluctant fellow traveller? Perhaps. Lord Halifax also held the view that 'keeping much company generally endeth in playing the fool or the knave with them' (Halifax 1969: 227).

EVERYBODY'S POLITICAL WHAT'S WHAT?

'Old men are dangerous: It doesn't matter to them what is going to happen to the world'. Or so Captain Shotover warned in *Heartbreak House* 1919. Was it true of Shaw? Was he too sailing out alone on God's open sea? Had the habit of mockery come to rule his soul, belittling everything; love, suffering, the fellowship of struggle and the warmth of friendship? 'A man's interest in the world is only the overflow from his interest in himself', Captain Shotover had said, adding that in old age such interest dies out and with it goes the concern for humanity: 'I no longer really care for anything but my own little wants and hobbies'. Were Shaw's late sallies into politics and playwriting mere indulgences, the habits and hobbies of a lifetime he could not bear to live without? Were they his drugs, to be taken daily and at regular intervals?

Yes and no. Shaw was certainly addicted to his work and perhaps even to the persona he had created through the fiction of GBS. His sympathies narrowed as his sensibility hardened. There was, too, a frivolousness and a petulance that accompanied his decline. Yet, in the dark years of war he settled down to write a long book, comparable in length to *The Guide* though broader in its concerns, encompassing the full range of his interests, from Fabian communism to creative evolutionism, a book which might yet serve as the foundation of human enlightenment.

Originally, the work was prompted by H.G. Wells's publication of a new Declaration of the Human Rights of Man in *The Times* on 23 October 1940. Writing to Beatrice Webb in February of the next year, Shaw said, 'The Wells Bill of Rights left me out of all patience with abstractions on which Stalin and Lord Halifax are perfectly agreed'. He was convinced that the real problem was the ignorance of statesman who lack the qualifications required for ruling a modern industrial nation. Shaw knew he could not solve the problem. On the other hand, he believed that 'Somebody must begin with a minimum list of things rulers must understand, no matter what their conclusions may be. I am drafting such a list, leaving those who can to amend it' (Shaw 1988: 595). Such were the origins and intentions underlying *Everybody's*. When it was completed, the claim Shaw made on its behalf was that it was but a 'Child's Guide to Politics', or an *a b c* of political terminology, written in second childhood, being a compendium of the scraps and leavings of what little wisdom he had acquired during his long life. It was too verbose, too diffuse, too much a statement of his failing powers. But for all that it seemed important to Shaw as a work of synthesis and reconstruction. And it sold remarkably well – at least 85,000 copies in a year.

As always with Shaw, opinion differed as to how the book was to be approached. His friend, Gilbert Murray, responding to the savage criticisms made by Walter Elliot in *The Spectator*, sought to comfort him with the thought: 'You were not writing a handbook for students but something to wake people up and make them think' (Shaw Papers: BM 50542). That is a view shared more recently by Eric Bentley who says even Shaw's 'lengthiest political works purport only to bring out points which the political scientists have neglected, not to state an alternative political philosophy' (Bentley 1967: 17). But that was written some years after the book was published. Nearer the time Bentley had taken a different line, describing *Everybody's* as 'an exposition of the whole philosophy of life which Shaw has advanced piece by piece in his plays' (Bentley 1944: 9). And that was the view accepted by most of the reviewers, sympathetic or otherwise, including among their number Leonard Woolf, Margaret Cole and Michael Foot. Woolf, writing in *The New Statesman*, described it as 'a compendium of Shaw's most important or persistent doctrines and dogmas' (Woolf 1944: 188), while a reviewer who signed himself R.P.A. in *Labour Monthly* thought the book was a conscious attempt to pre-empt the 'crowd of waiting anthologists and systematisers' (R.P.A. 1944: 319). Such was the majority view. And Shaw, when answering Murray, seemed unwilling to grasp at the straw of comfort offered in the intellectual downgrading of his work, preferring instead to argue a point of detail with Elliot in his most energetically egoistic fighting style. Because the book was 'not meant for people who want to know how far political thought can reach', it did not follow that it was to be read or defended as an unruly collection of eccentric ideas. Whatever its limitations (and there are many), it was intended as a serious work. (That Shaw was not always at his best when most 'serious' is another matter.)

Everybody's opens with the question 'Is Human Nature Incurably Depraved?', to which the answer reads, 'If it is, reading this book will be a waste of time, and it should be exchanged at once for a detective story or some pleasant classic, according to your taste'. Shaw then established the two assumptions at the heart of the work, namely, that we have both the political capacity and goodwill to remedy the mistakes 'that have landed us in a gross misdistribution of domestic income and in two world wars in twenty-five years'. This was his wall of rational hope, constructed to defend the citadel of progress from the forces of ignorance and despair. For assistance he called on the 'counsel of perfection'; the notion that the road to hell really is paved with good intentions and that our errors, evil as they seem, derive from inadequate information, and crucially, from disputes and uncertainties regarding the key concepts of social and political inquiry. An up-to-date political science, operating within a sophisticated conceptual framework, was the first step toward political order; human habits and ideas were to change synchronically with the facts. Beyond that it was implied that the state must ensure that common conclusions will be drawn from that pool of common knowledge. In a Hobbesian vein, it was assumed that the official view of social justice must prevail if order is to be maintained. In support of the argument the example of Russia was offered where the official economists rightly 'oppose and coerce' the people who feel production should be switched to luxury products before the urgent need for more factories, power stations, and railways had been met. Shaw did not claim that order required the eradication of all controversy. Nor did he say that political science, however sophisticated, will offer an infallible guide to practice. He drew back from an extreme kind of political rationalism when he explained 'the clearest knowledge of what needs to be done does not carry with it the knowledge of how to do it'. No intellectual blueprint can expel the need for good judgment on the part of the able statesman. Having opened the introductory chapter with a counsel of perfection, Shaw typically closed with the far more modest claim: 'There is nothing to be done but fence off as many of the pitfalls and signpost as many of the right roads as we can'. All of which was of course grounded on the assumption that all factions, dictators and democrats alike, 'have the best intentions, and believe they are ceasing to do evil and learning to do well'.

Everybody's was a peculiar mixture of naïvety and worldliness. In *The Guide* the emphasis was on the need to reform capitalist mankind, not just to present it with better information. But, then, the former was in many ways a pale shadow of the latter, lacking the structured elegance and precision of its argument. Writing in 1941 to Alfred Douglas, Shaw described his work-in-progress as 'a mass of senile rambling and repetitions; I shall never get it into any very orderly sequence' (Hyde 1982: 147). Obviously improvements were made in the two years before the book was sent to the printers. Yet, it still lacked the discipline and unity of *The Guide*. The opening chapter ranged across almost every Shavian concern, attacking Lloyd George, vaccination, the education system, Shakespeare's pessimism and all abstract declarations of rights. In doing so it set the pattern for the work as a whole, which wandered about all over the place, riding as many hobby-horses as Shaw could mount at his age. What is more, the opening chapter also signalled the danger points in his outlook. In particular, the brisk note on state coercion, coupled with the belated appeal for tolerance, left considerable scope for uncertainty. *Everbody's* was a serious work, but it was also the work of a rebel turned lawmaker, and as such it carried within itself the conflicting marks and signs of these contrasting perspectives. Ultimately, it seemed, the dilemmas and paradoxes which pervaded Shaw's work were not to be reconciled.

His views on democracy and education can be considered in this light.

DEMOCRACY

Nowhere do the many strands of Shaw's politics meet in so provocative and challenging a way as in his varied and controversial comments on democracy. There is no question of anything like a formal theory here. Although his comments were informed by broad doctrinal considerations, they remained tentative in nature. Similarly, though in 1927 he had recognized that a book was wanted on democracy 'and generally on the form of government appropriate to a Socialist State' (Shaw 1988: 81), the views expressed on these matters in *Everybody's* were no more than a sketch of an alternative scheme of things. They were certainly neither models of clarity or consistency. All the same, these reflections were the most constructive of his formulations, representing the culmination of his long discourse on the issues of order and enlightenment, the last attempt to disentangle the intractable problems of efficiency and participation which had troubled his mind for so many years.

Even in the early days of his social democracy, Shaw had enjoyed pouring the occasional bucket of cold water over the illusions of democracy. In the original edition of *Quintessence*, for example, he made the point that 'Democracy is really only an arrangement by which the whole people are given a certain share in the control of the government'. If that was not cool enough, he added 'It has never been proved that this is ideally the best arrangement: it became necessary because the people willed to have it; and it has been made effective only to the very limited extent short of which the dissatisfaction of the majority would have taken the form of actual violence' (Shaw 1965b: 253). Shaw modified the formulation in later editions (see *Major Critical Essays*, pp. 73–4). As early as 1891, therefore, democracy was seen to be for the satisfaction of the people and not necessarily for their good. By the turn of the century such views were more commonly expressed in the political arguments of the day as the cult of national efficiency gained ground in Britain. Shaw, never one to be denied his controversialist's habit of exploiting an intellectual fashion to its fullest extent, was among the most severe in his strictures against parliamentary democracy, doubting whether it was equipped to secure either the goals of happiness or perfection. Among his most forceful and extreme statements on the subject were those in *Man and Superman* where democracy was derided as 'the last refuge of cheap misgovernment' and the last bastion of ignorance and illusion: 'Democracy substitutes election by the incompetent many for appointment by the corrupt few' (Shaw 1931f). Parliamentary democracy was said to be a hindrance to both excellence and expertise.

Was there a Shavian remedy in sight? His view was that the one problem of government was the discovery of a trustworthy anthropometric method. But having formulated the problem so clearly, he offered no guidance in 1903 as to its solution. From then until 1944 Shaw's work was pitted with the salvoes he fired against the parliamentary system of government. At best it was only a negative and uncertain check on tyranny, instead of the positive organizing force required by socialism. During the Great War his views softened somewhat, though he still maintained that 'without qualified rulers a Socialist State is impossible'. In 1918 the choice of rulers was to be limited to 'persons who have passed certain tests and perhaps taken vows' (Shaw 1932c: 319). In *The Guide* he was to write of the need for a rational superpower to dominate the people, though he was careful to warn the intelligent woman to hang on to her vote so long as the present system lasts. In *Too True to be Good* he offered the skeleton of an alternative scheme, founded again on an anthropometric method and organized around the notion of a panel system of government. It was that notion which formed the basis of his reflections in *Everybody's*.

Underlying those reflections was a Platonic conception of the good society where the reconciliation of order with enlightenment was to be found through each of us 'knowing our places'. The assumption was that each individual is uniquely suited to some special function. The task of the social engineer was to match each individual with his right vocation, so ensuring a fusion of capacity with service. To this end Shaw produced a rough guide to aid the collectivist statisticians of the future, in the form of his classification of mental types which distinguished between the military, aesthetic, scientific and theocratic orders of men. Politics, too, was a vocation requiring special aptitudes and skills. Classification of those aptitudes and skills was 'the first step toward genuine democracy' (Shaw 1944: 46).

Fundamentally, the project of enlightenment entailed restricting power to the 5 per cent or so 'capable of some degree of government'. On this basis, the key question was not, who should be allowed to vote, rather, for whom should Everyman be allowed to vote. Shaw was not entirely consistent in this respect, however. In the main he supported a 'One Simpleton One Vote System', together with its accompanying fiction of popular consent which was too well-established and useful to be dispensed with altogether: 'I grant that Mr E. must be empowered to choose his rulers, were it only to save him from being ruled unbearably well'. But occasionally he digressed from this line, writing of 'registers of qualified voters', with some people (proven bigots and idiots incapable of reading the books of Wells, Shaw and their like) being disfranchised (Shaw 1944: 67, 165 and 331).

Similar uncertainty was evident in the more important (for Shaw) discussion on the minority allowed to stand as candidates for office. The Shavian system was to be based on a hierarchy of panels dealing with local issues at the bottom and national and international affairs at the top. Qualification to sit on any panel was to be determined by a census of political capacity, establishing at which level the members of the eligible minority were to be allowed to function. His discussion of the census was tantalizingly incomplete. Shaw believed a series of anthropometric tests should be devised which ought to be taken over a period of apprenticeship under critical observation. But so many details were not forthcoming. At what age were the panellists to receive their specialized education? Who were to act as judges or critical observers? Questions of this kind were left to the collective statisticians of the future.

One novel suggestion was that, having abolished Parliament and placed all the legislative and executive work in the hands of the panellists, a new talk-shop should be established where ordinary people could express their views with impunity. This talk-shop was to be called the 'Everyman's Congress'. It was not an elected body. On the contrary, to ensure its representative nature it was to be picked up haphazardly, so making party selection impossible. Its other feature was that it was to include men and women in equal numbers. The Congress's function was described in these unflattering terms:

> When the law becomes an instrument of oppression, as laws often do, especially before they have been amended in the light of experience of their working, it is the Everymans who know where the shoe pinches. For them there must be congresses in which they can squeal their complaints, agitate for their pet remedies, move resolutions and votes of confidence or the reverse, draft bills and call on the Government to adopt and enact them, and criticize the Government to their utmost with impunity. And as such congresses must be attended by the rulers, who could not possibly conduct the business of the country if they had to listen to Mr E. and Mrs E. and Miss E. 'ventilating their grievances' for longer or oftener than a few weeks every two years, a day-to-day ventilation and agitation must be effected by the newspapers and pamphlets, which should have the same privileges as the congresses.
>
> (Shaw 1944: 52)

Clearly, there was to be life for democracy beyond the congresses; 'freedom of congress, freedom of speech, freedom of agitation, freedom of the press are democratic necessities', Shaw wrote. The new order he envisaged, devoid of poverty and the extremes of wealth, was to be incorrigibly quarrelsome; 'all society will become polemical and partisan', he predicted, organized around creeds, trade unions, professional associations, clubs, sects and cliques. There would even be political parties, he suggested, though how exactly they would operate in relation to the panel system of government was not explained (Shaw 1944: 67).[8]

143

That was the problem. Shaw's speculations left a trail of confusion and ambiguity. 'Its chief demerit', wrote Margaret Cole, 'is that on its central theme it has literally nothing to say. Shaw wishes to abolish Parliament as a legislative body; he wishes laws to be made and men to be governed by a carefully educated and carefully selected minority, but on how these are to be selected he offers no suggestions whatever' (Cole 1945: 32). Another reviewer said Shaw was being 'wilfully obscurantist' on this point, while Walter Elliot remarked, 'No one has the right to propound such a solution seriously and bolt from the techniques involved' (Elliot 1944: 268).

Transcending these points of detail, the whole moral and intellectual framework in which the discussion of democracy was situated was also confused and ambiguous; the individualist and collectivist moralities were in a high state of tension. On his individualistic and rebellious side, Shaw offered a vision of a society of controversialists, enjoying the democratic freedoms to the full and using participation in political discourse as an opportunity for the development of character; as a collectivist and lawmaker, on the other hand, he sought a Platonic order which verged at times on a totalitarian scheme of things. Ultimately his republican vision was confused, inadequate and downright dangerous. By way of contrast to the statement on the democratic necessities (seen by Shaw as privileges not rights) there was a comment to the effect that the states of the future 'will tolerate hardly Free Anything that they can regulate with advantage to the general welfare' (Shaw 1944: 75). Having started with a conception of democracy as 'the organization of society for the benefit and at the expense of everybody indiscriminately and not for the benefit of a privileged class' (Shaw 1944: 40), he was in danger of emphasizing the imperatives of organization and collective duty at the expense of all else. Too often democracy was seen as simply a device for choosing among contending élites, with the vote supplying the illusion of government by popular consent (so diminishing the risk of sedition); a choice between capable legislators 'is all that is needed to give them [the people] as much control of their government as is good for them' (Shaw 1944: 352).

In this respect, Shaw was close to Schumpeter and the theorists of democratic élitism. However, the precise grounds for even limited conflict among members of the political élite were unclear in *Everybody's* because it was assumed that while they would proceed on a basis of trial and error they would none the less all accept socialism and creative evolutionism as provisional truths. A formidable degree of moral and intellectual consensus was built into the Shavian system, so placing even its minimal democracy at risk.

Indeed the limits on government power were not perceived in constitutional terms by Shaw. If anything, responsibility was established within a religious framework. 'Statesmen must be religious', he said, otherwise they will abuse their power, treating their fellow man simply as a means, or hindrance, or delay, without any intrinsic value. Without religion

144

as a guide, politics falls into the amoral realm of the emotivist self, becoming the plaything of personal ambition, preference and desire. The connections between Shaw's metaphysics and politics were at their strongest here. Above all, he argued, the panel system of government must restrict candidacy to the supreme cabinet to those who believe in and understand the vision encapsulated in the religion of creative evolution: where the statesman, who is the fallible instrument of the life force, has a duty, both to secure human welfare and to lead humanity toward the divine goals of evolutionary righteousness. Failing that, 'we shall become part of the Problem of Evil, and be exterminated like the mammoths and mastodons by some new species of greater political capacity' (Shaw 1944: 234). More mundanely, this religious sense of our common humanity was effectively the only guard Shaw placed against state corruption, even though he admitted that the extension of state power and activity under socialism 'carries with it a formidable extension of its possible abuse' (Shaw 1944: 260).

Remaining with the theme of religion, in 1933 Shaw had said that the statesman should not only have a sense of his own fallibility, but also a certain modesty; 'A vocation for politics, though essentially a religious vocation, must be on the same footing as a vocation for music or mathematics or cooking or nursing or acting or architecture or farming or billiards or any other born aptitude' (Shaw 1934d: 23). The point of this claim was to confirm the democratic nature of the Shavian system by mitigating the worst implications of differential rationality. Despite the apparent élitism, Shaw, it seemed, was only propounding a form of departmental excellence. He was not saying that the superior brains in politics were really superior to those of any other trade or profession. But this was a hopeless undertaking. More reasonably the claim could be seen as an attempt to save his work as a moralist from incoherence. Fundamental to his moralism was the insistence on individual responsibility. Fundamental to that was the capacity for rational choice. By operating with a form of differential rationality he effectively undermined his argument for responsibility. The note on departmental excellence went some way toward alleviating the problem, but in no way could it offer a solution, because the natural class distinctions within the vocations – between the super-average and sub-average – could not be eradicated. In this way, Shaw's project for moral revolution, culminating in the vision of a democracy of supermen, fell into disarray. Similarly, his emancipatory religion of creative evolution was transformed into a social creed, serving his overriding passion for the cult of superior brains.

Amidst the confusion, one is reminded of what John Plamenatz once wrote in relation to Rousseau: 'The rhetorical dealer in paradoxes is often the victim of his own eloquence' (Plamenatz 1963: 433).

EDUCATION

To hive off one facet of Shaw's argument to consider under the rubric of 'education' is an artificial exercise. Everything he wrote and said was infused with a passion to inform. His life's work was dedicated to the cause of enlightenment – 'I exist to be used', he said. He was for so many the archetypal prophet and teacher of his generation, a disseminator of knowledge in the grand tradition of Socrates and Voltaire. Modesty did not prevent him from seeing himself as belonging to that elect group of people 'who are building up the intellectual consciousness of the race'. All his activities were transformed into educational programmes. The theatre was for him, not a place of amusement, but a house of correction – 'a temple of the Ascent of Man' (Shaw 1932m: vii) he called it, a place where a new and higher conception of citizenship might be glimpsed. Such was the tenor of his argument for an endowed theatre at national and local levels, with that argument forming only one part of his general advocacy of moral and intellectual reform. Shaw was all to do with education. Yet, being Shaw, he certainly held strong views on educational matters in the narrower sense of the term. The critique of the education system was among his favourite themes. Added to which, he was scathing in his attacks on what he perceived to be conventional family life: 'I do not want any human child to be brought up as I was brought up, nor as any child I have known was brought up' (Shaw 1949a: 490). He took the view that a child was an experiment on the part of the life force, 'a fresh attempt', as he put it in 1928, 'to produce the just man made perfect: that is, to make humanity divine'. To date, the species had proved a dismal failure. Instead of heading for the divine goal, it had been diverted along the by-ways of corruption, aided and abetted by the morality of gangsterism, masquerading behind the frippery of romance. A child was so full of potential, almost all of which was stifled or perverted by the conventions and institutions of the adult world. Shaw was at his most fundamentalist here. The education system was a tyrannical sham, simply a means of keeping children out of the way of their parents for part or all the day, a system organized on the basis of rote learning and policed by the inhuman practices of corporal punishment. Of his own education, he declared: 'It was simply dragging a child's soul through the dirt'. Incompetent teachers teaching an unnatural curriculum, that was the sum of it. And for once there was no question of exaggeration. The school system made progress impossible. It destroyed responsibility, producing nothing but a lump of docile wage slaves, without self-respect or any regard for authority, wholly unsuited for citizenship in a modern state: 'the voters from the elementary schools and the governing classes from the public schools and universities have between them half-wrecked civilization' (Shaw 1922: 219). Of her own education at Cambridge, Vivie Warren said, 'Outside mathematics, lawn-tennis, eating, sleeping, cycling, walking, Im a more ignorant barbarian than any woman could possibly be who hadnt gone in for the tripos' (Shaw 1931h).

In its day, the power of Shaw's critique was considerable. If it was not original, it was at least trenchant and powered by bitter personal experience. On its constructive side, however, Shaw's argument was less successful, partly because it was pulled between the contrary forces of liberty and order. And further, that struggle increased in intensity over the years, with the cause of order predictably gaining the ascendancy by 1944.

Of the major statements on the subject, the *Treatise on Parents and Children* (Shaw 1932i) from 1914 was a relatively libertarian document, concerned to reorganize childhood so as to offer maximum opportunity for creativity and self-development. Instead of children being tied to a single school and one family, they were to be encouraged to explore the world, with children finding 'in every part of their native country, food, clothing, lodging, instruction, and parental kindness for the asking'. There was to be a child's Magna Carta, outlining the rights of children against parental and all institutional tyranny. Fundamental to the charter was tolerance of eccentricity; 'Every child has a right to its own bent', he wrote, 'It has a right to find its own way and go its own way, whether that way seems wise or foolish to others, exactly as an adult has. It has a right to privacy as to its own doings and its own affairs as much as if it were its own father' (Shaw 1932: 11). With such a system in operation, surprising developments in child laws, fashions, manners and morals were predicted. Who could tell what practices and institutions would be created by free children. The closest Shaw came to a depiction of the possibilities was in *You Never Can Tell* (Shaw 1931g) where the contrast was made between the gloriously free twins, Dolly and Philip, whose minds had successfully resisted all their mother's efforts to improve them, as against their sister, Gloria, who had for so long distorted her passionate character by trying to mould herself in the image of her mother's rational scheme of education. (Here Shaw was, perhaps, hinting at the limits to all progressive schemes of improvement, including his own).

Childhood was not seen by Shaw as a realm of freedom in any simple sense. It was not to be a perpetual holiday. With rights came certain duties. In particular, children were to be introduced to the morality of labour. Instead of spending long fruitless years in secondary education, taking subjects for which they had little or no aptitude, children were to be seconded to industry where they would learn the habit of work, along with the sense of repayable obligation to the community. It was not seen as an imposition on the child; on the contrary, Shaw reasoned that children were generally eager to substitute the dignity of adult work for the claustrophobic discipline of school life. Mental and manual labour were to be combined. So too was the sense of individual liberty (and the responsibility it entailed) on one side, with the spirit of service and with an appreciation of the value of communal life on the other. There was to be competition in Shaw's system, but he said this should be 'between teams, as this incites members to share their knowledge and help one another'.

A salient feature of his work was the critique of secondary education. He suggested it should be purely voluntary and conducted in voluntary organizations, at least as regards the optional subjects of liberal education for culture. Shaw had two points here. One was that school methods were entirely inappropriate where the appreciation of art and literature was concerned. Any child so inclined would be better off wandering around the art galleries and reading whatever books came to hand. That had sufficed for him, so why not for others? Self-education was really the only viable strategy where aesthetic instruction was concerned. Shaw's second point was that the distinction between optional liberal education and compulsory technical education should be redrawn. Here his main concern was to explain why civics and religion should join the three Rs as part of our technical education for civilized life. The teaching of science must include political science, 'not only in its elementary branch of police regulation, but in its modern constitutional developments as industrial democracy and socialism, which subjects, in a modern democratic state, should be as compulsory, up to the limit of the scholar's capacity for them, as the multiplication table' (Shaw 1932c: 303). As for religion, that was seen as fundamental to good ethics; if Shaw was convinced of anything, it was that 'all communities must live finally by their ethical values'. Through instruction in political science and religion, civil ignorance and amorality respectively were to be reduced to their natural minimum. As for the method of instruction, that was to be controversial in kind, entailing the toleration of all doctrines for the purpose of analysis and debate:

> Controversy is educational in itself: a controversially educated person with an open mind is better educated than a dogmatically educated one with a closed mind. The student should hear the case, but should never be asked for a verdict. It may take him forty years to arrive at one.
>
> (Shaw 1932c: 314)

This was Shaw at his best: open and stimulating, quite willing to admit he had no foolproof 'system ready to replace all the other systems', useful and constructive despite his eccentricities. His views on controversy in political education, for example, were a good guide for democratic practice. Through the prism of these reflections we gain the clearest sight of his vision of evolving free men in an evolving free society. We gain, too, a kinder and more constructive view of his republican politics of virtue, where the goal was to arrive, through open and free discourse, at a new understanding of citizenship, where the political realm was seen as a place of enlightenment inhabited by participants armed only with the power of committed reason.

By 1944 that vision was blurred and distorted; the cause of liberty seemed overwhelmed by the exigencies of order; individual rights were an alien intrusion into his scheme of things. The change in direction was related to the pressures Shaw faced as a socialist. In particular, as he came to recognize the need for a vigorous socialist creed to use in the propaganda war against capitalism, so increasingly education was identified with explaining the world from a definite point of view. He also recognized that the socialist state of the future would require its own official ideology with political, economic and religious dimensions. Neither of these were new insights. But they came to dominate Shaw's outlook, shifting the emphasis away from controversy towards the inculcation of an official creed. Functional and collectivist considerations had informed his Fabian views on education. The state had always played a part in his plans. As early as 1884, when protesting against the parental monopoly of authority over children, he had said 'that the state should compete with private individuals – especially with parents – in providing happy homes for children' (Joad 1953: 73). In *Everybody's* it was not so much the child's happiness that was at stake as the efficient functioning of the system of vocational élitism. This was the spirit that informed the proposal that child colonies be established to counter parental inexperience. Whereas in 1914 he was adamant that no adult should assume that 'the child does not know its own business', in 1944 he asserted that in the socialized states of the future, 'The State will insist on what we call forming the child's character as a citizen' (Shaw 1944: 152) (he even went on to say that the state would take a child from its parents if they were found inculcating subversive doctrines). The assumption was that 'Children must be obedient to adults, not because adults are physically stronger but because they know better'. In this revised system, the state was viewed as the repository of wisdom on human development. Collective organization of the child's working and leisure hours was to be the norm, with the family, schools and the socialist equivalents of the Boy Scout and Girl Guide movements functioning as state subsidiaries in this vast corporate enterprise. The state was even empowered to kill those children it classified 'as congenital and incurable idiots or criminals' (Shaw 1944: 177). The democratic free-for-all of 1914 was replaced by a strictly administered scheme of vocational education. The idea that a 'nation should always be healthily rebellious' was in retreat: 'the object of the sane state', Shaw said, 'is to make good citizens of its children: that is, to make them productive or serviceable members of the community' (Shaw 1944: 79).

As always, the case should not be overstated. Still basic to Shaw's argument was that 'children should live in an organized society with rights and constitutions, and be brought up neither as household pets nor as chattel slaves'. The difficulty was that he had already scrubbed rights off the doctrinal agenda. He continued to maintain that children should 'be educated to live more abundantly, not apprenticed to a life sentence of penal servitude'. Presumably, abundance was to be measured in terms of the individual's productive or serviceable contribution to the community. Also, Shaw still argued for controversy and tolerance in education, but only fitfully and without some of the earlier conviction. Now it was assumed that a democratic education would lead inevitably to communism. Besides, children were not to be 'bothered with controversy' (Shaw 1944: 70). They were to be taught in a dogmatic sense to accept the prevailing 'view of human nature and destiny'. It is worth noting in this respect that one of the main factors which drew him to the Russian experiment was that there 'They had got hold of the children', as Shaw put it; reverting to what Martin Hollis describes as the plastic model of man, Shaw said 'it is very easy to mould human nature if you catch it before it is set' (Shaw 1988: 273). It would appear that the cause of communal unity was to take precedence over that of individual self-development. Political education was part inculcation, part instruction for the masses on how to appreciate the good works of their rulers. Advancing was the darker side of the republican ideal. As Louis Simon said of the Shavian system, 'education could not influence the reformation of social policy or the redirection of social change'. In such a centralized scheme, 'the whole process of education could merely be designed to strengthen the hold of a dominant group' (Simon 1958: 263).

CONCLUSIONS

Originally Shaw had planned to subtitle *Everybody's* 'Machiavelli Modernised' (Laurence 1983: 245). Why he changed his mind we do not know. Perhaps he wanted to avoid the suggestion that his book was a mere supplement to H.G. Wells; the old rivalry still ran deep. Alternatively, and more fancifully, perhaps Shaw thought comparison with Machiavelli himself would have only served to underline his own failings. *Everybody's* was a mixed and mystic pot-pourri of ideas, at once idealistic and hard-faced, encompassing the many dilemmas and paradoxes which floated on the currents of Shavian rhetoric. It was supposedly addressed to Everyman, yet Shaw assumed that his readers formed the basis for an intellectual aristocracy of the future. Though critical of the 'Equality Merchants', it betrayed a distinct nostalgia for their company. Its intellectual seams were torn in the conflict between tolerance and social discipline. Its moral foundations were undermined in the struggle of individualism with collectivism. He still tried to build a meeting-house for happiness and perfection, but its foundations were decidedly shaky and flimsy. He tried also to retain a sense of our common humanity, though that buckled under the weight of his extreme and cheerless regard for meritocracy. For a man obsessed with law, he was cavalier in his approach to administrative and constitutional arrangements. For a vitalist so committed to the autonomy of the human will, he was oddly impressed by 'the possibility of changing human nature by improving its circumstances'. He created in 1944 in *Everybody's* a curious work, the flawed utopia of a pragmatist with fundamentalist tendencies. Above all, he was the victim of his own rhetorical method of reasoning. 'It is always necessary to overstate a case startlingly to make people sit up and listen to it, and to frighten them into acting on it', he said, adding 'I do this myself habitually and deliberately'. To which Leonard Woolf responded:

If you habitually and deliberately overstate your case, the form of your argument and of your own thought becomes stereotyped in the *reductio ad absurdum*. That is highly dangerous, particularly to your own mind and thought, for if you live and write long enough, you cease to be able to distinguish between your own sense and your own nonsense.

(Woolf 1944: 188)

Ultimately, Shaw lost the control he once had over his argument. For the rebel to turn lawmaker it required more careful thought and sober analysis than he could muster. The egalitarian doctrine was the prize exhibit of his political thought. That had been altered beyond recognition and with its demise the synthesis he sought between passionate commitment and critical distance assumed an air of waywardness and unreality. In his final years assessments of his achievements were tinged with regret. That the unwholesome statements of doctrine were often mitigated by the general tone and detailed characterization of his drama was accepted. That he could still write beautiful prose which buzzed with urgency was never denied. Yet, there was regret that somehow he had not quite kept the faith or quite fulfilled his promise. Shaw had entered the forum as a moral revolutionary. When he left it he carried with him many of the trophies of argument. But argument is a harsh and uncertain master. There is a sense in which the indefatigable controversialist was the victim of his own eloquence. How ironic, then, that his last will and testament of 1937 should have included a clause concerned to promote the endowment of a school of rhetoric (Chappelow 1969).

Politics, morals and metaphysics

Shaw was not the tidiest nor the most scrupulous of thinkers, 'a crow who has followed many ploughs' was how he described himself (Shaw 1931k: xxxvi). Also, he had the controversialist's habit of never discarding any line of argument in case it should prove useful in the future, 'you never can tell' was a favourite Shavian dictum. He was, in short, intellectually promiscuous, unwilling to admit to contradiction, to cast off old doctrines or to offer definitive statements on the relationship between elements of his work. All of which makes for the sort of confusion and uncertainty which cannot be dispelled by the invention of neat formulas. Three major themes, namely the relationship between theory and practice, the doctrine of evolutionary righteousness, and the cult of superior brains, can be identified as the underlying and perennial concerns of his work as a political thinker and artist-philosopher. But this is not to claim that his thought is neatly reducible to these themes. On the contrary, as guides to the creative contradictions in Shaw's work it could be argued that they present us with as many questions as answers.

Before moving on to consider the developing historical problems of Part

II we should pause to consider some of these loose ends, and, in doing so, to modify somewhat the brutal picture of Shaw which has emerged in the latter part of this chapter. It remains the case that the relationship between Shaw's politics, morals and metaphysics are far from clear-cut. Whilst it has been said that the religion of creative evolution gained a central place in the Shavian canon after 1918, it does not follow that the relationship between his socialism and vitalism was therefore consistent or straightforward. The two can be seen sometimes as complimentary partners in his argument and at other times as incompatible alternatives with very little in common. In one sense his creative evolutionism and socialism were alternative sources of hope: when humanity failed him, Shaw retreated into the shell of evolutionary optimism, deriding administrative socialism as 'fundamentally futile'; when his spirits were high, he trusted in man's capacity to carry the light of progress. This was his strategy for survival. Either way, the persona of GBS had the faith it needed to power the argument for progress. Certainly it would be wrong to suggest that creative evolution, with its curiously tragic yet optimistic vision of things, came to dominate every facet of his argument. The 1918 Fabian lecture was unusual in that respect. In *Back to Methuselah* Shaw was adamant that 'Our statesmen must get a religion by hook or by crook'. Seven years later in *The Guide* his approach was secular, more sober and limited: 'Both socialism and capitalism certainly do what they can to obtain credit for representing a divinely appointed order of the universe; but the pressure of facts is too strong for their pretentions: they are forced to present themselves at last as purely secular expedients for securing human welfare' (Shaw 1949a: 443). Clearly, in spite of all his dictates on evolutionary righteousness, the conception of goodness as happiness was never entirely overwhelmed in Shaw's work.

Nor was his politics ever to become the simple plaything of his metaphysics. Shaw's vitalist critique of economic determinism and the emphasis on personal righteousness in his progressive argument have been noted. But for all that he still insisted in a letter to H.G. Wells in 1917, 'we must reform society before we can reform ourselves ... personal righteousness is impossible in an unrighteous environment' (Shaw 1985b: 473). Added to this, a kind of residual economism was never far beneath the surface of his work, waiting to be called into action to meet the exigencies of argument. In *The Guide* he placed the responsibility for the Great War at the door of capitalism: 'the fault lay not so much in our characters as in the capitalist system which we had allowed to dominate our lives until it became a sort of blind monster which neither we nor the capitalists could control ... we were no more directly guilty of the war than we were guilty of the earthquake of Tokyo' (Shaw 1949a: 155). The tensions between the autonomous and plastic models of man were never eradicated from Shaw's work.

It would be convenient, especially in light of his reputation as an élitist, to say that Shaw placed such superior individuals as himself in the first category, and ordinary mortals, the dwarfs and giants of this world, into the second.

Something of the kind was certainly implicit in much of his work – 'whilst most people's minds succumb to inculcation and environment, a few react vigorously', he acknowledged in *Back to Methuselah*. Nevertheless, it must be said that such a categorical distinction was not consistently maintained. Picking up on this theme, perhaps Shaw also associated the selfish lower morality of happiness with Everyman, while restricting the higher perfectionist morality of service to the minority of superior brains. Again, there were hints of this in his work. Shaw was, for example, inclined to implore the common man to look to his own happiness and not to be duped by the middle-class ethos of altruism, while at the same time making such assertions as, 'Folly is the direct pursuit of Happiness and Beauty' (Shaw 1932f: 219); or, as he said in 1896, 'Philosophers have warned us that the pursuit of happiness is of all pursuits the most wretched, and that happiness has never yet been found except on the way to some other goal' (Shaw 1965b: 412).

Convenient as this is, the relationship between happiness and perfection in Shaw's outlook can also be seen in a more compatible light, with one serving as a necessary foundation for the other. Thus, in the distinctly socialist conception of happiness as material well-being, selfishness was a pre-requisite for the development of those spiritual and creative powers which might in time be employed for the common good. Socialism would not turn the ordinary woman into a Saint Joan, but hopefully it would establish the ground for a modest contribution to spiritual progress. The morality of happiness, understood as the self-interested pursuit of material welfare, was in that sense a foundation for the collectivist morality of perfection. Seen from another standpoint, the vital Mrs George from *Getting Married* offered her own formulation of how selfishness leads to selflessness when she declared, 'Ive been myself. Ive not been afraid of myself. And at last I have escaped from myself, and am become a voice for them that are afraid to speak, and cry for the hearts that break in silence' (Shaw 1932d: 338). Implicit in this argument is the view that happiness can only be found as a by-product of the search for the goal of moral self-discovery. Perhaps it would be better to consider self-interest as a necessary step toward a higher conception of life as one of service to community and, ultimately, to the righteous cause of evolutionary progress.

There are so many possibilities, so many trains of thought to spot and catch and ride from source to destination. There are so many Shaws. There is the hard Shaw, the stern moralist and collectivist lawmaker, impatient with the masses and with history, dismissive of sympathy and suffering, the tough republican possessed by a commitment to virtue and progress. There is, too, a softer Shaw, the rebel and humorist, the fighter and troublemaker, thundering and prodding against the cruel excesses of the men of power, the tender apostle of moderation and fair play. Commenting on Chesterton's portrait of him, Shaw said, 'Like all men, I play many parts; and none of them is more or less real than another' (Shaw 1932p: 82). Perhaps in old age the tougher elements in his public persona came to dominate over the tender, perfection over happiness, efficiency over enlightenment, order over subversive humour. Somehow the wit of the rebel was almost stifled by the lawmaker's creed. Almost, but not quite; for the sense of the ridiculous which made GBS a viable exercise in public relations for so long was never entirely lost; nor was the humility, still less the sense of the complexity of the world entailed in his self-deprecating humour.

Shaw's advice to the would-be lawmaker from *Everybody's* is worth noting because it sets the tone for his political argument, subject to so many lapses, open to countless temptations, cast as it is between paternalism and populism, dogma and doubt, pragmatism and idealism, the secular and the metaphysical: for the ruler, he declared:

> His God must not be an existing Omnipotent Omniscient Perfection, but as yet only an ideal towards which creative evolution is striving, with mankind merely its best attempt so far, and a very unsatisfactory one at that, liable to be replaced at any moment if creative evolution gives it up as hopeless. He must face the evil of the world, which apparently reduces the goodness of God to absurdity, as but the survival of errors originally well intended. He must treat life as everlasting, but treat his contemporaries as ephemeral mortals having no life beyond the grave to compensate them for any injustice they may suffer here and now.
>
> (Shaw 1944: 329)

Part II

3

SEXUAL EQUALITY

A COMPLEX LEGACY

Shaw's reflections on sexual equality are inherently controversial, inviting conflicting interpretations as to their meaning and worth. There are those who favour the ideas he formulated as a political thinker, while others find in these all the pitfalls and limitations of his Fabian socialism. Some disparage the portrayals of women in his plays, while others see them as model statements on the theme of female emancipation. Some find much to praise in a few plays and much to criticize in many more.

The confusion is not new. In his own day, activists struggling for the vote for women, for example, often canvassed his support, seeking to enlist the prestige of the great man of letters to their cause. Sometimes Shaw pleased them. Just as often his responses disappointed or perplexed these earnest women.

Traditionally, Shaw's contribution has been cast mainly in a positive light. The strong, dynamic women of the plays were said to have inspired many women to break the bonds of their Victorian upbringing. By the 1890s Shaw's name was connected intimately with the propaganda on behalf of 'the new woman'. As the arch-progressive he was eager to argue the case for radical feminism, to preach the rebel's gospel of liberation. Responding to these overtures, many women, young women especially, were enthusiastic in their support for Shaw, often treating him as a mentor from whom they could learn what to think, feel and do. F.C. Burnaud, writing of the audience at the Court Theatre during the Barker-Vedrenne regime, which Shaw so dominated, observed: 'The female element predominates over the inferior sex as something like twelve to one. The audience had not a theatre-going, but rather, a lecture-going, sermon loving appearance' (Ford 1983: 275).

Woman's cause and Shaw's were intertwined, it seems, held together by mutual need and admiration. As Wilma Meikle wrote in 1915, 'young women at the universities' around this time 'poured over' the works of Shaw and Wells, earnestly convinced that these were the true guides to emancipation (Meikle 1916: 87). In a less generous spirit, writing in *Time and Tide* in 1930, Lady Rhondda said Shaw's 'generalisations on these matters want watching'

157

because intelligent people take him 'seriously on women' (Lady Rhondda 1930a: 301).

Even in the Edwardian days, however, dissenting voices could be heard. For example the young Rebecca West, in the *Freewoman* in 1912, said that 'for all Shaw's audacious discussions, there is not one character in all his eighteen plays who infringes the conventions in practice'. Contrasting him with Granville Barker she wrote, 'Shaw never brought anything so anarchic as an unmarried mother on to his stage' (Marcus 1983: 20).

Comments of this sort have grown more insistent as Shaw's standing as an artist and thinker have declined. Some women remain enthusiastic about Shaw. Many more, while acknowledging his historical contribution, find too many problems in his work to see him as anything but a man pontificating on matters he did not and could not fully understand. A few even believe that Shaw used women as pawns in the drama of his own self-aggrandisement: 'Shaw was a pioneer feminist who exploited women' (Catling 1981: 12).

The enthusiasts and critics alike are to be found in a book edited by Rodelle Weintraub, entitled *Fabian Feminist*. Most notable among the former group is Barbara Bellow Watson who has written the one major study in this area. One claim she makes is that 'when Shaw thinks about women, something remarkable happens. He makes no assumptions'. Rather confusingly, Watson then goes on to cite with approval Shaw's comment that he always assumed 'that a woman is a person exactly like myself'; she concludes that all his doctrinal and dramatic reflections were founded on this androgynous principle (Watson 1977: 34). Watson accepts that Shaw is not a systematic thinker, but argues that his ideas on sexual equality 'have a superb coherence', synthesizing all the oppositions and tensions inherent in the cause of emancipation (Watson 1964: 34). She suggests that Shaw's revolutionary ideas were expressed through his female characters who stand outside the idealist world of male society (Watson 1964: 54). Shaw, in Watson's opinion, is a 'patron saint of the women's movement' (Watson 1977: 114).

Among the critics, Norbert Greiner says that, far from acting as mouthpieces for Shaw's ideas, his female characters should be seen rather as the last bastions of outmoded ideals in his work. Greiner's argument is that Shaw perceived woman's position as a product of male, middle-class society and, as such, her 'position as well as that of the proletariat is a mirror of the nineteenth-century social situation in general' (Greiner 1977: 96). Elsie Adams takes issues with the view that Shaw operated without assumptions or in keeping with an androgynous principle when dealing dramatically with women. What we find, Adams says, 'are permutations of basic literary types: temptress, mother, goddess' (Adams 1977: 157). Adams is not entirely critical. She argues we should distinguish between Shaw's traditional treatment of women in the plays and the 'feminist politics' of the essays and lectures, which were far more convincing and original (Adams 1977: 161). Germaine Greer is not so accommodating. Commenting upon *Mrs Warren's Profession* she writes 'Shaw could get no nearer the correct etiology of whoredom than the feeble Fabian diagnosis that women were overworked and undervalued and underpaid' (Greer 1977: 166). Shaw understood neither capitalism nor the sexism it engenders, Greer concluded.

What are we to make of this complex legacy? By way of introduction, it should be said that Shaw's reflections on sexual equality did not operate in relation to a unified feminist movement. In Shaw's day, in the late Victorian and Edwardian period specifically, feminist politics was split between competing factions and interests. There were those whose concerns were specific, limited to the vote for women or birth control, for example, whereas others had broader visions of radical emancipation. There were liberal feminists, socialist feminists, militant suffragettes and sexual radicals. Shaw's reflections operated within this spacious framework, touching – seriously, wittily, tentatively – on every point of interest.

COMPLEX RELATIONSHIPS

The Victorian theory about women is ludicrous delusion. She is the most dangerous of all the animals, if you come to that view of the situation. The attempt to hypnotize her into believing herself weak was bound to fail; and it *has*.

(Shaw 1985b: 898)

Such was the opinion Shaw expounded to his boyhood friend, Matthew Edward McNulty, in a letter written on Christmas Day 1924. In its deliciously enigmatic way, the statement, complete with its allusion to Kipling, hints at the undercurrents flowing beneath Shaw's doctrinal commitment to the emancipation of women. According to Margaret Walters, behind that commitment there lay a 'nervous hostility' towards women who aimed, consciously or otherwise, Shaw suspected, not for equality with men, but for domination over them. Thus, it is said that in Shaw's plays, notably *Candida* (Shaw 1931g), it is the men who are the dolls, trapped in a web of feminine mystery and machination without any real hope of escape. His formal regard for sexual equality was, in this respect, always qualified by a sense of the latent power of women, teasingly expressed in the Fabian *Manifesto* of 1884 where Shaw declared that men 'no longer need special political privileges to protect them against women'. For Walters, such views suggest that 'Shaw always suspected that, ultimately, power resides in the female'.[1] Articulation of that suspicion depended somewhat on the current intellectual vogue. When writing in 1906 to Clement Scott, for instance, Shaw packaged the argument in a Nietzschean guise, stating: 'The truth is that a Slave State is always ruled by those who can get round the masters, that is, by the more cunning of the slaves themselves'. In this way, Shaw continued, female slavery leads inevitably to female tyranny: 'no fascinating woman ever wants to emancipate

159

her sex: her object is to gather power into the hands of man, because she knows she can govern him' (Shaw 1972: 260). 'Is there any slavery on earth viler than this slavery of men to women?', asks the philandering Hector Hushabye in *Heartbreak House* in response to the irresistible Lady Utterwood's formulation of the scope and nature of woman's power over his unfortunate sex (Shaw 1931c: 121).

Personally, Shaw's relationships with women were extremely odd, a combination of fascination and wariness, candour and evasive charm, a curious mixture of lover and sprite, the emotional tease who made women fall for him only to toy with their affections, sending them on their way with but an armful of witty letters for company. He lost his virginity at twenty-nine years of age and then, according to Shaw's account of things, being a novice in sex, he was seduced by a woman fifteen years his senior, Mrs Jenny Patterson (Holroyd 1988: 161). She introduced him to the power of sex, a power he resented, says Michael Holroyd, because it 'unsteadied his self-sufficiency and exposed his loneliness' (Holroyd 1988: 161). Shaw was ready to advise any number of beautiful women, actresses especially (Florence Farr, Ellen Terry, Janet Achurch, Mrs Patrick Campbell and Molly Tompkins among others), but he was happiest leaving it at that and was relieved after his functional celibate marriage in 1898 to Charlotte Payne-Townshend to be able to plead the case of his wife's feelings whenever such a passionate huntress as Erica Cotterill threatened to disturb his routine and shatter his emotional brittleness. Sex was a trial to Shaw; 'Any sexual relationship that could not provide an alternative world, partly made out of words, tended to disgust him', writes Holroyd (Holroyd 1988: 108).

Yet despite his horror of sex, his suspicion of female intentions and the studied harshness he adopted in his emotional affairs, Shaw the realist, the destroyer of the illusions of romantic love, was himself under the spell of the romantic fascination of women. The stern advisor was liable at any moment to turn into the Irish gallant, full of displays of flattery and 'those philandering follies' which, he said, made him 'so ridiculous, so troublesome, so vulgar with women' (St John 1931: 90). Writing in 1923 to Mrs Patrick Campbell, perhaps the most powerful of all these spellbinders, her Joey (Shaw's pet-name) confessed all; 'I see women as I see other people. I always did, but with one eye only: the other eye was enchanted' (Dent 1952: 259).

On the other hand, he told Ellen Terry he doubted if women ever loved men at all in a romantic sense (St John 1931: 25).[2] His mother had not loved his father thus. What is more it seemed she did not love her only son at all, treating him with perfect indifference. In many respects, she was the model Shavian woman, both emotionally and economically self-sufficient. When Shaw arrived in London in 1876, in his mother's wake, and for years afterwards, he relied on her for the essentials of life, later boasting that he made a man of himself at his mother's expense; 'I did not throw myself into the struggle for life: I threw my mother into it', he said in the 1905 preface to his second novel, *The Irrational Knot* (Shaw 1931d: xv). What she threw back in return were the crumbs of her earnings, never the craved-for things of the heart. In Shaw's mythology at least, she was all strength, a source of cold, remote power, the begetter of tragic enchantment. He was the beggar at the door she could not open. Her influence on him was certainly profound, finding expression in his odd relationships with women, in particular in his attempts throughout the 1880s and 1890s to recreate the sort of *ménage a trois* his mother had established for herself in the Dublin home of his childhood with her drunken husband and her musical mentor, George John Vandeleur Lee.[3] Some glimpses of the odd nature of Shaw's difficult relationship with his mother were revealed in a long letter he wrote to Gilbert Murray in March 1911, which contained the confession:

> I very seldom dream of my mother; but when I do, she is my wife as well as my mother. When this first occurred to me (well on in my life), what surprised me when I awoke was that the notion of incest had not entered into the dream: I had taken it as a matter of course that the maternal function included the wifely one; and so did she. What is more, the sexual relation acquired all the innocence of the filial one, and the filial one all the completeness of the sexual one.
>
> (Shaw 1985b: 17)

In the light of this, something could be made of the fact that Mrs Patterson, Shaw's seductress, was his mother's best friend. But it is not our purpose here to explore at length the implications of Shaw's relationship with his mother, nor with any other woman. What matters is that we bear these complicating personal factors in mind when discussing Shaw's views on sexual equality, assuming in this instance that the connection between private experience and public utterance is especially intense. Shaw will insist on having the last word. Putting a brave face and a convenient gloss on the matter, he informed Ellen Terry in 1897 he was 'fond of women (or one in a thousand, say)', but added:

> but I am in earnest about quite other things. To most women one man and one lifetime make a world. I require whole populations and historical epochs to engage my interests seriously and make the writing machine (for that is what GBS is) work at full speed and pressure: love is only diversion and recreation to me.
>
> (St John 1931: 232)

A PERSON EXACTLY LIKE MYSELF

I do not regard women as animals of another species. I have no difficulty, as a playwright, in making female *dramatis personae* as easily as male ones: and I conclude that I could not do this if I had not a first-hand knowledge of both, being my mother's son as much as my father's. The sexes wear different boots and bonnets, not different souls.

(Shaw 1920b: 445)

Statements of this kind support the view that Shaw's reflections on women were based on an androgynous principle. When the actress Margaret Halston asked him to ghost write a short speech for her on 'The Women in Shaw's Plays', he revealed his secret:

> There are no women in Bernard Shaw's plays. Dont think that I mean they are untrue to life. I mean exactly the contrary. For I will tell you another secret. There are no women in the real world. Believe me, ladies and gentlemen, woman, of whom we hear so much is a stage invention, and, to me at least, a very tiresome one.
>
> (Shaw 1985b: 63)

Miss Halston was prompted to say that Shaw once told her 'that the reason the women in his plays were so uncommonly good is that he always assumes that a woman is just like a man'. Men, he admitted teasingly, were 'slightly more hysterical' than women, but this he attributed to their 'being coddled by women from their childhood' (Shaw 1985b: 64).

Shaw's radical feminist view was that human nature is neither exclusively masculine or feminine, but a mixture of the two, with the perceived attributes of womanliness and manliness owing more to the pressures of environment and convention than to any natural, deep-seated traits of personality. He had always assumed, Shaw said in a speech in 1927, that a 'woman is a person exactly like myself' (Shaw 1962b: 174).

This is not to suggest that the enchanted Shaw ever advocated a denial of femininity as such. As Watson points out, his 'belief in the androgynous nature of personality is by no means a plea for the masculine woman' (Watson 1964: 22). The vogue, current in the late nineteenth century and beyond, of women copying masculine attire and such vile habits as smoking never appealed to him. Woman's desire to beat man at his own absurd game was the path to true enslavement. 'Masculine affectations were always a mistake', he said; far from seeking to deny femininity, he championed the introduction of feminine qualities and experiences into every sphere of human life. What women should do at the start of the process of emancipation 'was not to repudiate their femininity, but to assert its social value; not to ape masculinity, but to demonstrate its insufficiency' (Shaw 1920b: 444). Putting aside the habits of rhetorical exaggeration for a moment, he was to admit that women were 'almost exactly' like men (Shaw 1928b: 101).

Bearing such qualifications in mind, it can be said that, on the constructive side, the defining features of his radical feminism were the substitution of equality for hierarchy together with an emphasis on similarity instead of difference. On the critical side, its main feature was the desire to undermine the Victorian ideal of the self-sacrificing 'womanly woman'. Basic to Shaw's radical feminism was the argument for freedom predicated on the principle of happiness. That happiness was not to be seen as an end in itself was especially clear in this context; its achievement would be accompanied by dignity and self-respect for the individual woman and, together, these attributes would transform family relationships and contribute to the making of a new society. The first step in the drama of emancipation, which had as its conclusion the creation of the new woman, was the stripping away of the invisible bonds of patriarchal illusion which held the women of the Victorian age in thrall.

My Dear Dorothea

Shaw's first foray into the field was in the 1878 *My Dear Dorothea* (Shaw 1956) where, as noted in Chapter 1, the young outsider set out to explain to a five-year-old girl the importance of selfishness and individuality. 'Let your rule of conduct always be to do whatever is best for yourself', he advised Dorothea, 'Be as selfish as you can'. Her most valuable possession was her individuality, he said, which she should cultivate by learning how to think for herself; and the quality she should especially strive to teach herself was that of self-control.

According to its sub-title, the essay purported to offer 'A Practical System of Moral Education for Females Embodied in a Letter to a Young Person of that Sex'. Whether Shaw thought that women were especially in need of enlightenment in these matters was not clear at this stage. Watson suggests that the choice of subject was part of a deliberate strategy on the part of the moral revolutionary, for 'in addressing the Victorian little girl, Shaw was approaching society through the being who stood at the bottom of a hierarchy of dominations' (Watson 1964: 41). Not quite: Dorothea arrived in Shaw's imagination complete with nurse and governess. None the less, as it is domination of mind and soul that is at issue here, the thesis that Shaw was framing his moral argument in relation to the most disadvantaged members of society has its point.

From another perspective, the essay, cast as it was in the form of a parody of the traditional Victorian tract on propriety and etiquette, was a vehicle through which Shaw expressed the basic tenets of his radicalism. In choosing to address a little girl he was imitating such moral tracts as George Augustus Sola's *Lady Chesterfield's Letters to Her Daughter*, thus establishing the trend in his work of setting a radical message in a conventional form (Holroyd 1988: 72). What is clear is that though 'Females' were its subject, the essay did not imply that men and women require different systems of moral education. Such rules of conduct as 'Hypocrisy is just like selfishness. It is only bad when it is improperly used' were precisely those which guided Shaw's own guarded affairs with the world.

Encapsulated in the essay were the many aspects of Shaw's family relationships. On the one hand there was the sad assumption that Dorothea's mother thinks of her 'only as a troublesome and inquisitive little creature', followed by the advice that the girl 'must be particularly careful not to form any warm affection' for such a parent: 'If you have any griefs, do not tell her of them . . . it is far better to bear sorrow in silence' (Shaw 1956: 18). In a more positive vein, the women of Shaw's family were in some respects prototypes of the new woman. During his impecunious youth in London his mother gave music lessons and his sister, Lucy, took up a career on the stage, working for Shaw's living instead of preaching that it was his duty to work for theirs. Consistent with the radical gospel of Shelley, Shaw's mentor at this time, their choice was not an expression of self-sacrifice, but an assertion of indomitable self- sufficiency. That, too, was the gospel according to *My Dear Dorothea*.

The Ibsen connection

The essence of Shaw's radical feminism is to be found in the chapter on 'the womanly woman' from *The Quintessence of Ibsenism*. It was for many reasons, the obvious context for such a doctrinal statement on sexual equality. In the late 1880s Ibsen was associated in the public mind with the cause of female emancipation, added to which, Shaw's association with Ibsenism and his estimation of its merits were especially strong. His diary shows that during the mid-1880s, when his lifelong beliefs on sexual politics were being formed, he was forever dropping round to see Edward Aveling and, more particularly, his common-law wife, Eleanor Marx, to discuss the marriage question. High on the agenda too was the first private reading of *A Doll's House* in England, which the Avelings were organizing and in which Shaw appeared in the role of Krogstad. Coincidentally, Eleanor's father, Karl Marx, was the only writer, in this period at least, to rival Ibsen in terms of the impact he made on Shaw. Marx challenges class respectability on economic grounds, whereas Ibsen challenges us as individuals on human grounds, Shaw noted on a lecture card, suggesting that these two were the complementary giants of moral revolution (Shaw Papers: BM 50743).[4]

In the dozen years or so that elapsed between *My Dear Dorothea* and *Quintessence* Shaw had embraced socialism as an economic doctrine and assumed the role of moral revolutionary. Ibsen was fundamental to the latter. In particular, Shaw's encounter with *A Doll's House* was crucial to the way he formulated woman's part in his dramatic argument for moral reform. What was only implicit or half-realized in the early essays and novels was now fully articulated, and in a form which set the argument for the emancipation of woman at the centre of the argument for the emancipation of humanity generally. In *Quintessence* women were sent to the frontline in the struggle for moral liberation, the order having been signed by the generalissimo, Henrik Ibsen.

The first English production of *A Doll's House* cast Shaw's friend, Janet Achurch, in the role of Nora. Shaw rejoiced in her performance and in the controversy that surrounded the play as a whole. His views on its importance were summed up in a review of its second English production at the Globe Theatre in 1897, where he said:

Nora's revolt is the end of a chapter of human history. The slam of the door behind her is more momentous than the 'cannon of Waterloo or Sedan', because when she comes back, it will not be to the old home; for when the patriarch no longer rules, and the 'breadwinner' acknowledges his dependence, there is an end of the old order; and an institution upon which so much human affection and suffering have been lavished, and about which so much experience of the holiest right and bitterest wrong has gathered, cannot fall without moving even its destroyers, much more those who believe that its extirpation is a mortal wound to society.

(Shaw 1932o: 131)

After Nora men had either to treat women as human beings like themselves, or else live without them; they must recognize that 'mankind is male and female, like other kinds, and that the inequality of the sexes is literally a cock and bull story' (Shaw 1932o: 130). All of which seemed quite straightforward. One problem was that relatively few people had heard of Ibsen, still less of Nora's revolt. Another was that Shaw was playing up the importance of the theatre in this respect. Perhaps it would be better to say that Nora's revolt was one incident foreshadowing the end of a chapter of human history, bearing in mind that some chapters can be tiresomely long.

In *Quintessence* Shaw maintained that the apparent dissimilarities between the sexes were the product of convention. He attacked too the traditional male idealization of women as paragons of virtue, as dutiful, self-sacrificing wives and daughters capable only of managing the immediate problems of domestic life. True to his vitalist doctrine he asserted: 'Only those who have helped themselves know how to help others, and to respect their right to help themselves'. Shaw explained that 'No man pretends that his soul finds its supreme satisfaction in self-sacrifice'; so why should women be made to suffer such delusion (Shaw 1932h: 33).

Only in free relationships can respect be found, he said, and this was out of the question in 'the legal marriage' of the day. Most marriages were for the gratification of the sexual appetite in its crudest form: 'This being so, it is not surprising that our society, being directly dominated by men, comes to regard woman, not as an end in herself like man, but solely as a means of ministering to his appetite'. This was tantamount to a denial of the wife's 'right to live', Shaw declared; either she must rebel or end up loathing herself as the slave of a conceited fool (Shaw 1932h: 36).

Few in fact rebel, Shaw admitted, because they have not the means to do so. And few women loath themselves. Instead they regain self-respect through motherhood, in which capacity, Shaw said, the woman's 'use and importance to the community compare favourably with those of most men in business' (Shaw 1932h: 38). In this way, women reinforce the ideal of marriage, the reality of which revolts them; they settle down to a narrow life of domestic management and child care which, in turn, reinforces the illusion of woman's peculiar fitness for that restricted sphere. Shaw moved on to the attack:

> If we have come to think that the nursery and the kitchen are the natural spheres of a woman, we have done so exactly as English children come to think that a cage is the natural sphere of a parrot: because they have never seen one anywhere else. No doubt there are Philistine parrots who agree with their owners that it is better to be in a cage than out, so long as there is plenty of hempseed and Indian corn there.... Still, the only parrot a free-souled person can sympathize with is the one that insists on being let out as the first condition of making itself agreeable.
>
> (Shaw 1932h: 39)

Such a bird may be selfish perhaps, putting its own gratification 'before that of the family which is so fond of it'; but, in its selfish insistence on happiness, there lies its only hope of self-respect and the respect of others. Shaw's argument was that woman was the slave of duty and she must repudiate it 'altogether'. He saw in this repudiation the gateway to a new kind of existence for men and women alike: 'A whole basketful of ideals of the most sacred quality will be smashed by the achievement of equality for men and women', he predicted (Shaw 1932h: 40). Out of the mutual recognition of our common humanity, a higher form of love, based as much on rational fellowship as on physical appetite, would develop. Family relations would change as a new freedom entered the marriage institution.

What is clear is that the cause of radical feminism was at the root of Shaw's vision of moral transformation. Indeed, as early as 1885 he said in an article on the future of marriage that equality between the sexes was an essential component of socialism itself (Shaw Papers: BM 50693). It is also clear that women, young middle-class women especially, were the infantry in Shaw's long revolution in conduct and morality. He explained why in the preface to *Plays Unpleasant* (1898): 'In the middle classes themselves the revolt of a single clever daughter ... and her insistence on qualifying herself for an independent working life, humanizes her whole family in an astonishingly short time' (Shaw 1931h: xvi).

Portraits from the early plays

Through work of this kind, in *Quintessence* and beyond, Shaw claimed his place in the vanguard of progressive opinion on sexual equality at the turn of the century. He was the quintessential apostle of rebellion, delivering his message of hope and liberation to the women of the nation.

None the less, if his message was one of hope, he at no time suggested that emancipation would be gained easily. As a radical diagnosis of the problems facing women in the patriarchal order Shaw's work had much to commend it. Considered as a strategy of rebellion, on the other hand, its value was less clear-cut. He had indicated in *Quintessence* that rebellion was not a political option for the majority of women under existing economic arrangements. Only a few women with special talents could afford to defy social convention, the rest had to make their compromise and survive behind their wall of illusion as best they could.

The portraits of women in Shaw's early plays often expressed the complications involved in the process of emancipation. Many of his female characters were highly conventional in their outlook, operating, like the proletariat, as the last bastions of outmoded ideals. One example from the early plays is Blanche Sartorius from *Widowers' Houses* (Shaw 1931h). While she is introduced as 'vital and energetic' in the stage notes, throughout the play these qualities are channelled into peevish hysterics. She is cruelly rude to her maid and, on learning that her wealth derives from the poverty of the slums, she responds with ruthless selfishness, stating she hates the poor: 'At least, I hate those dirty, drunken, disagreeable people who live like pigs', she declares. Her view is that 'If they must be provided for, let other people look after them'. Though her own family has only just risen from these ranks, she is indifferent to their fate: 'I don't want to know about them' (Shaw 1931h: 55). Blanche is both the ultimate defender of the rule of property and the perverse expositor of the Shavian doctrine of selfishness.

While Blanche is strong and clear-sighted in her way, Judith, the pretty minister's wife from *The Devil's Disciple* (1931k), is muddled and foolish. She understands none of the motives behind the actions of either her husband or Dick Dudgeon (with whom she falls in love). Unable to scratch beneath the surface of their statements, she judges both men by narrowly conventional standards of love, honour and duty. Judith even obliges the audience with a swoon.

The Philanderer (Shaw 1931h) also closes with a woman 'almost fainting'. That woman is Julia Craven, a character modelled on the seductress, Mrs Jenny Patterson. Set in the Ibsen Club and concerned mainly with the heartless philanderings of Charteris, Shaw's alter-ego in the piece, the play offers a range of insights, personal and doctrinal in kind, on the woman question. Through Julia, Shaw portrayed the womanly woman as huntress, using all her skills of calculated emotion and outrage in her pursuit of Charteris. She was every bit as vituperative and theatrically hysterical in her quest for her stage lover as the flouted Mrs Patterson was in her search for the elusive Shaw. Julia Craven, as her surname suggests, was an imposter in the Ibsen Club. She was incapable of conducting an honest and open relationship with men or women; she was the perfect manipulator of the established system, earning high praise from the manly man, Cuthbertson: 'A splendid fine creature: every inch a woman. No Ibsenism about her!' (Shaw 1931h: 95).

Grace Tranfield, the new woman of the play and Julia's rival, is a far more sympathetic character. At the outset she declares, 'No woman is the property of a man. A woman belongs to herself and to nobody else'. Subsequently she lectures Julia on her deplorable behaviour and informs Charteris at the close that nothing would induce her to marry him; 'we shall remain very good friends', she says, and sits down with perfect composure.

With respect to the issue of femininity, Shaw notes that Grace dresses without the slightest regard for fashion, 'though by no means without a careful concern for personal elegance' (Shaw 1931h: 107). Immediately following that description, however, the play hints at the tendency of the new woman to imitate male language and habits. As Grace enters the Ibsen Club, the following exchange takes place:

> Sylvia: (*running to her*) Here you are at last, Tranfield, old girl. I've been waiting for you this last hour. I'm starving.
> Grace: All right, dear. (*To Charteris*) Did you get my letter?
> Charteris: Yes. I wish you wouldn't write on those confounded blue letter-cards.
> Sylvia: (*to Grace*) Shall I go down first, and secure a table?
> Charteris: (*taking the reply out of Grace's mouth*) Do, old boy.

Such exchanges suggest that, in Shaw's view, the mimicking of male habits was an inevitable, if not welcome development in the struggle for emancipation from the mythology of the womanly woman. Even Vivie Warren of *Mrs Warren's Profession*, perhaps the most sympathetic of the new women portrayed in the plays of this period, takes up smoking which is described ironically as a 'nasty womanly habit'. After discovering that her wealth is based on prostitution, she turns obsessively to work as a means of salvation; we are left at the close with a brave but rather lonely and shallow young woman who prefers the company of the abstractions found in account books to the complexities found in human character.

Similar issues were canvassed in *You Never Can Tell*. There the character Mrs Clandon is introduced as a veteran of the old guard of the women's rights movement of the 1860s, which had for its Bible John Stuart Mill's treatise on *The Subjection of Women*. Shaw notes 'She has never made herself ugly or ridiculous by affecting masculine waistcoats, collars, and watch-chains, like some other old Comrades who had more aggressiveness than taste ...'; instead she dresses in a businesslike way, ruling out all attempt at 'sex attraction'. The portrait is not uncritical, however. We are told that Mrs Clandon 'feels strongly about social questions and principles, not about persons' (Shaw 1931g: 201–2). Moreover, the play itself shows how her attempt to force a rationalist system of education on her formidable and passionate daughter, Gloria, stifled the girl's true nature and instincts. Mrs Clandon is herself entrapped in the Victorian cult of reason and science and, to this extent, she presents a male-dominated agenda of liberation.

Responding to such portraits, Constance Barnicoat, writing in the *Fortnightly Review* in 1906, declared: 'If women as a sex are as Mr Shaw depicts them, taking the majority of his women characters, especially the early ones, then it is good-bye, "for always and always and always", to any real improvement in our position as a sex' (Barnicoat 1906: 519).

The odd fact is that, while Shaw was busy writing up the case for the new woman in his polemical work in the 1890s, the portraits of committed feminists found in the plays of that period were tinged with mockery and distaste. Better treated were those women of independent spirit, lacking ideological commitment maybe, yet determined to prove themselves by doing real work in the world. In the novels of his youth Shaw was fond of looking to the performing arts for prototypes of such women, with examples including Susanna Connolly from *The Irrational Knot* and Aurelia Szczymplica and Madge Brailsford from *Love Among the Artists.* Their spokeswoman from the plays was Lina Szczepenowska, the adventuress from *Misalliance* who literally drops out of the sky to enchant every male in the cast. Disgusted by their advances, she complains, 'I am an honest woman: I earn my living. I am a free woman: I live in my own house. I am a woman of the world . . . I am all that a woman ought to be' (Shaw 1932i: 196).

In the context of Shaw's drama, such especially gifted or spirited women were not representative of their sex in any strict sense: their way would not necessarily suit others. The moral of the plays seems to be that the ordinary women must travel a hard course, full of cul-de-sacs, backtracking and backsliding, where small victories may be matched by grand defeats: for them, the only rule of emancipation is that there is no golden rule; the only method will be that of trial and error.

STRATEGIC OPTIONS

With respect to Shaw's radical feminism there developed a variety of strategic options. Early on he seemed to advocate the abolition of marriage and the family. In an article in the *Practical Socialist* in 1886, for example, he noted his preference for 'organized or collective training for the young' (Shaw 1886b: 175). There was much bitterness in his critique of the family. His 1884 Fabian *Manifesto* declared 'That the State should compete with private individuals – especially with parents – in providing happy homes for children, so that every child may have a refuge from the tyranny or neglect of its natural custodians'; 'Let the family be rooted out of civilization! Let the human race be brought up in institutions!' announced the father from the 1910 *Misalliance*. Comments of this kind suggest Shaw's connections, personal and intellectual, with such sexual radicals as Edward Carpenter and Havelock Ellis, the eager apostles of free love and the bitter critics of family ties.[5] As already noted, another feature of Shaw's work in this period was the association of the cause of sexual equality with socialism itself. That was made clear in a paper on 'The Future of Marriage' from 1885 upon which, incidentally, Eleanor Marx made some constructive comments before Shaw presented it to William Morris for publication in the Socialist League's *The*

Commonweal.[6] There Shaw predicated that, 'when Socialism is realized, men, in spite of their professions, will probably try to exclude women, directly or indirectly, from perfect equality with their former masters'. Shaw added this warning, 'If they succeed, their success will be the failure of Socialism' (Shaw Papers: BM 50693).

The problem for the Fabian agitator and labour movement tactician was that such issues were hardly uppermost in the minds of the ultra-respectable rank-and-file: the last thing they wanted was to have the argument for an eight-hour day confused with supposedly evil ravings about free love. Characteristically, the Fabians tried to avoid such difficulties by denying their relevance to social democracy; the Fabian Society had no distinctive opinion on the marriage question, Shaw reported in Tract 70 in 1896. When H.G. Wells led his rigorous campaign against the policy, by word and deed, Shaw, in an explosive exchange between himself and the troublemaker in the February 1907 number of *Fabian News*, hastened to assure the confused members that the matter was 'not directly Fabian business, as the Fabian Society is not committed to any special views on the marriage question and remains, as far as that question is concerned, as open to the strictest Roman Catholic as it is to the most conscientiously polygamous Mohammedan' (Shaw 1907b: 22). A cautious approach was also adopted in *The Guide*. The chapter on 'socialism and marriage' opens with the statement, 'When promising new liberties, Socialists are apt to forget that people object even more strongly to new liberties than to new laws' (Shaw 1949a: 406). With this in mind, Shaw noted that 'marriage institutions are not a part of Socialism', thus contradicting his earlier stance. The most he was prepared to admit in 1928 was that 'Socialism must have a tremendous effect on marriage and the family' (Shaw 1949a: 406).

The views Shaw expressed on sexual relationships, here as elsewhere, can be characterized loosely as those of a Fabian feminist, having as their chief concern the reform and not the abolition of marriage and the family. Shaw had never overstated the case for sexual radicalism in a practical sense. In the 1885 paper, for instance, he had warned that free love had the same disadvantages for women as free contract had for workers; 'Woman may profit by the experience of man to the extent of feeling assured that whilst she remains virtually a slave she had better be a chattel slave, as wives are now, than a wage-slave, as 'free-labour' is now' (Shaw Papers: BM 50693). Considerations of this kind informed the 1908 preface to *Getting Married* where he concluded that 'Marriage remains practically inevitable'. There was no question of abolishing marriage, he said, but there was 'a very pressing question of improving its conditions' (Shaw 1932d: 182). Shaw went on to set out the case for rational divorce laws which would protect the welfare of adults and children alike.

The approach can be viewed as that of a responsible social reformer who preferred sober instruction to wild experimentation in these vital matters. Of course elements of timid conventionalism have been noted too. The near obsessive pre-occupation of the plays with marriage, as narrative subject and dénouement, is undeniable, as is the soundness of Rebecca West's view that none of Shaw's characters 'infringes the conventions in practice' (Marcus 1983: 20).

There can be no doubt that Shaw had personally infringed some of those conventions in his dangerous liaisons with married and unmarried women in the 1880s and 1890s. His marriage in 1898 changed that. Then the conventions, even the sacredness of marriage could be invoked when fending off the infatuated Erica Cotterill (Shaw 1972: 772). In any event, Shaw never encouraged personal scandal.[7] Once he admitted that 'the heroic impudence which is the quality most needed just now to ignore the taboos is beyond my strength' (Shaw 1908: 121). More usually he protested that sex scandals would not be tolerated in the largely puritanical labour movement, or else he explained, as in the preface to *Overruled*, that

> the friction set up between the individual and the community by the expression of unusual views of any sort is quite enough hindrance to the heretic without being complicated by personal scandals.
>
> (Shaw 1931a: 153)

From these observations it can be seen that at a practical, strategic level Shaw's radical feminist principles tended to be translated into reformist policies.

SOCIALIST FEMINISM

The distinctly socialist dimension to Shaw's reflections on sexual equality can be seen in his consistent argument for economic independence for women. He dealt directly with the economic plight of women in a capitalist society, working-class women in particular, in a Fabian lecture on the theme of 'Socialism and Human Nature' which he delivered in September 1890, that is, around the time he was writing *Quintessence*. The contrast he drew was between a 'great London landlord' earning a thousand a day perhaps for doing nothing and a labourer who could not hope to earn that much in fifty years, but who 'is yet three times as rich as women of his own class who work sixteen hours a day'. Women of this class were indeed at the bottom of a hierarchy of dominations; they owned nothing and were regarded as mere objects. Even their femininity was exploited. Shaw suggested that sexism was endemic in capitalism, noting that while we pretend to abhor lust:

> We then offer a pretty woman a position either behind the refreshment bar at a railway station for fourteen hours a day, or in some other place where her good looks will attract custom and make profit for us, assuring her at the same time that it would be the lowest infamy for her to use her good looks to make profits for herself. As to the man who would live

on her earnings in the event of her taking such a step, no words can express our loathing for him, though if he owned the refreshment bar or was a manufacturer employing women at wages which they could not live on without resorting to prostitution occasionally to bring them up to bare subsistence level, he would be a highly respected member of society.

(Shaw 1971: 98)

Putting the powerful engine of his rhetoric into overdrive, Shaw went on to spell out the deeper contrast brought about by capitalist economic arrangements. The contrast was not between rich and poor, but between poor women, on one side, and men of all classes, on the other:

on the one hand a female proletariat so ill paid and contemptuously treated that it matters little to them whether they sell themselves for one purpose to a brutal employer or for another to a drunken libertine, and on the other the whole male sex, headed by a contingent of gentlemen with a growing reluctance to marry before they are thirty-five, and seldom without a sovereign or two to spare.

(Shaw 1971: 99)

Under these conditions there was no hope for virtue among men or women, only the most sordid kind of interdependence would prevail. Rounding on the smug apostles of competitive scoundrelism, Shaw informed them that 'the one condition for giving lust its very widest scope is the reduction of women to two or three farthings an hour for the dullest sorts of drudgery'. In the absence of proper provision for the unemployed and a minimum wage, the idea that the path to emancipation was through an independent working life was but a bad joke.

In the 1890 lecture the particular concern was to warn the Fabians of the dangers involved in too close an association with the respectable, middle-class road to socialism. The plight of the ordinary middle-class woman, young or old, was not therefore high on the agenda. Elsewhere, however, he was critical of the cheap wages offered in the professions open to women – in teaching especially, but also in clerking and secretarial work. In this respect, cheap labour was the consistent theme, whether in relation to the factory or the office girl: 'the labor market is infested with subsidized wives and daughters willing to work for pocket money on which no independent solitary woman or widow can possible subsist', Shaw argued in *The Guide* (Shaw 1982: 221). Thus, under capitalism, women of all classes are 'the slave of a slave, which is the worst sort of slavery' (Shaw 1982: 219). At one level marriage was a compulsory profession. At another, prostitution was 'practically compulsory', the alternative being starvation (Shaw 1982: 223). The pretty factory girl was not to be admonished, Shaw said, if she took what 'district visitors' called 'the wages of sin rather than the wages of sweated labor', for the penalty of virtue was starvation and 'the reward of vice immediate relief' (Shaw 1982: 221).

Shaw's general point was that between them the search for financial security and the commercial exploitation of sex under capitalism tend to bring a woman's life down to the level of prostitution. The association of marriage with prostitution had a long history in Shaw's work, pre-dating even his conversion to socialism and reaching at least as far back as *The Irrational Knot* (1880). In the novel the struggling female writer, Neely McQuinch, speaks indignantly of a Parliamentary debate on marriage which she describes as 'the true profession of women'; she says, too, that in her view the bargain of marriage differs not a bit from prostitution (Shaw 1931d: 95).

Subsequently the argument was strengthened through Shaw's connection with the Avelings. At the height of their friendship with the Irish sprite, the couple were at work on a review of August Babel's influential *Women in the Past, Present and Future*. As Norbert Greiner has shown, Shaw has much in common with Babel, including the key observation that prostitution is a purely economic phenomenon, together with the general association of marriage with prostitution under capitalist conditions (Greiner 1977: 90). Marriage and prostitution were in this respect the two sides of the same coin. Far from prostitution being restricted to proletarian women, it was rather the general condition of the whole sex. The difference between marriage and prostitution, Shaw said in the preface to *Getting Married*, was the same as that 'between Trade Unionism and unorganized casual labour; a huge difference, no doubt, as to order and comfort, but not a difference in kind' (Shaw 1932d: 220). Mrs Warren, speaking on behalf of her profession and her sex, said that in polite society marriage is but a quest for security in which a woman's sex appeal is her only asset and that she must take her body to the market-place as the workman takes his labour. Summing up his views in *The Guide*, Shaw asserted: 'In short, Capitalism acts on women as a continual bribe to enter into sex relations for money, whether in or out of marriage' (Shaw 1982: 223).

CRITICAL ASSESSMENT

A number of criticisms have been levelled against Shaw's socialist feminism. It has been said, for example, that his analysis was rooted in the nineteenth century, and that in *The Guide* in particular he ignored contemporary developments, good or bad, in the condition of women. Margaret Walters has argued that Shaw neither recognized the contribution women had made to the war effort between 1914 and 1918, nor did he consider the way they had been 'pushed back, often reluctantly, into domestic life in the twenties' (Shaw 1982: xxxix). The double burden of housework and work outside the home, lack of training and union indifference to women, all of which combine to trap them in low paid work, were also ignored in *The Guide*. Further, when Shaw did try to account for the contemporary developments in the condition of women, his analysis often overshot the mark. For example, in a 1914 essay on 'the redistribution of income' he suggested that women had achieved a new position in the business world, acting as managers, sitting on committees and boards and generally running busy offices instead of being confined to routine work (Shaw 1971: 230).

Mrs Warren's Profession (1894) has also drawn fire. Germaine Greer has said that in concentrating on the affairs of a wealthy madam of a continental brothel the play ignored all but the tiniest minority of successful prostitutes; 'Shaw's argument seems to be that all working-class girls are whores who can be. The rest are the plain losers' (Greer 1977: 163). Central to Mrs Warren's outlook is the view that 'the only way for a woman to provide for herself decently is for her to be good to some man that can afford to be good to her', which does not seem to advance the socialist case very far (Shaw 1931h: 212). The argument was designed of course to dramatize the consequences of woman's economic dependence on man. That Shaw was aware of the brutalized existence of the ordinary prostitute was made clear in a letter he wrote in 1894 to the *Pall Mall Gazette*. There he said that any analysis of a prostitute's condition of life must include consideration of such factors as how much she must pay for the 'services of some man to protect her from violent and drunken visitors' as well as 'her relations with the police'. The choice facing many working-class girls was stark indeed, Shaw suggested; 'Marriage to these girls means living indecently in one room with a man legally licensed to abuse them as no frequenter of the Empire [Theatre] dare abuse a prostitute, and that, too, without her consent, and possibly in the presence of her children' (Shaw 1985a: 30–4).

Mrs Warren's Profession does make clear the association between capitalism, poverty and prostitution and, in presenting that association in a vivid, dramatic context, it succeeded in bringing it before a wider audience than such polemical works as Babel's could hope to reach. More specifically, although the play only dealt with a minority of prostitutes, it still highlighted the issue of the White Slave Trade of the period in which young British girls were shipped out to work in the legalized brothels on the continent. The hostility the play engendered in Establishment circles was expressed in the Lord Chamberlain's decision to ban it as 'immoral and otherwise improper for the stage'.

Shaw appreciated the subtle ways in which capitalism manipulates female sexuality. He recognized, too, the importance of organizing women in trade unions, as well as the difficulties involved. In 1907, in response to a letter from his old flame Florence Farr, he even considered the possibility of a trade union for prostitutes. He concluded, however, that the project was 'pretty utopian', especially when it was so hard to get women to join unions in socially tolerated occupations; Shaw explained 'It is always difficult to get women into a trade union, because none of them regard their occupation as permanent: they all intend to stop it and get married next month at latest' (Shaw 1972: 715).

The sexual dimension to Shaw's socialist politics was established in the novel *An Unsocial Socialist*. There the progress of the rebellious hero, Trefusis, is considered largely in terms of his interaction with the predominantly female cast of characters, notably his conventionally loving wife, Henrietta, the vivacious schoolgirl, Agatha Wylie, and her friends, June and Gertrude. Trefusis formulated the importance of women to the socialist cause thus:

> ... we Socialists need to study the romantic side of our movement to interest women in it. If you want to make a cause grow, instruct every woman you meet in it. She is or will one day be a wife, and will contradict her husband with scraps of your argument. A squabble will follow. The son will listen, and will be set thinking if he is capable of thought. And so the mind of the people gets leavened.
>
> (Shaw 1932a: 215)

According to this condescending formulation, romantic women, with their scraps of half-digested knowledge, were the means by which men would be brought to socialism. Seemingly, then, the superior brains of men were the reservoirs and the unstoppable mouths of women the conduits of socialist enlightenment. *The Guide* closes with the statement, 'By such ladies and their sons can the human race be saved, and not otherwise' (Shaw 1949a: 497). Why not their daughters? asked Lady Rhondda who commented that scarcely a woman in Shaw's plays seems to feel any comradeship with other women (Lady Rhondda 1930b: 332). She went on to remark that Shaw's female characters 'never want to talk to anything but men. When he thinks of a mother he almost instinctively thinks of her solely in relation to her sons' (Lady Rhondda 1930e: 437). Similarly, when Eve, in Part I of *Back to Methuselah*, expressed her dream of better things, it was in terms of 'My sons and my sons' sons'. With that in mind, it is worth noting that, whilst Shaw worked alongside women on equal terms as a Fabian and Vestryman, unlike the Avelings and Babel, he never championed a distinctly women's arm to the socialist movement. It is worth noting, too, the tendency in his work, dramatic or otherwise, to look upon men as the intellectually dominant partner in the relationship between the sexes. It can be argued that, in this respect at least, the relationship between the mentor, Henry Higgins, and his pupil, Eliza, in *Pygmalion* has a more general application than is usually supposed.

For all that, Shaw is an important socialist feminist and *The Guide* remains a landmark text in this context. Uniquely for its day it dealt with the peculiar economic standing of women in an original and forthright way, using the doctrine of equality of income to illustrate the value of women's contribution to the household economy and beyond. It is an innovative socialist document which succeeds in demonstrating the dignity and worth of woman's work.

THE COMPLEXITIES OF CLASS

Few, if any, of the plays Shaw wrote after the early 1890s touched directly on the theme of socialist feminism, at least in an explicit or concerted way. This has been explained in terms of Shaw's determination to capture a wider audience for his plays. Rarer still were depictions of working-class women in his drama; the voices of the countless women in England's army of industrial and rural workers were silent. One explanation for the omission is that such women were beyond Shaw's experience of life.

However, working women (in the narrower sense of the term) were not neglected altogether. Among their middle-class representatives was Vivie Warren, of course, though she was only about to embark on her working career at the close of the play; there was also Miss Proserpine Garnett, the pert and proper typist from *Candida* who seemed inclined to carry her affection for her employer, the Reverend James Morell, to the point of infatuation, and, from *Geneva*, the self-satisfied scholarship girl Begonia Brown, complete with her suburban accent and outlook which made her eminently unsuited to her post as secretary to the Committee for Intellectual Co-operation.

None of these were as endearing or formidable as the female representatives of the parasitic proletariat, in particular the deliciously ugly and unruly charwoman, Emmy, from *The Doctor's Dilemma* and her irrepressible counterpart in *Press Cuttings*, Mrs Farrell, who lectures General Mitchener of the War Office on the vital economy of motherhood.

More formidable still were Shaw's aristocratic women, for example Lady Cicely Waynflete from *Captain Brassbound's Conversion* (Shaw 1931k) who manages everyone in sight including the piratical captain and Sheikh Sidi el Assif, both of whom attempt to claim her for their own. Another example is Lady Britomart from *Major Barbara* who, like Lady Cicely, displays that air of authority natural to her station in life as she manages her family's affairs with impeccable skill. Often these aristocrats were free from the pettiness and snobbish illusions which tended to affect the women characters of straitened means. Occasionally they were the standard bearers of heroic unconventionality; Major Barbara herself was one instance of that tendency. A second was Lavinia from *Androcles and the Lion* (Shaw 1931a) who, having embraced the Christian faith in its profoundest sense, prepared to meet her fate in the Coliseum with the equanimity natural to a person of noble character. Lavinia is introduced as 'a good-looking resolute young woman, apparently of higher social standing than her fellow prisoners' (Shaw 1931a: 108). Whether it was beauty or resolution (or another unnamed quality) which served to indicate her noble lineage was not explained. Yet the remark does shed some light on the hold that certain deep-rooted conventions regarding the association between class and character had on Shaw.

With this in mind it can be said that, as a Fabian socialist with a special interest in those in the middle station in life, we might have expected Shaw to deal more fully and sympathetically with the social and economic experiences of middle-class women. In fact both the upwardly-mobile types such as Begonia Brown and the female 'skidders' tended to be rather dry and shallow, lacking the power of enchantment. A good example of Shaw's approach to the 'skidders' is to be found in *Pygmalion* in particular, in the contrast between Eliza and Clara Eynsford Hill, the sister of Eliza's future husband, Freddy. The Eynsford Hill's were essentially people of Shaw's own class, the shabby genteel folk of straitened means. They all lacked 'exchange value', to use Shaw's term (Shaw 1986b: 142). The mother, however, had a certain quiet dignity. Freddy had at least the charm of his devotion to Eliza to offset his useless absurdity. What of Clara? Along with Gunner from *Misalliace*, she was among the most heartfelt of Shaw's characters and one of the most painful to behold. Her want of social grace and understanding were revealed in the scene at Mrs Higgins's at-home in which Eliza utters her infamous expletive. Throughout the scene the pushy Clara interprets Eliza's comic low-life banter as evidence of the 'new small talk'. Pathetically equipped only with the gay bravado of genteel poverty she insists on imitating all that is up-to-date; as she is about to leave, therefore, Clara echoes Eliza's *faux pas* saying that Victorian prudery is 'such bloody nonsense!'

Shaw explained in the sequel to the play that Clara 'appeared to Higgins and his mother as a disagreeable and ridiculous person'. Even her mother looked upon her as a social failure; indeed she found it necessary to apologize for her daughter – 'We're so poor! and she gets so few parties, poor child! She doesn't quite know' (Shaw 1986b: 80). In the sequel Shaw, a little wickedly, tells us too of Clara's discovery of the novels of H.G. Wells and her subsequent transformation into a more or less useful person, still pushy, but free now of her former snobbery and illusion. As befits a 'new-born Wellsian' she takes a job in a furniture shop owned by a fellow admirer of the great man (Shaw 1986b: 142–4).

That sort of development of character was never to be the subject of Shaw's drama; for that purpose, the more colourful transformation of the flower girl was preferred. In the play, at least, the contrast between Clara and Eliza was profound. Eliza was poor and dirty when Higgins took her in, but she had pride, character and a sense of her own worth. She, too, was pushy, but in her it was rendered tolerable by innocence.

Largely through Eliza's father, Alfred Doolittle, the play operated as a critique of middle-class morality. Paradoxically, the sequel is largely a catalogue of how each of the characters, Doolittle among them, attained middle-class respectability. Eliza, being strong enough for two, married Freddy and, after some economic complications, she became a prosperous florist and greengrocer, a situation in life which allowed her to swank 'like anything' (Shaw 1986b: 147). By then, of course, the contrast with Clara was less than profound. None of that was of interest to Shaw the dramatist: for him to have brought the mundane experiences of such women on to the stage would have required a more radical break than he was prepared to admit with the conventional female stereotypes of the theatre.

RACE, PROGRESS AND THE MOTHER-WOMAN

From a feminist standpoint the most problematic of all the literary stereotypes found in Shaw's drama was that of the mother-woman, notably Ann Whitfield from *Man and Superman*. The theory that lay behind that stereotype was articulated in the *Epistle Dedicatory* to the play. It held that, contrary to convention, it is the woman who takes the initiative in the duel of sex; man is her unwitting prey. Contradicting the emphasis he put elsewhere on the forces of environemnt and convention, Shaw's explanation had to do with the division of biological functions between the sexes. It is the woman who is concerned with 'the serious business of sex', he said. What is more, as women break out of their Doll's House and assert themselves as individuals 'the enormous superiority' they enjoy as a result of 'woman's natural position in this matter is telling with greater and greater force' (Shaw 1931f: xiii). Shaw argued

> That the men, to protect themselves against a too aggressive prosecution of the women's business, have set up a feeble romantic convention that the initiative in sex business must always come from the man, is true; but the pretence is so shallow that even in the theatre, that last sanctuary of unreality, it imposes only on the inexperienced.
>
> (Shaw 1931f: xvii)

In their business dealings women are unscrupulous, Shaw said: no trick is too low, no web too intricate for the determined huntress as she ensnares the man most likely to father superior children. The broader point was that woman was in this respect the agent of the life force; her purpose was nature's purpose, her unscrupulousness was the product of her biologically-determined duty to ensure the welfare of the race: 'Women must marry because the race must perish without her travail'. Shaw equated the mother-woman's behaviour with that of the man of genius who is 'selected by Nature to carry on the work of building up an intellectual consciousness of her instinctive purpose'. He continued:

> I state the extreme case, of course; but what is true of the great man who incarnates the philosophic consciousness of Life and woman who incarnates its fecundity, is true in some degree of all geniuses and all women.
>
> (Shaw 1931f: xx)

Ann Whitfield was Shaw's Everywoman. Her pursuit and conquest of John Tanner, the play's supposed superman, was a model of its kind. No amount of clever talk, no plan of escape would suffice against her. She lied, cajoled and even pretended to faint in order to get her way. In desperation, Tanner called out, 'The Life Force. I am in the grip of the Life Force'. It was too late.

Moments later he had renounced 'the romantic possibilities of an unknown future, for the cares of a household and a family'. If Ann was more agreeable, Tanner's fate would not seem so bleak. As it is, his last testament – 'I am not a happy man' – would seem appropriate (Shaw 1931f: 161–6).

Feminists have abhorred the portrait of Ann and the attendant theory of the mother-woman which, among other things, seems to confirm the traditional view of man's superior capacity for abstract thought. Lady Rhondda said the mother-woman, as Shaw described her, 'was the product not of nature but of her environment'. As for Ann, 'She is a hypocrite, a sneak, a cad of the very first water' (Lady Rhondda 1930b: 334). Shaw's response was hardly calculated to placate his feminist critics; 'Ann is of course a cad; but it was not *qua* cad that I called her Everywoman, but as man huntress and slave of Nature' (Shaw 1988: 180).

The portrait had its positive side for Shaw. Thus, in *Man and Superman*, where his interest in eugenics was especially intense, he noted there was a political aspect to the sex question. He claimed in fact that the initiative in sex transactions 'is politically the most important of all the initiatives, because our political experiment of democracy, the last refuge of cheap misgovernment, will ruin us if our citizens are ill bred' (Shaw 1931f: xxii). The theory of the mother-woman can be seen, therefore, as one response to Shaw's despairing view of progress in this period. By equating woman's purpose with nature's purpose, Shaw uncovered at least one source of hope. He did not say that all women fitted neatly into the mother-woman mould, nor that women generally could not perform an infinite variety of tasks. None the less, the contribution most women would make to the life force's pursuit of progress would be the result of their own pursuit of the well-bred male.

The implication for Shaw's views on sex and marriage was that these matters were now cast into the eugenic equation. In *Man and Superman* he still considered the economic dimension to the marriage question, only now the emphasis was on the consequences of economic inequality for the welfare of the race. Observations of this kind were to lead Shaw down a number of unconventional paths. For example, he advised the 'immoral' statesman to cultivate a rational outlook on sex which would enable eugenic experiments to be undertaken irrespective of any love interest. Suggestions followed for permitting eugenically eligible individuals to procreate without having to suffer the inconveniences of marriage. In an address to the Eugenics Education Society in 1904,[8] he is reported to have said:

What we must fight for is freedom to breed the race without being hampered by the mass of irrelevant conditions implied by the institution of marriage . . . what we need is freedom for people who have never seen each other before and never intend to see one another again to produce children under certain definite public conditions, without loss of honour.

(Shaw 1904e: 74)

This was Shaw's way of combining the politics of virtue with a form of sexual radicalism.[9] He did not want to appear too outlandish. He claimed the arrangements he proposed were in fact more moral than the promiscuity of ordinary marriage, which is 'popular because it combines the maximum of temptation with the maximum of opportunity' (Shaw 1931: 214). Also, despite the rather threatening 'statist' aspects to his comments on eugenic experimentation, he assured his audience that the production of the superman did not 'involve the forcible coercion by the State of selected women to breed with selected men' (Shaw 1972: 509). Instead Shaw put his faith in the sex instincts of the mother-woman. At one point in the preface to *Getting Married* he suggested that the mother-woman might opt for a polygamous relationship on the grounds that she would naturally prefer 'a tenth share in a first-rate man' to 'a whole share in a tenth-rate man' (Shaw 1932d: 208). He argued, too, for the 'recognition of an absolute right to sexual experience', which, in the woman's case, may be taken to the point of childbearing:

> My own experience of discussing this question leads me to believe that the one point on which all women are in furious secret rebellion against the existing law is the saddling of the right to a child with the obligation to become the servant of a man.
>
> (Shaw 1932d: 206)

Shaw's advice to the immoral statesman was to disassociate the sex question from the subject of marriage and to look upon the former as a matter of practical race-welfare and not of ethics. The statesman Shaw said 'is bound to prefer one healthy illegitimate child to ten rickety legitimate ones, and one energetic and capable unmarried couple to a dozen inferior apathetic husbands and wives' (Shaw 1932d: 201). However, such advice was for the long term. When socialism secures economic independence for women marriage will fall into disuse, Shaw predicted tentatively (Shaw 1932d: 237). In the meantime the statesman must work for the reform of monogamous marriage, and for the endowment of motherhood which will place the work of a mother on the same footing as other work. The mother-woman, meanwhile, must deal with social institutions as she finds them. Writing in 1916 Shaw said he considered 'the status of a married woman as almost indispensable under existing circumstances to a woman's fullest possible freedom' (Shaw 1985b: 378).

What of birth control? How did it fit into Shaw's reflections on eugenics and the mother-woman. Rather awkwardly, is the short answer. On the one hand contraception represented another triumph for reason over nature and was in that sense conceptually compatible with his eugenic scheme.[10] On the other it fitted less neatly with that part of his work which he saw as belonging to 'the blessed reaction towards the cult of motherhood' (Shaw 1925: 850). His immediate concern was with the decline in the birth rate among the prudent middle classes where the use of birth control was most prevalent, as

SEXUAL EQUALITY

evidenced by personal experience and social statistics. The danger was that
the racial stock would be swamped by the 'reckless breeding' of the poor
(Shaw 1932d: 205). With that in mind Shaw, despite his personal regard for
Marie Stopes, was but a lukewarm supporter of the birth control movement
in the crucial years between 1918 and 1930. Also, whereas feminists have
welcomed contraception as contributing to the sexual liberation of women,
Shaw, like his fellow eugenicist, H.G. Wells, tended to emphasize national or
racial efficiency as against personal freedom and happiness in this context
(McLaren 1978: 254).

Shaw claimed that it was in *Man and Superman* that men were 'first warned
of woman's terrible strength and man's miserable weakness' (Shaw 1985a: 84).
Whether she would use her power for good or evil, in an enlightened or
reactionary way, would depend upon individual character and the forces of
circumstance. In *The Guide* Shaw suggested that women, 'even when they
are echoing male glory stuff', instinctively devote themselves to life's cause,
whereas the male still clings to the ideal of destructive heroism (Shaw 1949a:
439). Elsewhere he was less complimentary, speaking of the 'gratification that
war gives to the instinct of pugnacity and admiration of courage that are so
strong in women'. It was, he said, a natural survival from humanity's former
savagery when 'a woman's life and that of her children depended on the
courage and killing capacity of her mate' (Shaw 1962b: 283). When in 1902 he
posed the question, 'Should women stop war?', he answered simply that there
can be 'no feminine view of war', for on this, as on most other issues, 'women
think and feel exactly as men do' (Shaw 1902: 429). On balance, the conclusion
seems to be that the mother-woman shares the illusions of patriarchal society:
only in instinct does faint hope prevail.

DEMOCRACY FOR WOMEN

In 1903, the year Shaw published his views on the mother-woman, a
determined mother of four from Manchester, Mrs Emmaline Pankhurst,
founded the Women's Social and Political Union. While the title waited to be
coined, to all intent and purposes the suffragettes had arrived on the political
scene.

Shaw had always said that women should have the vote. In his Fabian
Manifesto of 1884 he had declared 'that the sexes should henceforth enjoy
equal political rights'. That was to remain his position throughout. The
alternative was to follow Prime Minister Asquith's view of things; as Shaw
explained in 1913, at the height of the women's war, Asquith seemed to place
his own mother 'on the footing of a rabbit' (Raeburn 1973: 221). Of course
the rabbit theory, which was tantamount to a denial of our common
humanity, was familiar enough. Shaw suggested it was implicit in the English
language itself, specifically in its lack of 'a word which includes men and
women'. He went on to say:

181

It just shows how little we realize men and women belong to the same species. No one denies that a stallion and a mare are both horses – they wear just the same kind of harness; but a woman is looked upon as an entirely different animal to a man. So everything – costume, coiffer, customs, political rights – everything is arranged as far as possible to accentuate the supposed difference between two human beings practically identical.

(Weintraub 1977: 238)

Shaw's view was that democracy for women was right both in principle and in terms of political efficiency. The latter was emphasized in Fabian Tract no. 93, *Women as Councillors* (1900). Its immediate concern was with the exclusion of women from the new metropolitan borough councils which replaced the vestries under the London Government Act, 1899. Shaw explained that as women had sat on the vestries since 1894, their subsequent exclusion was 'a withdrawal of an established right, and consequently a deliberate step backwards in political development'. That it was a step backwards in efficiency as well was illustrated with respect to the establishing and maintenance of public lavatory facilities for women. Shaw said that without the co-operation of women, as inspectors and councillors, these facilities would never be adequate and sanitary. It was a specific argument with general implications, which showed, *inter alia*, the variety of Shaw's work on sexual equality and the persistence of his interest in issues related to it.

When the suffragettes began their first major campaign in time for the 1906 general election, they might have expected Shaw's wholehearted support. In the event, his dealings with the militant suffragettes were mostly cautious and distanced by irony. When Mrs Shaw walked beside Mrs Pankhurst in the Great Hyde Park demonstration of 1908, Shaw raised his hat as she passed; but he refused to join her unless she consented to push him all the way in a Bath chair (Raeburn 1973: 74). When asked to speak on behalf of 'the cause' he refused invariably. His position on the matter was established back in the 1880s when he insisted that women should speak on their own behalf (Shaw 1965a: 204). In 1909 he explained to a Hungarian correspondent that, while his support for giving women the vote and enabling them to sit on all representative bodies was steadfast, he was convinced that the agitation must be undertaken by women themselves; 'Every time you ask a man to appear on your platform, you confirm the insufficiencies of women to plead their own cause'. Besides, he continued:

> many of the men who are most excited in their advocacy of the Feminist cause, are actuated by sentimental infatuation; and all of them without exception are suspected of it by the public. I strongly advise you to keep the movement altogether in the hands of women.

(Shaw 1972: 831)

Shaw's one platform appearance on behalf of 'the cause' was at the Queen's Hall, in a meeting held by the National Union of Women's Suffrage Societies on 26 March 1907, where he seconded a resolution that the meeting 'called upon the Government to introduce a Bill conferring the franchise upon women' (Shaw 1985b: 81). His speech was hardly the clarion call the audience probably expected. Central to it was the argument that the vote should be given to women to avoid the tragic waste of human talent which inevitably flows from the denial of political liberty; an analogy was made with the 'curse' of nationalism in Ireland. Shaw did say that social problems could only be solved with the help of women, but in this context his interest lay primarily with the minority of politically-able women. The average woman, like the average man, was hopelessly ignorant. Further, Shaw said he took a dim view of human nature:

> I quite grant that men and women are very little capable of governing either their own affairs or the affairs of a nation, and if I could find any superior class of beings to entrust the government to I would entrust the government to it.
>
> (Weintraub 1977: 249)

Having unveiled the illusions of democracy and declared the political ineptitude of the masses in *Man and Superman*, Shaw could not feign unbounded enthusiasm for 'the cause'. Far from being an end-in-itself, as it seemed to be for many of the suffragettes, the vote was but one rudimentary element of the politics of emancipation.

The coupled vote

Years later, in the 1945 preface to the minor play '*In Good King Charles's Golden Days*', Shaw said he had given great offence to the militants during the 'Suffragette revolt of 1913' by suggesting that, as a result of 'Feminine Mobocracy' (Shaw 1948: 224), the giving of the vote to women would actually have a negative influence on the representation of women on public bodies. Women would vote women out, he had predicted, and experience had proved the prediction right he now claimed. Shaw suggested, too, that he had presented the suffragettes with an alternative approach, namely, 'a constitutional amendment enacting that all representative bodies shall consist of women and men in equal numbers, whether elected or nominated or co-opted or registered or picked up in the street like a coroner's jury'. He elaborated:

> In the case of elected bodies the only way of effecting this is by the coupled vote. The representative unit must be not a man *or* a woman but a man *and* a woman. Every vote, to be valid, must be for a human pair, with the result that the elected body must consist of men and women in equal numbers.
>
> (Shaw 1946: 157)

The coupled vote was Shaw's one contribution to democratic theory. It represents an important suggestion on the vexed and, to Shaw's way of thinking, crucial issue of the political representation of the sexes. As he explained in the 1947 postscript to *Fabian Essays*, he operated on the assumption that equal representation was a political necessity as 'women are much more practical and less Party ridden, being trained managerially by housekeeping and childbearing' (Shaw 1948: 224). More generally, the merit of the coupled vote was that it would maximize the range of human experience which would be brought to bear upon social and political problems, thus hopefully facilitating better solutions and more sensible responses to these problems. Further, by counteracting the forces of mobocracy the coupled vote would promote the effective involvement of the politically-able women in public affairs; the assumption here was that nature's supply of the 5 per cent of born political thinkers and administrators was distributed more or less equally between the sexes (Shaw 1946: 159). Even if such an argument on its behalf is neither appealing nor compelling it remains the case that the coupled vote offers an interesting solution to the genuine problem of the unequal political representation of the sexes.

Shaw did indeed mention the idea of the coupled vote before the Great War, at least in an embryonic form. The first hint of it seems to arise in a letter he wrote in June 1914 to the puzzled suffragette, Ethel Smyth, who wondered why Shaw did not interest himself much in the cause. In reply he cautioned against concentrating on the vote, forecasting that its results would disappoint. What was wanted was 'a considerable proportion of women' on every public authority in the country, including the House of Parliament (Watson 1964: 194).

Whilst Barbara Bellow Watson suggests otherwise, Miss Smyth's very puzzlement would seem to confirm the view that Shaw's explanation of his tepid support for the Suffragettes was an isolated phenomenon (Watson 1964: 195). Even the leaders of the movement were not aware of it, it appears. When the proposal was first unveiled in public in Sylvia Pankhurst's *Women's Dreadnought* in 1916, the editor treated it as a new idea and put it under the heading of 'Bernard Shaw's strange suggestions'. After stating he was becoming convinced that elections are fatal to democracy, Shaw went on to say:

> I believe that what is wanted for women is an iron law that Parliament shall consist of a certain proportion of men and women; that there should be a list of qualified women; and that the M.P. s should be unselected, like jurors.

> (Shaw 1916: 547)

The strange suggestion surfaced again in a letter written in July 1933 to the former suffragette leader, Emmeline Pethick-Lawrence. However, while its formulation foreshadowed that in the 1945 preface, the precise proposal was for 'a proportion of women on every governing body' and not for equal representation as such (Shaw 1988: 346). It was in fact the mid-1940s before the coupled vote appeared decisively in Shaw's work, and then in such a way as to make it sound like a new idea. When he wrote in this vein in October 1946 to Lady Pethick-Lawrence, he made no mention of the earlier correspondence (Shaw 1988: 782). The same approach was taken in a letter he wrote in 1945 to the female candidate for the constituency of Flint at the forthcoming general election. He claimed the proportion of men to women in Parliament was 600 to 14, and said that the way to remedy 'that monstrosity is to make the electoral unit not One Man One Vote plus One Woman One Vote, but a man And a woman – a coupled vote' (Shaw 1988: 745). Only in this way would equal representation of the sexes be secured.

Three points can be made. First, that the idea of the coupled vote shows that in the 1940s Shaw still sought democratic solutions to political problems, thus offsetting the contrary tendency discussed elsewhere in this study. Second, if the idea was indeed of pre-Great War vintage, then it would surely have emerged in *The Guide*, either in the 1928 edition or in the 1937 chapter on fascism where he discusses women in Parliament. Of the major works, only *Everybody*'s touched on the subject, and then only as an afterthought in Chapter XLII, 'Political Summary', where Shaw comments that 'a representative popular parliament of men and women in equal numbers is necessary' (Shaw 1944: 352). Third, it follows that, in the absence of a constructive alternative, the qualifications that attended his support for 'the cause' between 1903 and 1914 would have been interpreted in a critical light. 'Shaw's attitude toward the struggle for women's suffrage ... seemed inexplicable to many women at the time', Barbara Bellow Watson admitted (Watson 1964: 177). Mrs Pankhurst was not amused.[11]

WOMEN ARISE!

On one occasion at least, in an interview in the *Tribune* in 1906, the temper of Shaw's reflections seemed to match the mood of the militants. Setting his doubts aside for a moment, he said:

> Of course, if I were a woman, I'd simply refuse to speak to any man or do anything for men until I'd got the vote. I'd make my husband's life a burden, and everybody miserable generally. Women should have a revolution – they should shoot, kill, maim, destroy – until they are given a vote'.
>
> (Weintraub 1977: 237)

For once, reality went more than half way to meet the inflammatory element in Shavian rhetoric. The women did arise and their revolt put violence back on the political agenda in mainland Britain. Forcible feeding, the *Cat and Mouse Act* of 1913, women in chains in the street, mass rallies, banners proclaiming sex war, these terrible and stirring things tore up the civil fabric of the British polity, stripped away the illusions of patriarchalism and turned the Victorian order inside out. That it was women in revolt and that their repression at the hands of the Government was so brutal and capricious served to intensify the sense of upheaval beyond measure.

That Shaw did not oppose political violence in principle is as clear as the fact that he abhorred it in practice. Thus, his reaction to the events surrounding the women's war was essentially that of a rational social democrat who could not endure the reality of violence, especially when it was obvious that it could be avoided. The political mess was a pathetic, tragic absurdity, an assertion of all that was wrong with Britain's parliamentary democracy. The Government's terror tactics were downright awful. Shaw's critique of forcible feeding, in particular, was among the strongest and most insistent to be heard. When the Home Secretary, Herbert Gladstone, suggested that the process was not seriously painful, Shaw treated him with the contemptuous ridicule he deserved, inviting him in the columns of *The Times* to personally test the truth of his views (Raeburn 1973: 142). In March 1913 Shaw spoke at a mass meeting at Kingsway Hall where he appeared not as 'a Suffragette speaker', he told the audience, but as one opposed to the torture of either sex. Sparing none of the graphic detail of the processes involved in forcible feeding, he concluded that the conscience of the community was not with the Government in this matter: 'The whole thing has now become propaganda of spite and rancour. It is a brutality that is degrading our national character'. He appealed finally to the oneness of human existence, stating:

> These denials of fundamental rights are really a violation of the soul and are an attack on that sacred part of life which is common to all of us, the thing of which you speak when you talk of the Life Everlasting. I say this is not a mystical sense, but the most obvious commonsense, that the denial of any fundamental rights to the person of a woman is practically the denial of the Life Everlasting.
>
> (Weintraub 1977: 228–35)

Shaw's contribution in this context was recognized by the Pankhursts. With respect to the *Cat and Mouse Act* of 1913 which the then Home Secretary, Reginald McKenna had steered through Parliament, Sylvia Pankhurst confirmed that 'again and again' Shaw wrote and spoke against it. His identification with the Suffragettes on this point was never in doubt (Pankhurst 1931: 451). At the first performance of *Androcles and the Lion* in 1913, there were cries of 'McKenna, McKenna!' when, on failing to persuade Lavinia to renounce her Christian faith, the Captain of the Guard said, 'Any person who perishes in the arena is not a martyr, but is committing suicide' (Pankhurst 1931: 510).

None the less, Shaw's rationalist predilections never allowed him to feel comfortable with the tactics of the militants, still less with the chiliastic temper which informed them. In 1908, subsequent to an episode when a muffin bell was used to stifle debate at an election meeting held by Winston Churchill, Shaw advised the Pankhursts not to introduce unreasonable methods into British politics (Raeburn 1973: 70). As matters worsened, so his concerns deepened. These were expressed in a private letter he wrote in September 1912 to a suffragette, Mary Gawthorpe, who was organizing a petition in aid of two activists who had been sentenced to penal servitude for attempted arson in a Dublin theatre. That the Government was basically responsible for allowing the situation to develop this far was clear. So, too, however, was the fact that the suffragettes could not be permitted to commit serious crimes with impunity simply 'because their motives are public motives'. The guilty parties must be restrained, Shaw wrote, and in this instance the prisoners, if determined to commit suicide by starvation, 'must be allowed to do so' (Shaw 1985b: 113–17). Looking back on those events in 1948, he described the activities of the WSPU as 'a grotesque campaign of feminine sabotage' (Shaw 1948: 224).

Neither the attitudes or activities of either the suffragettes or the Government appealed to Shaw. As a dramatist he revelled in the egalitarian duel of sex and in politics he had worked with women on equal terms. Surely, reasoned the social democrat, the sexes could find a safer path to emancipation. 'In the name of commonsense let us give them the vote and have done with it', he declared in exasperation (Raeburn 1973: 222).

Press Cuttings

The course that militancy was to take was foreshadowed in the one-act play, *Press Cuttings* (Shaw 1932r), which Shaw described as 'A Topical Sketch Compiled from the Editorial and Correspondence Columns of the Daily Papers During the Women's War in 1909'. The play was conceived as a fund raiser for the London Society for Women's Suffrage and it was planned to run over two matinées at the Court Theatre. In the event, the Lord Chamberlain objected to the play's allusions to the great men of the day and refused to license it.

The events in *Press Cuttings* take place on April Fool's Day in 1912: the country is under martial law and the Government is pondering the possibility of drawing a two-mile cordon round Westminster and turning all women out of it. The setting is the War Office where General Mitchener, who serves as a caricature of the militarist in politics, entertains a series of visitors. Outside, meanwhile, the agitators are heard shouting, 'Votes for Women!'

The first visitor is the Prime Minister, Balsquith (Balfour-Asquith) who enters dressed as a suffragette, this being the only way to get into Downing Street in 1912. There follows a discussion with Mitchener on the crisis in which Balsquith seeks to head off a militaristic solution to the problem on the ground that the public would never stand for it. Their conversation is conditioned by the social and intellectual conventions of their class. The greatest disaster they face is that the invitation for six garden parties and fourteen dances have been cancelled for all the subalterns in the regiment of an officer who had a pro-suffrage curate flogged, not realizing he had three aunts in the peerage. Mitchener would have the officer flogged, only Balsquith reminds him that his father subscribed a million to the party funds. For all that, both Mitchener and Balsquith are essentially men of good intentions; they are invariably silly, but never evil.

Balsquith is eventually replaced by the redoubtable Mrs Farrell. She is serious and clear-thinking. In fact, Shaw described her as the 'only really sympathetic woman' in the play. Of soldiering and childbearing, she says 'I wouldnt compare risks run to bear livin people into the world to risks run to blow them out of it. A mother's risk is jooty: a soldier's is nothin but divilmint'. Mrs Farrell represents the mother-woman. Interestingly, that aspect of Shaw's argument seems to have found considerable favour among the suffragettes. Mrs Pankhurst told Lillah McCarthy, who played Ann Whitfield in the 1903 production of *Man and Superman* at the Court Theatre, that the portrait 'had strengthened her purpose and fortified her courage'. The Court became 'the scene of women's emancipation', wrote Lillah McCarthy in her memoirs (McCarthy 1933: 64). It says something about Shaw's luck as a propagandist that even his most dubious doctrine found favour among the most dynamic, if intellectually limited, faction in the women's movement.[12]

Notable absentees from *Press Cuttings* are the suffragettes themselves. They are heard, but never seen. Instead, there are two representatives of the Anti-Suffrage League, the masculine Mrs Banger and the romantically beautiful aristocrat, Lady Corinthia. Between them, they succeed in converting the General to the cause of democracy for women; Mrs Banger by her insistence that all 'the really strong men of history have been disguised women'; Lady Corinthia by her snobbery and her conviction that the vote will undermine the power of really attractive and clever women like herself. Her belief is that man is 'ruled by beauty, by charm' and that 'the Suffragette movement is essentially a dowdy movement'.

All of which annoys Mitchener sufficiently to convert him to 'the cause'. He proposes to Mrs Farrell, primarily on the ground that she is the only woman he knows who can stand up to Mrs Banger (who is to marry Mitchener's arch-rival, Sandstone). When Balsquith returns, the transmogrified General has the pleasure of informing him that the moral he must learn is 'to give up treating women as if they were angels'; Mitchener, on the other hand, is told he must give up treating soldiers as if they were schoolboys. The last word goes to Mrs Farrell: 'It's a mercy you've found one another out at last. That's enough now'.

Press Cuttings seems to say that the case for democracy for women becomes irresistible once the arguments against it (and the proponents of those arguments) are brought out into the open. By implication, it suggests, too, that the play could not have delivered its 'rational' conclusion if it had brought a representative of the militant suffragettes on to the stage. Mrs Farrell indicated why when she said there was nothing to choose between the women who are for and those who are against the vote once 'they get into a state about it'. To have brought a suffragette on to the stage would have been to plunge the play into an endless round of irrational disputation: that was not the stuff of Shavian drama.

CONCLUSIONS

The obvious conclusion to Shaw's reflections on sexual equality is that there is no obvious conclusion. Perhaps that is appropriate to a subject which reaches across the totality of human experience and must, therefore, give rise to a vast range of ideas and sentiments. In this context, complexity is to be preferred to consistency, for surely the latter could only be attained by looking at experience through the blinkered spectacles of ideological commitment. Shaw's varied, often experimental and tentative approach to sexual equality was that of a critical ideologist determined to explore the boundaries of emancipation. In doing so, he did not ignore the difficulties raised by his male experience of the relationship between the sexes, nor did he forget the differences within the women's movement itself. Shaw operated within a rich framework of thought, encompassed by the personal and political, the polemical and the dramatic. The one certainty is that he envisaged the sexes working together to achieve the common goals of human happiness, welfare and perfection. Whether or not the partnership between the sexes would be one of equality could not be answered in the abstract. Shaw's tendency to set himself up as an intellectual mentor to so many women, from his first love, Alice Lockett, to Margaret Wheeler, a Workington housewife with whom he started to correspond in his eighty-seventh year, suggested a dominant intellectual role for the male. Also, aspects of the mother-woman theory would not contradict that view. Yet he was always the enchanted mentor, and he remained convinced that whenever women agitate for equality they achieve much more in fact. Shaw's argument in this context was for equality with difference, a goal which admitted of a huge variety of contrasting formulations, pitted with as many tensions as human relationships will allow.

Shaw's difficult relationship with the suffragette movement suggests he did not (on this occasion) seek to win golden opinions at the expense of intellectual integrity. His reflections on the practical options open to women in his own day were sober and typically Fabian in the way they translated questions of morality into matters of legal reform. Where H.G. Wells aimed to shock, Shaw chose relevance as his mark. If he was an enthusiast for women's liberation, Shaw managed to convey it in a muted form in his plays.

Very few of his female characters were paradigms of emancipation; but, then, he did not peddle false optimism. More damaging is the observation that his portraits were founded on literary stereotypes and, to that extent, tended to confirm established views of the categories of female personality.

Yet, whatever its faults and limitations, there is no doubt that Shaw's work as a whole made a difference in respect to the struggle for sexual equality in the twentieth century. That much was acknowledged by Rebecca West in her review of perhaps the most important and frustrating of Shaw's feminist statements, *The Guide*. She found it too cautious and a little dated, stating 'Curiously enough it is always Mr Shaw's own contribution to his age that he seems to ignore when he looks round on life' (West 1928: 514).

Taking a historical perspective, assessment of Shaw's influence is complicated by the fact that at different times different factions among the feminists have been attracted to different aspects of his work. Over the years women have found inspiration and frustration in it. It is probable that many were drawn to his work because they heard in it the voice of a friend who was honest enough to share his hopes, fears and vulnerabilities with women and who was wise enough not to take either himself or them too seriously. He did not pretend to be a man of good character where women were concerned. He insisted on the power of romantic enchantment. He was sometimes critical and even apprehensive of women. For all that, he never dreamed of excluding them from the charmed orbit of his universe of discourse. Similarly, women have often found fault with Shaw, but seldom have they fallen out with him. Thus, Lady Rhondda concluded, 'For when all is said and done, one must admit that the reason we ask so much of Shaw is that he has given us so much . . .' (Lady Rhondda 1930f: 470).

4

THE IRISH QUESTION

THE SERIOUSNESS OF THE LONG-DISTANCE WISECRACKER

Whatever we make of Shaw's views on women and the woman question generally, very few would doubt his abiding interest in the issues at stake. However perceived, women were never far from Shaw's mind. Whatever the shortcomings and pitfalls in his outlook, he was a committed participant in the great debate on sexual equality.

By way of contrast, conventional wisdom, at least until very recently, has held that Shaw was something of a dilettante where Ireland and the Irish question were concerned. Like Wilde, he is often seen as a British dramatist, conquering the London stage with his elegant and perceptive commentaries on English character and custom, commentaries that were written essentially with an English audience in mind. Like Wilde, he only rarely appears in books on Anglo-Irish literature. All he had done for Ireland was to send 'an occasional long-distance wisecrack' said one councillor when the Corporation of Dublin discussed offering Shaw the Honorary Freedom of the City in 1946 (Shaw 1962a: 293). Seen from this perspective, his relationship with his native land seems oddly cool and distant, a meagre thing of limited value in his struggle for personal ascendency over the world of English culture; his 'Irishness' was but a smooth accent, sedulously nurtured, with which he sought to beguile his London audience. How different this relationship seems to the romantic commitment of Yeats or the bitter-sweet intensity of Synge; how unlike O'Casey's hard love for Ireland or the sheer intimacy of Joyce's knowledge of her condition.

Continuing in this negative vein for a moment, it is certainly true that Shaw left Ireland in 1876 at the age of nineteen and only returned twenty-nine years later and then at his wife's insistence. If Fenian sentiments had moved his schoolboy heart, as he claimed in *Sixteen Self Sketches*, these were apparently soon ousted by the desire to be part of what Larry Doyle from *John Bull's Other Island* (*John Bull's*) calls 'the big world that belongs to the big powers'. Like Doyle Shaw seems to have taken England to his heart. Of all his plays, two only – *John Bull's* and *O'Flaherty VC* – were set in Ireland (though Part IV of *Back to Methuselah*, 'Tragedy Of An Elderly Gentleman', could be added to this list). Of these, the first was apparently written directly in response to a request from Yeats on behalf of the Abbey Theatre; the second was intended, however whimsically, as a recruiting pamphlet for the British Army during the Great War; and the last was a piece of futuristic speculation set in the year 3000. On this basis it would appear that Ireland and its affairs were peripheral to Shaw; Shaw peripheral to Ireland and to Irishmen. Though it may be admitted that as a political journalist Shaw wrote copiously on Ireland, the view has stuck somehow that these were more the belated reflections of a habitual meddler in events too tragic and too complex to be plummeted by his lightweight analysis than the work of a serious contributor to the subject. Brian Inglis holds that the well-being of the defendant was a secondary importance for Shaw when he wrote his discarded defence of Roger Casement in 1916; Shaw's true intention, according to Inglis, was to create a national dramatic event with himself as its star turn (Inglis 1974: 344). Shaw is in effect convicted on all counts: neglect, ignorance, opportunism and vanity.

Such is the case for the prosecution. Is it fair? Recently the critical tide has turned slightly in Shaw's favour as A.M. Gibbs, Nicholas Grene, Michael Holroyd and others have sought to explain the importance of Ireland to Shaw both as a man and as an artist. That Shaw found England a more congenial place to live is clear. But, as Gibbs argues, 'if the seventy-four years he spent in England makes us think of the land of his birth as Bernard Shaw's other island, it was 'other' only in a physical, not in a spiritual, sense' (Gibbs 1983: 123). His relationship with Ireland was difficult, admittedly, something of a love–hate affair, full of harsh thoughts and bad dreams, yet intense and powerful and fundamental to his being.

This more sympathetic view has been accompanied by the rediscovery of *John Bull's*, the most neglected of all Shaw's major works. The play had to wait until the 1980s before it appeared as a Penguin paperback in Britain, and it still awaits its revival in the West End. Such neglect is odd considering the tremendous interest generated by the original production of the play at the Court Theatre in 1904–5. Then it enjoyed one hundred and twenty-one performances, with the Prime Minister of the day, Arthur Balfour, being present at no fewer than five of these. King Edward VII also attended a special performance in March 1905, so elevating Shaw to the dubious ranks of the respectable literati. More importantly, the play, one of the most popular and provocative of its period, placed the Irish question firmly on the agenda of dramatic art. Praise arrived from many quarters. W.B. Yeats told Shaw that, contrary to received opinion, it showed that Ireland 'is the only subject on which you are really serious', and added 'You have said things in this play which are entirely true about Ireland, things which nobody has ever said before. . . . It astonishes me that you should have been so long in London and yet have remembered so much'. For the first time Shaw had found what Yeats described as 'a geographical conscience' (Shaw 1972: 453).

The achievement was literary and political. Contemporaries thought it not only a good piece of dramatic art but also, as with Yeats, a telling statement on the condition of Ireland. The trenchantly argued 'preface for politicians', which appeared in the published version of *John Bull's* in 1907, enhanced that political impact, reaching a far wider audience and touching on very different sensibilities with its unequivocal advocacy of home rule.

To place these comments in a broader socialist context, the preface was in fact something of a landmark in the social democratic analysis of Ireland. Shaw's importance in this respect is not to be underestimated. Though the Irish question was discussed in the labour movement, the approach was invariably sparse and unsatisfactory, relying for doctrinal guidance on the principles informing conventional radicalism. Shaw's reflections were not startlingly original, but they were searching and independent in spirit and he did confront the big doctrinal issues of nationalism and imperialism. In this respect, he used Ireland as a peg on which to hang a debate on arguably the most vital issues of contemporary politics. Shaw's expertise and commitment were acknowledged when, in 1920, he was asked to write a report outlining the policy of the Labour Party on Ireland, entitled *Irish Nationalism and Labour Internationalism*. Thus, far from the picture of Shaw as irrelevant to Ireland, a counterportrait emerges of a serious and responsible commentator. Despite their limitations, his reflections can be seen to have considerable historical interest, especially when viewed in relation to the neglect of doctrinal formulation in the labour movement as a whole. There are indeed good grounds for seeing Shaw as the leading Fabian thinker on Ireland during the first two decades of the twentieth century, with the pamphlet on *How to Settle the Irish Question* (1917) representing the culminating point of his work.

This chapter traces the development of Shaw's reflections on Ireland in all their varied forms – artistic and political, Shavian and Fabian – from the relative neglect of the early years, to the revival of interest in the Edwardian period, through the Great War and on to the foundation of the Irish Free State in 1921. Thereafter his interest waned once more as he turned again to the central egalitarian concerns of his socialism. Part of the purpose of this chapter is to show how even the periods of neglect are instructive as to the nature – the faults and predilections – of socialist thought and practice in Britain.

IMMATURITY

When Shaw's thoughts turned to Ireland they often strayed to Torca Cottage in Dalkey where he spent the happiest days of his childhood. Later in life he said he was 'a product of Dalkey', of the beauty of its landscape, its fine views out to sea and the clarity of the air which above all gave the place its special quality of splendour. Dalkey was a playground fit for a superior brain.

To Dalkey there belonged one set of memories, to Dublin and to Ireland generally there belonged another set, less pleasing and less positive in nature. Ireland as a whole had unhappy and disturbing associations for Shaw. Dalkey apart, it was there he spent 'the devil of a childhood' among a family in emotional and financial ruins. Perhaps his most trying experience came at the age of thirteen when he was sent, briefly, to a Roman Catholic school, so suffering the worst pangs of snob tragedy as an outcast from the Protestant garrison, a secret he was only to reveal eighty years later in *Sixteen Self Sketches*. It was in Dublin, that city of 'derision and invincible ignorance' as he described it in a letter to the editor of the *Irish Worker* in 1912, that he spent a frustrating adolescence as a clerk in a land agent's office (Shaw 1985b: 127). When he sailed for England in 1876 it was as if he had escaped from spiritual bondage, escaping from what A.M. Gibbs has called Dublin's 'prisons of the soul' (Gibbs 1983: 123).

Shaw's first novel, *Immaturity* (1879), published as late as 1930 with a long preface on his childhood years, throws some light on his difficult relationship with Ireland. In the novel the hero, Robert Smith, found employment as secretary to an Irish Protestant Member of Parliament, a Mr Woodward, who was said to represent a Dublin constituency. Smith, an Englishman with the archetypal English surname, seemed closely modelled on the young Shaw: argumentative, irreligious, a secretary with the soul of an artist, cast out into the business world at sixteen. Arguably, the description of him as 'the pale scholar of Islington, whose thoughts were like bloodless shadows of conscience and logic' is not irrelevant to a consideration of Shaw's character and art. There was a fine ironic touch in the portrayal of Robert Smith, nowhere more so than in those scenes depicting his interaction with the members of the Irish household, comprising of the MP's two daughters, Isabella and Clytie, and a 'very un-English manservant' called Cornelius Hamlet. Not only were these scenes the most convincing in a novel which substituted opinions for emotions, they were besides an acknowledgement of Ireland's hold on Shaw's youthful imagination. In this respect, tension, ambiguity and a sense of exorcism through art were evident throughout.

When Smith first entered the Woodward household the picture was one of friendly, informal slovenliness, such a juxtaposition of good humour and disorder as could only reaffirm the conventional Victorian view of the Irish as incapable of managing their own affairs. A similar appeal to the conventions of his would-be audience was apparent in the portrayal of the servant, Hamlet, full of blarney and indecorous intimacy, described by his employer as 'a great blackguard', so prone to social solecisms that he could not be trusted to answer the door after three in the afternoon in South Kensington.

Against this conventionalism, there was the portrayal of Isabella. Though initially presented as a shallow, clever girl, she was used in the novel to explore some of the complexities of the Irish question. She was, for example, a convert to Catholicism, so allowing Shaw to note the religious dimension to Irish politics. Her father only allowed her to return home on condition that he was 'at liberty to kick downstairs, break the neck of, or otherwise maim any emissary of the Pope who should presume to cross his threshold'. Isabella was also the vehicle used to present a paradoxical view of the Irish as intellectual and unromantic. However, her speech to this effect was not a defence of either Ireland or the Irish, for it culminated in a statement of hatred for the country as 'the slowest, furthest behind its time, dowdiest, and most detestably snobbish place on the surface of the earth'. There was an intensity of feeling in her conclusion: 'The only sensible institution in the emerald isle is absenteeism'. Isabella arrived at that view while on a visit to a village near Newry in the North. Shaw employed this episode to highlight the distinction between North and South, with the former receiving special condemnation: ill-mannered, thrifty, tasteless, false and ferocious were among the terms used in describing a people who were not Irish, 'only a sort of mongrel Scotch'. Isabella's Ireland was culturally backward and divided along religious and racial lines.

How much is to be gained from these ambiguous and fitful passages? Through Isabella we learn of Shaw's awareness of the multi-faceted character of the Irish question. But in 1879 the tragic potential of the religious and racial tensions was not realized. Instead, Shaw's achievement was in the expression of a sense of personal bitterness toward the country's cultural poverty. Through Hamlet and Mr Woodward we learn something of the conventions underlying the portrayal of Irishness in English literature of the period, and of Shaw's tacit acceptance of these conventions. In that sense he was a representative victim of English cultural imperialism. And through Smith, the novel's hero, Shaw explored the sheer alienness of the Irish sensibility to the English, which culminated in Smith's unsuccessful proposal of marriage to Isabella. Smith simply did not understand the Irish, though for all that he was of practical use to Mr Woodward, bringing a much-needed sense of routine and practicality to bear on his affairs.

Overall the impression was one of unresolved though potentially fruitful complexities, of an untidy mixture of radical and conventional perceptions, of pride and bitter loathing, leaving all the great questions of political reform unanswered.

THE CURSE OF NATIONALISM

Ireland withdrew into the shadows in Shaw's later novels, only surfacing again in his imaginative literature in a decisive way in *John Bull's* at the turn of the century. In the intervening years, consideration of the Irish question and its doctrinal implications was relegated to occasional speeches and articles: two of these from the 1880s are of interest, one dating from before his conversion to socialism, the other appearing just as he was starting work on *Fabian Essays*.

In the first, a speech delivered at the Zetetical Society in 1881, Shaw is reported as having opposed the view that the Irish belong to the 'lower races' and, accordingly, that neither land reform nor the reform of political institutions would alleviate their misery in the modern world (Shaw 1881: 2). Shaw, on the other hand, argued the case for reform. What was needed, he said, was better government and the investment of capital and intellect in Ireland. He was all for reasoned and urgent argument on home rule. This obscure exchange of views points to the less pleasing response in Victorian England to the alienness of the Irish, namely, the tendency to consider Ireland along social Darwinist and overtly racist lines, and this even in progressive circles where one might expect unconditional support for the Liberal argument for home rule.

In the second, an unsigned review from 1888 of a book by Robert Olivier on Ireland, Shaw set out the bare essentials of his mainstream social democratic doctrine on nationalism (Shaw 1962a: 20). At its heart was an acceptance of the development of national consciousness as an 'incident of organic growth', a necessary stage in the evolution of modern consciousness. Like most progressive thinkers of the age, Shaw accepted the coincidence of the territory of the state and nation as 'an inevitable phase of social organization', to be supported quite independently of any utilitarian considerations of material welfare. Shaw in fact wrote of an 'inevitable order of social growth' and offered a three-stage guide to this historicist scheme of things: (i) the destruction of the feudal order by the realization of individual liberty, (ii) the enlargement of the social consciousness from the individual self to the nation, and the consequent realization of national liberty, and (iii) the transcendence of national consciousness and the movement towards the federation of nationalities.

According to this ideally optimistic formulation, the birth of national consciousness and its expression in the national self-determination were inevitable and positive phases in human progress. Home rule for Ireland and eventually for all of Britain's colonies was to be accepted on these grounds. Otherwise, Shaw warned, 'the conquered races will destroy' those empires which 'persist in opposing them'. Failure to institute reform would lead to violence, he predicted. But not only that, with violence there would come the growth of nationalism as an ideology, that is 'the elevation of the interests of the unity and self-determination of the nation to the status of the supreme value' (Berlin 1981: 338). This was an essentially destructive and negative development in Shaw's mind.

His position was explained in full nearly twenty years later in the section on 'the curse of nationalism' from the preface to *John Bull's*. There he wrote of national self-determination as a 'natural right'. This was not the standard liberal argument. Instead, it was couched in social Darwinist terms, the argument being that the right had assumed the character of a 'natural function' in popular consciousness. The appeal for self-determination was irresistible because the nation was somehow a natural object of sympathy in modern politics, and social democracy must cut its doctrinal cloth accordingly. Again, it was not to be defended on utilitarian grounds; 'Like democracy, national self-government is not for the good of the people: it is for the satisfaction of the people', Shaw claimed.

The crucial point was that failure to satisfy the demand was an open invitation to an obsessive concern for national liberty which would then become the ultimate value in political agitation, resulting in the neglect of the politics of welfare and a decline in the regard for reason. Nationalism was the ideology of irrational nonsense: of separatism, of racial purity and superiority, of hearts enchanted to a stone by hatred of the English. In later years, subsequent to the Easter Rising, Shaw had not a good word to say for Sinn Fein, founded as it was on the romantic delusion 'that the world consists of Ireland and a few subordinate continents'. Sinn Fein was singled out for special attention when in 1916 he said he had 'attacked the romantic separatism of Ireland with every device of invective and irony and dialectic at my command' (Shaw 1962a: 111). A decade earlier Shaw said a nationalist movement is a 'curse' on the grounds that 'a healthy nation is as unconscious of its nationality as a healthy man of his bones'; it is when a nation is obsessed by its nationality that it loses its place in 'the world's march'. In this respect, the national question lay at the root of Ireland's backwardness: 'nationalism stands between Ireland and the light of the world', Shaw declared in the preface to *John Bull's*.

The framework within which the 1907 argument was set was more equivocal than its counterpart in 1888 when, as in the first edition of *Quintessence*, the discussion was framed in evolutionary terms and underpinned by a historicist optimism. By 1907 there was less certainty and a more urgent need to head-off the destructive potential of national consciousness. Strategically, the main object for social democracy was to defuse aggressive nationalism by legislative means, thus preventing the spread of racial, linguistic or religious bigotry; 'You cannot cure a dog's ferocity by chaining him', Shaw said in 1915, 'on the contrary, the chain is often the secret of the ferocity' (Shaw 1985b: 281). It was a policy of containment. The external threat of insurgent nationalism was to be defused by the same constitutional means as was the internal threat of insurgent poverty. Reason and civility were to prevail. National consciousness was to be endured so long as it was of a limited and undemanding kind, capable of being transcended by a more enlightened regard for our common humanity. Home rule was to be supported so long as it was seen as a prelude to a federation or commonwealth of nationalities.

This, in essence, was Shaw's mainstream social democratic outlook on the national question. As such, it was the doctrinal basis which guided his deliberations on Ireland. If it is not spectacular or original, it stands at least as a relatively clear statement on a woefully neglected subject among socialists.

FABIANISM AND THE EMPIRE REVISITED

What Shaw really offered in his 1907 'preface for politicians' was but a grudging approval of national consciousness, along with a grudging acceptance that the national question was an unavoidable fact of modern life. From the standpoint of rational, welfare socialism, the Irish question was indeed peripheral, something of a nuisance which, as Shaw told Sean O'Casey in 1919, 'will insist on getting settled before the Labour Question' (Krause 1975: 88). Its intrinsic interest was negligible. Thus Shaw claimed that, for the political scientist, Ireland is 'quite the dullest question there is on the face of the earth'.

This kind of hostility and exasperation was of course central to Shaw's Fabian response to nationalism and imperialism, at least in relation to the arguments surrounding the Boer War. As noted in Chapter 1, before then the Fabians had barely acknowledged the existence of the Empire, treating it as somehow irrelevant to their doctrine of national socialism. They had mounted an Irish campaign in 1892, but with uncertain results and little real doctrinal purpose. The underlying problem was the essentially insular and centrifugal nature of British socialism which made it shy away from exotic subjects. The early Fabians sought primarily to tailor their programme of reform to suit the preoccupations of their immediate audience in mainland Britain. In 'To Your Tents, Oh Israel!', which marked the Fabian break with the Liberals in 1893, Shaw wrote that the English workers 'did not and do not care a dump one way or the other about Irish Home Rule'. Ireland was but a hindrance to social reform, a costly irrelevance. Higher wages, improved working conditions, the extension of municipal services – these were the real issues of the day. There was no question of analysing the tangle of racialism involved in the British labour movement's response to Ireland, nor any consideration of the effect the grandeur of empire had on working-class consciousness.

During the Boer War Shaw had gone a step further, translating grudging approval into open hostility towards the principle of national self-determination. In a long article in *The Clarion* in May 1900 he explicitly argued for an end to socialism's traditional sympathy for such nationalist movements as those in Ireland and Poland. Socialism, he said, 'knows nothing of nationality or of independence'. Socialism was avowedly internationalist, standing for 'the identity of interests of all workers' and consequently opposed 'to nationalism, patriotism, wars for conquest and supremacy, pretensions to racial superiority, and the rest of the stock-in-trade of khaki politics and journalism' (Shaw 1900: 161). Strategically, the object was not to defend petty states, but to work for their inclusion under the trusteeship of a progressive empire. This was Shaw's maverick social democratic doctrine on the national question. The ultimate goal was the same as in the mainstream doctrine – a federal commonwealth of nations – only the path to its attainment was to be radically different.

In both the mainstream and the maverick doctrines alike, nationalism was seen predominantly as an unhealthy and unnecessary illusion, the sort of trinket that Loki might produce from his store of tricks to beguile the foolish giants of the world, disguising from them the true nature of Alberic's rule by creating a myth of false unity and purpose between the exploiting and the exploited classes. Shaw, while accepting their potential power, had not time for illusions of this sort. Nationalism, seen either as an expression of the unconscious self in mankind or as a species of political manipulation, was to be treated with care and suspicion.

It is worth emphasizing in this context that, while Shaw had no time for nationalism as such, his Fabian socialism did tend to show concern for the peculiar interests of the British working class. In the Irish context, for example, a central feature of his response was his emphasis on the innocence of the mass of Englishmen; 'the people of England have done the people of Ireland no wrong whatever'. Ireland, he said, was merely suffering the growing pains of capitalism and then in a far milder form than the people of England had experienced. In this way, the English working man was exonerated, his prejudices confirmed, even approved. Ireland's one genuine cause for grievance was in the export of capital from the country, which should have been channelled into investment and social reconstruction. But even here Shaw viewed the problem from a distinctly British perspective, using the example of Ireland to bolster the case for protectionism. Once again we encounter the tensions between Shaw's national and internationalist perspectives on socialism, tensions which filtered through to the whole range of his artistic and political reflections on Ireland.

JOHN BULL'S OTHER ISLAND

Whilst discoursing on the origin of justice Nietzsche observed, 'A poet could say that God has placed forgetfulness as a doorkeeper on the threshold of the temple of human dignity' (Nietzsche 1986: 49). When W.B. Yeats requested that Shaw write a play for the Abbey Theatre 'as a patriotic contribution to the repertory of the Irish Literary Theatre' it must have surprised Shaw. Yeats, after all, was not exactly an admirer of his art. Shaw was not exactly noted for his patriotism, still less as an enthusiast for the Celtic Twilight; the 'Irishness' of his literature was wholly a matter of style not of substance. Was the request, then, a piece of mischief on the poet's part, or was it only opportunism, an attempt on behalf of the infant Abbey Theatre to exploit the power of every rising star – however dim and distant – in the Anglo-Irish firmament? Whatever the reason, it certainly made Shaw think again about the disturbing subject of Ireland. That it proved a difficult undertaking was clear from the opening paragraphs of the preface, where Shaw gave an account of the play's origin and reception.

One difficulty was that, though *John Bull's* was commissioned by Yeats and admired by him personally, it was not in fact accepted for production at the Abbey. Shaw, in explanation, assumed that cocksure tone designed to deflect attention away from any hint of doubt or tension. 'Like most people who have asked me to write plays, Mr Yeats got rather more than he bargained for', he declared (Shaw 1931e: 13). The play was not only beyond the Abbey's technical resources, it was also in its 'very uncompromising presentment of the real old Ireland' quite 'uncongenial to the whole spirit of the neo-Gaelic movement, which is bent on creating a new Ireland after its own ideal'. Modest as ever, Shaw saw himself as too sophisticated, technically and morally, to be of any use to Yeats, secure in his dragon-guarded land. Instead of Dublin and the Abbey, the play was produced in London at the Court Theatre, where it gained 'immediate and enormous popularity with delighted and flattered English audiences' (Shaw 1931e: 13).

Shaw must surely have known that the play would prove unsuitable for the Abbey and that, despite his contrary claim in the preface, it was destined initially for an essentially English audience. This much was hinted at in his correspondence with Granville Barker and others (Shaw 1972: 423, 444). As Shaw's detractors suspected, he was not contributing to Anglo-Irish literature in an unequivocal sense. What, then, of the 'flattered English audiences'? Was flattery intended, or was it the product of the audience's limited perception of the work, as Shaw went on to suggest in the preface to *John Bull's*? Looked at from a different standpoint, perhaps the preface, which in some respects was as critical of the English as the play was of the Irish, was an attempt to defuse the notion that he was avowedly anti-Irish by redressing the critical balance between the two nationalities. Was it in that sense a scrap of clothing for Shaw's naked artistic consciousness, a brave disguise now that it was about to suffer the undignified glare of publication.

Comments of this kind reveal some of the problems in analysing the context and content of both play and preface. Are they even concerned with the same subject?

Preface and play

The preface, for example, was 'written by an Irishman of Protestant family and Protestant prejudices'. There was no question of impartiality. It dealt in large part with the religious dimension to Irish politics, in particular with the future of Protestant Ulster. The play, on the other hand, was set exclusively in the South, among the Catholic peasantry, where the immediate concern was not with the prospect of home rule, but with the effects of recent land reforms on patterns of ownership and standards of living. The only token Protestants in the cast were the two Englishmen, Broadbent and his valet, Hodson. What is more, these two were the only characters with more than a passing interest in home rule: Broadbent because it accorded with his shallow liberalism and political designs; Hodson because he was tired of the domination of Westminster by Irish affairs. In this way the play side-stepped the fundamental issue of the preface, namely, the hostility between the Catholic South and the Protestant community in the North. It was all very well for Shaw to make confident assertions in the preface that the Protestants would form the 'vanguard of Irish Nationalism and Democracy as against Romanism and Sacredotalism'; or to forecast that, far from there being a 'war of religion', the Protestant under home rule would 'be far safer and stronger than he is today', even with the acceptance of the Roman Catholic Church as the established church of Ireland. Forecasts and assertions were no substitute for consideration of these issues in a dramatic form. True, Shaw's distaste for the priest-ridden, superstitious Catholic peasantry was perfectly clear in the play; but nowhere was there an exploration of the Protestant response. All that was offered were a few dry comments on disestablishment from Broadbent's Irish partner, Larry Doyle, with Doyle being roundly denounced as a 'turncoat' by his audience of narrow-minded Catholic peasants. Indeed, it might be conjectured that the play's portrayal of the Catholic South was a reassertion of Protestant prejudices, pointing to an entirely different conclusion to that found in the preface, namely, for home rule for a united Ireland.

A common theme of play and preface was the comparison of English and Irish temperaments. More especially, Shaw was now concerned to reverse the conventional Victorian stereotype of the Irishman as simple, hearty, loquacious and at the mercy of his imagination, the antithesis of the practical, intelligent Englishman. The preface paints the Englishman as the most unrealistic, the least subtle and intellectual of creatures, sentimental to the core of his being; the Irishman as clear-sighted in politics, having a strong hold on the realities of life. It was not a racial doctrine (Shaw insisted there was no such thing as an Irish or Celtic race). Rather, the contrast had to do with the influence of climate and the variation in political circumstances. English stupidity, he suggested, derived from the extent of her worldly power, with the celebration of national glory ousting any need for intellectual subtlety in political life. Whereas Ireland's fortune places 'a premium on political ability', the fortune of England 'discount it' – so ran the Shavian formula, illustrated in the preface by a comparison of Nelson and Wellington as representatives of English romanticism and Irish realism respectively.

Much was also made of the romantic–realist dichotomy in the play. For example, in the discussion in the opening scene between Broadbent, Doyle and Tim Haffigan, Shaw debunked the conventional stage Irishman by exposing Haffigan's cultivated imprudence and fluent brogue as the humbug of a petty swindler who comes from Glasgow. Broadbent, of course, accepted Haffigan at face value precisely because he conformed to his own idealized conception of Irishness as a permanent state of slovenly, good-natured drunkenness. In using Doyle's clear-sighted cynicism to enlighten his partner of Haffigan's deception, Shaw immediately established the contrast between the English and Irish temperament which operated throughout the play. Broadbent was the comic invention, crude in perception and gullible, yet sympathetic to a degree; Doyle, his serious, subtle, rather disagreeable counterpart. This was an obvious advance on *Immaturity*, at least when considered in the light of Shaw's undermining of the conventional perceptions which underpinned contemporary English arrogance.

Of course the impact of this aspect of the play must have varied greatly. William Archer wrote that for some people 'the trenchancy of the caricature has been more apparent than its geniality, and they have bitterly resented the character of Broadbent' (Evans 1976: 127). Alternatively, with reference to an ill-conceived production of the play in Berlin in 1917, one critic observed that 'Shaw had made Broadbent, a pompous ass of an Englishman, the 'triumphant hero' of the play (Weintraub 1973: 210). Shaw, for his part, said 'The play cannot succeed unless Tom Broadbent is popular and genial in spite of his absurdities' (Shaw 1985b: 639).

Clearly, the central characters of the play and the relationships between them are open to conflicting interpretations. So too are the relationships between the more minor characters, especially where the romantic–realist dichotomy is concerned. In particular, comparison of the English valet, Hodson, and his Irish counterparts, Matthew Haffigan. (Tim's uncle) and Patsy Farrell, places the former at a considerable advantage in terms of the articulation of his real interests. Matt Haffigan was consumed by a narrow bitterness founded on a self-pitying conception of his own suffering, and Patsy, the young labourer employed by Matt, was consumed by superstitious terrors, believing a grasshopper to be 'the devil out of hell'. In the stage notes Shaw tells us that Patsy has 'an instinctively acquired air of helplessness and silliness, indicating, not his real character, but a cunning developed by his constant dread of a hostile dominance, which he habitually tries to disarm and tempt into unmasking by pretending to be a much greater fool than he already is'. Now this could be interpreted as another perspective on the way colonialism hampers authentic existence, to be read alongside Tim Haffigan's strategy of playing a character which he knows will satisfy the assumption of moral superiority common among a people of a dominant colonial power. However, such an interpretation of Patsy is not supported by the play itself. The hostile dominance he faced was clearly Irish in origin, not English. It was not colonial oppression that was at issue, but rather the exploitation, ignorance and cultural poverty suffered by the wage-labourer in a system of ownership dominated by peasants' proprietorship and a system of worship dominated by an archaic and corrupt church. The argument was socialistic in nature. Ireland's true need was for the investment of capital, a transformation in land ownership, a standard wage and an established church.

Anyone reading the full text of the preface would see Shaw as fundamentally anti-imperialist. Though it talks of nationalism as a curse and includes waspish remarks to the effect that England did Ireland a service in 'wrecking all the industries that were based on the poverty of our people', it does, nevertheless, close with a fierce critique of empire in relation to the Denshawi Horror of 1906. Shaw said that the denial of home rule leads inevitably to a military style of government, resulting in atrocities, chronic panic and cowardice. He ended with the assertion, 'the whole Imperial military system of coercion and terrorism is unnatural' (Shaw 1931e: 62).

The evidence from the play is more equivocal, however, suggesting some reluctance to deal with the colonial dimension to emancipation. Consider the confrontation between Hodson and Matt Haffigan at the close of Act III. There the former was a spokesman for Fabian national socialism, dismissing the Irishman's talk of injustice and starvation with the claim, 'You Awrish people are too well off: thets wots the metter with you'. Then with sudden passion, he tells of the suffering of his own family – his grandfather evicted by his landlord, his own seasonal unemployment, his wife's premature death – all aggravated by the rotten wages and conditions accepted by Irish immigrants into England. Hodson's answer was to give Ireland to the Kaiser 'and give poor aowld England a chawnce'. Haffigan, in response, could speak only of Coercion Acts and Dublin Castle. The debate between the valet and the smallholder ended in mutual contempt and simmering hatred.

This scene bears comparison with the confrontation between Malone Senior and Straker at the start of Act IV of *Man and Superman*. Again there is a breakdown in communication. Straker, the cockney chauffeur, treated Malone 'with the indulgence due to an inferior and unlucky species'. Malone, the self-made man, treated Straker with contempt, 'as a stupid Englishman who cannot even speak his own language properly'. Clearly, it is to Shaw's credit that he brought such tension on to the stage, suggesting as it does the problems that would be faced by socialist internationalism where relationships between working people on different sides of the colonial fence are at issue. Moreover, it indicated the strength of feeling behind formal political manoeuvering for self-determination. Such tensions and feelings were explored only fitfully in Shaw's drama. The Malone–Straker incident ended quickly with the intervention of a middle-class Englishwoman. The Haffigan–Hodson incident also ended quickly and very much to the latter's advantage, with Haffigan fleeing in terror from Broadbent's approaching motor car. In this way tragedy was dispelled by common farce.

Shaw's power to deal with the maze of suspicion and hatred engendered by colonialism was strictly limited. He could toy in a preface with the idea of using violence to secure home rule, to 'conspire and assassinate' if necessary. He could spin out elegant sentences on the appropriateness of political hatred among civilized people. To give full representation to assassination and hatred in his art was a different matter. Instead of dealing directly with the issue of political violence in an Irish context, he chose to take up the theme in *Major Barbara*, a play set in the relatively stable political framework of mainland Britain. This suggests in turn that the rationalist skeleton that rattled away in his intellectual cupboard prevented him from peering too long into chaos and nightmare; that expressions of mankind's unconscious self were all very well so long as they agreed with the consciously-expressed views of the superior brains. Otherwise they served only to reveal the heartbreaking gulf between vision and reality, thought and practice.

Broadbent, Doyle and Keegan

Interpretations of *John Bull's* centre invariably on the interaction between the play's three main protagonists – the civil engineers, Broadbent and Doyle, and the 'silenced' priest, Peter Keegan. In particular, the contrast between the serious, poetic qualities of Keegan, set against the unsympathetic cynicism of the 'Imperialist Irishman', Doyle, and the comic though effective blundering of Broadbent, is often viewed as an artistic reconstruction of the problematical relationship between thought and practice, or between idealism and pragmatism in Shaw's work. Keegan, it is said, represents the seer and moralist possessed of a republican vision of unity and service. Broadbent, on the other hand, is the dynamic, blundering pragmatist, the unconscious man of action, breaking through problems 'as an elephant breaks through a jungle'. Between these extremes there stands Doyle, a man of contrasts, a cool interlocutor who is forced to choose between Broadbent's dynamism and Keegan's vision, a predicament which many critics have associated with Shaw himself at this time. The closing scene has Keegan spelling out his madman's dream of heaven:

> In my dreams it is a country where the State is the Church and the Church the people; three in one and one in three. It is a commonwealth in which work is play and play is life: three in one and one in three. It is a temple in which the priest is the worshipper and the worshipper the worshipped: three in one and one in three. It is a godhead in which all life is human and humanity divine: three in one and one in three.
>
> (Shaw 1931e: 177)

It was a truly Catholic dream, transcending nationalities, implying that the heavenly state was to be world-wide, dedicated to emancipation, not efficiency. Doyle's reply was that it was all worthless talk. Broadbent responded with a volley of blundering hypocrisy. Having been chosen as Liberal candidate for Rosscullen and now that his plan for turning the place into a Garden City at a profit to the syndicate he represented (and at the expense of the likes of Haffigan) was in full swing, he was happy to conclude that Keegan's oratory had convinced him he was right in devoting his 'life to the cause of Ireland'. The play closed with a breakdown in communication between Keegan and Broadbent – the visionary and the man of action – seemingly as profound as that between Hodson and Haffigan; 'come along and help me to choose the site for the hotel', Broadbent tells the priest as the curtain falls.

204

This sense of incommensurable discourse was, however, modified slightly by Keegan's earlier, albeit qualified, endorsement of Broadbent's plan to modernize and sanitize Ireland. Broadbent at least had 'faith' in Ireland whereas, as Keegan remarks, the Irish themselves had 'only empty enthusiasms and patriotisms, and emptier memories and regrets'. Faced with a choice between a 'place of torment' that is clean and orderly against one that is squalid and chaotic, Keegan concludes 'perhaps I had better vote for an efficient devil that knows his own mind and his own business than for a foolish patriot who has no mind and no business.'

It would seem that whereas the preface looked toward a partnership between the two nations on an equal footing, the play effectively delivered Ireland's future into English hands. The triumph of power over sensitivity had a parallel in the play in Broadbent's courtship of the emotionally-starved Nora Reilly, perhaps the most pitiful of all Shaw's female characters, for she was no more than a pawn to be manipulated in her fiance's strategy of conquest. Whereas in the preface Broadbent was seen as outdated and unsatisfactory – 'much as I like him, I object to be governed by him, or entangled in his political destiny' – in the play, and here of course much would depend on the individual performance, he represented the dynamic, if unruly, forces of modernity. Keegan was altogether too shadowy and ambivalent a character, his constructive notions too idealistic to serve as any kind of practical counterweight. At the close, the only Irishman with any real future was Broadbent's partner, Doyle, who throughout the play preached an unsentimental doctrine of personal, political and financial dependance on England – 'the big world that belongs to the big Powers'. There was a clear echo here of Shaw's Fabian imperialism; 'The partition of the greater part of the globe among such powers is, as a matter of fact that must be faced, approvingly or deploringly, now only a question of time' (Fabian Society 1900: 3).

Unravelling the threads of Shaw's outlook on Ireland from the play and preface reveals a complex patchwork of contrasting and complementary stitches and designs. In the main the play was far bleaker. The preface at least allowed itself the luxury of rhetorical invective against empires, the comfort of unequivocal support for self-determination, together with the hope of reconciliation between the religious factions. In the words of one commentator it was 'as strongly worded as any anti-imperialist propaganda of that period' (Porter 1968: 113). In the play the rhetorical strategies of democracy and home rule were deflated, with the only determining factor being the power of capital. Far from pointing to reconciliation, it reinforced the picture of Catholic Ireland as backward and inhospitable. Ultimately its vision was one of Ireland drifting toward waste and exploitation, with no real hope of rational reconstruction. England's power was seen as wayward and ungovernable; Ireland's bitterness as futile and perverse. For Doyle, as for Isabella in *Immaturity*, the only sensible response was that of absenteeism from their native land.

The portrait of Doyle carries with it all the intensity, bitterness and heartbreak, the sour and sweet feelings Shaw felt for Ireland. Doyle's utterance are invariably hard and unsympathetic. If he is not exactly happy in his exile in England, he is at least fulfilled through his partnership with Broadbent. He has no regrets, it seems, no sentimental attachment either to Irish people or to Ireland itself. Doyle is unrelenting in his support for the harsh forces of modernity. Yet behind all that there lies, as Nicholas Grene suggests, a sub-text or a hidden agenda, for we are left with the suspicion, rare in Shaw, that Doyle's cryptic harshness conceals as much as it reveals about his true feelings. His whole relationship with Nora, for example, raises questions of motivation which are unusual for Shaw's characters, pointing to the depth and complexity of his own position as an exile. 'Larry Doyle is the most subtle study of the emotions of the Irish exile before Joyce', Grene writes, representing 'the dream of escape and the fear of return, the guilty shame and self-disgust of nationality' (Grene 1984: 75).

The comparison with Joyce is interesting. Joyce and Shaw are so different, yet in some ways they share the same bleak outlook on Ireland as a land which has missed the boat of modernity. In 'Ivy Day in the Committee Room' from *Dubliners* Joyce reproduced much of what we find in *John Bull's*, the same useless rhetoric, the sense of political futility and, too, an argument based on the overriding need for capital in a country which seems only to produce dreams and anger. Though in Joyce the scene has shifted to an urban landscape, we still encounter similar characters, most notably the shadowy Father Keon, 'a person resembling a poor clergyman or a poor actor', who drifts in and out of the narrative in a manner reminiscent of Shaw's Father Keegan. It is essentially a different scene haunted by the same ghosts (Joyce 1971: 439).

Connections of this sort indicate the extent to which we can place Shaw's bleak picture of Ireland in the general context of Anglo-Irish literature. Of all the major writers in this school perhaps only Yeats was openly optimistic and supportive of Irish nationalism, and even his optimism faltered badly immediately before the Great War. So much the worse for writers and their kind, may be the obvious response of the Irish patriot. However the realities and complexities portrayed in *John Bull's* and elsewhere cannot be set aside. Indeed the key to *John Bull's* lies in its complexity, pointing as it does to the impossibility of deriving a clear answer to the Irish question from neat ideological assumptions. As A.M. Gibbs says, Shaw provides in the play 'a deft, intimately knowledgeable portrait in miniature of Irish village life', at once 'highly critical and deeply sympathetic' (Gibbs 1983: 123). Bleak and limited though it may be, Shaw's portrait of 'real old Ireland' deserves serious consideration.

Of course certain features in that portrait were peculiar to Shaw. Its bleakness was perhaps deepened by his unhappy childhood on one side, and the pessimism he felt regarding the prospects for socialism at the time he was writing *John Bull's* on the other. Some view Shaw's ambiguities and complexities in relation to Fabian national socialism, rooted in contradiction. Others will see them as natural to his Protestant origins, rooted in the spirit of ascendancy. All these factors certainly impinged on *John Bull's*, rendering the relationship between the personal and the political especially difficult in this instance. What does emerge clearly from an analysis of the play and its preface is that by 1907 Shaw was a committed spokesman on Ireland, well-disposed if not exactly well-prepared to pursue the matter through more troubled times.

ULSTER AND THE THIRD HOME RULE BILL

When Shaw rose to address a meeting at the Memorial Hall in December 1912 he confessed, 'Though I have been before the British public as a political speaker for thirty years, this is the first time I have ever spoken in public on the subject of Home Rule'. The occasion was the controversy over the third Home Rule Bill introduced that year by the Liberals and vigorously contested by Sir Edward Carson and Bonar Law on behalf of the Ulster Protestants. In the same year Shaw also produced a special preface for a home rule edition of *John Bull's* where, as in the many articles he penned before the outbreak of the Great War, he tried to persuade the Orangemen to accept home rule as a challenge instead of rejecting it with fear and loathing.

Ulster, then, was the key issue. The people of the South, Shaw believed, were largely indifferent to nationalism, tired of the romantic rhetoric of the Gaelic League. Romantic Ireland was retreating in the face of industrial unrest, in the form of the Dublin lock-outs. Again Shaw looked at the possibility of breakdown and violence instigated by the North. Again his strategy was to stress his own Protestant origins, so implying a direct knowledge of the issues raised. In some passages he touched on the depth of feeling involved, noting the seriousness of political opinion for the Ulsterman, the moral, crusading sense of conviction behind his obstinacy, the righteousness at the core of his violence. The temper of Shaw's reflections had changed since 1907. The Ulsterman, he said, 'is inured to violence', and added:

> He has battered his political opponent with his fist and stick, and been battered himself in the same manner. Give him a machine gun, and he will not recoil with horror from the idea of mowing down his fellow townsmen with it; on the contrary, he will be delighted to substitute machinery for handwork; and he will not entertain a doubt that his views are completely reciprocated by the other side.
>
> (Shaw 1962a: 79)

The Ulsterman, then, fights 'not only as a fanatic, but as a stern moralist'. This was Shavian political realism at its most trenchant.

Nevertheless, the underlying assumption was that Ireland was 'politically one and indivisible', and that the Orangemen would have to make the best of whatever settlement was reached (Shaw 1931e: 3). Indeed it was assumed that a settlement had been reached in the passing of the Home Rule Act in 1914. It was the optimism that allowed Shaw to make forecasts which seem, in retrospect, terribly naïve: the Irish people, he said, were now rejecting the Nationalist and the Orangeman as equally insufferable – 'though the Protestant boys will still carry the drum' in the future, he announced in the *New Statesman*, 'they will carry it under the green flag, and realize that the harp, the hound, and the round tower are more satisfactory to the imagination' than the Union Jack (Shaw 1962a: 83). With the benefit of hindsight it looks like the crack-pated dream of a social democrat eager to 'mend whatever mischief seemed to afflict mankind' by bringing the world under the rule of a philosophy. Shaw was to admit that he had 'guessed ahead, and guessed wrongly', adding the peevish rejoinder 'whilst stupider and more ignorant fellow-pilgrims guessed rightly' (Shaw 1931e: 3).

EASTER 1916

The Irish question is not reducible to a single issue or perspective. Neither is it static – clear sky, still water, an unchanging reflection. Only fanaticism or the simple-mindedness of ideology can make it so. Change is of the essence of the living stream of Irish politics. In 1914 Shaw was right to identify the North as the chief threat to settlement, broadly correct in his estimation of the decline of aggressive nationalism in the South. In a few years the second half of the equation was transformed. The nationalist cause gained new impetus, pushing the possibility of moderation and reform into deep confusion. The turning point was the rising of Easter 1916 and the executions that followed.

Shaw's response to these events was mostly sensible and forthright. The rising itself he described as a 'harebrained romantic adventure', the executions as an error of judgement typical of the gentleman militarist mentality of the British army; 'Nothing more blindly savage, stupid, and terror-mad could have been devised by England's worst enemies' (Shaw 1931e: 65). It was of course a complicated matter. England was at war, having entered it originally in defence of 'little Belgium's' right to self-determination. Shaw supported England in the war, but did not entertain any sentimental attachment to the neutrality of small states. He also supported the Irish rebels, arguing they should be treated as prisoners of war. However he did not support the Sinn Fein ideal of a separate and neutral Ireland (a view he was to maintain throughout World War Two). Shaw said the goal of neutrality was a figment of the nationalist imagination (Shaw 1962a: 229). Neither England nor any Great Power would allow it, especially in a geo-political area as strategically sensitive as Ireland.

Points of detail and theoretical consistency were not Shaw's real concern

208

initially. His interest was in the practical outcome of any British response to the rising. He perceived from the outset that execution of the rebels would only heighten tension and make a political settlement harder to achieve. As a rationalist he sought to avoid the fury and the mire of nationalist politics. Concerning the rebels, he declared 'It is absolutely impossible to slaughter a man in this position without making him a martyr and a hero, even though the day before the rising he may have been only a minor poet' (Shaw 1962a: 112). His defence of Casement ran along the same prudential lines. Writing to the editor of the *Daily News*, A.G. Gardiner, in 1916, Shaw explained, 'I regard it as of extreme importance that Casement (whom I dont know personally) should not be hanged, as the mischief he will do as a martyr is incalculable. . . . His execution may make all the difference to the balance of power between Sinn Fein and Redmond-Dillon' (Shaw 1985b: 406). 'Ireland has enough heros and martyrs already', he said, and urged England to stop manufacturing any more, at the risk of a loss of all confidence in England's political abilities (Shaw 1962a: 129). In August 1916 his advice to the Prime Minister was to halt the escalation of bloodshed before the point of no return was reached; 'The Nationalist movement is still reasonable; and a friendly settlement is easy, provided no more executions take place' (Shaw 1962a: 125).

FEDERALISM

Shaw then proceeded to offer his most authoritative statement on Ireland, *How to Settle the Irish Question*, which appeared originally as a series of articles in the *Daily Express* and was subsequently published simultaneously in pamphlet form in England and in Ireland in November 1917 (Shaw 1962a: 140). Here Shaw outlined his federal scheme for the whole of the United Kingdom, a scheme which he attributed to his role as chairman of a committee of the Fabian Society called the Empire Reconstruction Committee. Writing now as a disinterested and disengaged observer of the political scene, Shaw proposed the federation of the UK into three or four distinct national parliaments. There would be no partition, no separation, but free partnership among free nations. The qualified freedom of devolution was rejected as 'irreconcilable with nationality', a half-way house that would satisfy nobody. Federalism alone, he said, would offer a partnership 'that does not obliterate the individuality of the nation that enters into it' (Shaw 1962a: 203). The argument was developed partly in terms of the satisfaction of the people's wants, partly in the name of good government. As a national socialist he was bound to say that Westminster was so overloaded that it neglected important business essential to the welfare of the English themselves. Federalism would not only satisfy the nationalist claim for self-determination, it would also deliver the most efficient units of government, capable of dealing with the growing burden of decision-making in an increasingly complex world. Joint affairs would be handled by a federal parliament (with defence and tariff reform high on the agenda). It would be this body that would send British representatives to the 'Imperial Conference of the Commonwealth' of the future. In this way, the federal scheme was offered as a model for the reconstruction of the Empire as a whole.

That Shaw was committed to the federation of the four kingdoms and serious about its practicality is clear from his efforts to become a member of the Irish Convention established by Lloyd George in 1917 (Holroyd 1991: 390). There Shaw planned to play the part of Ireland's saviour (Shaw 1985b: 478). In the event he was rejected and had to be satisfied with a lengthy correspondence with the Convention's chairman, Horace Plunkett, in which he was untiring in his pursuit of the federal solution, but to no avail.

One omission from his federal scheme was the right of nations to secede from the federal structure. Shaw considered the liberty it implied a fallacy in the modern world, and he told Horace Plunkett as much. Politically, however, its omission could have made the ideal of federalism hard to sell to those colonies suspicious of Britain's intentions. Otherwise the scheme in its outline form was a powerful statement of Shaw's political rationalism, a creditable if forlorn (in the Irish context) attempt to avoid the politics of bigotry and unreason.

IRISH NATIONALISM AND LABOUR INTERNATIONALISM

Shaw returned to the theme many times between 1917 and 1921, as his native country fell under the reign of terror. In particular, in the report he drafted for the Labour Party in 1920, *Irish Nationalism and Labour Internationalism*, he offered a summary of the full range of his views on Ireland.[1] Speaking on behalf of the Labour Party he asserted that it did not believe that the mere assertion of Irish nationality would do any more for the Irish workers than it had done for their British counterparts. Indeed, as a federalist and internationalist party, it was 'not concerned with nations except as units of organization for Labour throughout the world'. As for partition, even now Shaw dismissed it as 'impossible', primarily because it assumed an identity of interest among the people of the North which could not exist in reality. Here the argument took an economistic turn. The division between 'Capitalism and Labour', it was said, would undermine any temporary alliance against the South, with the industrialized North coming to play the key role in Ireland's development, all in keeping with good socialist principles. This was Shaw's residual economism again; 'the struggles for nationality', he predicted in 1917, 'will be forgotten in the clash of economic class war and the huge struggle for the integration of modern democratic civilization' (Shaw 1985b: 494). Shaw's claim was that 'the only grievances that really matter much politically are the common grievances of Labour throughout the capitalist world'. It was thus that his Fabian national socialism veered towards a complex internationalism.

One of his arguments on behalf of the federal scheme was that it would at last encourage the English workers to take an active interest in Ireland: 'When England sees in the Irish cause the image of her own, she will make it her own.'

ASSESSMENT

Sober reflections of this kind tend to conceal the sheer frustration Shaw felt at the development of Irish politics, with British mismanagement on one side only equalled by Irish intransigence on the other. Writing in 1929 he was to claim that recent events in Ireland had undermined the case for parliamentary democracy. Easter 1916 had placed violence firmly on the political agenda. The colonial problem would be settled as the Irish question had been settled, he suggested, not in a civilized and reasonable way, but 'as dogs settle a dispute over a bone' (Shaw 1931e: 67). Shaw realized now that no one had or ever would take much notice of his reformist proposals. It was all wasted effort. All that remained for Ireland was the distant dream that economic forces might yet overpower the religious and racial divisions.

There is a sense in which Shaw was at his best and at his most vulnerable in his reflections on Ireland. To his credit his qualified defence of nationalism and the ideal of a federation of nations remained relatively constant in his work. That he was not entirely consistent shows at least the extent to which he allowed the complexity of the world to impose on his thought. He was not a blinkered ideologist. His views were genuinely complex, the product of a multi-faceted perspective – Irishman, West Briton, Protestant and socialist. More-over, his constructive ideas were for the most part sensible and humane. In spite of his own doubts, the Fabian conception of a commonwealth of nations was to play an important part in the future British policy on the Empire.

Shaw's vulnerability was both intellectual and personal. Intellectually, his understanding of Ireland was restricted by the reformist assumptions which informed his social democracy. He was, in spite of all he said as an artist-philosopher, a rationalist in a storm of irrationality. Little wonder, then, that he sought refuge in economism in the 1920s and beyond. Little wonder, too, that socialism generally has found nationalism so troublesome a subject. Shaw's tendency to view it as an anachronism, or as a necessary evil at best, is after all the common doctrinal response among socialists who glimpse in nationalism the undoing of their vision of a rationally-ordered and morally-unified world.

Personally, the tensions inherent in his relationship with England and his English audience were most acute in this context. This was evident in his Fabian national socialism as well as in his plays, with the relationship becoming more strained as his confidence in England's democratic system declined. The theme was reworked many times in the plays. In 1915 in *O'Flaherty VC*, for example – that curious recruiting pamphlet for the English army – Irish involvement in England's war with Germany was depicted as an opportunity for the Irishman to escape the ignorance and poverty of Irish country life. If the play was not exactly pro-English in outlook, it was certainly designed to subvert the rhetoric of Irish nationalism by presenting the connection with England in an essentially positive light. Writing in 1915 to Lady Gregory, Shaw said of it:

> The picture of the Irish character will make the Playboy seem a patriotic rhapsody by comparison. The ending is cynical to the last possible degree. The idea is that O'Flaherty's experience in the trenches has induced in him a terrible realism and an unbearable candour. He sees Ireland as it is, his mother as she is, his sweetheart as she is; and he goes back to the dreadful trenches joyfully for the sake of peace and quietness.
>
> (Shaw 1985b: 309)

Shaw was at his most waspish in this little play, cutting the ground away from under the feet of nationalist rhetoric at every turn. In O'Flaherty's mother he portrays the most rabid kind of romantic nationalism. As her son explains, 'She says all the English generals is Irish. She says all the English poets and great men was Irish. She says the English never knew how to read their own books until we taught them. She says we're the lost tribes of the house of Israel and the chosen people of God'. It also transpires that she thought O'Flaherty was actually fighting on the German side in the war and she is scandalized to find papers full of her son 'shaking hands with the English King at Buckingham Palace' (Shaw 1931c: 208). Amidst the cruel humour Shaw did have a serious point to make. His portrayal of Irish womanhood, Nora from *John Bull's* and Mrs O'Flaherty in particular, were in part deliberate Shavian commentaries on the nationalist habit of presenting the romantic spirit of Ireland in a female form. More especially, his ignorant Nora and silly Mrs O'Flaherty were his own commentaries on Yeat's mythology of Cathleen Ni Hoolihan who calls the young men of Ireland to battle. Shaw's portraits of Irish womanhood were, by way of contrast, savagely critical. In a backward land the women were the most backward of all, symbolizing not romantic hope, but the waste that belongs to the bitter heart.

A different temper informed *Saint Joan* in 1923. Its connection with Ireland is more tenuous, of course. Nevertheless, Shaw does present his heroine as an ardent Protestant and nationalist, a martyr in love with war who takes up arms against the arrogance of the English imperialists, denying what the xenophobic Chaplain describes as England's 'legitimate conquest, given her by God because of her peculiar fitness to rule over less civilized races for their own good.' In statements of this kind Shaw was surely inviting us to draw parallels with recent Irish experience, with the link between the executions of Saint Joan and the rebels of 1916 being perhaps the most obvious of these. But recent events in Ireland seem to inform much of the dialogue generally. Arguably, it was Shaw's frustration at the sight of Ireland going from terror to civil war which guided the uncompromising tone of the play's more overtly political statements. The play is a curious sort of tragedy, typically Shavian in that it contrives in the epilogue to dispel the terror of execution. It has its limitations, therefore. Nevertheless, it was in the context of this history play that Shaw chose to confront the tragedy of political violence more or less directly. It is rumoured that the IRA leader, Michael Collins, carried in his wallet the caricature of the English national character from Shaw's *Man of Destiny* (1897) (Forester 1971: 21). If he had lived a little longer he might have added Saint Joan's battle cry to his collection, 'but the English will not yield to prayers', she tells Dunois, 'they understand nothing but hard knocks and slashes' (Shaw 1932q: 92).

O'Flaherty VC and *Saint Joan* represent the polarities of Shaw's response to the English dimension to the Irish question. It might seem a strange perspective on the subject. But it was important to Shaw, partly because he knew he would gain the bulk of his audience not among nationalists and Protestants in Ireland but among the English middle class. And on his reading of the situation these were the very people with the power to solve the Irish question if only their political will could be directed along intelligent lines. The English dimension was important because interdependence, political and personal, was the keyword for Shaw in this context. England and Ireland, Englishmen and Irishmen, were bound together in a symbiotic relationship. There could be no divorce. The choice was between creative partnership or sordid, even tragic cohabitation.

AD 3000

Part IV of Shaw's 'metabiological pentateuch', *Back to Methuselah*, is set in Galway Bay in the year AD 3000. The play opens with an elderly gentleman talking to a young woman who is obviously his superior in knowledge and insight. The gentleman is a visitor to Ireland. He introduces himself as a Briton living in Baghdad, which he says is the new capital of the British Commonwealth. The young woman, for whom all sense of nationhood is meaningless, listens patiently as the man delivers his version of British and Irish history. Even now, it seems, the two nations are bound in tortuous interdependence. Hence, when the British transferred their power to the East, the Irish actually pursued them, entering all those countries where the national question was still to be resolved as professional agitators. When all nations were free and nationalism itself was a thing of the past, the Irish were in a dilemma, because, as the gentleman said, they had 'lost all their political faculties by disuse except that of nationalist agitation'. They were, in effect, bores without a cause. They said they were the lost tribe of Israel and tried to claim Jerusalem, upon which the Jews redistributed themselves throughout Europe. Finally, on the advice of an English Archbishop, a group of devoted Irishmen decided to return to Ireland. But on arrival the starkness of the place so shocked them that they left for England the next day – 'and no Irishman ever again confessed to being Irish, even to his own children; so that when that generation passed away the Irish race vanished from human knowledge' (Shaw 1931b: 151). As the young woman explained, it was not literally so, but the story would suffice as a parable on the fate of a people possessed by the curse of nationalism. In the play, the Irish question was to be solved only by the eradication of both the English and Irish nations from history.

And Ireland itself? In AD 3000 it is the seat of a female oracle to which the politicians of the Commonwealth make regular visits. The gentleman had come with his son-in-law who is Prime Minister of the Commonwealth. The play proceeds to tell of how the gentleman discovers that politicians seek only to manipulate the wisdom of the oracle for their own ends. Filled with disgust at this corruption, he asks if he might stay in Ireland. His request is granted. But immediately he is exterminated by the oracle. He dies because he is unable to return to his own world of untruth, and is equally uncapable of being admitted to the kingdom of truth that is Ireland. Such was the 'tragedy of an elderly gentleman'.

The tale forms a curious backdrop to Shaw's own relationship with Ireland, characterized as it was by a brittle intensity. He was, in spite of himself, intensely proud of being Irish. He loved the landscape and the climate. However, in 1923, having completed *Saint Joan*, he sailed for England, never to return again to his native country. It was not the surfeit of truth which killed the elderly gentleman that caused Shaw to leave. On the contrary, it was his despair at the surfeit of passion and conceit that fuelled the real tragedy of Irish politics which speeded his departure. In 1914 he had said that Ireland had always 'suffered from a plague of clever fools always saying the wrong things in the most skilful way'. He had tried to reverse the trend. By 1918, however, he was ready to admit that the follies of rhetoric had turned Ireland into 'one huge Mutual Admiration Club of Stupendous futility' (Shaw 1985b: 561). It was a hard lesson to learn for one so confident of his powers of persuasion. Yet he came to understand that his own reasonable and often comic reflections were hopelessly inadequate in the circumstances: trying to reason with the Irish was like singing a Mozart aria against an Atlantic gale. 'I find myself without real influence in Ireland because I am without provincial illusions', Shaw concluded stoically (Shaw 1985b: 729).

There was no oracle to exterminate him, so instead he went of his own accord to England, his adopted home, where 'the lunatics ... are comparatively harmless' (Shaw 1985b: 583). As for Ireland, Shaw's conclusion was grim indeed. Writing to Sean O'Casey in May 1950 he suggested that the Republic was drifting towards a political and cultural vacuum. In the old days, when Ireland was under Dublin Castle and Grand Jury Government, it had the romantic sympathy of the rest of the world 'we were the first flower of the earth and the first gem of the sea, our only rival being Poland', Shaw explained. All that had changed. The only residual source of hope now was to be found in the economistic argument, and even that took a curious turn:

Now we are an insignificant cabbage garden in a little islet quite out of the headlines; and our Fianna Fail Party is now The Unionist Party and doesnt know it. I have nothing to tell them except that the Ulster capitalists will themselves abolish the Partition when the Labour Party is strong enough to threaten them with an Irish 1945 at the polls, and they must have the support of the Catholic agricultural south to avert it.

(Shaw 1988: 864)

5

WAR AND PEACE

ALL CHANGE

Throughout the first half of 1914 the political agenda in Britain was dominated by Ireland and controversy surrounding the third Home Rule Bill. Would Ulster fight?, that was the great question of the hour. There was of course talk of war with Germany. Yet it seemed unreal somehow, equally unthinkable and inevitable. The prospect of the civilized nations of Europe destroying each other was altogether too perverse to contemplate. Concerned voices were raised. Graham Wallas, among others, foresaw a terrible catastrophe ahead, smoldering on for as long as thirty years: 'What will be the population of London, or Manchester, or Chemnitz, or Breman, or Milan, at the end of it?', he asked. In the jingoistic press a different picture was painted, in which the Hun was dealt a bloody nose and the heroic boys would all be home by Christmas. The Edwardian summer was too long, the faith in progress and in the invincibility of the British Empire too deeply set for the warnings of cranky professors and their kind to be taken seriously. If only the Ulstermen could be persuaded to drop their unreasonable demand for partition, if some arrangement could be reached with the suffragettes, then life would be all gold and honey. It is something of a caricature, but in a sense it was a generation that hanged itself on the expectation of plenty. In the event, the coming troubles in Ireland, terrible though they were, were something of a local diversion amidst the greater tragedy of total war.

The Great War was for Shaw, as for so many others, the big divide in his life. The world changed in 1914; nothing could be the same again. Before then the world was a relatively ordered place where a vitalist philosopher might contemplate man's dangerous wilfulness with impunity. Politics was a frustrating business, darkened occasionally by government repression of the suffregettes or by the threat of violence in Ulster, but a realm of hope all the same, to be reformed by a combination of science and commonsense. All that was to change.

Before 1914 war had often formed the dramatic backdrop against which Shaw had sketched his moral tales which were designed to overturn the

216

popular romantic conventions of Victorian theatre. War, as depicted in the plays, was invariably limited in scale, little more than a harmless diversion from the affairs of the world. In *Arms and the Man* the professional soldiers all carried chocolate creams instead of bullets. *The Devil's Disciple* portrayed war as a bloodless pastiche of gentlemanly manoeuvrings. In *The Man of Destiny* and in *Caesar and Cleopatra*, one side, the French and the Romans respectively, were so superior in leadership and organization that the prospects of long and costly war were practically nil. All that changed too in the age of total war: the bullets were real, the manoeuvrings lethal, the leadership and organization muddled in the extreme. In *Heartbreak House*, the one major play Shaw worked on during the Great War, the promise of violence was all-pervasive, only there its significance was deeper and more sombre, symbolizing ultimately the destruction of the species if it did not mend its ways. For the prophet of evolutionary righteousness, total war had raised the spectre of total annihilation.

SHAW'S WAR RECORD

One question, among many, is how did Shaw – the socialist and political thinker – cope with this upheaval? Did he have a good war? Most commentators have in fact been critical of his war record. Edmund Wilson, for example, described 'Common Sense about the War' as a 'double-faced document', and wrote of its intellectual and moral chaos (Wilson 1962: 194). Many readers, according to A.J.P. Taylor, simply did not understand the intentions of 'the rigorous Bismarckian' (Taylor 1957: 137). More recently, Kenneth Miller noted that Shaw's ideas on war represented 'a somewhat discordant blend of idealism and economic determinism', thus calling the very possibility of a contribution to socialist doctrine into question (Miller 1967: 52).

Shaw did not agree. In 1930 he collected his reflections on international relations into a single volume, binding them together with an elaborate running commentary. The book was entitled *What I Really Wrote About the War*. It consisted of letters to the press – one written on behalf of Belgian refugees and addressed to Woodrow Wilson – book reviews, many newspaper articles, including the notorious 'Common Sense', a pamphlet on the Peace Conference and a Fabian tract on the League of Nations written in 1928. Shaw's view was that it furnished ample proof of a unique contribution to the debate on international relations. He claimed to be the only member of the British labour movement prepared to analyse war and its causes in a clear and constructive manner. While many indulged in the naïveties of patriotism or pacifism, and others reverted to crude economism, he alone tried to understand the subject in all its complexity. He was aware of many imperfections in his work. All the documents were reproduced in what he called 'their original casualness', indicating unevenness in quality, a lack of rigour, evidence and sufficient consultation with more institutionally-minded colleagues in the Fabian Society. The faults, he believed, were largely due to socialist neglect of international relations before 1914, leaving him to tackle the issue 'single-handed and dictatorially' (Shaw 1931l: 1–7). What emerged from the resulting dialogue with world events was not a socialist theory in the formal sense, but rather an attempt to formulate a practical doctrine which represented an accommodation between the loosely-defined general principles of reformist socialism and the realities of international affairs. It is best described, Shaw suggested, as an exercise in socialist realism, where the decisive factor is the skill of the interlocutor between thought and practice.

In a rare moment of modest appraisal from 1912 he was to admit that foreign policy was not his subject; 'I do not know enough about it to meddle effectively'. But he was quick to learn. By August 1914 he was already telling Beatrice Webb that 'nobody else seems to have any power of seeing what is really going on'. Of 'Common Sense', he was to say 'I think it brings out Socialism with something like an intelligible and distinctive foreign policy at last'. When assessing his war record in a letter to H.G. Wells in 1916, Shaw declared confidently:

> In this war I began by putting three months hard work into studying it; and I found that when I tried to fortify myself by facts and documents I could make nothing of it . . . and that when I went on my knowledge of human character and experience of the ways of men, and guessed and calculated accordingly, disregarding all except the quite unmistakable facts, I came out right enough for practical purposes.
>
> (Shaw 1985b: 72, 257 and 441)

Shaw's claims cannot be accepted at face value. There is a need both to explain his seemingly confused and confusing reflections on war and peace, and to reassess their historical and doctrinal significance. Are the detractors right, or is there something in Shaw's immodest claims? Here it is argued that in these reflections we find many of the doctrinal dilemmas facing the revisionist and reformist elements in the Second International, particularly those relating to the uncertain and largely unexplored relationship between the politics of class and nation. This is not to imply that Shaw's reflections on war and peace are of interest solely as a means of representing past confusion. Many of the dilemmas he faced as a realist and ethical rationalist seeking to deflate, understand and generally weather the storm or irrationality raised by war are still relevant today.

This chapter deals primarily with Shaw's reflections on the Great War. It begins with a brief intellectual biography of the period. This offers a canvas against which a more abstract or analytical picture of Shaw's reflections can be drawn. Subsequently, the debate is in three parts, looking first at his attempt as a realist to confront the major issues posed by the war. Second, it considers his attempt as a moralist to offer a constructive policy of intelligent patriotism. Finally, it presents his views, as a realist and as a moralist, on how to establish and maintain world peace.

JOURNEY TO HEARTBREAK

'Journey to Heartbreak' is the subtitle Stanley Weintraub chose for his fine biography of Shaw, dealing with the years of the Great War. That is what it was. Shaw counted many friends and colleagues among the dead and wounded. He saw old friendships perish in the heat of controversy. The souls of the young were filled with iron. Where there should be hope, honeyed memories and golden prospects, there was cynicism and despair. All that Shaw had said about the illusions of progress, the limits of reason and the corrupt manipulation of values under capitalism, was confirmed. Only the reality was far worse than the prophecy. Shaw's excursions into vitalism meant that he was better equipped, intellectually at least, than most socialists for the war, better than the Webbs, for example, as Beatrice herself acknowledged (Cole 1952: 31). In these excursions Shaw had not approached the reality of Ypres or the Somme, however. He had travelled in hope and he had arrived at heartbreak.

Like his friend, Graham Wallas, Shaw had read the warning signs early on. On a comic note, in the 1909 *Press Cuttings*, the representative militarist, General Mitchener, obsessed with the idea of war, confesses to the Prime Minister, Balsquith, that he has thought of nothing but invading Germany for 'the last ten years'. In a more sober vein, writing in March 1913 Shaw advised the politicians to form a triple alliance of Germany, France and Britain, the cornerstones of the highest civilization in Europe, he called them, to police the continent 'against war and the barbarians' (Shaw 1931l: 11). In some respects, statements of this kind represented Shaw at his best and worst. At his best, because it was both prescient and down-to-earth, especially in its concern for the organization of military force to guard the cause of peace. It was the policy of a good European, he said, neither pacifist nor militarist in nature. At his worst, because, in equating civilization with some European states, he disclosed a special interest in 'the civilizing mission of the Protestant North', which in turn revealed the dangerous and damaging influence of Houston Stewart Chamberlain on his thought at this time.[1] Lurking in these distant corners of Shaw's work were all the ambiguities and dilemmas over race, progress and civilization which habitually complicated his outlook on world affairs. They were in many ways the ambiguities and dilemmas of a Victorian mind cast adrift in an increasingly alien age.

Good or bad, his advice was ignored. When war was declared in August 1914, Shaw, on holiday at the time at the Hydro Hotel in Torquay, retreated from the bustle of patriotic fervour to write a long and considered pamphlet on the causes of war and the basis for peace. For three months he poured over official reports and books in what amounted to a crash course in international relations. The resulting pamphlet was the notorious 'Common Sense', published as a special supplement to the *New Statesman* in November 1914. The furore it caused was unprecedented in Shaw's long career as a rebel and trouble-maker. He had known notoriety before, most recently in relation to the use of the expletive 'bloody' in his hit play, *Pygmalion*. This was of a different order.

As Dan H. Laurence tells us, the pamphlet used as its model Tom Paine's essay, 'Common Sense', seeking to emulate the latter in its tone of reasoned radicalism, intended as it was to undermine the folly and ignorance of the press, the politicians and the cheering crowds (Shaw 1985b: 239). Shaw's 'Common Sense' opened with the quote from Wallas on the prospects of a new thirty years war in Europe. It then declared 'The time has now come to pluck up courage and begin to talk and write soberly about the war'. Next, Shaw claimed for himself a special vantage point for his view of events, 'until Home Rule emerges from its present suspended animation', he wrote waspishly, 'I shall retain my Irish capacity for criticizing England with something of the detachment of a foreigner, and perhaps with a certain slightly malicious taste for taking the conceit out of her' (Shaw 1931l: 22). That conceit took the form of pretending England had no share in the making of the war, that she had only been dragged into it at the eleventh hour and then only in defence of the neutrality of 'brave little Belgium'. The conceit also took the form of pretending the English were not a party to the militarist mentality of the Junker class, that England had not engaged in secret Junker diplomacy and that now she was a model of fairness in her treatment of ordinary soldiers and their dependants. If ordinary men were to fight for their country (as they would), and if Shaw was to offer his qualified support for their endeavours (as he would), it had to be on an honest basis and with a sensible purpose in mind. More specifically, that purpose ought to be in keeping with the application of the principles of social democracy at home and abroad. Shaw's vision was, therefore, both short and long term as he tried to steer his public away from mindless jingoism towards critical and intelligent patriotism.

In response, he met with a storm of abuse from all quarters. Such old friends as Henry James and H.G. Wells were indignant, while Arnold Bennett was shocked by his 'intellectual nimbleness'. Shaw was snubbed at the Society of Authors and cartoons depicting him wearing an Iron Cross appeared in the press. Also, Rowland Hunt, the MP for Ludlow, told the Solicitor General, to loud cheers in the House of Commons, that statements in the pamphlet were not only false but 'very injurious to this country' and that it should have been banned by the censor.

Shaw was not entirely alone in his views. Support did come from such like-minded men as Bertrand Russell and Kier Hardie. But it was the infamous Irish outsider who drew the brunt of the criticism. He was the sort of man who 'would write an advertisement on his mother's grave', *The Times* reported. If trying to reason with the Irish in the 1920s was like singing a Mozart aria against an Atlantic gale, trying to reason with the comparatively harmless lunatics over in England in 1914 was more hopeless still, like an old man puffing against a whirlwind. If truth is indeed the first victim of war, common sense runs it a close second, it seems (Weintraub 1973: 53–82).

Dan H. Laurence is surely right to say that Shaw's decision to publish 'Common Sense' was 'the most audacious and courageous action of his life' (Shaw 1985b: 239). Though it came down ultimately in Britain's favour, its tone and language were hardly calculated to blend in with the mood of the times. It was the critique of Britain that struck home and in return Shaw was branded a collaborator and as a known sympathizer with German culture – Wagner, Nietzsche, Schopenhauer, Strauss and the rest. Nor was his popularity as a dramatist in Germany and Austria forgotten. Partly as a consequence of the work of his translator, Siegfried Trebitsch, Shaw had gained a huge reputation in Berlin and Vienna, with a number of his plays, including *Pygmalion*, being produced there before they arrived in the West End. The editor of the *Westminster Gazette* christened him 'Bernardi Shaw' (Weintraub 1973: 63).

Even in Labour circles he was something of an outsider. Though 'Common Sense' was published in *New Statesman*, a weekly paper Shaw had helped to finance, his relations with its editor, Clifford Sharp, never good before the war, grew increasingly tense. When in 1915 Sharp refused to publish 'More Common Sense about the War', Shaw stopped writing for the paper altogether. There was some relief in *New Statesman* circles, even among the Webbs who had never really appreciated Shaw's critical stance on the war. Nor were his views welcomed amongst the pacifist section of the labour movement. Though Shaw's prestige was sometimes invoked in defence of conscientious objectors after 1916, he was never happy in the role. He had, after all, declared in March 1913 that as a socialist he was 'very strongly in favour of compulsory service' (Shaw 1931l: 12). For many, comments of this kind confirmed their opinion of Shaw as a perverse crank, vain and egotistical to the last degree, caring not for truth or principle, but the thrill and glitter of controversy at any cost.

Isolation was the order of the day. He stopped writing for the theatre in a serious way. Instead, his thoughts turned more and more on religious themes as the neglected prophet sought comfort in metaphysical reflection. Even here he could not escape the war, however. In the 1915 preface to *Androcles and the Lion* his sense of personal identification with Jesus, the martyred rebel and lawmaker, was sufficiently strong to be embarrassing at times. As Christ was crucified on the cross, so Shaw was crucified in the press.

That isolation should not be overstated. Shaw still lectured for the Fabian Society. He chaired meetings of the Fabian Research Department which offered a new forum for debate on international affairs, resulting in 1915 in the publication of Leonard Woolf's seminal work, *International Government*. Also, as the war dragged on Shaw's views seemed less perverse. After conscription was introduced in 1916 and with the massive casualties on the Somme, public opinion grew more critical and Shaw more acceptable again. He even found favour in official circles. Shaw tells us that, as a result of his one-act play *Augustus Does His Bit*, produced by the Stage Society in

January 1917, which caricatured the inefficiency of the amateur bureaucrat in khaki, he was invited to visit the theatre of war in Flanders by the Commander in Chief (Shaw 1931c: 251). He dined with Haig and saw the destruction at Ypres at first hand. On his return to England, Shaw published his impressions of the war in *The Daily Chronicle* in a series of articles called 'Joy Riding at the Front'. Though Rowland Hunt still raised the matter of Shaw's visit in the Commons, it was nevertheless the start of his rehabilitation with his adopted country. Slowly the rebel was transformed into the official gadfly, licenced to criticize within the limits of the Defence of the Realm Act. Shaw acknowledged that he operated within its restrictions, never seeking to fuel the cause of 'unreasoning disillusion' with the war as he had once stoked-up the attack on 'unreasoning patriotism' (Shaw 1931l: 246). Of Haig, he wrote:

> He seemed to me a first rate specimen of the British gentleman and conscientiously studious soldier, trained socially and professionally to behave and work in a groove from which nothing could move him, disconcerted and distressed by novelties and incredulous as to their military value, but always steadied by a well closed mind and an unquestioned code. Subject to these limitations he was, I should say, a man of chivalrous and unscrupulous character. He made me feel that the war would last thirty years, and that he would carry it on irreproachably until he was superannuated.
>
> (Shaw 1931l: 244)

When peace came finally, Shaw (showing less sense than the Kaiser, he said, for he at least had had the sense to recognize his irrelevance and had withdrawn to Holland), produced a pamphlet in 1919 called *Peace Conference Hints*. With one eye on his critics he admitted 'in spite of the obvious fact that nobody was paying the slightest attention to my criticisms and proposals, I was still self-important enough to offer my views on the impending Versailles Conference' (Shaw 1931l: 287). He was right, nobody did pay him any attention. Undaunted, once the Conference ended Shaw was busy predicting it had laid the foundations for the next world war.

Especially remarkable among much that is outstanding in Shaw's war record is the sheer constancy of his outlook. There were developments and there were, too, dilemmas, errors and contradictions. All the same, the constructive views expressed in *Peace Conference Hints* were not so significantly different to those presented in 'Common Sense'. This was not a matter of inflexibility on Shaw's part, but of his good sense, of his keeping his head when those about him were literally and metaphorically losing theirs. This constancy allows us to approach Shaw's reflections on war and peace in terms of the major themes and issues concerned, as expressed primarily in 'Common Sense' and elaborated upon elsewhere.

REALISM AND THE WAR

Wars generally, and the Great War in particular, posed many dilemmas of a personal and doctrinal kind for Shaw. All his adult life he had worked at undermining the established values of English society. England was corrupt, he said, and in need of fundamental reform along socialist lines. Moreover, as a socialist he gave his allegiance to the working people of the world and not to those in any one nation. Of course, as his reflections on the Irish question show, there were complications and bolt holes in this scheme of things. Fundamentally, England and Shaw's English audience held a special place in his work, both as an artist and as a political thinker. England was the stage on which GBS performed his role of the outraged moralist and wise jester, and his relationship with that stage was intimate and intense. On the outbreak of war, therefore, he sought not only to retain his critical distance from the hysteria of the patriots, but also, in his equivocal and obtuse way, to lend his support to his own side in the conflict.

This dilemma can be linked to the tension between realism and moralism in Shaw's outlook. In 1914 and beyond his critical and supportive response to Britain's involvement in the war operated at both these levels. Ideally, he said in 'Common Sense', the German and allied armies should have acted according to the dictates of international socialism, thus shooting their officers and going 'home to gather in their harvests in the villages and make a revolution in the towns'. But choosing such an option required special conditions. It was only feasible, Shaw suggested, in a 'defeated conscript army pushed by its officers beyond human endurance' (Shaw 1931l: 23). To have advocated the policy in Britain in 1914 would have been to prefer moral and doctrinal purity to political relevance. It was a luxury the socialist realist could not afford.

Instead, as a realist Shaw tried to come to terms with the overwhelming support for the war throughout British society. This he achieved by adapting his consequentialist morality of happiness or welfare to suit international relations. His response at the time of the Boer War was along narrow social Darwinist lines: 'The problem before us is how the world can be ordered by Great Powers of practically international extent', he said, taking the partition of the globe among those Great Powers as the inevitable fact against which any revolt for national self-determination was to be judged. Clearly, that approach would not suffice in 1914 when the war was not of a colonial kind, but involved the Great Powers themselves. Now his response was to retain the consequentialist outlook while effecting a break between public and private morality, stating as a good realist, 'the judgement of international relations by the ordinary morality of personal intercourse between fellow citizens in peace is as idle as taking the temperature of molten steel by a common bath thermometer' (Shaw 1931l: 195). The distinction was not explored in detail, but the implication was that public policy – war in particular – invoked consequences different in scope and kind to those ordinarily invoked in personal relationships, so different in fact as to require separate criteria of evaluation. A policy must be judged by its consequences, the most pressing in the event of a major war being that of self-preservation, for war of this kind calls the very existence of a community into question. Strictly speaking, he argued, war belongs to the realm of necessity which is beyond good and evil, and those responsible for policy must attend, however ruthlessly, to the goal of survival (Shaw 1962b: 100). In 1930 he described the Great War as 'an engagement between two pirate fleets with, however, the very important qualification that as I and my family and friends were on board British ships I did not intend the British section to be defeated if I could help it' (Shaw 1931l: 2). This was not a restatement of the Second International's resolution on the right to national self-defence, a resolution which Shaw considered so ambiguous as to furnish sufficient justification for all the European states to engage in hostility in 1914. Instead it was an appeal to the primitive ethic of survival irrespective of the wider issues involved. When Maxim Gorki wrote to him in 1915 saying that he had 'kept aloof from the chaos of passions' which the war had evoked, Shaw replied that he had done no such thing:

> That is too easy and too useless. If I had to live as one of the community of tigers, I should have to deal with public affairs from the tigerish point of view. Having to live as I do as part of a community of animals far more dangerous than tigers – to wit, men and women – I am compelled on pain of being wholly impracticable and useless, to put myself in their places by an act of dramatic sympathy, and deal with the war ... in the manner of our parliamentary representative statesmen, who have to accept popular passions, however unreasonable, ferocious, and finally disastrous, as real factors in the situation.
>
> (Shaw 1985b: 340)

This hard-nosed aspect of Shaw's response to war is often cited as evidence of the association between his thought and the policy of *realpolitik*, with its attendant philosophy of power. In fact, his stance was inherently ambivalent. Shaw hoped that in the long term international law would replace the rule of expediency in international affairs. He did not subscribe, therefore, to the pursuit of power for its own sake in the Machiavellian manner, nor did he believe that war is inevitable on the ground that international society is an arena of struggle in which states and their citizens are compelled to engage in conflict. Nor yet did Shaw think that the participants in war simply had no choice but to fight, that the imperative of survival would necessarily determine their response in the event of conflict. The realist accepted the possibility of choice, although he was convinced that choice itself was a matter of contingency. His argument in 'Common Sense' was not that national belligerence was the best option, only that it was the sole practical option in the circumstances. The basic fact all socialists, including pacifists and defeatists, had to recognize was that the state was the primary unit of international politics, as well as the major recipient of working-class loyalty.

Shaw would appear to be on firm ground. Historical evidence certainly indicates that the radicals in the anti-war movement had little influence on rank and file opinion. There were simply too many barriers of class, outlook and interest to overcome. As Marvin Swartz explains, trade union leaders saw the dissenters of the Union of Democratic Control as a threat to their own authority, while 'the union rank and file feared middle-class subversion of the working-class movement' (Swartz 1971: 148). Neither pacifist idealism, nor the policy of 'peace by negotiation' advocated by Ramsay MacDonald, were practical propositions in the circumstances.

Shaw argued the case for socialist involvement in the war with particular force in the 1915 draft manifesto of the British section of the International Socialist Bureau. It was an 'attempt to formulate the non-Pacifist socialist view' and was concerned not with 'the general principles of international fraternity', but with how far 'as a matter of hard fact, the socialists intend, rightly or wrongly, to support their national Governments in the war'. The manifesto accepted as a matter of course that socialists were hopelessly entangled in and identified with their respective nation states, and declared that in wartime 'we must each fight for our country and seek rather to be the bravest of the brave than the most lukewarm of the half-hearted' (Shaw 1915: 5). Survival was the only option in the circumstances, to be treated by socialists and statesmen alike as a moral imperative.

Of course the realist argument of necessity and circumstance is ambiguous and disturbing. Does consequentialism establish the boundaries of political ruthlessness, or set any limits on the means of prosecuting war? Does the principle of choice have any practical significance in this context? A common complaint against Shaw, for example, was that he invariably found good grounds for supporting the British state in any conflict. He had a habit, as Fenner Brockway recalls, of protesting against war generally while supporting the prosecution of the conflict at hand (Brockway 1942: 55). Moreover, the argument of necessity based as it is on the survival of the state poses particular problems for the socialist, especially in the reconciliation of the politics of class and nation. This was the central dilemma in 1914. In Shaw's Fabian mind the state was *the* instrument of social reform and fundamental to the goals and functions of political life. Nevertheless, the state was, to employ Robert Osgood's and Robert Tucker's distinction, the condition not the source of value in his Fabian socialism. This meant that it had only conditional justification and that its 'necessities' could be denied if the state itself threatened to destroy those values associated (in this instance) with human welfare. Apparently, therefore, the possibility of choosing a policy of revolutionary defeatism was a real one in Shaw's work. However, as Osgood and Tucker point out, in practice the result of this view was 'to permit its holder to enjoy the best of both worlds' because if the state was the condition of value then almost any action to preserve its independence and survival could be justified (Osgood and Tucker 1967: 284). There was no choice in fact. The just war was that which was necessary for the state's survival: 'When war overtakes you, you must fight, and fight to win, whether you are the aggressor or the aggrieved, whether you loathe war as the kingdom of hell on earth or regard it as the nursery of all the virtues' (Shaw 1931l: 263).

ARMS AND THE MAN

A feature of Shaw's realist analysis of war was the tendency to associate war with human nature: man (and woman) was the fundamental cause of war. That argument was not upheld consistently in his work. Indeed, of the many elements in Shaw's reflections on war and peace this was perhaps the least stable and the most open to revision according to the dictates of controversy. More generally, it has been explained that Shaw's whole approach to human nature was flexible in kind. For the most part he was neither tempted by the cynics to recognize only the selfish and aggressive side to human nature, nor still by the idealists to see only the possibility for goodness and co-operation. Shaw acknowledged instead a duality in man in terms of the tension between the social and anti-social elements in his nature, and recognized there were instincts and tendencies making for both war and peace. For example, in a dour formulation from the preface to *Heartbreak House* he said war destroys 'the pretenses of civilization' and 'puts a strain on human nature that breaks down the better half of it, and makes the worse half a diabolical virtue' (Shaw 1931c: 27). In the plays themselves, on the other hand, he worked out the dramatic tensions inherent in man in relation to such contrasting characters as Dick Dugeon and Anthony Anderson from *The Devil's Disciple*, with the latter announcing at the close 'I thought myself a decent minister of the gospel of peace; but when the hour of trial came to me, I found that it was my destiny to be a man of action, and that my place was amid the thunder of the captains and the shouting'. Dick Dugeon, on the other hand, was born a moralist: 'This foolish young man boasted himself the Devil's Disciple; but when the hour of trial came to him, he found that it was his destiny to suffer and be faithful to the death' (Shaw 1931k: 73). Perhaps the best example of the creative dialogue between the dualities in human nature was in *Androcles and the Lion*, especially in the contrast between the pacifist, Androcles, and Ferrovius, the man of war. Ferrovius is very much the man of the moment. He must worship Mars despite his best efforts to embrace Christianity: 'The Christian god is not yet. He will come when Mars and I are dust; but meanwhile I must serve the Gods that are, not the God that will be' (Shaw 1931a: 144).

Shaw exploited his flexible outlook to the full in his journalistic reflections on war and peace, emphasizing different possibilities and perspectives as the occasion demanded. It was a case of rhetorical license. He could be relatively

226

optimistic, as in the first part of 'Common Sense' where he explained war delirium as a product of the propaganda of militarism and so open, in part at least, to political reform. What was needed in this context was a critique of the romance of war similar in kind to the one on offer in *Arms and the Man*. At this stage there was cause for criticism but not for despair. He was also keen to avoid disillusion in the 1917 articles on 'Joy Riding at the Front'. There he wrote that man's fascination with war was rooted in the heroic instincts which might one day (as H.G. Wells had suggested) find a more constructive outlet in 'a decently organized civil life' (Shaw 1931l: 268). Evidently, a combination of gullibility and anachronistic virtue was at fault.

Elsewhere, Shaw was less sanguine, more inclined to emphasize human pugnacity as the key factor in any analysis of the actual or potential causes of war. This line of reasoning was especially important in his critique of disarmament where he struck a deeply Machiavellian note in the contemporary debate, in stark contrast, that is, to the general overture on the rationality of peace as performed by the leading socialist and liberal players of the period. As he informed those 'romantic novices in foreign policy', the pacifists, in 'Common Sense', it is not the arms which are to blame but man himself, 'What makes both war and the gun is the man behind them'. The point was made again in 1921 during the Washington Conference on disarmament when Shaw wrote, 'The notion that disarmament can put a stop to war is contradicted by the nearest dog fight. The story of Cain and Abel has been questioned by many honest Bible smashers, but never on the ground that Cain had no armament. . . . It is the man who fights, not the weapon. Also the woman' (Shaw 1931l: 374). The greatest danger in Shaw's mind was that 'created by inventing weapons capable of destroying civilization faster than we produce men who can be trusted to use them wisely', a danger which could only be averted by 'a general raising of human character'. Such was his sombre conclusion to 'Common Sense'. War, however, called the very possibility of such moral transformation into question; it demonstrated that civilization itself was but a pretence, a thin veil hiding the primitive forces in man which must be controlled by the threat of force itself.

Shaw understood, as few others at the time did, that military power could not be regulated by a naïve anti-militarism, and he was prepared to employ a partial conception of human nature in order to convey his ideas to the public. Force was an integral part of international politics and had to be considered on its own terms by those concerned to secure world peace. Their business was 'to organize a balance of military power against the war', something which could be done 'only by a combination of armed and fanatical Pacifists of all nations, not by a crowd of non-combatants wielding deprecations, remonstrances, and Christmas cards'. A statement to the effect that diplomats must prepare for the next war as a means of avoiding it was not a Shavian paradox. In the absence of an effective supernational authority, he said in *Peace Conference Hints*, even socialist governments should prepare for the worst on the ground that 'an army and navy in hand is worth ten League of Nations in the bush' (Shaw 1931l: 94).

His critique of disarmament and of the widespread aversion to the calculated management of force as an instrument of policy in liberal and socialist circles stands as one of the finest achievements of Shaw's self-styled realism. It also gives some indication of the part played by the factor of human nature in his multi-casual analysis of war. That his views on human nature varied so much does not make for theoretical elegance. But then Shaw's concern was not so much with theoretical consistency as with the practicalities of persuasion in the inherently untidy world of international politics. He was prepared, as he explained in 1930, to appeal to every morality in turn to carry his points, the major consideration (in this context) being the goals of happiness and security rather than those of moral or intellectual dignity. In the ill-fated 1915 'More Common Sense about the War' he claimed he was ready to shoot all pacifists (including MacDonald, Liebknecht and Luxembourg) 'ruthlessly rather than give them the slightest real power over foreign policy until they have an intelligible program which promises more prosperity and security than we, with all our faults, have won at Waterloo and Sedan and so many other stricken fields' (Shaw Papers: BM 50669B). All of which seems far removed from Kenneth Miller's 'discordant blend of idealism and economic determinism'.

MORALISM AND THE WAR

Nevertheless, Shaw's reflections on war and peace were indeed multi-faceted in nature. In 'Common Sense' he sought to legitimate his pro-British stance by supplementing the realist argument of necessity with a more general appeal to the principles of social democracy. As a moralist he sought to bring those ends associated with what he called 'the morality of peace' to bear on the necessities of war. In this respect, he maintained that the war could be justified (from his own side at least) not only in terms of survival or even material well-being, but also in relation to the broader goals of political rights and moral development which were fundamental to the social-democratic conception of human welfare. To this end he offered a characterization of the internal structures of those states vying for European hegemony, to which he added a minimal defence of the British state as the lesser of two evils (eschewing any reference to the 'just war' argument). Further, from a programmatic standpoint, he explained how reformist socialism should endeavour to employ the war as an opportunity to advance its own ends against those of its political opponents. In his view, the correct strategy for the Labour Party was to combine the pursuit of 'genuine working-class democracy' in domestic politics with the formulation of an 'intelligent and patriotic foreign policy – patriotic in the European as well as the insular sense' (Shaw Papers: BM 50669B). It was, of course, a controversial strategy which caused many on the Left to accuse him of opportunism and capitulation, the very creatures which had gnawed at the militancy of the Second International.

Starting with Shaw's views on Britain and Germany, his initial purpose in 'Common Sense' was to inject some coolness into the otherwise heated debate on the responsibility for war by explaining Britain's share of the guilt. Against the uncritical patriots, he established how Britain's involvement in the arms race and in secret diplomacy, together with the coarse temper of its jingoistic press, had all made for conflict. And he went on to register his debt to German culture and to affirm his friendship with the German people. Moreover, in order to draw a specifically socialist conclusion from his analysis, Shaw turned to the standard economistic identification of capitalism with war, stating 'The wise man looks for the cause of war not in Nietzsche's gospel of the Will to Power, or Lord Robert's far blunter gospel of the British Will to Conquer, but in the custom house'. Andrew Undershaft's creator was sure that 'Plutocracy makes for war because it offers prizes to the plurocrats', the implication being that the substitution of social democracy for plutocracy would result in 'the recognition of the identity of interests between all workers' and so signal an end to war (Shaw 1931l: 58). In the meantime, as both Britain and Germany were capitalist states, both were at fault, it seemed. It was in the light of such statements that Edmund Wilson claimed that Shaw's 'real interpretation of war was Marxist in nature' (Wilson 1932: 242).

In fact the status of the economic explanation was, to say the least, ambivalent in Shaw's work. He certainly used it, especially after 1920 when he sought to build a wall of rational hope around his political convictions. He was also its critic. For example, in 1885 he ridiculed the orthodox economic account of the Sudanese War held by William Morris and others: 'The Socialist League have unfortunately an official explanation for all wars; and they have forced it upon the Egyptian affair with the result of considerably extenuating its wickedness'. In Shaw's view, the war was 'a far lower form of villainy than commercial exploitation' (Shaw 1965a: 131). Clearly, the economistic approach cut against the grain of both his vitalism and his social democracy. As a social democrat, he believed that such reductionism stifled socialism's effectiveness and creativity, particularly in its refusal to accept a positive role for the state in the politics of welfare. According to his moderate strategy, the state was not only necessary for the efficient management of society, it also had a wider historical role to play as a moral force promoting humanitarian values. Obviously, all states would not promote humanitarian values in equal measure; it was possible, therefore, in principle, to prefer one capitalist state to another.

In this way he was able in 'Common Sense' to present his support for Britain in terms of a positive argument which accepted, on the one hand, Britain's share in the diplomatic and economic causes of war, while, on the other, explaining the relative superiority of its political, state structure in relation to the morality of peace. It was a qualified defence arrived at by an obscure and circuitous route, although its moral was plain for all that. In effect he sought to establish a special relationship between the internal structure and temper of the German state and the politics of militarism. Hohenzollernism, Shaw claimed, was controlled by 'the morality of feudal robber barons and gentleman conquerors'; it had made itself 'the exponent and champion in the modern world of the doctrine that military force is the basis and foundation of national greatness, and military conquest the method by which the nation of the highest culture can impose that culture on its neighbors' (Shaw 1931l: 102). The outlook was embedded in German caste politics, in the Junker tradition and the extent of aristocratic influence on policy.

It was not that Britain was free of such anachronisms. On the contrary, he spent a long time in 'Common Sense' vilifying Sir Edward Grey, the Foreign Secretary of the day, who, in Shaw's view, encapsulated all the limitations of the Junker class of politicians. In what amounted to a savage caricature of an old foe, Shaw poured scorn on Grey's mental and moral outlook. Many commentators, Arnold Bennett among them, disliked the caricature intensely, seeing it as the worst and most mistaken part of the pamphlet (Weintraub 1973: 62). But Shaw was adamant. Grey and his kind, in Britain and on the continent, were a public menace, remnants from another age who refused to quit a drama they could neither understand nor master. The caricature was supplemented by Shaw's treatment of the upper-class military men in his plays. There were exceptions, notably General Burgoyne from *The Devil's Disciple*, but usually this type represented the forces of reaction, as in the case of Colonel Craven from *The Philanderer* and General 'Boxer' Bridgenorth from *Getting Married*, the latter being introduced as 'ignorant, stupid, and prejudiced, having been carefully trained to be so' (Shaw 1932d: 260). The Junker spirit was not, therefore, exclusive to Germany.

The point Shaw tried to make in 'Common Sense' was that Britain and Germany differed significantly in the extent to which the militarist mentality achieved formal expression in state institutions and in the scope of its influence over every aspect of civilian life. Colonel Craven and General Bridgenorth were both portrayed as rather isolated figures barely able to cope, emotionally and intellectually, with developments in the world outside the officers' mess. The implication was that in Germany, on the other hand, the values and attitudes encapsulated by such characters were far more widespread, pervading every sphere of life. The philosophy of power, the belief that 'Providence is on the side of the big battalions', was endemic in German political life, dominated as it was by the outmoded ideals of aristocratic militarism.

INTELLIGENT PATRIOTISM

Shaw's doctrinal defence of Labour's intelligent patriotism developed from his identification of the relationship between monarchy and militarism, focusing in the first instance on the dissolution of the Prussian monarchy as the precondition for European security. His object was to exchange those moralities and institutions which were hopelessly out of date for more appropriate arrangements better suited to the goals of prosperity and moral development. Republicanism (in the narrow sense of the term) was fundamental to those aims. It formed the basis of his wartime propaganda which was concerned to eradicate the social roots of aristocratic militarism throughout Europe (Britain's constitutional monarchy was not excluded). Monarchy, according to Shaw, was both a symbol of inequality and of the idolatrous ethics of militarism. He even described war as a sport of kings. If the Great War was to achieve anything positive, it might at least destroy the myth of Prussian efficiency which implied the superiority of despotism over democracy, of arbitrary rule over the rule of law, a preference for authority before emancipation. However equivocal Shaw's support for democracy was before 1914 and after 1918, and however strongly his socialism was associated with the Prussian model of statism, during the Great War at least he was consistent in his advocacy of democracy against either oligarchy or autocracy. In *Peace Conference Hints*, for example, he made the point that 'Democracy as it exists today has little more to say for itself than that its hopes and possibilities are infinite, whereas the possibilities of oligarchy and autocracy are limited to such an extent by their fundamental economic and psychic unsoundness that they can hardly be said to hold out any hopes at all' (Shaw 1931l: 312). Parliamentary democracy was far from perfect, but at least it had potential for improvement, whereas alternative systems of government, however superficially efficient they might appear, had no real potential for moral and spiritual progress.

Moreover, from a practical standpoint, the very lack of political homogeneity in Europe placed undue stress on the balance of power, resulting in constant opposition between monarchial Germany and republican France, with Britain's uncertain position only adding to the state of tension. Evidently, the argument for republicanism was the practical moral to be gained from the militarist origins of war. In 1917 Shaw presented a draft manifesto to the Fabian Society entitled 'Fabianism and the War', where he said, 'socialism has always and necessarily been federalist and republican'. He went on to say that, unless modern civilization is constituted on this basis, then socialism 'will find itself helplessly entangled in dynastic wars' (Shaw 1917: A1/1).

The argument was hardly original. Most liberals, as Kenneth Waltz points out, believed that the militarist and authoritarian character of German politics was at the root of war, and many social democrats were inclined to agree (Waltz 1951: 10). But if the argument was not original, it at least had a good pedigree in Shaw's work. In *Arms and the Man*, for example, he portrayed the conflict between the idealism of the feudal aristocrat, Sergius, who claims that he went 'through the war like a knight in a tournament with his lady looking down at him', as against the prosaic Bluntschli, the free citizen of republican Switzerland, who undermines such ideals by stating the professional soldier's adherence to those conventions of war which limit its destructiveness. In this context the propaganda of republicanism was part of a general assault against conventional ethics and romantic logic, with Bluntschli serving as an illustration of the moral superiority of modern republican civilization over its aristocratic counterpart. In 'Common Sense', republicanism served the policy of intelligent patriotism by allowing the social democrat to use the critique of militarism as a means of pursuing those institutional reforms Shaw considered necessary for security and human development at home as well as abroad. And it was a double-edged policy in that it entailed a critique of Britain as well as of Germany, of the lesser along with the greater of the two evils, so dispelling some of the stigma of capitulation.

In the event his approach proved unique among the Fabians who declined to endorse his manifesto positively identifying socialism with the republican cause. Shaw knew they would. He believed Sidney Webb had no interest in foreign policy and was prepared to simply follow the Government line. It was because of this he said that Webb had withdrawn support for him in his argument with *New Statesman* over its refusal to publish his pamphlet, 'More Common Sense about the War', in 1915. Perhaps that in turn left Shaw in a mischievous frame of mind. Two years on he informed H.G. Wells, 'I am pulling the leg of the Fabian Society by proposing a republican manifesto to the Executive, but have no hope of creating anything thereby except an unquiet recalcitrance' (Shaw 1985b: 449). The moment for republicanism was not yet. It seemed a still more limited conception of the morality of peace was required if it was to agree with the narrow outlook which prevailed in influential sections of the British labour movement.

THE CITIZEN SOLDIER

J.M. Winter has argued that Sidney Webb's work on the War Emergency Committee avoided the broader policy issues, concentrating instead on the more immediate concerns of working-class welfare in the services as well as in industry (Winter 1974: 184–233). Winter notes Webb's propensity for turning moral questions into purely technical ones. Shaw, too, working in an independent capacity, touched on these matters, albeit from a rather idiosyncratic standpoint. In 'Common Sense' he offered a guide to the Labour Party on how to combine its pro-war stance with a policy best described as a form of parliamentary class confrontation. A set of objectives were provided, focusing on the conditions of those in the services and developing again his critique of militarism. He had for many years opposed the militarist soldier, that fighting automaton devoid of 'moral rights and moral duties'. In a series of powerful articles in *The Saturday Review* in 1897 he argued that the militarist soldier was a disgrace to civilized society: 'Some day when we get the better of our national cowardice, we shall give up the system of having our fighting done by slaves, and boldly make the soldier and sailor as free as the policeman' (Shaw 1897: 369). In 1914 he sought to persuade the Labour Party to press for major reform in the conditions of military service. Those in the services should retain their civil rights as a matter of course, including the right to join a trade union and to strike if necessary in order to secure the legal minimum wage. Further, in an unusually populist development, Shaw argued that the working class should be properly represented on all those committees of the War Office dealing with affairs directly affecting the welfare of the ordinary recruits, for only in this way could the interests of the common soldier and his dependants be protected. In the absence of such representation, policy would be considered on the basis of official ignorance of working-class life and probably to the detriment of working-class welfare. An example from 1914 was the War Office propaganda on the right to immediate discharge 'the minute the war is over', which, Shaw said, displayed total ignorance of the threat of unemployment facing the discharged soldier. Shaw's view was that the Labour Party should work to ensure that no man would be discharged from the services unless 'a job had been found for him in civil life' (Shaw 1931l: 65).

Abstracting from the many details of his proposals, they can be summarized in terms of the substitution of the citizen soldier for the militarist soldier. This in turn needs to be seen in relation to his broader commitment to compulsory military service, a policy which was part of the morality of service at the root of Shaw's socialism. His views were first formulated in *Fabianism and the Empire* where he established a doctrinal allegiance to military as well as industrial conscription, advocating the formulation of a small standing army of professional soldiers backed up by a militia of citizen soldiers with all their rights intact. Compulsory military service should be a socialist institution, he said in 'More Common Sense about the War', not 'a reckless imposition of one slavery the more on the proletariat'. Such were the ideal arrangements that would constitute an 'advance in social organization'. If the Labour Party adopted the policy it could then begin to use the war for its own ends by transforming military service from a condition of slavery to a training ground for civic virtue. The war could thus be made to serve the cause of the broader as well as the more limited conception of republicanism.

The reality was very different. When conscription was introduced in 1916 it was along conventional militarist lines. Shaw was not exactly supportive. True to his old obsessions, he despised the compulsory vaccination of all conscripts (Weintraub 1973: 156). He also recognized that conscription weakened his moral defence of Britain as a bastion, however flawed, of the democratic rights of the individual against arbitrary state power. Besides, it was too impractical, he said in 1915. But for all that he still accepted the reality of conscription on expedient grounds. When Bertrand Russell wrote to him in 1916 asking him to intervene on behalf of a conscientious objector, Shaw replied that, while he felt sorry for the man, he could only advise him to serve.

The unfortunate man would not be asked to kill anyone for a year or so, Shaw predicted, by which time 'he will either have been discharged as unfit for service or else have realized that a man living in society must act according to the collective conscience under whatever protest his individual conscience may impel him to make. I think that is what we are bound to tell all the pacific young men who apply to us' (Russell 1975: 289). Was it a case of expediency or of the morality of service masquerading as intelligent patriotism? Either way, the would-be conscientious objector received cold comfort from Shaw.

ASSESSMENT

Shaw's attempt to bring the morality of peace to bear on war is open to many interpretations. Considered as the basis of a practical doctrine for the British labour movement it was an abject failure; the doctrine of military and industrial conscription was as alien to the Labour mind as the ill-fated (in Britain) policy of republicanism. However, a different picture emerges when Shaw's socialist realism is viewed as an authentic expression of Fabian doctrine (on conscription, for example), something which Sidney Webb could not offer from within the War Emergency Committee. Despite the contradictions and comprises, Shaw at least tried to retain a distinctly socialist edge to his work. The war, he believed, had given a tremendous boost to collectivism in every sphere of life. The question the labour movement had to confront was not one of organization but of the ends which organization was designed to serve. Unless collectivism was allied to a clear egalitarian notion of distributive justice then it was just as likely to meet the needs of exploitation as of emancipation; 'The only outstanding question as to Collectivism in industry is as to whether it shall be applied as Socialism for the benefit of humanity or exploited by Capitalism and Privilege in the form of The Servile State', Shaw wrote in 1917 (Shaw 1917: A1/1). Bringing the ideals of socialism and republicanism together, he said 'ethical reconstruction will take the form of a substitution of the ethics of Communism for the ethics of commercialism, and of the ethics of democracy for those of feudalism' (Shaw 1962b: 109). All too often social democracy has allowed its consequentialist ethic to lead it into the fallacy of identifying its own ends with those of the established order. Shaw, it could be argued, sought to avoid that pitfall by seeking to direct the labour movement toward a social democratic conception of the morality of peace.

Against this picture of doctrinal scrupulousness, there is the left-wing critique of Shaw's work as a thinly veiled apology for the British state. Quite simply, it was too moderate and too equivocal as a guide to action. Shaw made no secret of the fact that, during the period of voluntary enlistment, in particular, he accepted a form of self-censorship purely because the danger of 'weakening the nation's morale' prevented him from stating all the faults of the British Government. In 1918, in a letter to the American socialist John

Spargo, he was to admit that 'the hatchet has to be buried between socialism and capitalism whilst the war is on' (Shaw 1985b: 556). Practically speaking, national unity outranked the policy of class confrontation, leading him directly into the consequentialist fallacy he sought to avoid. Unlike the militants, Shaw had no interest in using war to foster revolution simply because he denied the viability of the revolutionary road to socialism. Indeed, in *Peace Conference Hints* he lumped Bolshevism with Syndicalism, for they both abrogated the principle of gradualism and were timely warnings of what might befall democracy if its leaders failed to introduce effective political reform.

According to the left his analysis was superficial, failing to plumb the true economic depths of the matter. Shaw admitted as much (largely for tactical reasons) in the pamphlet *Irish Nationalism and Labour Internationalism*, where he said the Labour Party was right not to 'put Republicanism in the forefront of its political program' because 'only economic change can produce real political change' (Shaw 1920a: 6). Still, the relationship between economics and politics remained flexible, with the revolutionary vision of the peaceful socialist order being tempered by a realism which could not escape the exigencies of power politics. Writing at the end of the war, Shaw dispelled the orthodox identification of socialism with peace, stating:

> If every one of the Powers had in office a Labour Party boiling over with pacific enthusiasm, and had inscribed on its national arms 'Prole-tarians of all lands, unite', none the less their diplomatists and soldiers, in the absence of a League of Nations, would have to prepare for the worst as carefully as if Junkerism were still in command of all the earth.
>
> (Shaw 1931l: 306)

Generally, it was a sense of unresolved tensions and contradictory perspectives which pervaded his reflections on the morality of peace; the critical relationship between the appeal to morality and political rights, on one side, and to necessity and consequence, on the other, remained ambiguous; the conflicting demands of class and nation escaped resolution. There was a sense of struggle with a whole collection of intractable dilemmas which would not admit of a dignified solution from the standpoint of socialist realism. The policy of intelligent patriotism was more ingenious than convincing. A doubt even hung over socialism itself – a necessary though not sufficient condition of international order. At least the social democrat understood that economic determinism was no substitute for a combination of economic, political and moral reform.

Realism, moralism and international order

Nowhere are the tensions between the realist and moralist elements in Shaw's work more apparent than in a lecture he delivered to the Aristotelian Society on 'The Ethical Principles of Social Reconstruction' in April 1917. He began by establishing the classical realist view of war as governed by necessity, before posing the critical question of the moment as to whether 'it is not conceivable that a treaty concluding a war should have any higher ethic than war itself'. As a realist, he was bound to conclude that the victors should exploit their advantage to the full when dictating the terms of peace; it would be no less than a political crime, asserted the devil's advocate, 'if they sacrificed the smallest fraction of the fruits of victory'. Thus, in the event of a decisive victory there would be no ethical reconstruction, only a vengeful treaty which would ensure the immediate resumption of international anarchy. Stalemate alone offered any hope of order. Although he acknowledged that this was an unlikely contingency at best, Shaw still believed it was worth expounding his own version of the principles of reconstruction, based on yet another scheme involving 'the renunciation of sovereign nationality and the subordination of nationality to a supernational power' (Shaw 1962b: 105).

Such schemes were of course intrinsically problematical for revolutionary socialism because they not only entailed the use of bourgeois methods and institutions, but also implied the maintenance of the capitalist system itself. For the social democrats, there were no such inhibitions. Once their interest in international relations was aroused in 1914, many leading Fabians began research into the legal and institutional foundations of international order. The most celebrated product of their work was Leonard Woolf's *International Government*, written in 1915 and published a year later in America with an introduction by Shaw whose involvement ensured maximum publicity for the book. There was, in fact, much common ground between his own and Woolf's thinking on international order; both believed that security could be achieved through guarantees of mutual defence against aggression rather than through alliances and that the problem of deciding on the aggressor in a dispute should fall to a supernational tribunal.

However, two important differences must be noted, one of emphasis, the other of a substantive kind. First, Shaw's emphasis on the mobilization of force as the crucial element in the organization of order was certainly distinctive. The supernational authority 'must not be conceived as a Tolstoyan celebration', but as 'an attempt to focus the coercive forces, moral and physical, of idealism' (Shaw 1931l: 307) within a 'Hegemony of Peace' (Shaw 1931l: 78). This was the practical moral arising from the militarist balance of power; moral force alone was of no value unless it had the executive power to enforce its will on a chaotic world, unless it could serve the ends of human welfare in an effective way. The responsible statesman could accept no other basis for incursion into national sovereignty.

Second, Shaw was certain, as early as 1914, that any scheme looking toward a league of *all* nations would be undermined by the dual forces of political and ethical heterogeneity. His argument was that the many plans for international government circulating at the time all underestimated the sheer complexity of the world, in effect committing the cardinal rationalist error of neglecting the variety of political traditions and moralities which such a government would have to transcend. It was not that Shaw held a strict philosophical belief in moral relativism, rather he pointed out as a matter of contingency that the world was characterized by ethical heterogeneity, by different conceptions of justice, habits of mind and practices, all of which would make a League of Nations unwieldy and impractical. Such an organization simply could not act as an executive power in world affairs. Shaw's belief was that a measure of cultural, political and racial homogeneity was 'the first requisite of a stable political combination'. It would be unreasonable to expect a state to renounce sovereignty over collective security unless there was some firm basis for such a community of nations. Moreover, if international peace was to be kept by a system of guarantees then reliability was essential on the part of individual governments.

Concealed within this supposedly relativist doctrine was a decided preference for some forms of government and the values they represented. As noted above, before the war he had expressed the view, 'we can do nothing but clamour for an entente with Germany, and a revival of the great alliance of the Protestant North in defence of civilization' (Shaw 1985b: 72). This is an interesting example of Shaw's Eurocentric views. Also, in 'Common Sense' he argued that in the first instance political combination should be restricted to those nations which were ruled by law and governed by democratic procedures, and not by the personal caprice of a despotic monarch, as in the case of Tsarist Russia. The members of the original League of Nations 'must either be republics or constitutional monarchies' boasting 'a well-developed Labour movement, Socialist movement, and Science movement', and in April 1917 'the materials for such a League were to be found between the Carpathians and the Rocky Mountains, and not further afield'. Initially the world's peace must be secured by the high civilization of Western Europe and North America, although such a combination 'would have to be prepared for the formation of other Leagues of Nations in the yellow world, the Indian world, perhaps in the Slav world and the Spanish-Indian world' (no mention was made of the African or Arab worlds) (Shaw 1931l: 328). In time, Shaw speculated, 'it may be possible to induce the supernational groups to make pretersupernational compacts', thus hopefully eliminating international conflict (Shaw 1962b: 107). His view was that the goals of international socialism – of world federation or even of a Parliament of Man – could not be realized (if they could be realized at all) until man has become 'a much less miscellaneous lot than he is at present'.

There was something oddly Fabian about Shaw's scheme, particularly in its appeal to gradualism and in its recognition of the importance of cultural and historical differences for any major political reform. Consideration of the uniqueness of the British political tradition and its implications for socialism was of course crucial to Fabianism's national socialism and it is interesting to note that Shaw alone seemed prepared to apply such notions to the analysis of international politics. In doing so he gained an original perspective on the difficulties encountered in bringing morality to bear on the problem of order.

Loose ends

Though original and often sensible, ultimately Shaw's reflections on war and peace were marred by gaps and confusions. There were too many loose ends in his work for it to be called a socialist theory of international relations. The relationship between the legalistic conception of the supernational authority and the internal state structures remained ill-defined – ideally, all those states participating in the combination should be democratic and socialist in nature, but in practice he was prepared to accept more or less any arrangement which might further the minimal goal of security in an uncertain world. In this respect, the process of transition, together with the means of applying the principle of political homogeneity, remained unclear. Shaw wrote of the need for a well-developed socialist movement, but he did not explain under what conditions, if any, a social democratic state was expected to renounce sovereignty in matters relating to collective security when other member states in the combination remained essentially capitalist in nature. Indeed, in light of his commitment to the state as the condition of value, his analysis of the limitations on sovereignty entailed by a supernational authority was woefully inadequate. In one sense he appeared to sanction the customary social democratic argument that socialism was an internal matter and that domestic and foreign politics should be treated in two separate compartments; in another, he seemed prepared to forego doctrinal issues altogether for the sake of peace. He disagreed with the structure and terms of reference of the League of Nations, yet he always urged nations, groups and individuals to use its organs in the settlement of disputes on the basis that it might, despite its imperfections, make some contribution to human welfare (a tendency encapsulated in the play *Geneva* in 1938, which is discussed in Chapter 6). It was the obvious response for a Fabian desperate to avoid another war, eager to accommodate the shifting realities of power politics within the framework of his thought. In the 1930s, when the quality of Shaw's reflections on war and peace declined markedly, he was to be found oscillating between the League of Nations and Stalinist Russia as the greatest hope for peace in an increasingly hostile and alien world.

Among the early British socialists Shaw was renowned for his attempts to reconcile the competing claims of power and reason, order and morality, to effect some compromise that might be described as a form of progressive *realpolitik*, or as an exercise in socialist realism. His intention was to explore neglected avenues of thought, to confront those practical obstacles to socialism which others preferred to ignore. From this standpoint, the most serious flaw in his scheme in 1917 was its lack of serious consideration of empire. Much of the globe was at that time divided into imperial spheres of interests, a fact which any scheme seeking to establish politically homogeneous combinations could not ignore. The matter was especially significant for Shaw because he had supported British imperialism in 1900. As noted in Chapter 1, that support is open to conflicting interpretations. What is clear is that Shaw did not reconcile these views on empire with his later thoughts on political homogeneity, and in this respect his reflections on international order must be said to be radically inconsistent and incomplete. Original or not, sensible or otherwise, his reflections terminated in confusion. When he confronted the problem of Britain's imperialist future in a radio broadcast in 1934 he confidently announced that lack of racial and political homogeneity would inevitably destroy the Empire. But instead of recommending a drastic limitation of Britain's influence to the North Atlantic, he preferred instead to appeal for imperial federation (Shaw 1934a: 1). This was the long-term outcome of Shaw's accommodation of power to reason in relation to international order.

Aftermath

Shaw's critics are surely right to note the confusion in his reflections on war and peace. Though his concerns were in their way remarkably constant, he approached these from different perspectives, seeking to combine seemingly irreconcilable standpoints. Critics say he was too impressed by power, too eager ultimately to resort to a consequentialist mode of reasoning which could establish no firm boundaries to political ruthlessness. Was the policy of intelligent patriotism anything but plain political opportunism?

Perhaps not. But in its way the very untidiness of Shaw's reflections and the openness with which he courted contradiction made him a good guide to many of the dilemmas facing reformist socialism in relation to international politics. The conflicting claims of the politics of class and nation were evident in Shaw's work, as was the uncertain relationship between capitalism and war in social democratic thought. There was much that was representative of reformist socialism together with some original and sensible insights on disarmament and other issues. Perhaps his reflections are simply out of date. After all, almost as he was rising to address the Aristotelian Society, comrade Lenin was speeding toward the Finland Station intent on changing the face of world politics to a degree which seems beyond the scope of the Fabian imagination. Yet, curiously, the tensions within Shaw's socialist realism appear remarkably resilient to revolutionary transformation. The difficulties he faced in formulating the policy of intelligent patriotism are not unknown to socialists who operate in a world where the state remains the major recipient of working-class loyalty and where the ideal of internationalism found expression in the Soviet Empire founded on a system best characterized as a form of bureaucratic state socialism. His treatment of force as an integral part of international politics is certainly relevant to socialism in the nuclear age.

Thomas Nagel has said that 'the world can present us with situations in which there is no honorable or moral course for a man to take, no course free of guilt and responsibility for evil' (Walzer 1977: 326). This, in essence, was Shaw's predicament in 1914. It is a predicament socialism itself cannot escape so long as it seeks to accommodate its vision of justice to the realities of power politics.

The Great War left an indelible mark on Shaw. Writing to the humanitarian socialist Henry Salt in 1919, on the death of his wife, Kate, he said he hoped it was not the war that killed her: 'A good many people have died of simple horror, mercifully without quite knowing it'. Those who had done the fighting were far from hateful. That epithet was reserved for those renegades who had written of Shelley and Tolstoy before 1914 and had succumbed so readily to the temptations of mindless patriotism. 'Four years of mud bath and blood bath, of intellectual and spiritual looting' was how Shaw described the war, closing with the remark, 'We two have survived our wounds so far; but we shall always be revenging them' (Shaw 1985b: 591). His new maxim was to be 'I never grieve; and I never forget' (Shaw 1988: 798).

6

FASCISM AND SOVIETISM

HEARTBREAK HOUSE

The development in Shaw's political outlook after 1918 can be approached through the one major play he worked on during the Great War, namely *Heartbreak House*.[1] Modelled as it is on Chekhov, the play is among the most complex Shaw wrote, combining a wide range of themes and sentiments to create 'A Fantasia in the Russian Manner on English Themes'.

The play's unifying feature is the promise of violence which pervades its mood and symbolism. Central to the play is Captain Shotover and his eccentric family. For their livelihood they depended on the money earned from the Captain's destructive inventions. Ironically, his paymasters – 'those hogs to whom the universe is nothing but a machine for greasing their bristles and filling their snouts' – are the very people the Captain hopes eventually to annihilate by means of his ultimate invention, 'a mind ray that will explode the ammunition in the belt of my adversary before he can point his gun at me'.

Heartbreak House closes with an explosion, or rather with a series of explosions, one destroying the rectory, the other killing the counterfeit capitalist Boss Mangan and the burglar who was hiding with him in the gravel pit. The first explosion, which leaves the rector homeless, was caused, again ironically, by a bomb falling out of the heavens. The second was caused by a combination of such a bomb with thirty pounds of the Captain's good dynamite. 'The judgement has come', the Captain says. Evidently the church had been found wanting, so too had the economic system and its representative dealers in fraud and waste. In opting for this kind of selective violence Shaw was perhaps seeking to draw a socialistic moral from a tale depicting a general state of breakdown and decay, with democracy in ruins and the ship of state heading for the rocks. Violence was the means by which this degenerate system was to be destroyed, it seemed. This is not to suggest that violence operated in a purely negative way in the play. On the contrary, in that act of destruction there was also the hope of renewal. It was almost as if violence was to act as a cathartic agent, cleansing the world of impurity, signalling a departure into a new era of adventure and creativity. The penultimate line belongs to the Captain's bewitching daughter, Mrs Hushabye: 'But what a glorious experience! I hope they'll come again tomorrow night'; 'Oh, I hope so', responds young Ellie Dunn, radiant at the prospect.

The last Act of *Heartbreak House* opens with the unmasking of the supposedly wealthy Boss Mangan who turns out to be the mere employee of a financial syndicate who lives off travelling expenses and a trifle of commission. What emerges in the debate is that Mangan, acting as the agent of plutocracy, has immense influence in politics, and that influence is of a peculiarly unwholesome kind. He claims his main achievement was in sticking a ramrod into the administrative machinery of all those fellows who thought they were 'going to save the country'. At this, Lady Utterword, the seemingly more conventional of Shotover's daughters whose husband 'has been governor of all the crown colonies in succession', enquires of Mangan, 'Do you expect to save the country, Mr Mangan?': 'Well, who else will', he replies, assuming only the practical businessman has any real experience of administration. Lady Utterword reminds him of her husband, Hastings: 'Get rid of your ridiculous sham democracy; and give Hastings the necessary powers, and a good supply of bamboo to bring the British native to his senses: he will save the country with the greatest ease'. Captain Shotover, who has hardly said a word all this time, speaks out: 'It had better be lost. Any fool can govern with a stick in his hand. *I* could govern that way. It is not God's way'. From there the conversation drifts into a chorus of denials and recriminations, punctuated by conflicting statements of faith, notably the false optimism of the liberal Mazzini Dunn, who thinks we shall muddle through, and the apocalyptic utterances of the Captain. Only the explosions, Mrs Hushabye's 'splendid drumming in the sky', disrupt the chaotic flow of clear ideas, though even the explosions only lead ultimately to a new round of competing interpretations. There is no unambiguous political conclusion to be drawn from *Heartbreak House*. What does emerge is a sense of crisis and imminent collapse. Neither plutocracy nor the reactionary violence of the colonialist offer any hope; nor does liberalism. Even the play's socialistic moral is presented in an oddly negative light, that is, by the death of Mangan and the burglar in the gravel pit. The paradox is that while violence is not an answer to the problem of government, it is perhaps the door through which we must pass if a new moral order is to be created. Hope is to be found only in the Captain's mind ray, or else in the explosions in the heavens.

THE NEW POLITICS

Through this darkening glass we glimpse the concerns underlying Shaw's post-war politics. These were to operate as a kind of sub-text behind the egalitarian doctrine, pulling him towards still more dramatic responses to the political problems of the day. According to the sub-text, the prospect of gradual, rationally-conceived reform was minimal.

Shaw started work on *Heartbreak House* in 1916. By the time it was published three years later the Bolsheviks were clinging to power in Russia, the Austrio-Hungarian and Ottoman empires had been dismantled, and the new German republic was set on an uncertain course, probably heading for a new war to undo the wrongs of the Versailles Treaty. By 1922 Mussolini had marched on Rome, adding a new term, fascism, to contemporary political vocabulary, as well as a new dimension to the critique of liberal democracy. In Britain, meanwhile, there was the usual round of party wranglings, strikes, scandal and stupidity, all the paraphenalia belonging to the politics of waste and decline; even the imminent prospect of a Labour Government in office was only a marginal source of comfort. That at least was Shaw's view of the post-war political madhouse in Europe. What is more, he was confidently predicting a major war between Britain and America for world supremacy. These were desperate times. Panic and confusion were to be encountered in the sub-text.

Shaw believed the Great War had changed more than just the political map. The map of human consciousness too was different now. Writing in *The Guide*, he said: 'The post-Marxian, post-Ibsen psychology gave way in 1914–18 to the post-war psychology'. And, echoing the Captain, he added: 'It is very curious; but it is too young, and I am too old, for more than this bare mention of its existence and its literature'. Perhaps he should have left it at that and not become too entangled in post-war politics, certainly not beyond the formulation of his argument for equal incomes. But he did and at great cost to his reputation. By the 1920s he apparently preferred anything to liberal democracy and was prepared to say so in the most extreme language. Consequently, his work as a prophet of social democracy has been largely overshadowed by his enthusiasm for various forms of dictatorship – proletarian or otherwise. Now, in so far as Shaw is mentioned in works on the history of political thought, it is either in connection with the élitist tendencies in Fabianism, which culminated in his support for the Stalinist conception of state-worship in the 1930s, or else his name is to be found in the long list of literary proto-fascists, fellow travellers with Hitler and Mussolini, those fake emblems of the collectivist politics of virtue.

The latter claim is the more controversial of the two. Though Shaw's allegiance to Stalin's Russia was not entirely straightforward, it was still clear and unwavering. It has also attracted much criticism. Among the most strongly worded was Eugene Lyons's comment on Shaw's visit to Russia in 1931: 'The lengthening obscenity of ignorant or indifferent tourists, disporting themselves cheerily on the aching body of Russia, seemed summed up in this cavorting old man, in his blanket endorsement of what he would not understand' (Lyons 1937: 429). There is no record of his four-hour interview with Stalin, but it appears to have been a facetious, uncritical affair, with the old heretic siding with the man of power against the questioning Lady Astor. According to Lyons, it was 'understood that he was not taken in, but himself collaborating in the deception, with the world at large as the common dupe'.

Shaw was to tell Molly Tompkins 'never in my life have I enjoyed a journey so much. You would have been disgusted at my reception as a Grand Old Man of Socialism, my smilings and wavings and posing and speech makings; but it made things very smooth for us all' (Shaw 1960: 150).

His keen eyes were prepared to overlook so much and, in time, to accept so much false propaganda. Privately, he admitted to Beatrice Webb in September 1936 that he found the whole business of the show trials 'very puzzling', saying that the claim that level-headed men like Sokolnikoff had planned to kill Stalin suggested that the Russian leaders were 'relapsing into pre-Marxian conceptions of politics' (Shaw 1988: 441). Publically, however, he accepted the Stalinist account of the show trials as exposing a treasonous conspiracy on the part of the old Bolsheviks: 'revolutionary habits are hard to change', he said, 'it still holds good that one of the first jobs of a successful revolution is to get rid of the revolutionists' (Shaw 1949a: 464).

Shaw was in many respects a model fellow traveller. According to David Caute, the typical symptoms of that ailment were a contempt for the Communist Party of one's own country, coupled to a revolutionary commitment that is at a distance – geographical, emotional and intellectual (Caute 1973: 3). Trotsky said that the fellow traveller's loyalty is not 'so much to the revolutionary working class as to the victorious revolution' (Caute 1973: 3). All that is true of Shaw. Though the Soviet experiment answered a deep chord of idealistic fervour within him, it did not prompt him to join the Communist Party, nor was he reconverted to Marxism. Quizzical to the last, the critical ideologist claimed that Stalin was really a good Fabian, the disciple of a certain Irish prophet, combining political opportunism with the doctrine of socialism in one country: 'there ran the pride of authorship' in his praise of the Soviet regime, it was reported at the time (Shaw 1931j: 30). In short, his response reflected the complexities within his own personality, mixing idealistic praise with critical appraisal. Shaw lampooned the Soviet belief in Marxism as the true basis of scientific socialism. All the same, writing from his sparse outhouse in a Hertfordshire village, Shaw gave Stalin his full backing, consistently describing the Soviet system as 'the only hope of the world'. His regard for Sovietism was not straightforward, but, publically at least, it was unequivocal.

What makes the claim of proto-fascism more controversial is that Shaw's response was muddled in the extreme. Some inkling of the confusion generated by his comments is gained from his attempt in 1935 to set the record straight:

It is this confounded association of ideas as opposed to my analytical method that gets me into trouble in England. If I say (as I did) that the fascist government of Italy really governed, and in some respects governed very efficiently, where the Italian parliament had governed either very ineffectively, or not at all, and that the conception of the Corporate State is an evident advance towards socialism and away from laissez-faire, I am immediately accused of having, in effect, murdered Matteotti and exiled Salvemini.

(Shaw 1935c: 10)

Concealed in the argument was the claim that, as a realist, Shaw was able to distinguish whatever was progressive and valuable in a regime from the (in his view) relatively minor incidents of political exile and assassination which the ordinary Englishman mistakenly equates with fascism itself. As a socialist realist, Shaw said he was bound to conclude that fascism's dynamism as well as its commitment to a form of collectivism were to be preferred to the muddle of liberal or capitalist democracy.

Many interpretations of Shaw's relationship with fascism have emerged. On the defensive side, Eric Bentley is certain that 'Shaw is neither a fascist nor an academic proto-fascist', he had no time for heroism, no patience with anti-modernism (Bentley 1947: 177).[2] Similarly, Gerard Pilecki says that Shaw 'could hardly be called a fascist, since fascism for him meant simply state capitalism or capitalism with a dictatorship' (Pilecki 1965: 150; Nickson 1959: 14). Both Bentley and Pilecki recognize that Shaw made some fascistic utterances, but these arose more from his habit of startling democrats (British democrats especially) out of their complacency with a show of exaggerated hostility, than from a real intellectual affinity. It is unfortunate, Bentley argues, that 'what Shaw actually says about fascism when not playing advocate to Mussolini's devil has been much less heeded'.

Against this, Oswald Spengler saw 'Shaw as one of the seminal figures in the development of what was subsequently dubbed fascism'; and 'he was right to do so', asserts Paul Hayes (Hayes 1973: 76). Whereas Pilecki argues that Shaw's admiration (such as it was) was limited to Mussolini as an individual and that it did not extend to fascist ideology, the Italian exile, Gaetano Salvemini, believed Shaw had 'discovered embodied in fascism his ideal of civil life' (Shaw 1927a: 9). In the British context, Robert Skidelsky writes that for Mosley's Union of Fascists Shaw was 'the most famous example of intellectual sympathy from the left': he epitomized the socialistic contribution to fascist thought in Britain in terms of the fusion of social imperialist and social Darwinist ideas in the name of collective national welfare. Skidelsky writes: 'The failure of democratic politicians had long convinced him that this creed could be implemented only by heroic realists. His collectivism and his doctrine of the superman thus combined to make him look with favour on the social experiments initiated by Hitler and Mussolini' (Skidelsky 1975: 348). Skidelsky goes on to insist that Shaw was certainly a major influence on Mosley. In return, Shaw was to assert in 1940 that nine-tenths of what Mosley (and Hitler) said was true – it was sound national socialism marred only by an unfortunate allegiance to bogus racialism. Picking up on this kind of statement, George Orwell was to say that Shaw alone in the inter-war years, 'for some years at any rate, declared Communism and Fascism to be much the same thing, and was in favour of both of them' (Orwell 1971: 208). A sense of the bewilderment he caused is found in an entry from Beatrice Webb's diary from 1934, where she asks 'Why does GBS uphold not only Mussolini but also Hitler and Mosley as leaders to be followed? Why does he imply that their leadership is as valuable as Lenin's, that they also have a vision of a new and more desirable civilization? (MacKenzie and MacKenzie 1985: 334).

This chapter looks first at Shaw's views on fascism and Sovietism, as expressed in the 1928 and 1937 editions of *The Guide*. Here, if anywhere, we would expect a serious and coherent analysis of the issues involved. The gaps and ambiguities we find in this analysis offer a basis for looking next at the whole range of Shaw's reflections on 'the new politics' from 1917 to 1950.

THE RELIABLE GUIDE?

If we were to use only *The Guide* as a source for Shaw's views on fascism, then we might be hard put to explain what all the fuss is about. Certainly this is the case with the original edition of 1928 where the few, brief comments on fascism were all hostile in nature. There it was seen as a form of capitalist dictatorship, competing for approval with socialism 'by cleaning up some of the dirtiest of our present conditions: raising wages; reducing death rates; opening the career to the talents; and ruthlessly cashiering inefficiency, before in the long run succumbing to the bane of inequality, against which no civilization can finally stand out' (Shaw 1949a: 298). In the same edition Shaw went on to refer to fascism as 'a call to a new Theocracy', to be viewed in the same disparaging light as such fanaticisms as Marxism, Mormonism and Imperialism (Shaw 1949a: 443).

In 1937 he added two new chapters to *The Guide*, one on Sovietism, the other on Fascism. As one might expect in the light of his 1931 visit to the Soviet Union, the contrast Shaw drew between the two models of the new politics was unmistakable. He stated 'We only have to compare the development of Russia since the slump of 1929 with the utmost that Fascism has been able to accomplish in double that period to see that Fascism is subject to all the limitations and vices of capitalism, and can no more save civilization today than it could save all the earlier civilizations it has wrecked' (Shaw 1949a: 485). In the fully Sovietized regions of Russia there was not a hungry nor a ragged child, Shaw claimed. Its five-year plans and its educational system were models for the world, transforming the children of peasants into 'persons quite different from themselves, and indeed as incapable of living like themselves as a hunter or a racehorse of stabling in a pigsty' (Shaw 1949a: 459). This was praise indeed. The Russians were proving the truth of socialism in practice. Fascism, by way of contrast, was merely 'the latest mask of Capitalism' (Shaw 1949a: 488), dedicated ultimately to the preservation of private property. What else was a socialist to say.

The 1937 chapter on fascism is important because, being part of the Shavian

Bible of socialism, it was relatively sober and authoritative in its approach. Whereas elsewhere Shaw might have been less than scrupulous in his comments, here at least he was concerned not to undermine the consistency and seriousness of his work. Though hardly one of the glories of Shavian prose, the chapter does appear to support Bentley and Pilecki's thesis: fascism was only capitalism with a dictatorship.

However, while it was certainly critical in its main conclusion, the chapter on fascism contains much that is ambiguous and more that is disturbing. For example, it was withering in its contempt for parliamentary democracy, clearly relishing in the actions of any impatient genius, be it Cromwell or Kamal Ataturk, when cutting through its morass of talk and indecision. This of course was in a work which still offered no constructive alternative to parliamentary democracy. It was also contemptuous of the 'negative traditions' of rights and liberties operating under liberalism, with these being dismissed as pernicious illusions: 'Fascism is better than Liberalism', Shaw asserted. This was because it 'produces a United Front with a public outlook', dispensing with useless opposition 'by simple violence' (Shaw 1949a: 479). Shaw wrote casually of young and athletic men, devoted to the dictator, 'quite simply and naïvely' breaking into the offices of all opposition institutions, beating up the occupants and smashing the furniture. Only the liberals complain, raising their usual ballyhoo against infringements of those negative principles 'on which their Capitalism is founded' (Shaw 1949a: 479).

There was a parallel here with Sovietism. Shaw dismissed Stalin's 1936 Constitution as 'a feat of window dressing to conciliate Liberal opinion in Europe and America', and went on to say he was not convinced of the prudence of resurrecting the 'Rights of Man' (Shaw 1949a: 475). He also noted the good work done by the Soviet secret police, the Tcheka, in dealing with 'slackers and would-be Sinecurists' (Shaw 1949a: 466). Positive things could emerge from a terror campaign, it seemed, in Russia as in Italy. Thus, after noting in the chapter on fascism that 'nothing shocks our notions of liberty and order so much as the extinction of working-class organizations by violence and plunder', Shaw added reassuringly, 'their reconstruction as State departments produces what is called a United Front, and collects into a solid mass the fluctuating and often jarring fragments of organizations into which the immense forces of the proletariat have quarrelsomely split' (Shaw 1949a: 481). In this respect at least, fascism and communism were alike.

But Shaw made it plain that fascism's united front was of a corrupt kind, representing the 'organization of popular ignorance and romantic folly' (Shaw 1949a: 482). His argument here was that the fascist leader finds his natural constituency among the mass of ordinary people who are 'Fascist by nature and schooling', despising liberty, agreeing instinctively with the leader's 'calls for discipline, order, silence, patriotism, and devotion to the State of which he is the embodiment'. Fascism was really perfectly democratic, being founded on the support of the masses against the

247

opposition of the seditious few. All the leader must do is deal with fools according to their folly, taking 'care that there shall be plenty of pageantry, of romantic oratory, of press propaganda, of fascist teaching in the schools and universities, and as little criticism of his rule as possible' (Shaw 1949a: 480).

The contrast with the Soviet system, where education was used to transform consciousness instead of simply reproducing its worst aspects, could not have been greater. Under fascism, it appeared, the leader was more or less obliged to deal in the sort of humbug which would appeal to the masses. In Russia, on the other hand, the leadership was honest and straightforward, admitting its mistakes openly and 'solving problem after problem by trial and error'. Stalin and his colleagues were models of Fabian realism, an energetic minority of superior brains dedicated to the cause of progress through social experimentation.

It should not be deduced from this that Shaw was actually critical of any fascist leader. The odd feature of the 1937 statement on fascism was that almost every reference to any dictator was quite complimentary. At the outset they were introduced, not as ambitious scoundrels, but as ardent and able reformers 'seeing civilization falling to pieces under an effete monarchy or a parliament capable of nothing but playing the Party game and talking'. The violence they employ was not exceptional – ask any Irishman, Shaw said – nor were the gimmicks the leader uses to keep the masses amused 'whilst he sets to work energetically on reforms that appeal to everyone's commonsense and comfort, and stops the more obvious abuses of the existing order' (Shaw 1949a: 479). True, the dictator's achievements may be superficial and he may ultimately be wrecked by the need to engage in some war or other to maintain his support, but Shaw implied that the fault lies not in the leader, who 'may be quite sincerely desirous that history shall record of him that he put down the mighty from their seats and exalted them of low degree', but in the movement and regime he leads (Shaw 1949a: 483).

On this point Shaw's analysis was terribly thin, however. Why should the average citizen who supported fascism as a mass movement be so committed to the institution of private property and the inequality it maintains? Shaw explained more or less why the hypocritical liberals were so inclined, but not the mass of people in the fascist movement itself, most of whom must have been both propertyless and poor. Was Shaw referring to the more exclusive fascist regime when he said, regarding the leader's sincere desire for social reform, 'But the Fascists will have none of this. Of them it shall be said that they filled the overfed with good things, and the poor they sent empty away'. Members of the fascist regime, the core of leaders behind the mass movement, would sanction attacks against left-wing targets, 'But ask them to burn a country-house, or sack the Bank of England, or lynch a Conservative Cabinet Minister, and they will conclude that you have gone mad or joined the Reds' (Shaw 1949a: 483).

The conclusion seems to be that any major achievements the fascist dictator could claim were only accomplished in the face of opposition from his supporters who suspected him of socialist leanings. The leader was thus trapped in a web of progress and reaction; like the sorcerer's apprentice he 'finds that he can call up the demons easily enough, but knows no spell by which he can exorcise them when they have served his turn'. In this way, two faces of fascism emerge from the 1937 chapter on fascism, one more or less progressive and associated with the dictator, the other reactionary and linked either to the movement or the regime.

There was, too, a decidedly economistic element in Shaw's analysis, which was very much in keeping with the general tenor of *The Guide*. Notions of this kind illuminated his brief and anodyne comments on Hitler's persecution of the Jews (the product of mass discontent over Jewish wealth, he said).[3] More surprisingly, perhaps, this trend was also apparent in the way he underplayed Stalin's importance to the Soviet system in 1937. Whereas in speeches and articles from the period he lavished praise on Stalin as the most able ruler in the world, 'the one inevitable man for the job he holds' (Shaw 1933b: 10; Shaw 1976: 228), in *The Guide* he was barely mentioned at all. It was the system, not the man, that Shaw's audience was invited to applaud. Stalin's one acknowledged achievement was in formulating the ultra-Shavian programme of socialism in one country.

Against this, considerations of a more flexible, vitalistic nature seem also to inform the chapter on fascism, especially in the section dealing with Mussolini's achievements. He, surely, was not a tool of the plutocracy as the economistic analysis would have us believe. Shaw's comments were in fact quite encouraging, citing no specific failings in *Il Duce*'s policies and noting that he had not been tempted into the kind of idiosyncratic escapade which tended to wreck fascist regimes. The war in Ethiopia was ignored when Shaw claimed 'So far, the Italian leader has kept his head' (Shaw 1949a: 486). On balance, the suggestion was that in politics the power of personality might yet transcend the constraints of its economic base.[4]

The chapter, therefore, hinted at the interplay of the economistic and vitalistic elements in Shaw's analysis of fascism which were to surface more obviously elsewhere. For example, in the preface to *Geneva* (1945) he said the German plutocracy had made a 'bad bargain' with Hitler because once he had achieved 'real personal power' he then set off on his own ruinous course of imperial expansion (Shaw 1946: 20). *The Guide* also hinted at a view of fascism (in Italy at least) as a form of developmental dictatorship guided in its policy-making by the ideal of a corporate state. The exact function of this potentially revolutionary doctrine was not explained. More obvious was the downright hostile view of liberalism which went far beyond Bentley's notion of devil's advocacy. Further, Shaw's attitude to violence was equivocal, neither openly supportive nor yet clearly critical. The average citizen was lampooned. Indeed, it could be claimed that only the fundamentalist critique

249

of private property and the remaining commitment to equal distribution prevented Shaw from welcoming fascism as an interesting, if short-term, experiment in social and political organization. Anything was better than the drift and talk of parliamentary democracy. The concerns of the sub-text were not to be silenced.

For all that, Shaw was clearly not a fascist in 1937. Fortunately for him (in this context) the Soviet experiment allowed him to steer a reasonably certain if unruly course. But then Shaw's commitment to that alternative had not existed for long. The question arises, therefore, as to how he responded to fascism before he visited Russia in 1931. Besides, there are enough ambiguities and points of affiliation with fascism in the 1937 edition of *The Guide* to support a still broader survey of his reflections on the matter in the plays and prefaces of the period, as well as in the endless articles and speeches Shaw produced in the inter-war years and beyond.

FASCISM OR BOLSHEVISM?

Not unreasonably, Shaw equated fascism with the Italian model. He assumed it was in Mussolini's experiment in social organization that its essential character was to be found. Initially, Shaw was slow to react to that experiment. He was 'horribly ignorant of Italian politics', he said. Writing to a correspondent in 1917 he remarked that if he was asked to comment on Italy 'This ignorance of mine would certainly be found out: in fact I should confess from the start that neither I nor anyone else in England knows anything about Italian public life or has heard of any Italian later than Garibaldi' (Shaw 1985b: 465). Mussolini changed that, but not immediately, and Shaw never quite lost that sense of his limited grasp of Italian affairs.

His first public announcement on fascism was in an interview with his biographer, Archibald Henderson, in 1924. It was non-committal. On balance, Shaw thought it best to suspend judgement, though in the event the temptation to say something proved too hard to resist. The style and temper of fascist politics were both terrible and ridiculous, he said. However, to Mussolini's credit he had opposed the absurd syndicalist threat of factory occupation and in that respect his regime did represent a more or less healthy 'reaction against Anarchism towards devotion and discipline'. After acknowledging the positive, socialist aspects of Mussolini's intellectual heritage which had served him well during the time of crisis, Shaw observed:

> But the danger is over, the fundamental difference of opinion between the bourgeoisie and the socialist is bound to come to the surface. Mussolini may sell out and become a mere careerist-opportunist like the rest of the politicians. He may stand by his guns.
>
> (Henderson 1925: 31)

From this it would seem that fascism was to be preferred to non-Shavian, non-statist forms of socialism, especially those committed to the absurdities of worker's control. Shaw also suggested that Mussolini's future depended more on his own intellect and will-power than on the forces of economism, the implication being that the strong man could act as an autonomous political force. Picking up on this vitalistic point, it is worth noting that Shaw and Mussolini shared a common affinity with Bergson and Nietzsche and the whole anti-positivist, anti-rationalist element in European intellectual life. That Mussolini carried the critique of reason so much further than Shaw is clear. Yet that affinity, and with it the underlying belief in the intervention of the strong man in politics – Shaw's man of destiny – indicates why he was not prepared to dismiss Mussolini out of hand, even though the fascist terror was directed primarily against Shaw's fellow (if misguided) socialists.

Shaw drew an interesting parallel in his conversation with his biographer, stating that, in its infancy, Italian fascism was, like Bolshevism, an emergency policy, a form of martial law, a species of 'middle-class Bolshevism' to be precise. In fact his early response to Bolshevism was in many ways as qualified and tentative as was his response to fascism. He had no information on Russia, he told Maxim Gorki in 1917. His one firm expectation was that the revolutionary government – provisional or Bolshevik – would proceed with the war as a means of securing national unity: 'a war is the first necessity of life to a revolutionary government' (Shaw 1985b: 474). He made the same point in the short 1918 play, *Annajanska, the Bolshevik Empress*.[5] The fact that he chose a young, female member of the deposed royal family as a vehicle to comment on the advent of the first socialist revolution suggests an equivocal attitude to the proceedings. None the less, on balance Shaw supported the Bolsheviks in his public pronouncements. Lenin, he said, was the only interesting statesman in Europe. In 1919, in an article in *The Labour Leader* which asked, 'Are we Bolshevisks?', Shaw dutifully answered in the affirmative. There he sided with Lenin against Kautsky in the argument over the place of democracy in the revolutionary process. Dictatorship was perfectly acceptable in principle; other things being equal, the ordinary man must be bullied into submitting to positive government by somebody, and in Shaw's view 'he had better be bullied into submitting to honest rather than dishonest government' (Shaw 1919: 1). In Shaw's mind, there was no question of the dictatorship of the proletariat representing some higher form of democracy. It was a dictatorship, plain and simple. As Annajanska was to elaborate, 'some energetic and capable minority must always be in power. Well, I am on the side of the energetic minority whose principles I agree with' (Shaw 1928c: 168).

Whether the Bolshevik dictatorship would succeed in its long-term goals was another matter. Russia held a special place in Shaw's scheme of things. Its artists were the finest in the world. Yet, economically and politically it was so backward that he refused to admit it into his exclusive 'Hegemony of Peace'. In 1914 it was Russian autocracy, not German militarism, which he identified as the real enemy. That a group of administrative novices could turn such a country into a socialist model was just incredible to a Fabian of the old gang. The Bolshevik advocacy of compulsory labour as the basis of a creed to be imposed on the masses was welcomed as a step in the right direction. What was less acceptable was the slavish pursuit of a Marxist dogma enshrined in the High Church of the Third International, complete with its icons and its own Pope. Summing up his views in *The Sphere* in 1928 Shaw said that Bolshevik eccentricities were foolish and their methods often deplorable. The Government would almost certainly fall. Only the Bolshevik 'idea' would survive to take root in a more hospitable environment. It was the most interesting experiment of its kind, but it was doomed to failure (Shaw 1928c: 168). Little wonder, then, that he should have spent so much time in 1937 explaining the mistakes of the Bolsheviks, detailing their contempt for Fabianism and their hostility to the intellectual proletariat as evidence of their incompetence. In a rare (in this context) moment of compassion he wrote of the 'thousands who must have perished miserably from disease, exposure and starvation' after the revolution. It was Stalin, above all, who changed all that and it was precisely his near omission from the 1937 chapter on Sovietism which made that account of the miraculous transformation from failure to resounding success so implausible.

Little wonder, too, that Shaw should have looked elsewhere in the late 1920s for a working alternative to parliamentary democracy. Intellectually, fascism lacked the calibre of Bolshevism. In practice, however, it was arguably the better example of strong, positive government, combining dynamic leadership with the sort of principles Shaw more or less agreed with.

LETTERS TO THE PRESS

The storm broke early in 1927 when, shortly after a visit to Italy, Shaw published a brief statement in the *Daily News* under the title 'Mussolini: a defence'. The title was the sub-editor's work. The rest was Shaw's. The piece was written in his most agressively 'realist' manner. Its gist was that fascist violence and curtailments of rights in Mussolini's Italy were no different to those experienced under the British ruling class. Mussolini was simply less hypocritical. Otherwise, 'the only visible difference is that the British Oligarch kicks constitutional rights out of his way to secure the ascendency of his class, whereas the Italian Dictator does it to get public business done diligently for the public benefit'. According to Shaw, the Italian people tolerated *Il Duce* because he served the cause of national efficiency and not through fear of the Blackshirts; the people, tired of parliament, 'feel the need for a strenuous tyranny, and think Mussolini the right sort of tyrant'. That at least was Shaw's 'very superficial tourist's contemplation of the situation' (Shaw 1927a: 7).[6] Policy and good manners demand that we treat Mussolini civilly, the realist concluded.

Subsequently, Shaw had to defend his position against a barrage of criticism, notably from the Austrian socialist, Friederick Adler, and the exiled Gaetano Salvemini. In February Shaw wrote a still more aggressive rejoinder: 'it is clear that our attitude towards a regime cannot be determined by the means employed to establish it', he declared, 'the only question for us is whether he is doing his job well enough to induce the Italian nation to accept him *faute de mieux*' (Shaw 1927a: 4). From the ordinary middle-aged citizen Mussolini had received a pragmatic sanction. As for the young, Shaw said they had a Boy Scout mentality and associated their *esprit de corps* with fascism. Did Shaw's critics seriously expect him to compromise his reputation for good sense by refusing to accept an accomplished fact? Besides, he asked Friederick Adler in October 1927, 'are you not delighted to find at last a Socialist who speaks and thinks as responsible rulers do and not as resentful slaves do?' (Shaw 1927a: 8).

His critics were not impressed. They looked in vain for the rebel who had railed so forcibly against the Denshawi Horror of 1906. Instead they found a maverick elder statesman who admitted he knew of the many 'revolting incidents of the Fascist terror', but was ready to assume that these belonged only to the period of crisis. Shaw showed no understanding of the inherent fascist craving for forceful action, his critics argued. There was a resounding complacency in his final assessment of Mussolini: 'The blots on his rule are neither specifically Fascist nor specifically Italian: they are blots on human nature' (Shaw 1927a: 9).

More controversial still, Shaw argued in February that 'Some of the things Mussolini has done, and some of the things he is threatening to do go further in the direction of Socialism than the English Labour Party could yet venture if they were in power'. And he added (directly contradicting his argument in *The Guide*), 'They will bring him presently into serious conflict with capitalism; and it is certainly not my business nor that of any Socialist to weaken him in view of such a conflict'. Writing in *The Manchester Guardian* he was to say that Mussolini was 'farther to the Left in his political opinions than any' of his socialist rivals (Shaw 1927a: 17). But could he break the control of *laissez-faire* capitalism? Anything seemed possible in the light of Shaw's commendation of Mussolini as a man 'who had achieved a dictatorship in a great modern state without a single advantage, social, official, or academic, to assist him'. In response, Salvemini considered it an astounding assertion, disregarding the assistance Mussolini had recieved from the banks, the big industrialists and landowners. But is was important to Shaw. Mussolini, like Hitler later, was an outsider, a quintessential Shavian rebel in many respects, a rebel turned lawmaker in fact, as determined to set the nation's affairs straight as the men of the establishment were to keep them crooked. Mussolini is a man of the people, he told Adler, 'and *knows them*'. It was not just a question of personal sympathy. Shaw was adamant that fascism had much in common with socialism. Adler was left in no doubt that socialists 'have nothing to do with liberty'. Shaw went on to say 'Our message, like Mussolini's, is one of discipline, of service, of ruthless refusal to acknowledge any natural right of competence'.

The discrepancy between these views and those expressed in the original edition of *The Guide* is puzzling. Why was Shaw so expansive and sympathetic in one and so prefunctory and critical in the other? Are the comments from the letters to be discounted as journalistic half-truths written to provoke thought among British democrats and socialists? Writing to Ramsay MacDonald in October 1927, Shaw stated:

> My letters about Mussolini, which have raised a considerable flutter, were really written at our own people. At bottom the people know that what they need is not more paper liberty and democracy, but more discipline; and Mussolini's grip of this fact is the whole secret of his command.
>
> (Shaw 1988: 75)

The fact that the letters about Mussolini were directed torwards his British audience does not, however, support the idea that the views he expressed therein were anything less than serious. Indeed Shaw seemed to underline his intellectual agreement with Mussolini in his letters to MacDonald. Further, regarding Shaw's letter of 7 February, he is reported to have said he 'would not be sorry to see it given the same publicity as the telegram of Signor Turati' (Shaw 1927b: 968). If Adler had taken up the suggestion, the letter would have amounted to nothing less than a Shavian policy statement to the Socialist International. It should be noted, too, that the sections dealing with fascism from *The Guide* were almost certainly written before Shaw visited Italy in 1927 and certainly before the formulation of the first Charter of Labour which outlined Mussolini's corporatist policy on working-class organizations.

That policy clearly impressed Shaw, as did Mussolini's economic record prior to the 1929 crash, especially when compared to that of the liberal democracies. Shaw might have poked fun at Mussolini's posturings in private. The public message was different. Ultimately, 'Caesarian theocracies' would not work in the modern world, he admitted rather belatedly in October 1927, 'they all come to some sort of parliamentary complexion at last'. In the meantime, however, the Italian people were right to trust in Mussolini's personal dynamism. What is more, in stark contrast to the 1937 edition of *The Guide*, in these letters to the press the political judgement of the masses was presented in a more or less positive light.

Clearly, the views Shaw expressed in 1927 caused great confusion and concern. Beatrice Webb was to say that Shaw 'puts forward the Mussolini regime as the *New Model* which all other countries ought to follow' (Cole 1956: 155). Adler's comment was that Shaw's opinions were 'really astonishing' for a militant socialist.

CORPORATISM

Over the next few years it was Shaw's interest in the corporate state, as well as his regard for the force of personality in politics, which fuelled his reputation as a proto-fascist. Both were to feature in *The Apple Cart* (1930). That is not to say that either the play or its preface can be seen as extended discussions on these themes in any simple sense. The preface was initially concerned with refuting the claim that the play was an apology for royalty, which would have contradicted Shaw's life-long commitment to republicanism – 'the conflict is not really between royalty and democracy', he said, 'It is between both and plutocracy' (Shaw 1932q). The latter was represented by the mythical Breakages Ltd., a corporate successor to Boss Mangan from *Heartbreak House*. Having made the point, Shaw then offered an account of his thoughts on democracy, culminating with an outline of his views on the panel system of government. Mussolini was mentioned here, though only in those passages criticizing contemporary democratic practices. Here, at least, Shaw was clearly not advocating dictatorship as the 'new model'. The preface closed with an account of how Breakages Ltd. operates, with Shaw using the experience of an acquaintance, A.W. Gattie, to show how capitalism stifles inventive genius and so undermines national efficiency.

Corporatism emerged from the preface primarily as a vogue word to represent any and every form of collectivism: 'the civilized way of getting along is the way of corporate action, not individual action; and corporate action involves more government than individual action'. It was the old Fabian message. Only now in his choice of terminology the controversialist courted the many dangers of intellectual affiliation. Arguably, that danger was also implicit in the discussion of Gattie and Breakages Ltd. The example was supposed to demonstrate the power of corrupt plutocracy over industry and politics. It did nothing of the sort. Instead it accused organized labour and unimaginative officialdom of wrecking Gattie's revolutionary scheme for transporting glass bulbs. These were the real breaks on national efficiency. In the play itself, however, Lysistrata, the Powermistress General, identified Breakages Ltd. with the sinister interests of big business. It was all rather confusing. What was needed, apparently, was a new sort of state capable of directing all these forces towards the goal of technological progress – something along the lines of Mussolini's corporate state perhaps.

There is certainly some truth in the view that before 1931 Mussolini's regime was the only working approximation to Shaw's conception of positive statism. There were some striking similarities between the two. Shavianism and corporatism shared a commitment to national unity and the collective organizations of civil life. Moreover, it could be argued that anti-unionism, centralization, planned growth, the élitist manipulation of public opinion, as well as a belief in a form of vocational differentiation were all common features of the Shavian and fascist political agendas. Shaw, the national

255

socialist, even shared the fascist ideal of self-sufficiency, a point aptly illustrated by his life-long hostility to foreign trade (Shaw 1976: 238). Many of these themes were evident in *Major Barbara*, in particular in those scenes at Undershaft's munitions works where the future is presented in microcosm in terms of a hierarchical, perfectly functioning unit dedicated to techno-logical progress and underpinned by a common reliance on violence. Of Mussolini's regime, Shaw was to ask in a Fabian lecture in 1933:

> What has he built up? He is trying to build in Italy what he calls a corporate state. He wants to put all the different industries into the hands of corporations as he calls them, and then, finally to create a council of Corporations to succeed Parliament. I approve of that, because it is precisely what the Fabian Society wants, and it is clearly a necessary part of socialism, no matter what you call it.
>
> (Shaw 1976: 236)

That the ideal corporate state could only be achieved through communism was clear.

However, it is worth noting that in 1933 Shaw was of the opinion that 'Fascism is still wavering between Empire and Church, between private property and Communism' (Shaw 1934d: 24). The corporate state was one of the 'modern progressive and revolutionary movements' which were 'at bottom attacks on private property' (Shaw 1934d: 150). In December of that year he informed his German translator, Siegfried Trebitsch, that:

> Fascism, or the organization of the State as a hierarchy of industrial and professional corporations, is right as far as it goes; but what real power will the corporations have unless they own the land and control the industries – unless, that is, the State is Socialist as well as Fascist? . . . if Fascism is to come to anything it must come to communism finally.
>
> (Shaw 1988: 359)

In May of 1934 he seemed to be more positive still in his evaluation of fascism. Thus, in a letter to a British communist, Christina Walshe, Shaw advised that the Communist Party 'should not have attacked the Fascists'. He went on to explain:

> Before any serious changes can be made in England, the Parliamentary party system, with its mask of democracy, liberty, and all the rest of it, must be smashed, and replaced by a constitution which will have a good deal in common not only with the Russian constitution but also with our own municipal government and with the Corporate State of Mussolini and the National Socialist State of Hitler. As against our Parliamentary pretences Communists, Fascists and Nazis have a common cause. The blind attack on Fascism in the name of Liberty is not Communism: it is old fashioned Radicalism and Anarchism.
>
> (Shaw 1988: 374)

Such statements were political dynamite in the supercharged atmosphere of the 1930s. A.K. Chesterton, writing in *Fascist Week*, was only too pleased to assert that there was much in Shaw's vision of an organic state 'which Fascists will not fail to acclaim' (Chesterton 1934: 4).

In fairness, less sympathetic views were also to be found in Shaw's work from the period. Taking his lead from the Webbs, he told Sylvia Pankhurst in 1935 that fascism's corporate state is 'conceived as the organization and domination of producers, and not of the consumer, who is the true democratic political unit' (Shaw 1935a: 12). In *The Guide* his views were still less friendly, though even there his ingrained collectivism led him to choose the most uninviting line of argument: all that could be said for fascism was that it trained 'citizens to take the corporate view of themselves, looking to the State – the Totalitarian State, as it is tautologically called – instead of their private individual competitive efforts to make their lives tolerable' (Shaw 1949a: 488).

In 1934 Shaw said that, as a communist, he was naturally in favour of fascism. Some commentators have turned this around, arguing that in some respects he had more in common with corporatism than with the classical theory of communism. Nigel Harris, for example, says that it was the *étatiste*, corporatist elements in Stalin's Russia which gained Shaw's support (Harris 1971: 125). It was not the revolutionary tradition that attracted the fellow traveller so much as the power of the state militant. And on a slightly different note, it is worth recording that Shaw often equated the Soviet system with the Catholic Church and that Catholicism is in turn often cited as a major influence in the history of corporatism. His references to this theme were sometimes (as in 1928) critical. By 1933, however, they were far more positive, as his own commitment to a creed-inspired élite took shape. Was it Father Keegan's old dream of a 'country where the State is the Church and the Church the people: three in one and one in three'? Certainly Shaw's socialist commonwealth was in many ways closer to the corporatist ideal than to anything envisaged by Marx.

In the mid-1930s the prevailing theme in Shaw's work was that fascism was still wavering between Church and empire. Ultimately, its version of the state militant was judged by Shaw to be a failure. Yet it pointed the way towards the collectivist vision of strong organic life and, for a time at least, operated as a positive force in Shaw's increasingly rhetorical argument: 'the Corporate State is an evident advance towards Socialism' (Shaw 1935c: 10).

THE APPLE CART

When Beatrice Webb confronted Shaw on a July morning in 1934 to ask him exactly why he admired the dictators, he was said to have admitted that they had no economic principle, but to have countered with the claim that 'they had personality and it was personality that was needed to save the world'. It was the old idea of the superman, Beatrice concluded.

The problem was that Shaw's views were so unstable as to generate any number of interpretations of his views on democracy and dictatorship. As we have seen, even when he sought to synthesize his ideas they remained terribly ambiguous and incomplete, pointing towards contradictory political strategies. When explaining his proposed hierarchy of cabinets or panels in 1932 he referred to the 'hierarchy of dictators' to be found in Russia where there is 'no opposition, no obstruction, no talking out of Bills' (Shaw 1962b: 247). He said he did not advocate dictatorship by one man as a solution to the problem of government. All the same, in 1934 he did advise W.A. Robson to turn *The Political Quarterly* into the 'organ of all the dictators' (Robson 1951: 234). No wonder Beatrice Webb was confused.

These conjectures and departures were played out in the political extravaganzas of the 1920s and 1930s, *The Apple Cart*, *On the Rocks* and *Geneva*. Together they show just how difficult it is to reconstruct Shaw's reflections on fascism and dictatorship generally, with each suggesting a different conclusion. Of the three, *The Apple Cart* is perhaps the most subtle and complex work and, therefore, the least suited to one-dimensional analysis. Though it is often cited as evidence of his belief in the strong man, it is hardly convincing as such. At one level it was a commentary on MacDonald's unruly Labour cabinets. At another it was a dialogue on the ritualistic world of politics, with its sham imagery and false scenes, the realm of appearances, set against the underlying realities considered (purportedly) in the preface. The conventions of dress, manners and style, the many props of the political orator, were among the key issues of the play. Many of the characters were like music hall 'turns', double acts and choruses, turning to mimicry and song at the slightest provocation, seemingly confirming Shaw's view that 'The art of government is the organization of idolatry'. He had warned in 1903 that the people 'can only worship the national idols'. Now contemporary politics was like a theatre of illusion controlled by the masters of political symbolism. In *The Guide*, at least, Shaw insisted that the theatrical manipulation of the prejudices and sentiments of the masses was encapsulated in fascism itself.

In effect, in presenting a critical discourse on these issues Shaw revealed the gulf between the style and temper of Shavian and fascist politics. He, too, believed in strong leadership and inspiring creeds, but it had to be the right sort of leadership with the right sort of creed, founded on a progressive iconography. Royalty, another central theme of *The Apple Cart*, was for him the ultimate form of anachronistic political idolatry: 'Kings are not born: they are made by artificial hallucination'.

The play opens with a discussion between two of the king's secretaries, Pamphilius and Sempronius. We are told that the latter's father was a ritualist by conviction and profession, the man responsible for staging the major ceremonies of state, the chief purveyor of illusions. Having thus set the scene, the secretaries then introduce the play's supposedly strong men and potential rivals for popular support, namely, the President of the Board of Trade, that 'bull-roarer' Boanerges, dressed in a Russian blouse and peaked cap, and the mannered and gracious King Magnus. They engage initially in a mild verbal tussle where the king plays on the vanity of the mass orator before arranging for Alice, a young princess, to mock his rival for dressing so badly (subsequently Boanerges appears in Act II in a brilliant uniform). Before separating they acknowledge the power of personality in politics: 'there is a divine spark in us all', the king argues in his refutation of the 'india rubber stamp theory' which reduces the individual to a passive instrument of plutocracy.

The chorus then enters in the form of the Cabinet headed by the Prime Minister, Proteus. His business is to attempt to avert the constitutional crisis caused by the king's criticism of government policy in the press. His undertaking seems hopeless, primarily because his cause is weakened by internal dissent, mostly orchestrated by the two women in the Cabinet who openly support the king. Also, Boanerges has, in the meantime, been converted to the strong man solution to political crisis. Adding to Proteus's problems, the king too refuses to co-operate. When put to the test he prefers abdication to silence and decides to stand as a candidate in the forthcoming general election, confident he will win and that the forces of popular idolatry will soon bring him more power than he ever enjoyed as a constitutional monarch.

Throughout, parliamentary democracy is criticized. But so in many ways is the strong man thesis. Boanerges is made vaguely ridiculous in all his finery; so too is the king, though less obviously. At the close he accepts passively when commanded by Proteus to withdraw his abdication. He is not the man to upset the apple cart after all. In fact, the play ends on a maternal note, with the Queen telling Magnus to put his playthings aside and to prepare for dinner: 'Now, now, now! Dont be naughty. I mustnt be late for dinner. Come on, like a good little boy'. The most positive comment on his character is made during the Interlude by the other woman in his life, Orinthia, who tells him 'You have almost the makings of a first rate women in you'. Almost, but not quite. Compared to Shaw's Caesar his greatness lies in his name only. He is the prisoner of his role, prepared ultimately to act as 'An idol set up by a group of plutocrats so that they can rule the country with the king as their scapegoat and puppet'. It is suggested in the play that these plutocrats will in the future be American not British. Ultimately, the king is 'too old fashioned' to take on Breakages Ltd.: 'This is a farce that younger men must finish'.

There was little encouragement for any form of extremism in *The Apple Cart*. The play's spirit is experimental, playful and essentially civil. Typically, the heros are all flawed, with the central character shying away from the vulgarities of action and the upheaval it entails. The political farce goes on. That is not to say that the possibility of intervention by a strong man or men is discounted altogether. But it will not be heroic in the usual sense. Revolutionary politics will be as farcical as any other, and thus a proper subject for extravagant political comedy. As Bentley indicated, Shaw was too much of a humourist and rationalist to fall under the spell of a heroic political theatre. With this in mind, it can be said that fascism's appeal to Shaw was not aesthetic in nature.

ON THE ROCKS

By the time Shaw started work on *On the Rocks* in 1933 circumstances were very different. For the western world economic ruin was now visible. Shaw, meanwhile, had found the right sort of dictator in distant Russia – a prosaic hero in the Fabian mould – with the right sort of creed. Echoes of these developments are found in the new play. Whereas *The Apple Cart* was set in the uncertain future, making the crisis somewhat unreal, in *On the Rocks* collapse was imminent and unavoidable. In the former the workers enjoyed the rewards of corrupt plutocracy, now there was mass unemployment. Quiescence had turned to revolt. Violence was firmly on the political agenda. Such contrived interventions as the American proposal to rejoin the British Empire were not required any longer. Whereas *The Apple Cart* was extravagant and expansive, *On the Rocks* was more insular and claustrophobic, set in the one dark room and assailed by mass unrest. There was the usual Shavian diversion – the question of marriage between the younger characters – but this was incidental to the main concern with the condition of England. The play was in many ways the perfect artistic companion to Shaw's doctrine of national socialism. Whereas in 1930 the issue of dictatorship was used mainly as a vehicle in the pursuit of artistic ends, now, arguably, it had become a serious political option, thus making far deeper inroads into Shaw's artistic consciousness. *On the Rocks* was set in the world of Shotover's lucid ravings. The sub-text had emerged from the shadows.

The action revolves around Sir Arthur Chavender who is the Liberal Prime Minister of a national government. In Act I he is introduced as a typical parliamentarian, described by the Chief Commissioner of Police, Sir Broadfoot Basham, as the best man in England 'that could be trusted to talk and say nothing, to thump the table and do nothing'. Sir Arthur is seen to be wasting his time on the farce of politics, playing the game as astutely as Proteus, but to no great effect. He uses all his suavity to deal with the deputation of the representatives of the unemployed from the Isle of Cats, avoiding any commitment to do anything at all about the subject at hand. By Act II, however, he has been transformed into a paragon of Shavian socialism, armed with a programme of wholesale nationalization backed up by the doctrine of compulsory public service. There are four stages in the transformation. First, his wife, Lady Chavender, derides his pointless fairyland world where he is busy doing nothing. Second, the younger radical members of the deputation, disgusted by his complacency, nettle him with their parting remark that they had got his measure. Their departure leaves the stage clear for Old Hipney, the third factor in Chavender's transformation. He is a curious and sinister figure. He could be seen simply as a repository of political experience gained from a lifetime's involvement in working-class politics, or else as a grander Mephistopholean figure tempting Chavender to assume absolute power. His message is that the parliamentary 'game is up' and Chavender must face the real challenge posed by the angry unemployed and the educated radicals full of the conceit of Marx. Finally, Chavender is confronted by a lady doctor, a self-professed messenger of death, sent by his wife to tell him he is dying from a lack of mental exercise – a common English complaint. What he needs is a long stay at her retreat in Wales. Of Chavender's kind she says, 'On the Great Day of Judgement the speechmakers will stand with the seducers and the ravishers, with the traffickers in maddening drugs, with those who make men drunk and rob them, who entice children and violate them'. The choice facing Chavender, then, is between damnation and transformation.

He chooses the latter. Act II plays out the consequences in a series of discussions between various 'representative' figures, including Basham, Sir Dexter Rightside, leader of the Conservative Party, a half-witted admiral, Sir Bemrose Hotspit and the aristocratic His Grace the Duke of Domesday. All of these, with the exception of Sir Dexter, initially support Chavender's scheme, though purely on grounds of self-interest. Support also comes from a curious quarter, namely, an Indian plutocrat, Sir Jafna Pandranath. His purpose in the play, like Hipney's, is distinctly ambiguous. On one side he points to the imperial dimension to British politics, showing up the parochialism of much of the debate, as well as revealing the ingrained racism of Sir Dexter who dismisses him as 'a silly nigger pretending to be an English gentleman'. At another level Sir Jafna represents two contrary forces: the superior mystical wisdom of the East, on the one hand, and the power of plutocracy, on the other, a power which in this instance is prepared to co-operate with Chavender's new-found progressivism. Curiously, only Sir Jafna does not renounce Chavender when he reveals his plan to establish a radical dictatorship. Chavender only mentions this plan after the tide of debate has turned decisively against him. This change in fortune is itself the result of an intervention by the Mayor of the Isle of Cats who tells him: 'Of course we're against you. Do you expect me to go back to my people and tell them they should vote for compulsory labour and doing away with strikes'. The upshot is that the Labour and Conservative Parties combine to defeat the cause of national efficiency, so forcing Chavender to reveal his 'ace of trumps', namely his plans for a radical dictatorship. In response, Sir Dexter, in an oddly populist turn to his conservatism, threatens to 'put fifty thousand patriotic young Londoners into Union Jack shirts' if parliament is prorogued. Shaw seems to be saying that traditional conservatism, not radical dictatorship, will manipulate the ingrained fascist sentiments of ordinary people. But to complicate things still further, Chavender had asserted a few moments before that the people of Europe and America 'are ready to go mad with enthusiasm for any man strong enough to make them do anything, even if it is only Jew-baiting, provided it's something tyrannical, something coercive, something that we all pretend no Englishman would submit to, though we've known ever since we gave them the vote that theyd submit to anything'.

Like Magnus, Chavender eventually backs down; he sees what has to be done, but does not feel that he is the man to do it. At this point Old Hipney returns to the stage and offers a long critique of democracy, similar in temper to the vituperative moralism of Thomas Carlyle, which culminates in the statement: 'Now I'm for any Napoleon or Mussolini or Lenin or Chavender that has the stuff in him to take both the people and the spoilers and oppressors by the scruff of their silly necks and just sling them into the way they should go with as many kicks as may be needful to make a thorough job of it'. What are we to make of Old Hipney and of his implications for Shaw's political outlook in this period? M.M. Morgan, favouring the Mephistopholean interpretation of the character, holds the view that as Chavender fails to take up this tempting offer and closes the play with an appeal against the hypocrisy which enmeshes modern politics, then the work's message is clearly anti-fascist in nature, pointing towards an alternative strategy to be sought by all 'responsible minds' (Morgan 1974: 286). Is the message so clear cut? It is worth noting the parallels between Hipney's views and those Shaw expressed in a controversial Fabian lecture, 'In Praise of Guy Fawkes', from November 1932, just a few weeks before he started work on the play. Old Hipney also praises Guy Fawkes as the only man with any understanding of Parliament. Like Shaw, he too sees dictatorship as the last hope of responsible government and, significantly, does not really discriminate between communist and fascist forms of dictatorship. Both cite the harnessing of volcanic power as evidence of fascism's dynamism and capacity for positive government. Both view the prospect of violent upheaval as imminent. The parallels are remarkable, tempting one to conclude that Old Hipney is the artistic *alter ego* of Shaw in his more Mephistopholean moments. It is also worth noting that Chavender ultimately agrees with Old Hipney that the work of political reconstruction will be undertaken by a strong man: 'And I shall hate the man who will carry it through for his cruelty and the desolation he will bring on us and our like', he tells his wife. It is then that the unemployed mob breaks into Downing Street smashing windows and singing not 'The Red Flag', but 'England, Arise!' (much to A.K. Chesterton's delight).

Surely the play's message is not as obviously salutary as Morgan suggests. Again, Shaw does not bring the political hero on to the stage. But this, perhaps, was as much a problem of artistic method as commitment. The strong implication is that, while dictatorship may not be a long-term political solution, it is necessary as a means of transition. The work is critical of the hypocrisy and trappings of politics and does appeal for study and meditation as a basis for enlightened action. Yet it also contains an underlying commitment to ruthlessness in public life, a commitment which found full expression in the preface to *On the Rocks* as well as in *The Millionairess*.

Shaw was poised on a knife-edge in 1933.

SIR OSWALD MOSLEY

The temptation is to proceed by asking if Mosley was the man of action, the new Arthur, for whom England awaited? Certainly, as Skidelsky noted, he had much in common with Shaw. The BUF programme was in many ways a restatement of Shaw's social imperialism, with its concern for social reform, protectionism, racial fitness and national efficiency. Shaw's national socialism was something of a model for Mosley. Was Mosley the living embodiment of his maverick socialism, with its combination of economic collectivism and political vitalism? Many contemporary commentators suspected as much, viewing Shaw as an intellectual patron of British fascism.

The lecture 'In Praise of Guy Fawkes' was central to that claim. There Shaw described Mosley as 'a very interesting man to read just now: one of the few people who is writing and thinking about real things, and not about figments and phrases'. He told this Fabian audience:

> You will hear something of Sir Oswald Mosley before you are through with him. I know you dislike him, because he looks like a man who has some physical courage and is going to do something; and that is a terrible thing. You instinctively hate him, because you do not know where he will land you; and he evidently means to uproot some of you. Instead of talking round and round political subjects and obscuring them with bunk verbiage without ever touching them, and without understanding them, all the time assuming states of things which ceased to exist from twenty to six hundred and fifty years ago, he keeps hard down on the actual facts of the situation. When you pose him with the American question, 'What's the Big Idea?' he replies at once, 'Fascism'; for he sees that Fascism is a Big Idea, and that it is the only visible practical alternative to Communism – if it really is an alternative and not a halfway house.
>
> (Shaw 1962b: 242)

This more or less sums up the case for Shaw's reputation as a proto-fascist, or, as Orwell has it, as a man who 'declared Communism and Fascism to be much the same thing, and was in favour of both of them'. This startling lecture was the high point of that trend in Shaw's thinking. Beatrice Webb called it 'a painfully incoherent tirade about nothing in particular, except for the laudation of Oswald Mosley as "the man of the future"!' (MacKenzie and MacKenzie 1985: 202). That was the sort of impact the lecture made on Shaw's friends. In an interesting aside, Beatrice added that Mosley and his wife were among Mrs Shaw's social pets at this time, 'their good looks, luxurious living and aristocratic ensemble appeal to her and this influences GBS'. Shaw's links with British fascism were social and personal, as well as intellectual, it seems. Mosley was quick to capitalize on the association, using Shaw's laudation of him as a motto for the fascist publication, *BUF: Oswald Mosley and British Fascism*.

Returning to Beatrice Webb's diary for a moment, she suggested that Shaw's public advocacy of Mosley as a possible future dictator proved short-lived. By May 1933, when work on *On the Rocks* was in full swing, he was already 'a little shy about Mosley'. Perhaps the main reason was the advent of Hitler as Chancellor in January of that year. Two points can be made here. First, it was one thing to indulge in provocative pro-fascist statements when fascism itself was only to be found in a relatively distant and minor Mediterranean nation, or else among a group of adventurers at home with little or no hope of success. A militant and rampant Germany was a different matter. Second, Hitler's rise to power highlighted the anti-semitic elements among Mosley's followers and even in Mosley himself. This was unacceptable to Shaw.

From then on he said hardly anything about Mosley (publicly at least). In January 1934 he suggested Mosley should be included in a series of radio talks for the BBC titled 'Whither Britain?': 'He is said to be a very good speaker; and he puts real work into his speeches', Shaw informed Charles Siepmann (Shaw 1988: 362). Also, in the war years Shaw was to criticize Mosley's imprisonment – what kind of people were the British to be frightened by one man, he asked? (Shaw 1943: 2). Otherwise Shaw contented himself with this reply to *The News Chronicle* on 'The Blackshirt Challenge' from January 1934: 'As a red hot Communist I am in favour of Fascism. The only drawback to Sir Oswald's movement is that it is not quite British enough. We do not like black shirts in this country. The Englishman likes a white shirt – or a moderately white shirt' (Shaw 1934c: 2). After that, this particular rhetorical gate was closed tight. Evidently Mosley was no longer even a candidate for the title 'once and future king'. He had returned to the chorus line.

The initial attraction – personal and doctrinal – should not be under-estimated, however. Shaw was lucky not to make an even bigger fool of himself than he did over Mosley. Just as his 1931 visit to Russia distanced him initially from fascism, so Hitler may have parted him still further, and just at the crucial moment where his relationship with Mosley was concerned, it seems. The evidence is not compelling. However, it can be argued that, but for Hitler, the knife-edge Shaw was poised on in 1933 could have been sharper still.

ANTI-SEMITISM

Shaw was particularly sensitive about the charge of anti-semitism. When in 1925 he was accused (somewhat incredibly) in the French press of exploiting anti-semitism for the mob, he was swift to respond, stating that in England 'the Jews always treat me as conspicuously pro-Jew'. So eager was he to refute the charge that he appended the equally incredible comment, 'The truth is that there is no anti-semitism in England' (Shaw 1988: 922).

Shaw had in fact queered his own pitch rather by his silly and provocative advocacy of Houston Stewart Chamberlain's *The Foundations of the Nineteenth Century*, in *Fabian News* in 1911. He said the book should be read by all good Fabians as 'a masterpiece of really scientific history'; its unconcealed bias and bold generalizations raised it above the work of mere specialists and 'accumulators of hard data'. Shaw was using Chamberlain to bolster his own case for the methods of the artist-philosopher against those of the empiricist. It was another dangerous tactic, especially as he proceeded to say that Chamberlain was right to protest 'against the lumping together under the general name of 'Humanity' of people who have different souls'. Considerations of this sort seem to have informed Shaw's proposal for a number of Leagues of Nations, each founded on the principle of cultural homogeneity, with the world's peace being secured in the first instance by the higher civilization of the Protestant North. The continuing influence of Chamberlain's work on Shaw in this respect was evident in the unpublished 'More Common Sense about the War' where Shaw argued that Chamberlain 'is interesting only to readers of genius, or the high intelligence to which genius appeals' (Shaw Papers: BM 50669B). It was an astonishing assertion. So too in its way was Shaw's protest against the general concept of 'humanity'. Elsewhere he had, after all, denied the existence of distinct races. It was all rather messy. Shaw did not go so far as to accept Chamberlain's chief contention that the struggle between the races was the main propelling force of history. However, in the broader context of his argument, Shaw's interest in eugenics at this time did lead him to speak of racial fitness, and in some Fabian circles this concern had anti-semitic overtones: for example, Sidney Webb in 1907 cited the high birth-rate among the Jews and Irish as a significant factor in England's racial degeneration (Webb 1907: 17). Shaw, fortunately, avoided making that precise connection. Indeed, as Geoffrey Field notes, he ultimately rejected Chamberlain's thesis that 'the battle between Teuton and Chaos still raged, concluding that Chaos had triumphed and with it superstition, national conceit, militarism and mediocrity' (Field 1981: 464). And, typically, Shaw turned the argument around, stating that none of these were specifically Jewish complaints, but were instead to be traced to the advent of the 'Short round skull' of the British greengrocer. How like Shaw to court disaster only to twist the tail of his English audience. It was the habit of the controversialist which was to serve him so badly in his dealings with fascism.

The escapade was not forgotten and he was to spend a lot of time and energy setting the record straight. He never again indulged in paradox and wild assertion where the Jews were concerned. He was to be consistent in his critique of anti-semitism, calling in 1921 for a 'powerful counterblast to the Anti-Semites' (Shaw 1985b: 714). On the other side, he invariably noted the Zionist predilection for viewing the Jews as a chosen race – a monstrous presumption, he called it, useful as an illusion when in captivity, but now a 'dangerous paranoic delusion' (Shaw 1928: 16). He was against all forms of racial snobbery: 'I have never taught the biological gospel of a new race-aristocracy', he declared in 1933 (Shaw 1933a: 879).

Considerations of this kind informed his response to Hitler. He had warned in 1931 that Hitler would triumph in Germany if the democratic system was not reformed. Writing in *The Jewish Chronicle* a year later, Shaw blasted the Nazis as a 'mentally bankrupt party' capable only of exploiting the phobias of the masses against the Jews (Shaw 1932f: 23). Nazi anti-semitism was the political tactic of desperate men. He made this point again in the *New York Times* in April 1933, saying that 'the Nazis had no real plan of action, and after they had aroused enthusiasm and obtained support, had to resort to an attack on the Jews because they had nothing better of offer'. It was a 'disgrace', Shaw declared (Shaw 1933d: 19).

There was, however, another side to Shaw's response to Hitler. He often described him as an able statesman, especially whenever his actions contradicted the Versailles Treaty. On these occasions, Hitler had Shaw's complete support. More revealingly still, when interviewed in *The Sunday Dispatch* in June 1933, he was to acknowledge Hitler as a fellow national socialist: 'The Nazi movement is in many respects one which has my warm sympathy; in fact, I might fairly claim that Herr Hitler has repudiated Karl Marx to enlist under the banner of Bernard Shaw'. Furthermore, he said that the Nazis, 'as socialists using Bolshevik dictatorial tactics', had 'the sympathy of Russia, in spite of the rivalry of Fascism and Communism'. Shaw was on a knife-edge again.

Shaw did part company with Hitler over the Jewish question and in this respect his criticism of the Nazis was even more severe than in 1931. He began by denouncing Hitler's Judophobia as a form of insanity which had nothing to do with fascism and against which one could not hope to reason; it was 'an incomprehensible excrescence' on the doctrine of fascism which must deny to the Nazis the sympathy they otherwise deserve. The idea that Hitler only used the raids on the Jews as a tactic to repay the loyalty of his followers or to retain mass support was not to be countenanced. In Shaw's view, Hitler's hatred of the Jews was genuine enough. It was a kind of madness, not just a political tactic to be manipulated in a more or less rational way. Hitler's thoughts on the Jews were 'stark raving nonsense' Shaw told Trebitsch in 1939: 'he is mad on that subject' (Shaw 1988: 525).

In the event, this line of argument proved hard to maintain. As in *The Guide*, elsewhere Shaw was tempted on the one hand to explain away the Jewish question in economistic terms while, on the other, highlighting the racial arrogance of the Jews themselves and minimizing the violence done to them under Hitler: Einstein's expulsion, for example, was passed off as a 'silly gaffe'. In another letter to Siegfried Trebitsch, written in June 1935, Shaw commented:

Tell Colonel Goering with my compliments that I have backed his regime in England to the point of making myself unpopular, and shall continue to do so on all matters in which he and Hitler stand for permanent truths and genuine Realpolitik. But this racial stuff is damned English nonsense, foisted on Germany by Houston Chamberlain. The future is to the mongrel, not the Junker.

(Shaw 1988: 413)

As if Colonel Goering would listen.[7] Was Shaw once again the rationalist in a storm of irrationality?

MUSSOLINI'S AFRICAN ADVENTURE

These dilemmas were to find full expression in the play *Geneva*. Before Shaw started work on it he had to deal with still another new development in the fascist saga, namely Mussolini's declaration of war in Ethiopia (or Abyssinia as it then was) in October 1935. Shaw's response was predictably odd. Against the hypocrisy of outraged British opinion, he resurrected the old social Darwinist argument of the Boer War as a means of defending Italy's aggression; he said the British more than anyone should know that the spread of civilization through colonization must involve violence and 'even the extermination of the uncivilized'. Writing in *The Times* in his most Euro-centric vein, he portrayed the conflict as one between savage Danakil warriors waving spears and Italian engineers paving the way for modern trade and communication (Shaw 1935d: 12). He had to side with the engineers against the tribesmen in 'their hopeless conflict with the march of bourgeois civilization'. Victory for the engineers was simply 'inevitable' he declared in a long article in *Time and Tide*. As a realist, he was bound to conclude that 'The Italians must allow us to slaughter the Momands, because, if we do not kill the warlike hillmen, they will kill us. And we must allow the Italians to slaughter the Danakils for the same reason' (Shaw 1935b: 1423). Similar views were expressed in his private correspondence. For example, when comparing the relative significance of the Spanish Civil War and the Ethiopian affair in a letter to Beatrice Webb from September 1936, Shaw said the former was 'much more important' that the latter, 'which was merely an incident in the inevitable erosion of tribal savagery by police and engineering' (Shaw 1988: 441).

Shaw's response was not racist as such. He was quick to note in the *Time and Tide* article that 'the next great civilization may be a negro civilization; for there is not the smallest scientific ground for the notion that pink or olive men are any better cogenitally than brown, yellow or black men'. Nor was it specifically pro-fascist: fascism was lumped with 'predatory nationalism' as a force hostile to the Kantian rule of supernational law. It was just that the war demonstrated the obvious superiority of 'Capitalism over Tribalism'. As for the instrument of supernational law, the League of Nations, the conflict only confirmed its impotence in Shaw's eyes. The League was ill-conceived: 'A

League of Nations must by definition consist of nations; and by a nation is meant a homogeneous political unit with a political territory and a responsible government capable of making elaborate treaties and enforcing them'. Italy was a nation, Ethiopia was not, and should never have been admitted to the League.

In such circumstances the prospects for maintaining world peace were grim, Shaw calculated. Arguably, this was a major factor in his support for Italy in the Ethiopian affair. Naïvely, Shaw seemed to believe that appeasement with the fascists was the only means of avoiding world war. More specifically, he thought British hostility to Mussolini over Ethiopia would only drive him closer to Hitler and by the mid-1930s Shaw seriously feared a combination of the fascist nations with Japan in a war against Russia (Shaw 1936a: 252). He did not always admit these fears, especially as the actual conflict drew nearer, but they were real enough and seemed to trap his mind in a stranglehold, apparently locked in the grip of a brutal realism which yet served his underlying quest for peace and order. Limited war in Africa was to be preferred to total war in Europe and beyond. That at least is one rationalization of his views on Mussolini's African adventure (Pilecki 1965: 146).

That adventure made Shaw more wary still of fascism. After 1935 he was more eager to discriminate between the fascist and Soviet forms of dictatorship. There were still hints of praise for Mussolini, but these were mixed with a view of fascism as predatory – having chosen empire instead of Church – and of *Il Duce* as a political humbug: 'He is like an old-fashioned automobile', Shaw told a *New York Times* reporter in June 1936, 'a wonderfully awesome thing to watch, and the explosions are thrilling, but it never took you where you wanted to go' (Shaw 1936c: 5). Mussolini was becoming a liability, fostering civil war in Spain and failing to implement the corporatist policy in its integrity at home.

It was against this backdrop that Shaw wrote the 1937 chapter on fascism in *The Guide*. Clearly, he had the ammunition and, presumably, the motivation to offer a really decisive critique of every facet of fascist politics. All of which makes the ambivalent nature of the statement more surprising. The Ethiopian war was ignored. So too was Mosley's increasingly disreputable record. The Jewish question was deliberately underplayed. Meanwhile, faith of a kind in Mussolini's political acumen remained intact. The logic of the argument dictated that fascism would lead inevitably to war. But that was to countenance disaster and the wounds Shaw carried from the Great War were too deep for that. All the faults of fascism were placed at the door of capitalism and its average citizen. Together, Shaw's vitalism and rationalism conspired to grant a reprieve to the leader, so building some flexibility as well as hope into the argument as a whole.

Shaw continued in the same vein beyond 1937. He supported Hitler's invasion of Austria on the basis of his economic record, describing it as a 'highly desirable event' (Shaw 1938c: 18). Even stranger, he told the *Daily Herald* in 1938 'If you ask me the difference between Russian Bolshevism and German national socialism, I cannot for the life of me tell you' (Shaw 1938b: 9). Right up to the war he continued to advise the Jews that their best response to anti-semitism was to ignore it (Shaw 1939a: 12). Similarly, he doggedly predicted that war would not be declared, until the position simply could not be sustained any longer. Stalin was his main hope. That Shaw had less trouble than other fellow travellers in hailing Stalin's pact with Hitler as a masterstroke of a prince of peace was only to be expected. It was 'joyful news'. Writing in the *New York Times* in August 1939, Shaw said the 'unfortunate Fuehrer' was 'now under the powerful thumb of Stalin, whose interest in peace is overwhelming' (Shaw 1939c: 4). More surprisingly perhaps, he continued almost until the outbreak of war to see Mussolini as the senior partner in the fascist alliance. When applauding Neville Chamberlain's mission of appeasement to Munich in October 1938, Shaw said he believed Mussolini had more to do with the settlement than anybody: Italy had not the counters to play the game of war, he reasoned, and this made Mussolini 'the most ardent pacifist in Europe'. Even at this stage Shaw still described Hitler and Mussolini as 'two highly capable revolutionary and proletarian leaders, who are giving their people as big a dose of socialism as they can stand' (Shaw 1938d: 3).

All of which goes to show just how wrong a clever man can be.

GENEVA AND BEYOND

Shaw's position was hopeless; the conflicting forces of socialist realism and ethical rationalism were in disarray. That hopelessness was encapsulated in *Geneva*, a play he started in 1936 but one he continued to work on beyond the outbreak of war in a vain attempt to keep it abreast of the times. More than that, as his wife said, he just could not get it right. This was because it encompassed the impossible polarities of his thought, with its logic being pulled between hope and despair, happiness and perfection.

Geneva's central concern was with the accountability of the men of power to a higher supernational law. The action revolves around the efforts of a number of complainants – a Jew and a traditional democrat among them – to use the offices of the League of Nations to bring Hitler, Mussolini and Franco before the International Court at The Hague. The play is cast in the form of a caricature, somewhat in the manner of a David Low cartoon (only Low was far more consistent in his attitude to dictatorship). The dictators are portrayed as Battler, Bombardone and Flanco respectively, with other representative figures – including a British Foreign Secretary and a Russian Commissar – making up the cast. The judge is the Shavian idealist, the man of eternal if uncertain hope, looking at one point to the perfecting of human nature, at another deciding that 'man is a failure as a political animal' and looking to the life force to produce something better. The Commissar is the prophet of happiness, arguing that 'Russia – Holy Russia – will save the soul of the world by teaching it to feed its people instead of robbing them'. As for the British characters, they represent mostly the forces of hypocrisy and stupidity in the world: that at least was the case in the original version of the play.

Pilecki has shown how the many revisions to *Geneva* reveal the difficulties Shaw faced in treating the issues at hand. This is especially true of the scene where the Jew and Battler confront the matter of anti-semitism. In some ways the difficulties Shaw faced over the Jewish question were more intense in the drama than elsewhere. In his polemical work he could acknowledge, if only fitfully, that some problems were beyond the bounds of reason; it was harder in the drama because the dialectic of the plays was grounded on rational discourse. Originally, therefore, the scene depicted a venomous exchange between the Jew and Battler, with both making strong claims to racial superiority: the Jew says he represents the 'Upper layer of the human race', while Battler maintains he exterminates only sub-humans, poisonous vermin and Jews. No further discourse was possible. Shaw subsequently revised the scene, playing down the Jew's arrogance and allowing Battler a far more reasoned stance: he was merely following the rational policy of excluding unwanted foreigners from his country, a policy no different in fact to the British exclusion of the Chinese from Australia. According to Pilecki, 'Shaw had converted a blind hatred into a rational point of view', thus allowing the dialectic of Shavian discourse to unfold within the usual framework of his drama (Pilecki 1965: 28). Of course in doing so he undermined the power of his critique of anti-semitism, so rendering the play's treatment of the issue irrelevant. Anti-semitism was caused by some of Battler's wayward followers. It was a tactical problem once again.

Another dimension to the debate was that after 1938 Shaw had to account (in *Geneva* as elsewhere) for Mussolini's apparent conversion to anti-semitism. 'Musso let me down completely by going anti-Semite on me', Shaw told Lawrence Langer in September 1938, 'and I have had to revise the third act [of *Geneva*] to such an extent that you may now put the copy I sent to you in the fire as useless, or, better still, sell it as a curiosity' (Shaw 1988: 511). Even so, Bombardone's treatment in the play is in fact quite sympathetic; he is introduced as a paragon of Shavian virtue, preaching nationalism only as a prelude to the federation of empires. Not unexpectedly, then, his new-found anti-semitism is explained away in terms of the practical difficulties faced by Italy in accommodating the Jews expelled by Germany.

In a similar vein, in an article in *Time and Tide* around the same time, Shaw said a committee of the League of Nations should be established 'to determine whether the anti-semite measures taken by Germany and Italy are legitimate legislation or pathological phobia'. If the committee decided it was a phobia, then the measures would have to be cancelled, or else the dictators must 'stand before Europe as certified lunatics' (Shaw 1938a: 1653). The scheme's implausibility speaks for itself and shows again Shaw's drift into political irrelevance. After 1945 he was to explain the horrors of the concentration camps as a problem of organization: 'Had there been efficient handling of the situation by the authorities (assuming this to have been possible) none of these atrocities would have occurred' (Shaw 1946: 17; 1988: 752). The political world Shaw had constructed had fallen apart.

Ultimately, he could not deal with political fanaticism on its own terms, either in his drama or elsewhere. As in *Three Plays for the Puritans* it had to be dispelled by laughter or by love;[8] or, as in *Geneva*, by the sweet reasoning of the Judge who views all the participants as 'personally harmless human beings'. Pilecki was right to detail the conflict between the forces of optimism and despair in the plays. He was also correct in noting the drift in successive versions of *Geneva* towards an idealistic resolution to the conflict. As in *Everybody's*, the themes of the sub-text were submerged under the burden of Shaw's desperate hope.

Two other issues raised in *Geneva* should also be mentioned. One is that, as war drew nearer, the critique of the British faction in the play grew less intense. Shaw took a very different stance in his polemical work. Pilecki has cited the criticism of the reviewers who attended the first performance in August 1938, complaining *Geneva* was 'overly critical of the British and generally sympathetic toward the dictators', whereas by 1940 a New York production was blasted as 'a British propaganda mission'. Perhaps Neville Chamberlain's policy of appeasement or simply the threat of censorship was responsible. Whatever the reason, Shaw again managed somehow to support his own side in time of war. In 1945 he even neglected momentarily to praise Stalin and decided instead to suggest that England defeated Hitler single-handedly. The argument should not be overstated. Shaw saw Hitler's declaration of war on Soviet Russia as the turning point of the war. His confidence in the latter was absolute. Writing in the *New York Times* on 23 June 1941, he declared 'Today, owing to the inconceivable folly of Hitler, we've nothing to do but sit and smile' while Stalin smashes Hitler. Now we'll see what will happen. Germany hasn't a dog's chance'. All the same there was a hint of patriotism in the assertion from the preface to *Geneva*, 'when England is frightened England is capable of anything' (Shaw 1946: 5). As Shaw said in his will, his domicile of choice was England and he was privileged to remain a British subject by the special order of the Home Secretary.

Nor was *Geneva* entirely uncritical of Russia. When disaster threatens at the close, the Commissar cannot act without instructions from Moscow. He is locked into orthodoxies of the Marxian dialectic. The Shavian dialectic would be much more suitable, it is implied. But that was the only criticism Shaw levelled against Sovietism, here or elsewhere. In *Everbody's* the contrast between it and fascism was more severe than in 1937. Now fascism was the great corruption of socialism, using collectivist means for plutocratic ends and finding expression, not only in Italy and Germany, but also in the welfarism of the New Deal in the USA. Basically, Shaw was merely reproducing the redundant Stalinist theory of social fascism which blurred the distinction between capitalism and fascism. The western fascists (Britain included) should have combined to defeat 'the genuine democratic socialism of the USSR' and partition Russia among themselves, Shaw said (Shaw 1944: 264). Instead they defied reason and fought alongside Stalin against their own kind. This was Shaw at his worst, expecting life to conform to his own faulty logic.

In this respect, *Geneva* and *Everybody's* were among Shaw's least convincing yet most revealing works.

CONCLUSIONS

To claim that Shaw was a seminal figure in the development of fascism is to overstate the case. Nevertheless, he did have more affinity with fascism than the apologists suggest. Both the fascist ideology and its leaders gained his support to some degree, although that support was uncertain and it varied according to time and context. Some of it belonged to Shaw's controversialist habit of chiding his British audience. Beyond that, however, there was a genuine match between aspects of fascism and Shaw's own odd amalgamation of vitalism with economism. Together, his natural sympathy for the individual rebel and his regard for the collectivist lawmaker drew him towards Hitler and Mussolini. Their conception of strong, organic life was imperfect. Compared to liberal democracy, however, it was at least a step in the direction towards Shaw's vision of the politics of virtue. What is more, he never quite lost the sympathy he felt for the dictators. The offer of political asylum in Ireland for Hitler was about the only thing he found to applaud in Eamon de Valera's presidency. Shaw opposed the war crimes trials at Nuremburg, always maintaining that the horror of the concentration camps was wholly a matter of administrative inefficiency. The trials, therefore, would have more to do with martyrdom than with justice, he said, returning to the familiar territory he had occupied in his defence of Casement and the Irish rebels back in 1916. All of which suggests that Shaw's mind was trapped in a time-lock. As H.M. Geduld puts it, 'between creative evolution and Alfred Rosenberg's *Myth of the Twentieth Century* is an unfathomable abyss of horror which Shaw was never able to comprehend' (Geduld 1961: 18).

Writing to Nancy Astor in 1942, Shaw said he was reading Hitler's *Mein Kampf* 'really attentively instead of dipping into it' and 'had come to the conclusion that':

> He is the greatest living Tory, and a wonderful preacher of everything that is right and best in Toryism. Your Party should capture him and keep him as a teacher and leader whilst check-mating his phobias. On the need for religion, and on the sham democracy of votes for everybody, on unemployment and casual labour, he is superb ... we

must lick his rabble of Rosenberg's and ruffians; but we really mustnt hang him. But there is not much danger of that: When his army cracks, he will turn up in Ireland, renting the Vice Regal Lodge like Louis Napolean at Chislehurst or the Kaiser at Doorn; and who can touch him?

(Shaw 1988: 643)

'These two poor devils' was how Shaw described Mussolini and Hitler in 1945. What they lacked finally was a creed to keep them within the bounds of reason, Shaw said. That was where Stalin held the advantage over them. Paradoxically, however, Shaw did not admire Stalin's Marxism. Indeed he maintained that Stalin's success was due largely to his ability to transcend its dictates. Stalin was a Shavian by default. Moreover, the system he ruled was Shavian in all but name. It demonstrated the chilling truth of Shaw's vision of socialism as a bureaucratic Leviathan governed by the intellectual proletariat for the good of the masses. As always, there was room for improvement, and here too Shaw was intent on showing the way.

That Shaw would not have survived the rigours of his own utopia is clear. So too is the fact that his support for totalitarian regimes could only have existed at a safe distance. In the end the position he occupied was contradictory and unsatisfactory. The question mark which accompanied the title of *Everybody's* confirms that Shaw was no intellectual dictator at heart. His mind was too critical and his wit too quizzical for that. But he wanted to instruct, to cajole and to offer new hope; he needed to express his commitment to the righteous cause of collectivism and to celebrate the hard-won victories gained by the superior brains; he was not a man of power but he believed vainly he understood their world; and he could not avoid avenging the wounds he suffered in the Great War. Together, this combination of motives and impulses allowed him to excuse the inexcusable excesses of fascism and Sovietism.

Part III

7

CONCLUSION

What Shaw's political thought lacks in originality, it gains in terms of its representativeness. He was the multi-media, multi-faceted, multi-talented phenomenon of his times. He said so much about almost everything, he played such a multitude of parts, he was so much in earnest, a righteous jester at modernity's court, that he managed somehow, by dint of energy and intellectual enthusiasm, to carry within himself the dilemmas and complexities which beset and characterize our age. The persona of GBS, through which Shaw's dealings with the world were carried out, was too fantastic to be representative of anything but itself: the persona's outpourings, however, touched the nerve ends of the human condition, tragic and magnificent in its brave mask of hope. Whatever the persona said, its master felt; whatever the master could not digest emotionally was fed into the persona's unnatural maw. Shaw was anything but typical, yet the themes which underpin his work, the intractable tensions we find in it, are the staple diet of the twentieth century debate on modernity, morality and citizenship.

Central to that debate is the concern that in modern times the public realm has degenerated, undermined by the decline of citizenship and the collapse of values as evidenced by the development of relativistic and utilitarian moralities. Borrowing and adapting the terminology formulated by J.G.A. Pocock in his study of early modern political thought, the debate can be construed in terms of the still pressing conflict between the juristic (mainly liberal) and the civic or republican humanist vocabularies in political thought. Pocock describes the liberal, law-centred model, with its negative conception of freedom, as 'predominantly social, concerned with the administration of things and with human relations conducted through the mediation of things'. In opposition, there stands the republican model based on the classical Greek sense of citizenship, entailing active political life within a civil polity, in which liberty is understood to consist in 'freedom from restraints upon the practice of such a life'. Against liberalism's predominately social vocabulary, republic-anism presents a 'civic vocabulary of the purely political, concerned with the unmediatated personal reactions entailed by equality and by ruling and being ruled'. Where liberalism presents a theory of rights in which morality is reduced to a system of legal rules, republicanism, on the other hand, speaks of the virtues and the human good, the realization of which is understood in terms of moral self-discovery, participation and self-rule (Pocock 1985: 42).

In recent times, eloquent versions of the classical Greek model have been championed by Ronald Beiner and Alasdair MacIntyre, both of whom seek to reformulate the idea of citizenship and to reconstruct the public realm in opposition to what MacIntyre calls 'the dominant individualist and bureaucratic models of modern culture' (MacIntyre 1981: 211). Differences in emphasis and outlook notwithstanding, Beiner and MacIntyre share a common idiom, critical of the domination of political discourse by experts and the consequent alienation of citizens from the public realm. Of the two, MacIntyre is less forthcoming in his identification with the republican tradition. None the less, through the darkness of modern emotivism, the obsession with rules and expertise, he applauds the older conception of justice based on public desert and public merit, that republican understanding of political life where 'Equality of respect provided the ground for service to the corporate community' (MacIntyre 1981: 220). Beiner explains that 'Here politics functions as a normative concept, describing what collective agency should be like, rather than abiding by its present devalued meaning. The political expression of this ideal is the republican tradition' (Beiner 1983: 152).

Shaw was a player on this stage – a jester maybe; but then the jester often has the best lines which, however complex and equivocal, deliver the true lesson of the play. Shaw's universe of discourse was a realm of creative tensions. From the republican standpoint, much of his work encapsulates what is negative and destructive in modern culture: on a partial reading his moral outlook was a seemingly chaotic concoction of emotivism, relativism and a form of utilitarianism which perceived the good in consequentialist terms, in relation to the happiness of the individual. Alternatively, he presented his republican vision of civic virtue in the form of the ideal of the gentleman. Similarly, Shaw embodied the contrast between the Fabian tendency to interpret social reform in the language of the social engineer, the bureaucrat and manager in terms of the regulation of social intercourse, and the republican vocabulary of virtuous conduct to be achieved by means of the participation of all citizens in the project of communal enlightenment. Ultimately, Shaw's goal of combining individual moral responsibility with the morality of service within the framework of the good polity, foundered on the rocks of these unresolved tensions.

Shaw's importance lies more in his inclusiveness, as the embodiment of representative tensions, than in terms of his resolution to these. Thus, only at the mythical, transcendental level of the democracy of supermen could the conflict between expertise and enlightenment be resolved. Social inquisition and compulsory labour were the processes through which the typically anarchic, individualist personality of the capitalist order would be transformed into one appropriate to the collectivist community of civic virtue. Despite his commitment to what he called the New Protestantism, it seemed that in Shaw's scheme of things ordinary beings lacked the personality required to participate fully in the quest for moral self-discovery and self-rule.

As a product of the Enlightenment, Shaw looked to reason and science as the forces which would cure the evils (or were they errors) which beset the world; at the same time, he saw the political realm as one of dramatic argument grounded upon conflicting values and governed, not by reason, but by the illusions or myths which bring hope to men and women and inspire them to act. On the subject of illusions, he said progress was exactly that, though that did not prevent him, as a political commentator, from preferring the dynamism of the British or Italian imperialist to the static native orders they overturned. Shaw did not trust technology in the hands of the medical profession; engineers working in distant lands, lacking modern means of communication, were another matter. In his reflections on imperialism we see too the conflict between the socialist politics of class and the national socialist politics of nation. It was the nation that was to be the repository and beneficiary of the virtue of the Shavian 'gentleman'. The complete sense of citizenship and the positive conception of freedom entailed in that vision were expressed through Shaw's own politically active life; and yet, as a socialist theorist, he associated liberty with leisure, the very epitome of the negative conception of freedom. As a Fabian he maintained that socialism was from beginning to end a matter of law and emphasized the need for appropriate institutional mechanisms to ensure the healthy functioning of the social organism. As an independent thinker, however, especially in the 1930s and 1940s, he tended to underplay the importance of the legalistic and institutional approach, preferring instead to rely on the power of a progressive creed to keep his scientifically-chosen, vocationally-suitable leaders within the bounds of justice. Shaw owned an inadequate theory of democratic élitism which really amounted to no more than an inconsistent patchwork of views on related themes. He seemed to despair of democracy, yet he propounded the doctrine of the coupled vote. Invention was within his reach. Shaw knew that what he called 'Caesarian theocracies' would not wash in the modern age, that 'they all come to some sort of parliamentary complexion at last' (Shaw 1927a: 18). For all that, he could not deny the fascination of the great man in politics, his ridiculous magic, his drama and vitality, the rich combination of superficialities which in Shaw's mind characterized the super-charged kings of illusions, armed with their fake visions of authentic collective life. Above all, perhaps, through his reflections on the dictators we see how the commitment to individual welfare can be complicated and sometimes compromised both by the exigencies of power and by the perfectionist ideas of evolutionary righteousness. Shaw was an optimist who said he should despair if he did not know that all the classes of modern society 'will die presently, and that there is no need on earth why they should be replaced by people like themselves' (Shaw 1949a: 490).

Shaw did not cultivate paradox for its own sake. His confusions were genuine and instructive. The tussle between happiness and perfection, the love–hate relationship with democracy and the bureaucratic model of reform, the troubled legacy of the Enlightenment, all these were the dilemmas inherent in socialism itself.

There is some truth in the view that Shaw's craving was not for paradox but for logic. Rare among social democrats, he tended to unravel the philosophical underpinnings of his thought, more it must be said by the simple pursuit of a line of reasoning to its extreme conclusion, than by the processes associated with detailed theoretical analysis. In doing so he revealed many of the gaps and contradictions in the Fabian model of socialism. At the heart of that model was the collectivist doctrine of the state. The lack of anything like an adequate theory of the state was the central flaw in Shaw's (and by extension, Fabianism's) socialist realism. Where his reflections were theoretically naïve, they were also revealing in so far as their extremist tendencies suggested from a very early date the dangers inherent in the collectivist vision. Ultimately, there was to be no limited liability in morals in the Shavian polity; indicating the darker side of the republican ideal, he said the concept of the totalitarian state was a mere tautology. The fact that his collectivism travelled so far in the directions of both socialism and fascism suggests that the gulf in moral outlook between the founders of social democracy and the liberal tradition they are often said to have inherited was much deeper than is usually supposed; virtues not rights were the central component of the socialist visions of Shaw, Wells, and the Webbs.

It has been noted that Shaw, like the Webbs, placed great emphasis on the bureaucracy as the agent of socialist transformation, but that, in contrast to them, he recognized from an early date the even greater importance of political leadership in this respect. Thus, whereas the significance of the creed-inspired élite for the Soviet Revolution was something of a revelation to the Webbs in the 1930s, in Shaw's case it confirmed a long-standing tendancy in his thought. This difference in outlook had many consequences for their political ideas, for example with regard to their contrasting views on empiricism and political consensus. While the Webbs were not crass empiricists, they did tend to assume that open reflection upon factual data would generate political consensus, thus largely eliminating party rivalries and the use of coercive measures from their socialist commonwealth; future government, in the Webb scheme of things, was associated almost entirely with the administration of things. Shaw was less sanguine. At the establishment of the London School of Economics in 1895 he informed Sidney of his reservations, suggesting that the institution would only serve the goals of socialism if it were inspired and guided by the right sort of ideological leadership. Affirming his view that controversy in political matters could not be eradicated by commitment to a value-free social science, Shaw insisted 'Any pretence about having no bias at all, about "pure" or "abstract" research, or the like evasions and unrealities must be kept for the enemy . . . the Collectivist flag must be waved, and the Marseillaise played if necessary to attract fresh bequests' (MacKenzie and MacKenzie 1977: 217). At times, notably in *Everybody's*, Shaw moved closer to the Webb standpoint, though even in that work there operated the countervailing view that consensus must be imposed in some way from above, with the political élite using the education system as a vehicle of social order. This suggests further that Shaw was a more thorough-going centralist than the Webbs who, in *A Constitution for the Socialist Commonwealth of Great Britain* (1920), formulated their vision of functional democracy in pluralist terms, with power being divided amongst the different levels of government. Shaw, on the other hand, was at best an irregular advocate of the cause of local government, preferring ultimately to retain the power to mould the illusions of socialism in the hands of a few superior brains.

Like the Webbs, in later years Shaw pondered the impossibility of Fabianism itself. The combination of moral fundamentalism and socialist realism left him dissatisfied with the policies of the Labour Governments of the 1920s and 1940s. In the 1931 preface to *Fabian Essays* he doubted the efficacy of Fabian constitutionalism. After noting that two of the essayists were in the House of Lords, one of them a Cabinet minister, and that parliament, from the Prime Minister down was swimming with Fabians, Shaw warned:

> If all this change were part of a developing Socialism it would be a matter for rejoicing. But being as it is an attempt to gain the benefits of Socialism under Capitalism and at its expense: a policy which has for its real slogan 'What a thief stole steal thou from the thief', there is more threat of bankruptcy in it than promise of the millennium.
>
> (Shaw 1932e: 302)

He stuck to this view, more or less. During the 1940s, while sending forth bitter complaints about paying supertax, Shaw maintained that the burgeoning welfare state was a corruption of authentic Fabian values. This is not to suggest that the socialist realist, the purveyor of compromise and expediency, preferred in the final analysis the fundamentalist impossibilism of the political Brands of this world. His humour and common sense saved him much of the embarrassment of dogma. It confirms rather Shaw's own prognostication from *Man and Superman*, that 'The most distinguished persons become more revolutionary as they grow older, though they are commonly supposed to become more conservative owing to their loss of faith in conventional methods of reform' (Shaw 1931f: 169).

The extent of Shaw's revolutionary commitment was encapsulated in the doctrine of equality of income. He ultimately allowed the forces of expediency and idealism to compromise its integrity, but none the less, it operated in his work as a constant reminder of an alternative conception of social justice, as a practical utopian measure by which the standards of capitalist and socialist polities alike could be gauged. The extent of Shaw's loss of faith in conventional methods of reform was evident in many facets of his argument, including his metaphysical speculations where he transformed his religion of creative evolution from a creed of liberation into an instrument of moral inquisition.

What emerged was a deeply divided vision. On one side Shaw was the master of rational socialism, concerned to establish a collectivist state, dedicated to the elimination of waste based on a communal commitment to the morality of service and organized (ideally at least) around the principle of equality of income. Against all that there ran the concerns of the sub-text, wherein violence and unreason lurked to spoil the vision of the moral polity. More conventional and circumspect socialists sublimated or ignored such complexities. Shaw allowed them to invade his kingdom of words, using the drama and tension they created to feed his insatiable discourse with experience. In the final analysis, of course, he could not abandon optimism altogether. To that end Shaw built a wall of rational hope around his collectivist doctrine. Yet, that wall itself was brittle and transparent. We glimpse his kindly, Mephistophelian features peering out from behind their protective screen, his fingers pressing at it, almost daring to reach out into the world of chaos that was rising about him.

When Shaw died in 1950 the press boomed with tales of his achievement. The unsigned leading article in the *Manchester Guardian* said of him:

> The degree to which he was an original thinker is probably negligible, but he was so admirable a verbal artist, so brilliant in controversy and satire (the greatest master since Swift), so ready to invert the conventional view and trust to what might happen, that there can be few forward-thinking minds for two generations that have not been at some period affected by his influence.
>
> (Evans 1976: 387)

Neither comments of this kind, nor the emphasis on the representative quality of Shaw's work, should blot out the innovative and inventive nature of his engagement with ideas. In his position as master Fabian propagandist Shaw took it upon himself to formulate a philosophical defence of the Society's pragmatic approach to socialism. The importance of the insights he gained from work of this kind into the relationship between socialist theory and practice should not be understated.

All the same, Shaw is not a political theorist of note. Though his work encompassed a vast territory usually associated with political theory, his natural domain was more that of rhetoric and argument. It was not proof so much as persuasion that enthralled him. Controversy more than contemplation excited his passion for reform. His mission, as well as his personal path to salvation, was to transform the world by exposing its contradictions, poking fun at its absurdities and railing in the face of its evils. He owned every explosive device in rhetoric's vast armoury. His contribution to the long revolution of our times has few rivals.

The exact extent of his influence is impossible to calculate. Writing in 1930 Lady Rhondda commented, 'The England of today is in part a Shaw-made and a Wells-made democracy' (Lady Rhondda 1930a: 300). Impressionistic comments of this kind can be multiplied almost indefinetly. Shaw made a difference, it seems. That at least was the overwhelming view of his contemporaries.

In some areas his influence has probably been overstated, for example with respect to the suffragette movement. In others it may not have been altogether to the good, particularly with respect to the labour movement's propensity to seek technological solutions to moral questions. There was another side to Shaw, concerned with the soul of man under socialism. That is not to deny, however, that he contributed to that aspect of the Labour Party's outlook which has constructed socialism in impersonal terms as the administration of things. Shaw made a difference. Yet predictably, in no instance did his intervention dramatically affect the course of history. The Irish question was as impervious to his wisdom as to anyone else's, unless that is one counts the gunman's wisdom. The Great War pursued its murderous course in spite of him.

In old age Shaw dwelt on the negligible impact he had made on British political life. In those comments we hear the voice of the frustrated ideologist, the rebel turned lawmaker. What he neglected, of course, was the impact he had made as artist and critical realist in plays, prefaces and countless journalistic sallies, where he challenged, rebutted and unravelled the spiritual, moral, economic, social and political foundations of capitalist society: 'the most remarkable running critique of imperialist civilization from within, that has so far appeared' was Eric Hobsbawm's Leninist estimation of Shaw's achievement (Hobsbawm 1947: 326); 'unlike his contemporaries, he has not timidly attacked or tinkered at isolated abuses, but rushed upon the whole group of conceptions upon which our tottering society rests', commented the literary critic, Bonamy Dubree (Evans 1976: 344).

Through the persona of GBS, Shaw lived out the role of world betterer on a grand scale. Yet a recurring theme of this study has been his special connection with England and the English people. It may be that in the early years his plays were more popular in the United States and Germany than in his adopted home. No matter; be it as moral heretic, artist-philosopher or socialist tactician, England was the focus of his work. England was Shaw's stage, the English middle class was his core audience, English foibles and hypocricies were the necessary targets of his righteous wit. He was puritan England's puritan conscience; Bunyan with a sense of humour. Like his fellow Irish outsider Edmund Burke, Shaw worked himself into the bones and sinews of England's body politic, to attain not the position of apologist but that of gadfly and gospeller.

England, then, was the mightiest planet in his universe of discourse. The mightiest star was Shaw's superior brain. Observing its surface, we see incessant explosions of intellectual fire sending forth a mass of high-energy words. Analysing its processes, we find these are a product of a complex fusion. Unlike Marx, he did not attempt to formulate new concepts to describe the social realities he believed he had uncovered, nor as a playwright did he stray far beyond the established forms of Victorian drama. Conventional forms and modes of discourse were the core materials of the Shavian inferno. His gift lay in his ability to mould these to his radical purpose. That process of fusion had its costs and limitations. It had its glories too. Much of Shaw's influence derived from the sheer accessibility of his message. If his thought was élitist in substance, its method of expression was decidedly populist. He had no jargon to peddle; his audience was not required to master any mystifying technicalities. Shaw brought socialism to the world dressed in plain English, wrapped in a style so brilliant it seemed blessed with the power of perpetual flight. In essence, his idiom was the common idiom of his day, purged of corruption so that it might reflect the realities of human existence. He believed in the power of clear language to dispel the socially generated mists of confusion. The Shavian universe of discourse was a transparent realm of light.

Unsatisfactory as this may be as a philosophy of language, it still suggests many of the strengths of Shaw's political argument. In particular, he understood that a form of life can only be transformed from within, that the transformation must be gradual, and pulling back from an extreme form of 'rationalism in politics' that it will not be guided solely by the dictates of theory. Compulsive intellectual that he was, his chief concern was not with abstract ideas for their own sake, but with the impact they made on the lives of ordinary men and women. His lapses have been recorded.

For the most part he was a critical ideologist, tolerant and questioning in outlook. Marx converted Shaw to socialism, but not even that intellectual colossus overpowered his quizzical mind. He presented the first critique of Marx from within the English socialist movement. More than that, he kept his mind open to a vast array of influences, from William Morris to Samuel Butler, Webb to Nietzsche. Shaw's eclecticism is legendary. It brought him into contact with the many strands of progressive thought in the last quarter of the nineteenth century, political and philosophical. So much was absorbed into his skinny frame, is it any wonder it cast such a big shadow across the stage of modern culture?

Shaw's influence has diminished in recent years. There can be no doubt that the shadow he cast across modernity's stage will recede even further in the future. History devours its propagandists. Of course he will not be forgotten, nor should he be. He is an important figure in the history of modern socialism and progressive thought generally. He made a difference. There are cautionary tales to be read in Shaw's work, in particular with respect to his evolutionary righteousness and his cult of superior brains. As an educator who perceived the forum of education in controversial terms and himself as a communicative learner in that forum, he remains a positive force.

Shaw's achievements as a political thinker are scattered, embodied largely in the tensions his thought encapsulates. Perhaps the jester's truth derives from the fact that his own reputation is no more secure than socialism's itself.

In many ways Shaw's socialism exemplifies R.N. Berki's argument that the 'contradictions of socialism are the contradictions of the age' (Berki 1975: 20). Berki discussed those contradictions in relation to what he called the four basic tendencies of socialist thought, namely, libertarianism, rationalism, egalitarianism and moralism. All these tendencies are to be found to some degree among Shaw's political ideas; they can be used here to reconstruct the essential tenets of his socialism. Libertarianism, Berki's romantic principle of socialism, was the subterranean element in Shaw's work, finding expression in the anarchic episodes from the plays, as well as in the vision of communism Shaw inherited from Morris and Kropotkin. Seeing the problems entailed in attaining that ideal, Shaw pursued the compromise order of social democracy where the rationalist, Enlightenment goals of individual happiness and welfare were to be realized. Further, because he was discontented with that compromise, he reformulated his communitarian vision in terms which satisfied his desire for a form of literal egalitarianism; the moral polity organized around the principle of equality of income was, in this respect, Shaw's alternative to Fabian social democracy and communism alike, transcending the ethical and practical pitfalls associated with each of them respectively. Fundamental to that egalitarian argument was the quality of moralism which sought to eradicate idleness and greed – the mainfold corruption of capitalism – and to replace these with the civic ideals of public honour, duty and service to the common good. First and last, Shaw was a moral revolutionary; his socialism was, in essence, a plea for virtue.

NOTES

1 SHAW'S FABIANISM

1 With respect to Shaw's conversion to the Fabian theory of rent, it should be noted that the moralism he inherited from Ruskin served as a vital socialist corollary to the marginal utility theory of Stanley Jevons. Shaw discussed the connection between Ruskin and Jevons in 1906, stating, *inter alia*, 'Ruskin's advance was reduced to pure economics by Stanley Jevons, who treated Ruskin's wealth and *illth* as utility and disutility . . .'. (Shaw 1976: 8) The influence of Ruskin and Carlyle on Shaw is discussed in Griffith (1979).

2 Echoes of this debate on strategy were to be heard in the career he was forging as a dramatist. *Plays Unpleasant*, which he introduced as 'facts for playgoers' on slum landlordism, marriage and prostitution, were designed to instruct a minority audience of sympathetic enthusiasts. However, by 1893 he was already writing the first of his *Plays Pleasant*, *Arms and the Man*, where a very different approach was adopted, more populist and playful and less explicitly socialistic. Proceeding with this broader conception of the policy of permeation, Shaw was to turn to the popular form of the melodrama for inspiration in two of his *Three Plays for Puritans* – *The Devil's Disciple* and *Captain Brassbound's Conversion*; there was nothing exclusive or élitist here.

3 Association of the Fabian model of socialism with élitist paternalism, efficiency and organization (as opposed to emancipation) is central to the interpretation found in Greenleaf (1983). This line of interpretation is taken up with respect to the views of five prominent Fabians (including Shaw) on the issue of eugenics in C. Shaw (1987). The Fabian interest in eugenics certainly highlights the anti-egalitarian and undemocratic strands in the thought of its leading exponents. None the less, as Michael Freeden has said, 'The Mental Climate concerning efficiency has to be borne in mind when examining the issue of the unfit.' Freeden considers the influence of eugenics on social democratic and liberal thought alike in this period, stating 'in the first great enthusiasm for eugenics liberals were prominently to the fore, simply because what appealed to them was the rationality of the science, the possibility that man could now control a new aspect of his 'environment' – his own body' (Freeden, 1978: 185).

4 Shaw did not explicitly link the elimination of the 'Yahoo' to the extermination of the poor at this time. Such a connection was common among eugenicists (including Sidney Webb) and it does surface in *The Guide* (see Chapter 2).

2 SHAVIAN SOCIALISM

1 Winter cites a letter from Beatrice Webb to Shaw in June 1914, noting that the Webb partnership was to work on the distribution of power among classes, while Shaw 'must work out the distribution of wealth or the pleasure of consumption, and the effect of this on such eternal institutions as the family, religion, etc.'.

2 Margaret Walters in her recent Introduction to *The Guide* spends ten pages discussing Shaw's feminism but only two pages discussing his egalitarianism (Walters 1982).

3 Shaw does contradict this at one point when he writes 'the less we have, the more important it is that it should be equally divided, so as to make it go as far as possible, and avoid adding the evils of inequality to those of scarcity' (Shaw 1949a: 113). On balance, however, the evidence is firmly against the equality of misery strategy.

4 In June 1928 Beatrice told Sidney that Shaw 'believes his book will have a great effect on the results of the general election – for good among the Have-nots and for bad among the Haves'. By 1929 Shaw was even advising the Conservative, Lady Astor, to use his work, telling her the public 'neither know nor care whether it is Socialism or Conservatism if you dont tell them' (Sykes 1972: 300). See also Brockway (1963).

5 McBriar notes the problem of reconciling equality of income with Rent Theory which assumes 'that the contribution of factors of production is at least theoretically capable of being measured'. There are in fact other contradictions of this kind. For example, the categorization of class according to distinctions in income contradicts the categorization of class in terms of social functions which Shaw employs elsewhere.

6 For a discussion of Butler's influence on Shaw see G. Griffith (1979). Shaw first encountered Butler when he reviewed *Luck or Cunning?* for the *Pall Mall Gazette* in 1887. Impressed by Butler's style and the substance of his argument, Shaw explained his defence of evolutionism against the orthodox Darwinian interpretation in these terms:

> He admits pure luck as a factor in evolution, but denies its sufficiency as an explanation of all the phenomena, and insists that organisms that have the luck to be cunning make further luck for themselves by the deliberate exercise of that cunning, and so introduce design into the universe – not design as we used to conceive it, all-foreseeing from the first, but a 'piecemeal *solvitur ambulando* design', which as it becomes more self-conscious and intelligent tends to supplant natural selection by functional modification.
>
> (Shaw 1887d: 5)

Shaw appears to have met Butler some time in the early 1890s, though the latter's influence seems to surface first in *The Perfect Wagnerite* (1898). Shaw's praise of Butler was extravagent: *The Way of all Flesh* was one of the great books of the world, Shaw maintained, as he elevated Butler's work to prophetic status. His impact on Shaw is evident in many areas, for example, in Shaw's treatment of the importance of money in the preface to *Major Barbara*; also, in the view, expressed in the preface to *Back to Methuselah*, that progress is attained by 'consigning our earliest and most important habits to the realm of the unconsciousness'. Shaw's hero-worship of Butler was not reciprocated in any way, it seems. Shaw repelled Butler who, though he smashed many idols in his time, did not care to join the charmed circle of Shavian pioneers.

7 See also a letter to his wife, Charlotte, dated 24 July 1931, where Shaw mentions Nancy Astor's groundless concerns for the wife of an émigré: Nancy Astor's 'head is full of Bolshevik horrors in spite of what we see here', Shaw remarked (Shaw 1988: 250–2).

8 Shaw wrote: 'Classes under Socialism? Parties, creeds, trade unions, professional associations, clubs, sects, and cliques, plus the new panels and registers? Yes: plenty of them, possibly on fighting terms, but always on speaking and marrying terms: that is, on equal terms' (Shaw 1944: 67).

3 SEXUAL EQUALITY

1 A feature of Shaw's work was the claim that whenever women seek equality they invariably overshoot the mark. As Walters says, he was more than half serious when he protested that 'the Married Women's Property Act had freed women only to put intolerable legal and financial burdens on men' (Walters 1982: xxx–xxxiii).

2 Shaw said he believed women pitied men and mothered them. The theme recurs many times in the plays: in *Heartbreak House*, for example, now that he is in his second childhood, Captain Shotover is treated like a baby by his daughter – 'I only want a cap to put on daddiest', says Mrs Hushabye, 'The sun is setting; and he'll catch cold'.

3 Shaw's relationships with married couples included his friendship with Henry and Kate Salt, Edward Aveling and his common-law wife, Eleanor Marx, and, perhaps most tragically, with May Morris and her new husband, Henry Sparling.

4 This note was probably written in 1888. Forty years later Shaw said: 'There was only one other man who had the same vital effect as Ibsen during the nineteenth century, and he was not a story teller. He was Karl Marx' (Shaw 1928b: 101).

5 Shaw's name is still associated with these writers in this context. Sheila Rowbotham has recounted that in 1970 she attended meetings of a women's liberation group where men and women read the works of Shaw, Carpenter and Ellis: 'Reading these writers led us on to thinking about the family' (Rowbotham 1983: 88).

6 Consult the entry for 9 March 1885 from Shaw's diary (at the London School of Economics) where he acknowledges that Mrs Aveling suggested some changes to the proposed article. He notes, too, that Morris refused to publish it in *The Commonweal*. Morris's refusal was a consequence of the uncertain state of the Socialist League's views on the marriage question (Shaw Papers: BM 50541).

7 Shaw advised Erica Cotterill to get married, as celibacy for her would mean 'morbidezza and imperfect development' (Shaw 1972: 734). Something of the chaotic impact she made on the Shaw household is indicated in a letter Shaw wrote to John Wardrope in 1942 (Shaw 1988: 637).

8 The other speakers included H.G. Wells and Benjamin Kidd. According to Karl Pearson, Shaw went 'further than Galton certainly approved' in indicating methods for improving the race. Pearson reminded the editor of *Fabian Essays* that 'the doctrine of Eugenics will best be served like those of socialism, by a slow process of impenetration' (Pearson 1930: 427).

9 The theme of the impersonality of sex was to remain in Shaw's work to the end. Thus, in the 1945 preface to the play *In Good King Charles's Golden Days* (Shaw 1949) he said the King's sexual adventures were 'in the line of evolution, which leads to an increasing separation of the unique and intensely personal and permanent marriage relation from the casual intercourse described in Shakespeare's sonnet'.

10 Ruth Hall has said that Shaw gave his nominal support to Marie Stopes on the ground that 'he did not like to see human beings as slaves to nature' (Hall 1977: 199). A letter Shaw wrote to Margaret Sanger seems to confirm this view: 'Birth control should be advocated for its own sake, on the general ground that the difference between voluntary, irrational, uncontrolled activity is the difference between an amoeba and a man; and if we believe that the more highly evolved creature is the better we may as well act accordingly' (Sanger 1971: 372).

NOTES

11 It has been said that Mrs Pankhurst never forgave Shaw for refusing to participate more actively in the movement (Mitchell 1967: 160). On the other hand, Shaw's views on the Pankhursts were not altogether complimentary. Thus, writing in 1920 to Boris Lebedoff, his Russian translator, Shaw vilified Sylvia Pankhurst for her naïve socialist militancy. He concluded:

> My own sympathies are a good deal with Sylvia; but she does not stand for anything effective in England, and as she is a spoilt child, like all the Pankhursts, she refuses to recognize anyone or study anything that does not happen to interest her temperament.
>
> (Shaw 1985b: 703)

12 The liberal feminist, Millicent Garrett Fawcett, concluded her discussion of the mother-woman with a quote from *Press Cuttings* (Fawcett 1910: 6).

4 THE IRISH QUESTION

1 In fact some of Shaw's views, on republicanism and political violence in particular, were modified in this document which reflected the position of the Labour Party on Ireland. Besides, he had already decided that republicanism was 'bad policy' in the Irish context (Shaw 1985b: 493).

5 WAR AND PEACE

1 Chamberlain's influence on Shaw is considered in Chapter 6. In fact Shaw's thoughts had run along similar lines back in 1898 when he had written: 'What we have to aim at, then, is not disarmament, but a combination of America and the Western Powers to supress civilized war by internationalized force of arms, and to dispassionately extirpate barbarous races, whose heroism, chivalry, patriotism, and religion forbid them to live and let live' (Shaw 1985a: 53). Chamberlain's influence was limited, therefore, to the use of the vogue term 'Protestant North'.

6 FASCISM AND SOVIETISM

1 This interpretation of *Heartbreak House* is indebted to A. Wright (1984).
2 The relationship between fascism and anti-modernism is of course complex. Many see Mussolini's futuristic claims as a source of Shaw's sympathy for him (Crick 1970: 31).
3 The anology Shaw went on to draw between Hitler's persecution of the Jews and the treatment of the Catholic Church by Henry VIII was fraught with confusion.
4 Shaw recognized that, in combination, Hitler's persecution of the Jews and the Churches along with his attempt 'to organize a European crusade against Russia' could well 'prove the undoing of German Fascism' (Shaw 1949a: 486).
5 J. W. Hulse argues in keeping with his thesis on the revisionist versus anarchist Shaw, that on the one side his Fabian gradualism made him fear a Bolshevik victory in 1917, while on the other the anarchic rebel of the drama allowed him to accept the challenge of revolution in the play *Annajanska*. However, here as elsewhere, the evidence does not admit such a neat dualism in the interpretation. Shaw's letters from the period do not suggest he feared a Bolshevik victory and, though the play does affirm the challenge of revolution, that affirmation was far from straightforward (Hulse 1970: 217).
6 Subsequent letters were collected in *Bernard Shaw and Fascism* (Shaw 1927a). The

first letter therein was dated 7 February 1927. The second was a letter written to Friederich Adler from Stresa, Italy on 2 October 1927. The third was published originally in the *Manchester Guardian* on 28 October 1927. Other letters in the volume were from Gaetano Salvemini (19 and 31 October 1927), together with comments and correspondence from other Italian socialists, including Arturo Labriola and Filippo Turati, none of which addressed Shaw's claims directly, but were used rather to support Salvemini's case concerning fascist terror. Shaw's correspondence with Adler is found in *Collected Letters, 1926–1950* (Shaw 1988: 67–74).

7 Shaw's reputation in Nazi Germany is discussed in detail by Samuel A. Weiss who notes that 'Shaw was *persona grata*, but within limits'. Shaw was criticized by Alfred Rosenberg for such qualities as his pro-semitism and Bolshevism, yet, even during the war, Goebbels rejected banning Shaw, whom he justified as 'antiplutocratic', as Irish rather than English, and as a satirist of Britain. Shaw's *Geneva* was banned, but generally his new plays were performed and published in Nazi Germany. Goebbels saw *The Millionairess* and Hitler attended a performance of *Caesar and Cleopatra* in 1939 (Shaw 1986a: 331).

8 Both Richard Dudgeon and Sidi el Assif are introduced as fanatics, but the latter succumbs hopelessly to Lady Cicely Waynflete's charm, while the former turns out to be quite a humane moralist destined for the clergy.

BIBLIOGRAPHY

PRIMARY SOURCES

Fabian Papers, Nuffield College, Oxford.
Shaw Papers, British Museum (BM).

OTHER SOURCES

Adams, E. (1977) 'Feminism and Female Stereotypes', in R. Weintraub (ed.) *Fabian Feminist: Bernard Shaw and Woman*, London: Pennsylvania State University Press.

Alexander, K.J.W. and Hobbs, A. (1962) 'What Influences Labour MP's', *New Society*, 13 December: 11–14.

Anonymous (1928) 'Book Reviews', *Life and Letters*, June: 56.

Arnot, R.P. (1964) *William Morris: The Man and the Myth*, London: Lawrence and Wishart.

Arthur, J. and Shaw, W.H. (eds) (1978) *Justice and Economic Distribution*, New Jersey: Prentice Hall.

Barker, R. (1984) 'The Fabian State', in B. Pimlott (ed.) *Fabian Essays in Socialist Thought*, London: Heinemann.

Barnes, T.R. (1983) 'Shaw and the London Theatre', in B. Ford (ed.) *The New Pelican Guide to English Literature Volume 7*, Harmondsworth: Penguin Books.

Barnicoat, C.A. (1906) 'Mr Bernard Shaw's Counterfeit Presentation of Women', *Fortnightly Review*, March: 516–27.

Barry, B. (1965) *Political Argument*, London: Routledge & Kegan Paul.

Beiner, R. (1983) *Political Judgment*, London: Methuen.

Bentley, E. (1944) 'Bernard Shaw's Fabian Platonism', *The Saturday Review of Literature*, 28 October: 9.

—— (1946) 'Shaw's Politics', *Kenyon Review*, 8, 3: 347–71.

—— (1947) *The Cult of the Superman*, London: Robert Hall.

—— (1967) *Bernard Shaw*, 2nd edn, London: Methuen.

Berki, R.N. (1975) *Socialism*, London: Dent.

Berlin, I. (1981) *Against the Current*, Oxford: Oxford University Press.

Bernstein, E. (1921) *My Years of Exile*, London: Leonard Parsons.

Briggs, J. (1986) 'A Life Based on Sound Principles', *Times Higher Education Supplement*, 7 November: 15.

Britain, I. (1982) *Fabianism and Culture*, Cambridge: Cambridge University Press.

Brockway, F. (1942) *Inside the Left*, London: George Allen & Unwin.

—— (1963) *Outside the Right*, London: George Allen & Unwin.

Brustein, R. (1964) *The Theatre of Revolt*, Boston: Little, Brown & Co.
Catling, P.S. (1981) 'Love by Letter', *Sunday Telegraph*, 12 April: 256.
Caute, D. (1973) *The Fellow Travellers*, London: Weidenfeld & Nicolson.
Chappelow, A. (1969) *Shaw – 'The Chucker-Out'*, London: Allen & Unwin.
Chesterton, A.K. (1934) 'G.B.S. on the Brink', *The Fascist Week*, 23 February–1 March: 4.
Chesterton, G.K. (1910) *George Bernard Shaw*, London: John Lane.
Clarke, P. (1978) *Liberals and Social Democrats*, Cambridge: Cambridge University Press.
Cole, G.D.H. (1956) *Socialist Thought: The Second International 1889–1914*, London: Macmillan.
Cole, M. (1945) 'Review', *Fabian Quarterly*, January: 32.
—— (ed.) (1952) *Beatrice Webb's Diaries, 1912–1924*, London: Longmans.
—— (ed.) (1956) *Beatrice Webb's Diaries, 1924–1932*, London: Longmans.
Crick, B. (1970) 'Introduction', in N. Machiavelli *The Discourses*, Harmondsworth: Penguin Books.
Crosland, C.A.R. (1956) *The Future of Socialism*, London: Jonathan Cape.
Dent, A. (ed.) (1952) *Bernard Shaw and Mrs Patrick Campbell: Their Correspondence*, London: Gollancz.
De Wolfe Howe, M. (ed.) (1953) *Holmes-Laski Letters*, Oxford: Oxford University Press.
Dutt, R.P. (1928) 'Notes of the Month', *Labour Monthly*, July: 387–411.
Elliot, W. (1944) 'The Sage of Eyot St. Lawrence', *The Spectator*, 22 September: 268.
Ellis, R.W. (ed.) (1930) *Bernard Shaw and Karl Marx: A Symposium*, New York: Random House.
Evans, T.F. (ed.) (1976) *Shaw and the Critical Heritage*, London: Routledge & Kegan Paul.
Fabian Society (1892) *Fabian Election Manifesto*, London: Fabian Society.
—— (1896) *Report on Fabian Policy*, London: Fabian Sociey.
—— (1900) *Fabianism and the Empire*, London: Grant Richards.
—— (1904) *Fabianism and the Fiscal Question*, London: Fabian Society.
Fawcett, M.G. (1901) 'Women, Politics and the Vote', *The Times*, 25 June: 306.
Feuer, L.S. (1975) *Ideology and the Ideologists*, New York: Harper & Row.
Field, A. (1893) 'Comments on the Conference', *Workman's Times*, 4 February: 2.
Field, G.G. (1981) *Evangelist of Race: The Germanic Vision of Houston Stewart Chamberlain*, London: Columbia University Press.
Ford, B. (ed.) (1983) *The New Pelican Guide to English Literature Volume 7*, Harmondsworth: Penguin Books.
Forester, M. (1971) *Michael Collins – The Lost Leader*, London: Sidgwick & Jackson.
Freeden, M. (1978) *The New Liberalism*, Oxford: Clarendon Press.
Geduld, H.M. (1961) 'Bernard Shaw and Adolf Hitler', *The Shaw Review*, January: 11–20.
George, H. (1880) *Progress and Poverty*, London: Reeves.
Gibbs, A.M. (1983) 'Bernard Shaw's Other Island', in O. MacDonagh (ed.) *Irish Culture and Nationalism 1750–1950*, London: Macmillan.
Greenleaf, W.H. (1983) *The British Political Tradition: Volume 2, The Ideological Heritage*, London: Methuen.
Greer, G. (1977) 'A Whore in Every Home', in R. Weintraub (ed.) *Fabian Feminist: Bernard Shaw and Woman*, London: Pennsylvania State University Press.
Greiner, N. (1977) 'Mill, Marx and Babel: Early Influences on Shaw's Characterization of Women', in R. Weintraub (ed.) *Fabian Feminist: Bernard Shaw and Woman*, London: Pennsylvania State University Press.
Grene, N. (1984) *Bernard Shaw: A Critical View*, London: Macmillan.
Griffith, G. (1979) 'The Political Thought of George Bernard Shaw', unpublished Ph.D. thesis, University of Wales.

—— (1984) 'Socialism and International Relations: Bernard Shaw's Reflections on War and Peace', *Review of International Studies*, October: 253–68.

—— (1985) 'George Bernard Shaw's Argument for Equality of Income', *History of Political Thought*, 6: 551–74.

Halévy, E. (1961) *Imperialism and the Rise of Labour*, London: Ernest Benn.

Halifax, Marquis of (1969) *Complete Works*, Harmondsworth: Penguin Books.

Hall, R. (1977) *Marie Stopes, a Biography*, London: Andre Deutsch.

Harris, N. (1971) *Beliefs in Society*, Harmondsworth: Penguin Books.

Hayes, P.M. (1973) *Fascism*, London: George Allen & Unwin.

Henderson, A. (1925) *Table-Talk of G.B.S.*, London: Chapman and Hall.

—— (1956) *George Bernard Shaw – Man of the Century*, New York: Appleton/Century/Crofts.

Hobhouse, L.T. (1913) 'Equality of Income', *The Nation*, 7 June: 384.

Hobsbawm, E.J. (1947) 'Bernard Shaw's Socialism', *Science and Society*, 11: 306–26.

—— (1950) 'Fabianism and the Fabians, 1884–1914', unpublished Ph.D. thesis, Cambridge University.

—— (1964) *Labouring Men*, London: Weidenfeld & Nicholson.

Hollis, M. (1980) *Models of Man*, Cambridge: Cambridge University Press.

Holroyd, M. (1988) *Bernard Shaw: Volume I – 1856–1898, The Search for Love*, London: Chatto & Windus.

—— (1989) *Bernard Shaw: Volume II – 1898–1918, The Pursuit of Power*, London: Chatto & Windus.

—— (1991) *Bernard Shaw: Volume III – 1918–1950, The Lure of Fantasy*, London: Chatto & Windus.

Howell, D. (1983) *British Workers and the Independent Labour Party, 1888–1906*, Manchester: Manchester University Press.

Hulse, J.W. (1970) *Revolutionists in London*, Oxford: Clarendon Press.

Hyde, M. (ed.) (1982) *Bernard Shaw and Alfred Douglas: A Correspondence*, New York: Ticknor & Fields.

Ingle, S. (1975) 'Socialist Man: William Morris and Bernard Shaw', in B. Parekh (ed.) *The Concept of Socialism*, London: Croom Helm.

—— (1979) *Socialist Thought in Imaginative Literature*, London: Macmillan.

Inglis, B. (1974) *Roger Casement*, London: Cornet Books.

Irvine, W. (1968) *The Universe of G.B.S.*, New York: Russell & Russell.

Jackson, H. (1909) *Bernard Shaw*, London: Grant Richards.

Joad, C.E.M. (ed.) (1953) *Shaw and Society*, London: Odhams Press.

Jones, G. (1980) *Social Darwinism and English Thought*, Sussex: Harvester Press.

Joyce, J. (1971) *The Essential James Joyce*, Harmondsworth: Penguin Books.

Kaufmann, W. (ed.) (1968) *Basic Writings of Neitzsche*, New York: Random House.

Kaye, J.B. (1958) *Bernard Shaw and the Nineteenth Century Tradition*, Norman: Oklahoma University Press.

Kennedy, A. (1975) *Six Dramatists in Search of a Language*, Cambridge: Cambridge University Press.

Kilroy Silk, R. (1972) *Socialism Since Marx*, London: Allen Lane & The Penguin Press.

Knowlton, C. (1877) *The Fruits of Philosophy*, London: Free Thought Publishing Co.

Krause, D. (ed.) (1975) *The Letters of Sean O'Casey, 1910–1941*, London: Cassell & Co.

Lady Rhondda (1930a) 'Shaw's Women', *Time and Tide*, 7 March: 300–1.

—— (1930b) 'Shaw's Women', *Time and Tide*, 14 March: 331–4.

—— (1930c) 'Shaw's Women', *Time and Tide*, 21 March: 364–6.

—— (1930d) 'Shaw's Women', *Time and Tide*, 28 March: 395–6.

—— (1930e) 'Shaw's Women', *Time and Tide*, 4 April: 436–8.

—— (1930f) 'Shaw's Women', *Time and Tide*, 11 April: 468–70.

Laski, H.J. (1928) 'Mr Shaw as a Socialist', *Labour Magazine*, June: 67–8.
Laurence, D.H. (1983) *Bernard Shaw: A Bibliography in Two Volumes*, Oxford: Clarendon Press.
Le Mesurier, L. (1929) *The Socialist Woman's Guide to Intelligence: A Reply to Mr Shaw*, London: Ernest Benn.
Lichtheim, G. (1975) *A Short History of Socialism*, London: Fontana.
Lloyd, H.J. and Scouller, R.E. (1919) *Trade Unionism for Clerks*, London: Palmer & Hayward.
Lyons, E. (1937) *Assignment to Utopia*, London: Harrap.
McBriar, A.M. (1962) *Fabian Socialism and English Politics 1884–1918*, Cambridge: Cambridge University Press.
McCarthy, L. (1933) *Myself and My Friends*, London: Thorton Butterworth.
MacIntyre, A. (1981) *After Virtue*, London: Duckworth.
MacKenzie, N. (ed.) (1978) *The Letters of Sidney and Beatrice Webb, Volume III*, Cambridge: Cambridge University Press.
MacKenzie, N. and MacKenzie, J. (1977) *The First Fabians*, London: Weidenfeld & Nicolson.
—— (eds) (1985) *The Diary of Beatrice Webb, Volume IV*, London: Virago.
McLaren, A. (1978) *Birth Control in Nineteenth Century Britain*, London: Croom Helm.
Marcus, J. (ed.) (1983) *The Young Rebecca*, London: Virago Press.
Martin, D.E. and Rubernstein, D. (1979) *Ideology and the Labour Movement*, London: Croom Helm.
Meikle, W. (1916) *Towards a Sane Feminism*, London: Grant Richards.
Meisel, M. (1971) 'Shaw and Revolution: The Politics of the Plays', in N. Rosenblood (ed.) *Shaw: Seven Critical Essays*, Toronto: University of Toronto Press.
Miller, K.E. (1967) *Socialism and Foreign Policy: Theory and Practice in Britain to 1931*, The Hague: Martin Nijhoff.
Mitchell, D. (1967) *The Fighting Pankhursts*, London: Jonathan Cape.
Moore, D.L. (1933) *Edith Nesbit*, London: Ernest Benn.
Morgan, M.M. (1974) *The Shavian Playground*, London: Methuen.
Nickson, R. (1959) 'G.B.S. : British Fascist?', *The Shavian*, October: 9–15.
Nietzsche, F. (1986) *Human, All Too Human*, Cambridge: Cambridge University Press.
Ohmann, R. (1962) *Shaw: The Style and the Man*, Middletown: Weslayan University Press.
Orwell, G. (1971) *The Collected Essays, Journalism and Letters: Volume IV*, Harmondsworth: Penguin Books.
Osgood, R.E. and Tucker, R.W. (1967) *Force and Justice*, Baltimore: The Johns Hopkins Press.
Pankhurst, E.S. (1931) *The Suffragette Movement*, London: Longmans, Green & Co.
Parkin, F. (1975) *Class Inequality and Political Order*, St Albans: Paladin.
Pearson, K. (1901) *National Life from the Standpoint of Science*, London: Adam and Charles Black.
—— (1930) *Life of Francis Galton, Volume IIIA*, Cambridge: Cambridge University Press.
Pease, E.R. (1963) *The History of the Fabian Society*, London: Frank Cass.
Perelman, C. (1977) *The Idea of Justice and the Problem of Argument*, London: Routledge & Kegan Paul.
Pierson, S. (1973) *Marxism and the Origins of British Socialism*, Ithaca and London: Cornell University Press.
Pilecki, G.A. (1965) *Shaw's Geneva*, London: Mouton.
Pimlott, B. (ed.) (1984) *Fabian Essays in Socialist Thought*, London: Heinemann.
Plamenatz, J. (1963) *Man and Society, Volume I*, London: Longman.

Pocock, J.G.A. (1985) *Virtue, Commerce, and History*, Cambridge: Cambridge University Press.

Porter, B. (1968) *Critics of Empire*, London: Macmillan.

—— (1984) 'Fabians, Imperialists and the International Order', in B. Pimlott (ed.) *Fabian Essays in Socialist Thought*, London: Heinemann.

Pugh, P. (1984) *Educate, Agitate, Organize: 100 Years of Fabian Socialism*, London: Methuen.

Radice, L. (1984) *Beatrice and Sidney Webb: Fabian Socialists*, London: Macmillan.

Raeburn, A (1973) *Militant Suffragettes*, London: New English Library.

Riewald, J.G. (1977) *Beerbohm's Literary Caricatures*, London: Allen Lane.

Robson, W.A. (1951) 'Bernard Shaw and the Political Quarterly', *The Political Quarterly*, xxii: 221–39.

Rosenblood, N. (ed.) (1971) *Shaw: Seven Critical Essays*, Toronto: University of Toronto Press.

Rowbotham, S. (1983) *Dreams and Dilemmas*, London: Virago Press.

R.P.A. (1944) 'G.B.S. Boiled Down', *Labour Monthly*, October: 319.

Ruskin, J. (1906) *A Joy For Ever*, London: George Allen.

Russell, B. (1975) *The Autobiography of Betrand Russell*, London: George Allen & Unwin.

—— (1976) *Unpopular Essays*, London: George Allen & Unwin.

St John, C. (ed.) (1931) *Ellen Terry and Bernard Shaw, A Correspondence*, London: Reinhardt & Evans.

Salt, H.S. (ed.) (1915) *Killing for Sport*, London: Bell and Sons.

Sanger, M. (1971) *An Autobiography*, London: Dover Publications.

Semmel, B. (1960) *Imperialism and Social Reform*, London: George Allen & Unwin.

Shaw, C. (1987) 'Eliminating the Yahoo', *History of Political Thought*, Winter: 521–44.

Shaw, G.B. (1881) 'Miss Helen Taylor and the Land League', *The Radical*, 30 July: 2.

—— (1884) 'Who is the Thief', *Justice*, 15 March: 6.

—— (1885) 'What's in a Name?', *The Anarchist*, March: 2.

—— (1886a) 'A Socialist on the Unemployed', *Pall Mall Gazette*, 11 February: 4.

—— (1886b) 'Socialism in the Family', *The Practical Socialist*, 1: 175.

—— (1887a) 'A Word for War', *To Day*, September: 8.

—— (1887b) 'Concerning Interest', *Our Corner*, September: 162–75.

—— (1887c) 'Concerning Interest', *Our Corner*, October: 193–207.

—— (1887d) 'Darwin Denounced', *Pall Mall Gazette*, 31 May: 5.

—— (1887e) 'Karl Marx and Das Kapital', *The National Reformer*, 7 August: 84–6.

—— (1887f) 'Socialists at Home', *Pall Mall Gazette*, 12 May: 11.

—— (1888a) 'A Refutation of Anarchism', *Our Corner*, June: 374–81.

—— (1888b) 'My friend Fitzthunder', *To Day*, August: 39.

—— (1889a) 'Bluffing the Value Theory', *To Day*, May: 128–35.

—— (1889b) 'To the Editor', *Justice*, 20 July: 3.

—— (1891) 'The Socialist Ideal: Politics', *The New Review*, January: 9–18.

—— (1894) 'Why I am a Social Democrat', *Liberty*, January: 5.

—— (1895) 'The Political Situation – A Fabian View', *Daily Chronicle*, 5 October: 7.

—— (1896) 'Socialism at the International Congress', *Cosmopolis*, September: 664.

—— (1897) 'Discipline in the Services', *The Saturday Review*, 2 October: 369.

—— (1900) 'Shaw on South Africa', *The Clarion*, 26 May: 161.

—— (1902) 'Should Women Stop the War?', *The Freelance*, 25 January: 429.

—— (1903) 'Preface', in W. Morris *Communism*, London: Fabian Society.

—— (1904a) 'Bernard Shaw on Incomes', *The New York Times*, 23 December: 8.

—— (1904b) 'The Class War', *The Clarion*, 30 September: 1–3.

—— (1904c) 'The Class War', *The Clarion*, 21 October: 5–6.

—— (1904d) 'The Class War', *The Clarion*, 4 November: 1–2.

—— (1904e) 'Eugenics: Its Definition and Aims', *Sociological Papers*, 1: 74–5.

—— (1904f) 'Mr Bernard Shaw on Equality', *The Daily News*, 8 December: 12.

—— (1906) 'Fabian Notes – the Election', *The Clarion*, 2 February: 5.

—— (1907a) 'Fabian Notes – The Moral of the LCC Election', *The Clarion*, 5 April: 1–3.

—— (1907b) 'Untitled', *Fabian News*, February: 22.

—— (1908) 'The Unmentionable Case for Women's Suffrage', *Englishwoman*, March: 121.

—— (1909) 'What I Think of the Minority Report', *Christian Commonwealth*, 30 June: 685.

—— (1914) 'Common Sense about the War', *New Statesman*, 14 November: 3–29.

—— (1915) 'Draft Manifesto', International Socialist Bureau.

—— (1916) 'Is the Servile State Coming?', *Woman's Dreadnought*, 16 September: 547.

—— (1917) 'Fabianism and the War', *Fabian Papers*.

—— (1919) 'Are We Bolshevists?', *Labour Leader*, 24 April: 1.

—— (1920a) *Irish Nationalism and Labour Internationalism*, London: The Labour Party.

—— (1920b) 'Women Since 1860', *Time and Tide*, 8 October: 443–5.

—— (1922) 'The Limits to Education', *The Survey*, 6 May: 219.

—— (1925) 'Shaw versus Roosevelt on Birth Control', *The World Today*, September: 845–50.

—— *et al.* (1927a) *Bernard Shaw and Fascism*, London: Favil Press.

—— (1927b) 'Mr Shaw and Mr Mussolini', *The Living Age*, December: 968.

—— (1928a) 'G.B.S. on Jews', *The Jewish Chronicle*, 28 December: 16.

—— (1928b) 'Ibsen and After', *Drama*, April: 101.

—— (1928c) 'On Bolshevism', *The Sphere*, 28 July: 168.

—— (1930) *Immaturity*, London: Constable.

—— (1931a) *Androcles and the Lion, Overruled and Pygmalion*, London: Constable.

—— (1931b) *Back to Methuselah*, London: Constable.

—— (1931c) *Heartbreak House*, London: Constable.

—— (1931d) *The Irrational Knot*, London: Constable.

—— (1931e) *John Bull's Other Island, How He Lied to Her Husband and Major Barbara*, London: Constable.

—— (1931f) *Man and Superman*, London: Constable.

—— (1931g) *Plays Pleasant*, London: Constable.

—— (1931h) *Plays Unpleasant*, London: Constable.

—— (1931i) 'Reflections on the Crisis: A Symposium', *Political Quarterly*, 11: 457–62.

—— (1931j) 'Shaw Twits America on Red's Prosperity', *The New York Times*, 12 October: 30.

—— (1931k) *Three Plays for Puritans*, London: Constable.

—— (1931l) *What I Really Wrote About The War*, London: Constable.

—— (1932a) *An Unsocial Socialist*, London: Constable.

—— (1932b) *Cashel Byron's Profession*, London: Constable.

—— (1932c) *Doctors' Delusions, Crude Criminology, and Sham Education*, London: Constable.

—— (1932d) *The Doctor's Dilemma, Getting Married, and the Shewing-Up of Blanco Posnet*, London: Constable.

—— (1932e) *Essays in Fabian Socialism*, London: Constable.

—— (1932f) 'G.B.S. on the Nazis', *The Jewish Chronicle*, 2 December: 23.

—— (1932g) *Love Among the Artists*, London: Constable.

—— (1932h) *Major Critical Essays*, London: Constable.

—— (1932i) *Misalliance, The Dark Lady of the Sonnets, and Fanny's First Play*, London: Constable.

—— (1932j) *Music in London 1890–94, Volume I*, London: Constable.

—— (1932k) *Music in London 1890–94, Volume II*, London: Constable.
—— (1932l) *Music in London 1890–94, Volume III*, London: Constable.
—— (1932m) *Our Theatre in the Nineties, Volume I*, London: Constable.
—— (1932n) *Our Theatre in the Nineties, Volume II*, London: Constable.
—— (1932o) *Our Theatre in the Nineties, Volume III*, London: Constable.
—— (1932p) *Pen Portraits and Reviews*, London: Constable.
—— (1932q) *Saint Joan and the Apple Cart*, London: Constable.
—— (1932r) *Translations and Tomfooleries*, London: Constable.
—— (1933a) 'Hitlerism and the Nordic Myth', *Time and Tide*, 22 July: 879–80.
—— (1933b) 'I Warn the World', *The Sunday Chronicle*, 30 July: 10.
—— (1933c) *The Political Madhouse in America and Nearer Home*, London: Constable.
—— (1933d) 'Shaw sees America as Speech of Future', *New York Times*, 4 April: 19.
—— (1934a) *Are We Heading for War?*, London: Constable.
—— (1934b) *The Black Girl In Search of God and Some Lesser Tales*, London: Constable.
—— (1934c) 'The Blackshirt Challenge', *The News Chronicle*, 17 January: 2.
—— (1934d) *Too True To Be Good, Village Wooing & On The Rocks*, London: Constable.
—— (1935a) 'I Am Not a Fascist, But . . .', *The Sunday Referee*, 21 July: 12.
—— (1935b) 'Notes on the Way', *Time and Tide*, 12 October: 1423.
—— (1935c) 'Provocations', *G.K.'s Weekly*, 21 March: 8–11.
—— (1935d) 'To the Editor', *The Times*, 22 October: 12.
—— (1936a) 'The Case for Russia', *G.K.'s Weekly*, 3 December: 250–2.
—— (1936b) *The Simpleton, The Six, and The Millionairess*, London: Constable.
—— (1936c) 'Communist World is Shaw's Utopia', *New York Times*, 26 July: 5.
—— (1937) *London Music in 1888–89 as heard by Corno di Bassetto*, London: Constable.
—— (1938a) 'How to deal with the Jewish Question', *Time and Tide*, 26 November: 1653–4.
—— (1938b) 'Mussolini Makes Shaw Rewrite Play', *Daily Herald*, 12 October: 9.
—— (1938c) 'Nazi Racial Ideas Assailed by Shaw', *The New York Times*, 10 July: 18.
—— (1938d) 'Shaw Says Mussolini Did It', *Sunday Referee*, 2 October: 3.
—— (1939a) 'Shaw speaks his mind on Russia', *Daily Express*, 26 May: 12.
—— (1939b) 'Uncommon Sense about the War', *New Statesman*, 7 October: 483–4
—— (1939c) 'Shaw Hails Soviet Pact', *New York Times*, 28 August: 4.
—— (1943) 'Mosley by Shaw', *Daily Express*, 26 November: 2.
—— (1944) *Everybody's Political What's What?*, London: Constable.
—— (1945) *Back to Methuselah*, Oxford: Oxford University Press.
—— (1946) *Geneva, Cymbaline Refinished, & Good King Charles*, London: Constable.
—— (ed.) (1948) *Fabian Essays*, Jubilee Ed., London: George Allen & Unwin.
—— (1949a) *The Intelligent Woman's Guide to Socialism, Capitalism, Sovietism and Fascism*, London: Constable.
—— (1949b) *Sixteen Self Sketches*, London: Constable.
—— (1950) *Buoyant Billions, Farfetched Fables, and Shakes versus Shav*, London: Constable.
—— (1956) *My Dear Dorothea*, London: Phoenix House.
—— (1960) *To A Young Actress: The Letters of Bernard Shaw to Molly Tompkins*, ed. P. Tompkins, London: Constable.
—— (1962a) *The Matter with Ireland*, ed. D.H. Greene and D.H. Laurence, London: Rupert Hart-Davis.

—— (1962b) *Platform and Pulpit*, ed. D.H. Laurence, London: Rupert Hart-Davis.
—— (1963) 'Appendix', in E.R. Pease, *The History of the Fabian Society*, London: Frank Cass.
—— (1964) *The Rationalization of Russia*, ed. H.M. Geduld, Bloomington: Indiana University Press.
—— (1965a) *Collected Letters 1874–1897*, ed. D.H. Laurence, London: Max Reinhardt.
—— (1965b) *Selected Non-Dramatic Writings*, ed. D.H. Laurence, Boston: Houghton Mifflin.
—— (1971) *The Road to Equality*, ed. L. Crompton, Boston: Beacon Press.
—— (1972) *Collected Letters 1898–1910*, ed. D.H. Laurence, London: Max Reinhardt.
—— (1976) *Practical Politics*, ed. L.J. Hubenka, Lincoln: University of Nebraska Press.
—— (1985a) *Agitations: Letters to the Press, 1875–1950*, ed. D.H. Laurence and J. Rambeau, New York: Frederick Ungar.
—— (1985b) *Collected Letters 1911–1925*, ed. D.H. Laurence, London: Max Reinhardt.
—— (1986a) *Bernard Shaw's Letters to Siegfried Trebitsch*, ed. S.A. Weiss, Stanford: Stanford University Press.
—— (1986b) *Pygmalion*, Harmondsworth: Penguin Books.
—— (1988) *Collected Letters 1926–1950*, ed. D.H. Laurence, London: Max Reinhardt.
Simon, L. (1958) *Shaw on Education*, New York: Columbia University Press.
Skidelsky, R. (1975) *Oswald Mosley*, London: Macmillan.
Strauss, E. (1942) *Bernard Shaw: Art and Socialism*, London: Gollancz.
Swartz, M. (1971) *The Union of Democratic Control in British Politics During the First World War*, Oxford: Clarendon Press.
Sykes, C. (1972) *Nancy: The Life of Lady Astor*, London: Collins.
Taylor, A.J.P. (1957) *The Trouble Makers*, London: Hamish Hamilton.
Thompson, E.P. (1955) *William Morris: Romantic to Revolutionary*, London: Lawrence and Wishart.
Turco, A. (1976) *Shaw's Moral Vision*, Ithaca and London: Cornell University Press.
Walters, M. (1982) 'Introduction', in G.B. Shaw, *The Intelligent Woman's Guide to Socialism, Capitalism, Sovietism and Fascism*, Harmondsworth: Penguin Books.
Waltz, K. (1951) *Man, the State and War*, New York: Columbia University Press.
Walzer, M. (1977) *Just and Unjust Wars*, Harmondsworth: Penguin Books.
Watson, B.B. (1964) *A Shavian Guide to the Intelligent Woman*, London: Chatto & Windus.
—— (1977) 'The New Woman and the New Comedy', in R. Weintraub (ed.) *Fabian Feminist: Bernard Shaw and Woman*, London: Pennsylvania University Press.
Webb, B. (1975) *Our Partnership*, Cambridge: Cambridge University Press.
Webb, S. (1887) *Facts for Socialists*, London: Fabian Society.
—— (1901) *Twentieth Century Politics: A Policy of National Efficiency*, London: Fabian society.
—— (1907) *The Decline in the Birth-Rate*, London: Fabian Society.
Webb, S. and Webb, B. (1975) *A Constitution for the Socialist Commonwealth of Great Britain*, Cambridge: Cambridge University Press.
Weintraub, R. (ed.) (1977) *Fabian Feminist: Bernard Shaw and Woman*, London: Pennsylvania State University Press.
Weintraub, S. (1973) *Bernard Shaw 1914–1918: Journey to Heartbreak*, London: Routledge & Kegan Paul.
Wells, H.G. (1932) *The Work, Wealth and Happiness of Mankind*, London: Heinemann.
—— (1970) *The New Machiavelli*, Harmondsworth: Penguin Books.

West, A. (1974) *A Good Man Fallen Among Fabians*, London: Lawrence & Wishart.
West, R. (1928) 'Contesting Mr Shaw's Will', *Bookman*, 67: 513–20.
Whitman, R.F. (1977) *Shaw and the Play of Ideas*, Ithaca and London: Cornell University Press.
Wilson, E. (1932) 'Bernard Shaw and the War', *New Republic*, 13 April: 241–2.
—— (1962) *The Triple Thinkers*, Harmondsworth: Penguin Books.
Winsten, S. (ed.) (1946) *G.B.S. 90*, London: Hutchinson.
Winter, J.M. (1974) *Socialism and the Challenge of War*, London: Routledge & Kegan Paul.
Wolfe, W. (1975) *From Radicalism to Socialism*, New Haven and London: Yale University Press.
Woolf, L. (1944) 'Review', *New Statesman*, 16 September: 188.
Wright, A. (1979) *G.D.H. Cole and Socialist Democracy*, Oxford: Oxford University Press.
—— (1984) *Literature of Crisis*, London: Macmillan.

INDEX

Achurch, J. 160, 164
Adams, E. 158
Adler, F. 252–4
anarchism 34–5, 50–1
Androcles and the Lion 14, 52, 102, 176, 186, 221, 226
Annajanska, The Bolshevik Empress 251
anti-semitism 264–7, 270
Apple Cart, The 82, 132, 135, 255, 257–60
Archer, W. 202
Arms and the Man 14, 65, 81, 217, 227, 231
Astor, N. 137, 243, 272
Ataturk, K. 247
audience, Shaw's need for and identification of 10–12, 14, 91, 109, 112–13, 200
Augustus Does His Bit 221
Aveling, E. 42, 45, 164, 175

Babel, A. 173–75
Back To Methuselah 3, 14, 57, 102, 126–8, 133, 152–3, 175, 192, 213
Balfour, A. 187, 192
Barker, G. 200
Barker, R. 72–3
Barnes, T.R. 15
Barnicoat, C. 168
Bax, B. 33, 40, 47
Beerbohm, M. 10
Beiner, R. 8, 278
Belloc, H. 12
Bennett, A. 230
Bentley, E. 2, 11, 139, 245, 247, 249, 259
Bergson, H. 9, 127, 251
Berki, R.N. 285

Berlin, I. 16
Bernstein, E. 3, 31, 101
Besant, A. 38–9
Black Girl in Search of God, The 136
Bland, H. 54, 68
Blatchford, R. 4, 69
Bolshevism 250–2
Bradlaugh, C. 38
Briggs, J. 10
Brockway, F. 225
Brustein, R. 13
Bunyan, J. 23, 283
Burke, E. 283
Burnaud, F.C. 157
Butler, S. 126, 284, 287

Caesar and Cleopatra 64, 217
Campbell, P. (Mrs) 160
Candida 54, 159, 176
capitalism, moral critique of 29–30
Captain Brassbound's Conversion 176
Carlyle, T. 3, 29, 262
Carpenter, E. 33, 169
Casement, R. 192, 209, 272
Caute, D. 244
Chamberlain, H.S. 219, 265, 267
Chamberlain, J. 67
Chamberlain, N. 269, 271
Chesterton, A.K. 256, 262
Chesterton, G.K. 3, 12, 105, 153
Churchill, W. 187
citizen soldier, theory of 232–4
Clarke, P. 83
Cole, G.D.H. 1–2, 6, 69, 76, 88, 108
Cole, M. 139, 144
collectivism, moral theory of 104–6
'Common Sense About the War' 217–24, 227–30, 232, 237

Common Sense of Municipal Trading, The 71, 99
compulsory labour, doctrine of 77, 116–17, 252, 278
Comte, A. 40
conscription 233–4
consequentialism 48, 58, 104, 223
Constitution for the Socialist Commonwealth of Great Britain, A 112, 281
corporatism 254–7
Cotterill, E. 160, 171
coupled vote, theory of 183–5
Cox, H. 110
Crane, W. 69
creative evolution, religion of 125–31, 152
Cromwell, O. 247
Crosland, C.A.R. 115

Dalton, H. 122
Darwin, C. 25
Darwinism, critique of 126–9
de Valera, E. 272
Death of an Old Revolutionary Hero 46, 85
Deck, R. 35
Decline in the Birth Rate, The (Fabian Tract No. 131) 119
democracy 76–7, 89, 141–5, 181–5
Devil's Disciple, The 167, 217, 226, 230
Dialectical Society, 24
Dickens, C. 23
Dobb, M. 6
Doctor's Dilemma, The 4, 94, 99, 176
Doll's House, A 164–5
Douglas, A. 140
Dutt, R.P. 11, 112

economic theory 40–4
education 86, 146–50
élitism 6, 135, 142–5
Elliot, W. 139, 144
Ellis, H. 169
Engels, F. 26
equality of income, doctrine of 105–25, 135; argument, doctrine characterised as 107–8; audience for 112–13, 120–1; biological argument for 118–20; communism, and 116–17; compulsory labour, and 116–17; economic argument for 114–16; Fabianism, and 108–9;

morality of service, and 105–6, 110, 119; perfectionism, and 120; political argument for 117–18; principle of distributive justice, as 112; reception and reputation of doctrine 120–3; repudiation of doctrine 123–5; social democracy, and 111; socialist ideology, as 110
eugenics 57–8, 63, 71, 118–20, 178–81
Everybody's Political What's What? 12, 18, 76, 125, 131, 138–45, 148–51, 154, 185, 271–3, 281
evolutionary righteousness, doctrine of 57–8, 102, 137, 151

Fabian Election Manifesto (Fabian Tract No. 40) 45, 54, 86
Fabian Essays 30, 36–8, 40, 44, 48, 54–5, 64, 72–4, 76, 79, 97, 99, 108, 124, 132, 184, 195, 281
Fabianism: Annie Besant's contribution to 38–9; audience, middle class nature of 32; bureaucratic socialism, and 278; complex moral nature of 70–2; compulsory arbitration, and 89; creative evolution, and 127–8; economic theory, the making of 40–4; elitist socialism, and 6, 71; equality of income, and 106–9, 124; Fabian realism, its nature and Shaw's role in the formulation of 44–53; feminism, and 170; 'gas and water' socialism 45; imperialism, and 65–70; intellectual proletariat, and 96; international peace, and 236–7; Irish question, and 198, 203; Labour Party, neglect of 86; Lassalle's influence on 36; middle class propaganda, and 91–3; modern socialism, and 20, 98; moral reformism, and 5; neglect of political theory 77, 98; permeation, as preferred strategy of 64; politics of gradualism, and 36–7; politics of national efficiency, and 64–5; politics of welfare, and 29, 48, 70–2, 98, 106; pragmatism, as Fabian approach to politics 44–53, 101, 106; protectionism and free trade, and 67–8; republicanism, and 231–2; Shaw resigns from Fabian executive 99–100; Shaw's membership of 31–2; Shaw's militancy, and 90; Shaw's

moral radicalism contrasted with 103; Shaw's political pessimism, and 62–3; social democracy, and 50–1; state, as basis of Fabian collectivism 72–3, 78; strategic dilemmas in the 1890s 53–6; style, middle class nature of 32; Wells, H.G., and 92–6
Fabianism and the Empire 6, 65–9, 79–80, 198, 233
Fabianism and the Fiscal Question (Fabian Tract No. 116) 67
Farr, F. 160, 174
fascism 8, 241–73: anti-semitism, and 264–7, 270; corporatism, and 254–7; Jewish question, and 249, 264–8, 270; national socialism, and 260–3; reputation of Shaw, and 245–6; social fascism, as theory of 272
federalism 209–10
Field, G. 265
Foot, M. 139
Franco, General 269

Gaelic League 207
Gardiner, A.G. 209
Gattie, A.W. 255
Gawthorpe, M. 187
Geduld, H.M. 272
Geneva 135, 238, 249, 267, 269–72
George, H. 25, 33
Getting Married 153, 170, 173, 180, 230
Gibbs, A.M. 192, 194, 206
Gorki, M. 224, 251
Greer, G. 158–9, 174
Gregory, Lady 212
Greiner, N. 158, 173
Grene, N. 192, 206
guild socialism 76, 82, 108

Haig, A. 222
Halifax, Lord 131, 138
Halston, M. 162
Hampstead Historic Club 39–40
Hardie, K. 80, 220
Harris, N. 257
Hayes, P. 245
Headlam, S. 33, 106
Heartbreak House 63, 133, 138, 160, 217, 226, 241–3, 255
Hegel, G.W.F. 73–4
Henderson, A. 250
Hitler, A. 11, 19, 68, 131, 137, 243, 245–6, 249, 256, 264, 266–9, 271–3

Hobbes, T. 7–8
Hobhouse, L.T. 12, 110, 115
Hobsbawm, E.J. 2, 5, 96, 283
Hobson, J.A. 67, 69, 132
Hobson, S.G. 68
Hoggart, R. 11
Hollis, M. 18, 150
Holroyd, M. 20, 160, 192
How to Settle the Irish Question 193, 209
Howell, D. 55–6
Hulse, J.W. 5, 20, 32–3, 36, 51, 62
Human Nature in Politics 64
human nature, views on 16–17, 51, 64, 139, 226–7
Hunt, R. 220, 222
Hyndman, H.M. 10, 12, 25, 31, 33–4, 41, 45, 48, 80

Ibsen, H. 4, 9, 33, 47–9, 52, 164–5
idleness, critique of 29
Illusions of Socialism, The 46, 51–2, 82–3, 105, 110
Immaturity 193–5, 202, 205
imperialism 64–70, 86, 198–9, 202–3, 239
Impossibilities of Anarchism (Fabian Tract No. 45) 46, 50, 73, 77, 79, 117
In Good King Charles's Golden Days 183
Independent Labour Party (ILP) 14, 53–6, 84
individual rights 58, 75, 148
Ingle, S. 38, 87
Inglis, B. 192
Intelligent Woman's Guide to Socialism, Capitalism, Sovietism and Fascism, The 11, 18, 58, 76, 81, 85, 95, 106–9, 112–23, 130–1, 138, 140, 142, 152, 170, 172–3, 175, 181, 185, 190, 243, 246–50, 258, 266, 268
international socialism 64–70
Irish Nationalism and Labour Internationalism 193, 210–11, 235
Irish question, the 191–215: absenteeism, and 205; audience, and 200; federalism, and 209–10; imperialism, and 198–9, 202–3; national character, and 201, 213; national socialism, and 198–9, 203, 207; nationalism, and 195–9, 211; political violence, and 203–4, 207–9; religious rivalries, and 194–5, 200–1;

Shaw's reputation, and 191–3; socialism, and 210–11; Ulster, and 207–8; women, and 212
Irrational Knot, The 47, 160, 169, 173

Jackson, H. 6
James, H. 128, 220
Jevons, S. 36, 40–4
Jewish question, the 119–20, 249, 264–7, 270
John Bull's Other Island 16, 62, 191–3, 195–7, 199–207
Jones, G. 119
Joyce, J. 191, 206
Joynes, J.L. 33

Kautsky, K. 79, 251
Kennedy, A. 15
Kiernan, V. 2
Kipling, R. 159
Kropotkin, P. 16, 50–1, 285

Labour Party 85–6, 91, 99, 109
Labour Representation Committee 68
Land Nationalization Society 25
Land Reform Union 39
Laski, H. 122
Lassalle, F. 36, 74
Laurence, Dan H. 12, 20, 220–1
League of Nations 236–8, 267–70
Lee, G.J.V. 23, 161
Lenin, V.I. 68, 239, 251, 262
Lessnoff, M. 117
Liberal Imperialists 65
Liebknecht, K. 228
Life Force philosophy 60, 101–2, 126–31
Lloyd George, D. 140, 210
Locke, J. 129, 132
Lockett, A. 189
Love Among the Artists 46
Low, D. 269
Luxembourg, R. 228
Lyons, E. 243, 281

McBriar, A.M. 7, 20, 50, 54, 68, 122
McCarthy, L. 188
MacDonald, R. 121, 132–3, 225, 228, 254, 258
MacIntyre, A. 278
McKenna, R. 186
Mackenzie, N. and J. 5, 20, 25, 27, 38, 77
McNulty, E. 23, 36, 94, 159

Major Barbara 1, 16, 28, 57, 62–3, 79, 85, 88–90, 111, 176, 203, 255
Major Critical Essays 141
Mallock, W.H. 97
Man and Superman 4, 13–14, 16, 26, 28, 57–9, 62–3, 99, 101, 119, 126–8, 130, 141, 178–81, 183, 188, 203,
Man of Destiny 14, 213, 217
Manifesto, A. (Fabian Tract No. 2) 32, 35, 37, 159, 169, 181
marriage, views on 169–71, 173
Martin, K. 1
Marx, K. 25, 29, 36, 41–4, 52, 78, 80–1, 98, 116–17, 119, 164, 266, 284
Marx-Aveling, E. 33, 164, 169, 175
Meikle, W. 157
Meisel, M. 62
middle class, views on 91–8
Mill, J.S. 35, 40, 42
Miller, K. 217, 228
Millionairess 136–7, 262
Misalliance 76, 94, 99, 169, 177
monarchy 230–2, 257–9
morality of service, collectivist doctrine of 5, 29–30, 89, 105–6, 110, 119–20
'More Common Sense About the War' 221, 228, 232–3, 265
Morgan, M.M. 20, 136, 262
Morris, W. 2, 30–1, 33, 35, 37–8, 50, 72, 76, 90, 98, 111, 116, 132, 169, 229, 284–5
Mosley, O. 245–6, 263–4, 268
mother-woman, theory of 178–81
Mrs Warren's Profession 158, 168, 174
Murray, G. 12, 139, 161
Mussolini, B. 19, 90, 131, 135, 243–5, 249–56, 262, 267–70, 273
My Dear Dorothea 47, 163–4

Nagel, T. 240
national socialism, Shaw's doctrine of 64–70, 86, 198–9, 203, 207, 237, 260–3
national efficiency, doctrine of 64–5, 71–2
nationalism 195–9, 211
Nietzsche, F. 9, 10, 58, 199, 221, 229, 251, 284

O'Casey, S. 191, 198, 214
O'Flaherty VC 192, 211–12
Ohmann, R. 7, 11, 20
Olivier, S. 39–40, 55

On the Rocks 17, 90, 135–6, 260–2, 264
Orwell, G. 3, 245
Osgood, R. 225
Overruled 171
Owen, R. 29

Paine, T. 220
Pankhurst, E. 181–2, 185, 187–8
Pankhurst, S. 184, 186–7, 257
Patterson, J. 160–1, 167
Peace Conference Hints 222, 227, 231, 235
Pearson, K. 119
Pease, E. 100
Perelman, C. 10
perfectionism 99, 120
Perfect Wagnerite, The 52, 57–62, 129
Pethick-Lawrence, E. 184–5
Philanderer, The 167, 230
Pilecki, G. 245, 247, 270
Plamenatz, J. 145
Plato 7
Plays Unpleasant 14, 64, 166
Plunkett, H. 210
Pocock, J.G.A. 277
political violence 185–7, 203–4, 207–9, 241–2
Porter, B. 69
pragmatism 49, 102–3, 282
Press Cuttings 176, 187–9, 219
Priestley, J.B. 1
Pritchett, V.S. 2
protectionism 67, 86
Proudhon, P.J. 35
Pugh, P. 68–9
Pygmalion 14, 70, 81, 87, 175, 177, 220–1

Quintessence of Ibsenism, The 33–4, 46–7, 49, 51, 56–7, 76, 83, 102–5, 141, 164–6, 171, 197

radical feminism 162–6
Radice, L. 68
Rationalization of Russia, The 135
rent of ability, theory of 97, 124
rent, Fabian theory of 43–4
Report on Fabian Policy (Fabian Tract No. 96) 46, 73, 78, 107
republicanism 105, 148, 277–8
Revolutionist's Handbook, The 90
Rhondda, Lady 157, 175, 179, 190, 283
Ricardo, D. 25, 42–3

Robson, W.A. 132, 258
Rosebery, Lord 65, 68, 101
Rosenberg, A. 272
Rousseau, J.J. 117–18, 145
Ruskin, J. 3, 29–30, 114
Russell, B. 220, 233

Saint Joan 1, 131, 212–14
Salt, H. 33, 58, 240
Salvemini, G. 245, 252–3
Scheu, A. 31, 35
Schopenhauer, A. 9–10, 47–8, 221
Schumpeter, J.A. 144
Scott, C. 159
Semmel, B. 69
sexual equality 157–90: class, and 171–3, 176–8; coupled vote, theory of 183–5; democracy, and 181–5; early plays, and 166–9; eugenics, and 178–81; femininity, and 162; marriage 169–71, 173; mother-woman, theory of 178–81; political violence, and 185–7; prostitution 172–4; radical feminism 162–6; Shaw's reputation, and 157–9; socialist feminism 171–5; Suffragette movement 181–9
Seymour, H. 34
Shakespeare, W. 13, 23
Sharp, C. 221
Shaw, G. B: aesthetic theory 13; anarchism, views on 34–5, 50–1; argument, Shavianism characterized as 7; audience, Shaw's need for and identification of 10–12, 14, 91, 109, 112–13, 200; capitalism, moral critique of 29–30; childhood 23; citizen soldier 232–4; collectivism, moral theory of 104–6; compulsory labour, theory of 77, 116–17, 252, 278; conscription 233–4; consequentialism, and moral vision 48, 58, 104, 223; corporatism 254–7; coupled vote, theory of 183–5; creative evolution, religion of 125–31, 152; critical ideologist, described as 31, 37; democracy, views on 76–7, 89, 141–5, 181–5; early radicalism 24; economic theory 40–4; education, views on 86, 146–50; élitism 61, 135, 142–5; equality of income, argument for 105–25, 135; eugenics 57–8, 63, 71,

118–20, 178–81; evolutionary righteousness, doctrine of 57–8, 102, 137, 151; Fabian executive, he resigns from 99–100; Fabian realism, Shaw's role in the formulation of 44–53; Fabian Society, he joins 32; Fabian strategy, views on 54–6, 63–4, 86, 92–3; federalism 209–10; gentleman, theory of 29, 104–5, 110; happiness, and moral vision 70–2; human nature, views on 16–17, 51, 64, 139, 226–7; idealism, and 9; idleness, critique of 29; imperialism, views on 64–70, 239; individual rights, views on 58, 75, 148; intellectual proletariat, place in Shaw's socialism 95–7; intelligent patriotism, as response to war 230–2; international socialism, views on 64–70; Jewish question, and 119–20, 249, 264–7, 270; labourism, contrasted with socialism 83–90; Life Force philosophy 60, 101–2, 126–31; literature and politics, relationship between 13–16; marriage 169–71, 173; Marx, and Shaw's conversion to socialism 25, and Shaw's critique of his theory of surplus value 31; middle class, views on 91–8; moral absolutes, critique of 48; moral revolutionary, discussed as 4–5; moral vision 4–5, 28–30, 102–6, 119, 152–4, 280; morality of service, collectivist doctrine of 5, 29–30, 89, 105–6, 110, 119–20; mother-woman, theory of 178–81; national efficiency, politics of 64–5, 71–2; national socialism, doctrine of 64–70, 86, 198–9, 203, 207, 237, 260–3; perfectionism, and 99, 120; political myths, value for socialism 52–3; political science 52–3, 140, 280; political violence, views on 185–7, 203–4, 207–9, 241–2; poverty, hatred of 29; pragmatism, views on 49, 102–3, 282; progress, loss of faith in 57, 64, 103, 179; protectionism, support for 120; radical feminism 162–6; rationalism, views on 47, 127, 203; rent of ability, views on 97; rent theory 43–4; republicanism, support for 105, 148, 277–8; reputation, as a political thinker 1–3; Sidney Webb,

his relationship with 39; social conflict, views on 80–3, 90; social democracy, as Shaw's compromise political order 50–1, 285; Social Democratic Federation, Shaw's critique of 31; socialist fundamentalism, and ethical basis of Shaw's socialism 26–30; socialist realism 9, 61, 102; Soviet Union, visit to 134–5, 243–50; state, theory of 72–9; superman, theory of 56–7, 60–1, 63, 118–19; technocratic socialism 124, 135; trade unionism, views on 84–6, 94–5; vitalism 9–10, 47, 102, 126–31, 268; Webb, S. and B., their socialism contrasted with Shaw's 280–1; Wells, H.G. and Fabianism 92–3; women, relationships with 159–61; working class, views on 83–90
Shelley, P.B. 9, 23–4, 47–9, 164, 240
Simon, L. 150
Simpleton of the Unexpected Isles, The 130, 135–6
Sinn Fein 208–9
Sixteen Self Sketches 191, 194
Skidelsky, R. 245
Smyth, E. 184
Social Democratic Federation (SDF) 25, 31, 33, 37, 48, 72
social conflict 80–3
social Darwinism 64, 87, 136, 196, 223, 245
social democracy: compromise political order for Shaw 50–1, 285; élitist socialism, and 63–4; equality, and 111; middle class, and 91; war, and 234–5
Socialism and Superior Brains (Fabian Tract No. 146) 95, 97
Socialism for Millionaires (Fabian Tract No. 107) 70
Socialist League 33, 37, 39, 72, 169
Sola, G.A. 163
Sorel, G. 9, 52, 131
Sovietism 243–4
Spargo, J. 235
Spencer, H. 50, 75
Spengler, O. 245
Stalin, J. 19, 124, 131, 134–5, 138, 243–4, 248–9, 257, 269, 271–3
state, theory of 72–9, 225–6
Stopes, M. 181

strike, right to 89–90
Suffragette movement 181–9, 283
superman, theory of 56–7, 60–1, 63
Swartz, M. 225
syndicalism 108–9, 235
Synge, J.M. 191

Tawney, R.H. 123
Taylor, A.J.P. 217
technocratic socialism 97–8
Terry, E. 160–1
Three Plays for Puritans 271
To Your Tents, Oh Israel! 56, 84, 198
Tompkins, M. 160, 244
Too True To Be Good 133–5, 142
Trade Unionism for Clerks 95
trade unionism 84–6, 94–5
Treatise on Parents and Children 147
Trebitsch, S. 221, 256, 266
Trotsky, L. 244
Tucker, B.K. 34, 53
Tucker, R. 225
Turco, A. 20, 49–50, 103
Twentieth Century Politics: A Policy of National Efficiency (Fabian Tract No. 108) 65, 71

Unsocial Socialist, An 26–8, 33, 175

vitalism 9–10, 47, 102, 126–31, 268

Wagner, R. 57–61, 221
Walker, E. 132
Wallas, G. 39–40, 64, 68, 103, 121, 216, 220
Walshe, C. 256
Walters, M. 11, 112–13, 159, 173
Waltz, K. 231
war 216–40: citizen soldier, and 232–4; conscription 233–4; disarmament 227–8; economism, and 229, 235; human nature, and 226–7; imperialism, and 239; intelligent patriotism, and 230–2; League of Nations, and 236–8; militarism, and 230–2; monarchy, and 230–2; moralism, and 228–30; reactions to Shaw's views on 220–2; realism, and 223–6; social democracy, and 231, 236; state, and 225–6
Watson, B.B. 158, 162, 164, 184–5
Webb, B. 56–7, 63–4, 71, 109, 113, 119, 122, 133, 138, 218, 244, 246, 254, 257, 263–4, 267
Webb, S. 2–3, 39–40, 42, 44–6, 54, 64–5, 71, 83, 92–4, 119, 232, 234, 265, 280, 284
Webb, B. and S. 72, 74–5, 78, 90, 92, 96, 99, 101, 112, 138, 219, 221, 257, 280–1
Weintraub, R. 158
Weintraub, S. 219
Wells, H.G. 1–3, 12, 63, 71, 84, 92–3, 96, 100, 121, 138, 142, 150, 152, 157, 170, 177, 181, 189, 218, 220, 227, 232, 280, 283
West, A. 27
West, R. 122, 158, 171, 190
What I Really Wrote About the War 217
Wheeler, M. 189
Whelan, F. 68
Why Are The Many Poor? (Fabian Tract No. 1) 29
Wicksteed, P.H. 41
Widowers' Houses 167
Wilde, O. 191
Wilson, C. 34, 40
Wilson, E. 2, 15, 217, 229
Wilson, W. 217
Winter, J.M. 232
Wolfe, W. 20, 34–5, 38
Women as Councillors (Fabian Tract No. 93) 71, 182
Woolf, L. 2, 139, 150–1, 221, 236
You Never Can Tell 147, 168

Yeats, W.B. 191–3, 199–200, 206

Zetetical Society 24, 35, 40, 196